Managerial economics
for business, management and accounting

SECOND EDITION

Howard Davies

Head of the Department of Business Studies
Hong Kong Polytechnic

Pitman

Pitman Publishing
128 Long Acre, London WC2E 9AN
A Division of Longman Group UK Limited

First published by Longman Group UK Limited 1989
Reprint published by Pitman Publishing 1990
Second edition 1991

© Longman Group UK Limited 1989
© Longman Group UK Limited 1990
© Howard Davies 1991

British Library Cataloguing in Publication Data

Davies, Howard
  Managerial economics for business, management and
  accounting.
  I. Title
  658.15

ISBN 0 273 03510 X

Typeset, printed and bound in Great Britain

Contents

Figures

Tables

Preface

Managerial economics is a subject which relates very closely to more directly practical business disciplines including management accounting, marketing, and corporate strategy. Indeed, many economists would insist that in so far as these other subjects have sound theoretical foundations they are usually to be found in economics.

Nevertheless, the relationship between the different disciplines is often an uneasy one. Economic models were not originally intended to provide prescriptions for managers, and yet they have often been used for that purpose when translated into the other disciplines. To the chagrin of the economists they find that their beloved models are used for purposes for which they were never intended and are then castigated for not fulfilling those purposes well. At the same time economists have tended to sell themselves short in terms of the potential practical usefulness of the subject by insisting on a very high degree of rigour, at the expense of usefulness. Marketing analysts and corporate strategists pick out some of the key qualitative insights of the economic models, and flesh them out with a level of detail which managers can recognise, to produce a highly saleable product which the economists rather wish they had thought of themselves.

This book aims to show how managerial economic analysis can be of relevance to decision-making, without attempting to make pretentious claims for its practical application, which would not bear scrutiny. In doing so, it attempts to differentiate itself from other texts on the subject by incorporating material not usually included in managerial economics textbooks written to date. This material includes aspects of marketing, like 'the marketing mix' and decisions associated with it. It also includes an introduction to Porter's work on the structural analysis of industries, and an outline of the basic elements of corporate strategy. Linking to that analysis is a treatment of the 'scope' of the firm which introduces the transactions cost framework of analysis, and its application to the theory of the multinational enterprise.

This mix of material should make the book useful to those involved in a variety of courses. Undergraduates in business studies will find it most useful at second year level, but can also use many sections in their first year. Post-experience courses such as the Master's in Business Administration (MBA) or the Diploma in Management Studies (DMS) should also find that while the material can be used by those with no background in theoretical economics, it develops their knowledge to a level which is appropriate for a general management student at master's level.

Each chapter contains a list of self-test questions, which should assist the student in checking that they have grasped the vocabulary and some of the fundamental analytical issues. There is also a question of examination standard at the end of each chapter, for which answers have been provided at the end of the book.

Howard Davies
October 1990

1 The definition and scope of managerial economics

A definition of managerial economics

Managerial economics is most easily defined as the application of economic analysis to business problems. This very general definition covers a wide variety of subject matter and a number of very different approaches to the subject, reflected in the range of textbooks available. Before proceeding it is useful to set them in context.

The origins and methods of managerial economic analysis

Managerial economics and microeconomics

Most of the economic analysis to be found in textbooks on managerial economics has its origins in theoretical microeconomics. Topics like the theory of demand, the profit-maximising model of the firm, optimal prices and advertising expenditures and the impact of market structure on firms' behaviour are all approached using the economist's standard intellectual 'tool-kit', which consists of building and testing *models*.

The process of model-building

The use of models is a common feature of widely different types of investigation. Engineers build scaled-down replicas of aeroplanes and motor-cars, or computerised simulations, in order to examine their behaviour. Meteorologists use computer models of weather patterns in order to make forecasts. Accountants build financial models of companies, in order to examine the impact of different decisions or different external events on their financial position. Economic models are just another example of this very widely used technique.

The process of building and testing an economic model can be described in the diagram shown in Fig. 1.1. The first step is to establish a set of definitions and a set of assumptions about the entity to be modelled, which could be an individual

1

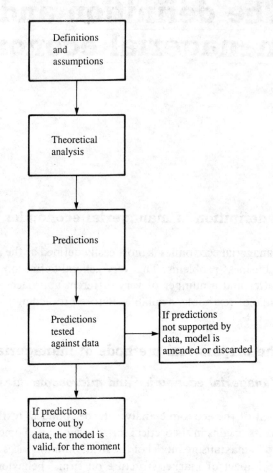

Fig. 1.1 Building and testing economic models

household, the market for an individual product, the national economy as a whole, or an individual firm. Having established a set of assumptions the next stage in the process is one of theoretical analysis, or logical deduction, whereby the logical implications of the assumptions are followed through and identified. This can be a very difficult process, as the implications of the assumptions may be hard to unravel, and they may change dramatically with slight changes in the details of the assumptions made. As a result, this process takes up a very substantial proportion of the total effort involved and many economists specialise in this particular aspect of model-building. A brief examination of most learned journals in economics shows that a very high proportion of articles published are solely concerned with theoretical issues, unconnected with any empirical evidence. Nevertheless, despite economists' professional enjoyment of the theoretical aspects of model-building ('illicit relationships with beautiful models'), a model has little value until it has been tested against data on the actual behaviour of the entity being modelled. If a model provides a better explanation of the facts than the alternatives then it can be regarded as a useful means of explaining and predicting the behaviour which has been modelled.

The use of economic models for decision-making purposes

It is clear that the various different models explored in this book are in some sense 'about' aspects of business decision-making, including decisions on price and output, the scope of the firm and strategies for competition. However, that is not enough to demonstrate that the models can be used 'for' business in the improvement of decision-making. Such a claim is highly problematical, for a number of reasons. Most fundamentally, there is a wide gulf between the original aims of the model-builders and the attempt to use them directly for management purposes. The initial objective of economic models of the firm has been to act as a building block in our understanding of how the economic system as a whole works to allocate resources. This is a very different aim from that of assisting managers to take better decisions, and as a result there is considerable tension between the major objectives of the models and the attempt to use them for decision-making.

This tension is most apparent in the contrast between 'normative' and 'positive' approaches to theory, and the different types of methodology associated with each approach. A 'positive' theory is essentially one which is concerned to explain what 'is', while a 'normative' theory is concerned with what 'ought to be'. In the positive approach to theory, which dominates mainstream economics, the main concern of the theory of the firm is to provide models which produce testable hypotheses. If a model produces predictions about firms' behaviour which are testable, and if these predictions are supported by the evidence, then the model can be pronounced a success, for the time being at least. This approach to theory, and to model-building, has a number of implications which can cause difficulties if the same models are used directly to help decision-makers in firms. Most obviously, there is no need for the assumptions in such a theory of the firm to be realistic. The test of a 'good' model is its ability to generate testable predictions, and the success of those predictions. As a result, the firm described in theory need bear no descriptive similarity to any recognisable real firm. Indeed, the very purpose of theory is to cut through the complexities of real life in order to get to the essence of the way in which the world works. To do that successfully may well demand the adoption of wholly unrealistic assumptions. Indeed, some theorists go so far as to aver that the best theories are likely to be based on the most unrealistic assumptions!

Clearly, then, given the basic aims and methods of mainstream economic analysis, it is perfectly legitimate to construct a model of the firm which is wholly unrealistic. Real firms are assumed to behave 'as if' they conform to the assumptions of the model, and the process of deducing and testing predictions can follow from that assumption. If prediction of firms' behaviour, from the perspective of an outsider, is accepted as the purpose of the theory, then the analysis is immune to the common lay criticism that it is unrealistic. The economist has a cast-iron defence. However, if the same models are used without amendment for the 'normative' purposes often attributed to managerial economics or management accounting, there is much more substance to the criticism. If the aim is to improve the quality of decision-making there is very little purpose in simply declaring that managers should behave 'as if' they had perfect information, for instance. Such an injunction is not operational and cannot be acted upon. In this sense the criticism of 'unrealism', which is often levelled at economic models by those concerned with other business disciplines, is perfectly valid if those models are used to derive prescriptions for managers to follow.

If many economic models cannot be put to direct use by managers, how can their use be justified in the context of decision-making? There are a number of possible defences. The first is to argue that the adoption of the positive methodology, and the acceptance of an external perspective, is itself useful for decision-makers. By stepping outside their own highly individual circumstances, and adopting a more general perspective, managers may be able to avoid the common fault of generalising from an unrepresentative sample of one (their own experience). A second argument is that simple but unrealistic models provide a stepping stone towards more realistic and complex models, which can provide usable normative guidelines. A third argument stresses the value of thinking logically through a problem, even if the example given is far more simple than the actual problems faced in practice. Some of the work carried out by organisational psychologists has suggested that the use of even simple formal models may lead to better decision-making than unaided human intuition and judgment.

Taking these arguments together, it is clear that there is considerable value to be had in using the methods of economic analysis to tackle the problems facing decision-makers. What would be entirely misleading and dishonest would be to claim that the analysis can produce a set of normative decision-rules which provide 'off-the-shelf' answers to complex business problems. It is as well to remember Lord Keynes' remark that economics is essentially a way of thinking about problems, rather than a set of solutions.

The links between managerial economics and industrial economics

In managerial economics, the emphasis is upon the firm, the environment in which the firm finds itself, and the decisions which individual firms have to take. In industrial economics, the emphasis is upon the behaviour of whole industries, in which the firm is simply a component. The most common approach adopted by industrial economists is known as the **structure – conduct – performance** approach, in which the structure of an industry is seen as an important determinant of its conduct and performance. The **structure** of an industry has a number of different dimensions, including most notably:

- the level of concentration
- the height of barriers to entry
- the degree of product differentiation
- the extent of vertical integration
- the extent of diversification

The **conduct** of an industry refers to the type of behaviour engaged in by its component firms, including:

- company objectives
- collusive versus competitive behaviour
- pricing policies
- advertising policies
- competitive strategies.

The **performance** of an industry refers to its results, the most common measures of performance being:

- profitability
- growth
- productivity increases
- export performance and international competitiveness.

In the simplest applications of the structure – conduct – performance approach, the structure of an industry is treated as exogenous and structure is seen as the cause of conduct or performance. For instance, a very wide range of studies have examined the links between the level of concentration across industries, and their performance in terms of profitability. The basic theoretical proposition which is being tested in this case is that higher levels of concentration give firms in an industry a greater degree of market power, which will be reflected in higher profits.

Clearly, the concerns of industrial economics are rather different to the concerns of managerial economics, in that the focus lies with the industry, rather than the firm. Nevertheless, in building industrial economic models, economists have to take into account the behaviour of individual firms, so that there is a considerable link between the two branches of the discipline. As managerial economics has to pay considerable attention to the environment of the firm, and as the structure of the industries in which it is operating is the most important determinant of that environment, managerial economists need to be aware of both industrial structure and competitive conduct.

The links between managerial economics and management science

Just as there are overlaps between managerial economics and industrial economics, so there are overlaps between managerial economics and *management science* or the *decision sciences*. Management science is essentially concerned with techniques for the improvement of decision-making and is therefore almost entirely normative. Techniques used in operational research, like linear programming, goal programming, queueing theory and forecasting are all aspects of management science, which tends to have a heavily quantitative bias. In so far as managerial economics is often concerned with finding optimal solutions to decision problems, the boundaries between the two subjects are not clearly defined. Many managerial economics texts contain sections which could also be found in books on management science or quantitative methods, making use of techniques drawn from those disciplines to solve business problems.

Illustration

Economic theory and business practice: the overtaking analogy

One of the earliest contributions to the debate on the relationship between theory and practice, written by Fritz Machlup in 1946, still provides one of the most vivid illustrations of a point which many students find difficult.

Machlup drew an analogy between profit-maximising behaviour and the situation of a motorist deciding whether or not to overtake on a two-lane highway. If we attempted to model the overtaking decision we would have to construct a very complex set of equations, which took into account a long list of factors including the weight, power, speed and acceleration of the vehicle being driven, the weather, the condition of the road and its gradient, plus the same information about any oncoming vehicles and a series of assumptions about the behaviour and objectives of the drivers. The model would then have to make the unrealistic assumption that the overtaking driver has all of this information and it would be tempting to conclude that the decision on whether or not to overtake is so difficult that it cannot be done successfully! And yet millions of drivers make such decisions dozens of times every day and those decisions are the correct ones in the vast majority of cases.

The overtaking decision is rather like the attempt to make maximum profit. The model of the profit-maximising firm assumes that decision-makers have perfect information about costs and revenue conditions, which is unrealistic. Nevertheless, that does not prove that firms are unable to profit-maximise. Like the driver taking the decision to overtake, managers behave 'as if' they had the relevant information, in which case they will behave like the profit-maximising model and that model will be a good predictor of their behaviour.

References and further reading

Each of the following chapters include a list of sources for the references made in the text.

In addition to these references to original material there are a number of textbooks which provide good coverage of some, although not all, of the topics, at an appropriate level. In order to avoid making laborious and repetitive reference to these at the end of every chapter a listing is set out below.

J. Bates and J.R. Parkinson, *Business Economics* (Oxford, Basil Blackwell, 1983)

P.J. Devine, N. Lee, R.M. Jones and W.J. Tyson, *An Introduction to Industrial Economics* (London, George Allen and Unwin, 1979)

E. Douglas, *Managerial Economics* (London, Prentice-Hall, 1979)

K.D. George and C. Joll, *Industrial Organisation: Competition, Growth and Structural Change*, (London, George Allen and Unwin, 1983)

D. Hay and D. Morris, *Industrial Economics: Theory and Evidence* (Oxford, Oxford UP, 1980)

A. Koutsoyannis, *Modern Microeconomics* (London, Macmillan, 1978)

F. Machlup, 'Marginal Analysis and Empirical Research' *American Economic Review*, vol. 36, September 1946, pp. 519–554.

J.L. Pappas, E.F. Brigham and B. Shipley, *Managerial Economics: UK Edition* (London, Cassell, 1983)

J. Pickering, *Industrial Structure and Market Conduct* (Oxford, Martin Robertson, 1980)

W.D. Reekie and J.N. Crook, *Managerial Economics* (Oxford, Philip Allan, 1982)

J.H. Wilson and S.G. Darr, *Managerial Economics: Concepts, Applications and Cases*, (London, Harper and Row, 1979)

2 Basic features of the firm and its environment

This chapter begins by examining the various legal forms which the firm may take and goes on to consider the major features of ownership and control. This is followed by an outline of the environment in which firms operate, taking account of structural changes in the economy and the level of industrial concentration.

Alternative types of firm

Managerial economics frequently analyses the activity of 'the firm' without any explicit reference to the different legal and organisational forms which the firm may take. Nevertheless, these forms may be an important determinant of firms' behaviour and they need to be outlined before proceeding to more detailed analysis. A more comprehensive treatment of the legal issues is to be found within textbooks on company law. The legal framework within which firms operate varies from country to country and this section is set against the English legal system. Nevertheless, the features described are very general and apply to a greater or lesser extent in most economies based upon private enterprise.

The sole proprietorship

The sole proprietorship is the simplest form of business organisation, based around a single individual who provides the capital, takes the decisions, has the sole right to any profits and bears the risks of, and liability for, any losses which might be made. Ownership and control are united in this one individual, who is easily identifiable as 'the entrepreneur'. Governments, who are often committed to the development of a healthy small business sector, frequently extol the virtues of the sole proprietor and point to the personal commitment to success implied by this form of organisation, the speed with which decisions can be taken in such a simple organisation and the potential flexibility of owner-managed firms in responding quickly to changes in the market environment. On the other hand, sole proprietorships may be rendered cautious by the owner's total liability for any losses and this form of enterprise is hampered by the fact that finance can only be raised from the owner's own resources or by borrowing on his own personal security.

The sole proprietorship is a very common form of organisation in unconcentrated industries, being most heavily represented in farming, retailing, building and the non-financial services sector.

Partnerships

The partnership was defined in England under the Partnership Act of 1890 as, 'the relation which subsists between persons carrying on business with a common view to profit.'

This form of organisation goes beyond the sole proprietorship in that capital may be provided by a number of individuals and decision-making can be shared. Not all partners need to play an active role as some may simply provide capital and act as 'sleeping partners.' The major advantage over the sole proprietorship is that each partner may specialise in a particular aspect of the business, leading to an improvement in efficiency, but in many other respects the partnership has the same advantages and disadvantages as sole proprietorship. As the number of partners is usually relatively small (except in the notable case of the large accountancy practices) decision-making can be speedy and flexible, but the partners also have unlimited liability for losses, which can be a major disadvantage. (Some partners may limit their liability to a fixed sum, but at least one of the partners must assume unlimited liability.) Partnerships rely for their existence upon a large measure of agreement amongst the partners which may be difficult to sustain in turbulent market circumstances.

Partnerships are a particularly common form of business organisation in the professions of accountancy, law and medicine.

The joint stock company

The development of the joint stock company marks one of the most significant innovations in the history of economic development. Under this form of organisation a distinct 'legal person' is created, having legal duties and legal rights separate from those of its members. A distinction may be drawn between private companies and public companies. In the case of the public company, shares and debentures can be offered for sale to the general public and such a company's shares are generally quoted on the Stock Exchange. In England a public company must have a minimum issued capital of at least £50,000, at least one quarter of which is 'paid up'. In the case of a private company the public cannot be asked to subscribe for shares. In order to protect shareholders and others, companies are under legal obligations to provide regular and considerable amounts of financial information to the authorities, so that the fraudulent promotion of companies may be controlled. Since the Companies Act 1980 public companies have been required to include the words 'public limited company' or the letters 'plc' as the last part of their name. Private companies continue to use the word 'limited' or 'Ltd'.

In order to form a company, its promoters are required to submit a number of documents, the most important of which are the **Memorandum of Association** and the **Articles of Association**. The memorandum is essentially concerned with the external affairs of the company, regulating its relationships with outsiders. It defines the company's name and the location of its address, states the number of shares the company may issue and their nominal value (the 'authorised capital') and sets out the 'objects' of the company, which are the purposes for which it is being established.

The Articles of Association are concerned with the internal regulations for the management of the company's affairs and the conduct of its business. This includes the number and powers of directors, the rights of different classes of shareholders, the means by which shares are to be issued and transferred, the election of officers and the holding of meetings. Articles of Association bind the company and its members as if they had been signed, sealed and delivered by all the members. They may be amended by a special resolution of the company, involving a 75 per cent majority of the shareholders present and voting.

Perhaps the most important advantage of the joint stock company is that it establishes 'limited liability'. The company, as a legal person in its own right, is fully liable for its debts. However, the liability of the shareholders is restricted to the amount which they have agreed to subscribe. This principle removes a major disincentive to provide capital for economic development as in its absence an individual making a small investment could find himself liable to the full extent of his personal possessions for any liabilities incurred by the business. It was the development of the joint stock company which provided, and continues to provide, for the mobilisation of savings to fund business investment.

Companies may tap the pool of savings by raising capital in a number of ways. The 'authorised capital', or nominal capital is the amount set out in the Memorandum of Association. When shares are issued they need not be fully paid for. A company may simply ask for a proportion to be paid on application for the shares and a further proportion when they are alloted to the applicant. This amount is known in total as the 'paid-up' capital. The remainder acts as a reserve which may be called upon if required. Shares may take a number of forms, the more common types of which are:

- preference shares
- ordinary shares
- debentures (which are not strictly shares).

Holders of preference shares take precedence over holders of other types of shares in respect of the payment of dividends. In most cases the rate of return on preference shares is set as a fixed percentage of their nominal values. If no profit is made, holders of preference shares will receive no dividend (unless they hold special cumulative preference shares, in which case arrears of dividend will be paid in later years). If profits are particularly high, holders of preference shares receive no additional payment (unless they hold another special class of preference shares, called participating preference shares).

As the returns to preference shares are quite loosely linked to the performance of the company, the Articles of Association usually provide them with more limited voting rights than other shareholders, allowing them to vote at the annual meeting only if they have not received their dividends.

Holders of ordinary shares bear most of the risk associated with the company's activities in that their entitlement is to the residue of profits after all other claims on them have been met. Their dividends depend upon how profitable the company is and upon the directors' decisions with respect to the amount of profit which should be retained within the company. Most ordinary shares carry voting rights and a company's ordinary share capital is referred to as its 'equity'.

Debentures are not strictly shares in that the purchaser of a debenture is making a loan to the company, rather than buying a share in it. A debenture holder is therefore a creditor, rather than an owner. The rate of return on a debenture is fixed and payment on debentures takes precedence over payment on shares of all types. Clearly, the attraction of debentures is to investors who seek security and in reinforcement of this companies may attach some of their valuable assets to their debentures so that if the company is unable to make the required payments, debenture holders have the right to sell those assets in order to receive the payments due to them.

Co-operatives

Co-operatives account for a very small proportion of economic activity, but merit consideration as they are an unusual form of venture which may offer a way into business for individuals and groups who would otherwise be unable to consider work options other than employment.

In the case of **producer co-operatives**, a group of workers join together to raise capital, elect managers rather than appoint them in the usual way, take decisions through some form of democratic process and share the profits according to some agreed formula. There are only about 500 such co-operatives in the United Kingdom, concentrated in retailing and catering, craft activities, printing and publishing and other creative work like photography and film-making.

In the case of **retail co-operatives** or **consumer co-operatives** a group of consumers rather than producers join together to form a society which establishes retail outlets. These are usually managed by full-time salaried managers, appointed by a management committee of part-time members which is elected by the full membership of the society on a 'one member − one vote' basis. One of the unique features of the retail co-operative societies is that profits are not distributed in accordance with ownership, but in relation to the volume of purchases, so that the 'dividend' in effect becomes a discount on the purchase price of commodities bought in the society's retail outlets.

Public corporations

The different types of company described above make up the private sector of the economy. In the public sector, a substantial part of the activity which takes place is carried out directly by government departments. However, when public sector operations involve commercial activities, as in the case of the railways or the public utilities, these *nationalised industries* are often organised in the form of public corporations. Such corporations exist as separate legal entities, like companies, but there are no private shareholders as ownership lies with the government. Finance is usually provided directly by the Exchequer. Such corporations have a controlling Board whose members report to the government and the policy of each public corporation is usually the responsibility of a minister, whose department may take a close interest in the activities of the corporation.

Public corporations usually have objectives other than profit, which may be set out in the nationalisation statutes, or in Government White Papers issued from time to time, or in policy statements emanating directly from government. While this forms part of an attempt to achieve a compromise between securing social objectives and ensuring commercial viability, there can be conflict between the objectives set which can make it very difficult for the Board of a public corporation to take decisions and manage effectively, especially if government alters the priorities given to the different objectives from time to time. One of the major arguments in favour of *privatisation* is that multiple and possibly confusing objectives are replaced by an unambiguous emphasis on profit, which allows policies and operations to be more tightly focused and more efficiently managed.

Ownership and control of companies

The implications of the joint stock company for ownership and control

In the case of the sole proprietor the firm consists essentially of an 'owner-manager' and both ownership and control are vested in a single individual. Most economic analyses of the firm appear to be couched in terms of this type of firm, as the firm in theory is viewed in a 'holistic' way. The firm is modelled as a single entity which can have objectives and take decisions. However, the development and widespread adoption of the joint stock company as a form of organisation raises important questions with respect to the realism and usefulness of this approach. More than 50 years ago, Berle and Means (1932) pointed out that in a very substantial proportion of major companies in the United States no single individual, family, or group of associates held more than 20 per cent of the voting strength. In that situation, it was argued, with shareholdings widely diffused, and shareholders relatively ill-informed about the operations of the companies they own, control would effectively reside with the management of the company who have the important advantage of inside information with respect to the firm's activities.

The debate on owner-versus-manager control

While the Berle and Means findings drew attention to the 'managerial revolution', and provided the basis for a number of alternative approaches to modelling the firm, described in Chapter 2, the question of whether control lies with ownership or with management is a complex one. The Berle and Means approach, whereby a firm is described as 'manager-controlled' unless a 'compact group of individuals' holds at least 20 per cent of the voting rights involves the adoption of an entirely arbitrary criterion, which may bear little relationship to the realities of control. Other observers (Gordon (1961)) have suggested that much smaller holdings, as low as three per cent, may be sufficient to give the owners of those shares effective control, in which case many more firms are 'owner-controlled' than would be so classified under the Berle and Means approach. To complicate matters further, the influence of shareholders depends not only upon the size of their holdings, as a proportion of the voting rights, but upon who they are, and their possible influence on the opinions of other shareholders. Individual shareholders may have quite substantial proportions of the voting rights, but exert little control over management (except in times of major crisis) because they have neither the time nor the inclination to take a close interest in the firm's activities. On the other hand, institutional investors like pension funds, insurance companies, investment trusts and banks may own a relatively small holding in a firm and yet wield substantial influence through their monitoring of the firm's activities and through other shareholders' acceptance of their judgments on the company's policies and performance.

Given the potential importance of institutional shareholdings, the extent of their ownership of industry is of considerable interest. Table 2.1 shows the distribution of ownership of ordinary shares quoted on the UK Stock Exchange over the period 1957 to 1975.

Table 2.1 The ownership of UK ordinary shares

Owners, by sector	% of market value			
	1957	1963	1969	1975
Personal sector	67.7	56.1	49.5	39.8
Financial sector of which:	21.3	30.4	35.9	47.9
Pension funds	3.4	6.4	9.0	16.8
Insurance companies	8.8	10.0	12.2	15.9
Investment trusts	6.8	10.0	8.7	10.0
Overseas sector	4.4	7.0	6.6	5.6
Public sector	3.9	1.5	2.6	3.6
Industrial and commercial sector	2.7	5.1	5.4	3.0
Totals	100.0	100.0	100.0	100.0

Source: Reproduced by permission of the Department of Applied Economics, Cambridge from J. Moyle, *The Pattern of Ordinary Share Ownership 1957–70*, CUP 1971.

As the table shows, share ownership in the United Kingdom shifted overwhelmingly in this period towards the financial institutions, with the implication that control through ownership has become more powerful, rather than less.

The argument that control resides with management rather than with the owners is only of any significance for firms' behaviour if the managers have substantially different objectives to the owners, and the discretion to pursue those objectives without being disciplined. If the objectives of the two groups are similar, or if managers have no discretion, then companies will behave in the same way, regardless of which group is in control. The 'managerial school' of economic thought (see Chapter 3 for details), building on the work of Berle and Means, has tended to argue that owners and managers are different groups of individuals, or organisations, and that they do have conflicting interests. Owners are seen as primarily interested in profits, while managers are seen to be interested in status, prestige, power and the general ability to control the firm in their own interests. Certainly it is true that the owners of a joint stock company are not the same set of individuals as the managers. However, the set of 'owners' and the set of 'managers' do overlap in that senior managers, especially the directors, often hold shares in the firm, being both owners and managers. The separation of ownership and control is therefore incomplete. If the managers who are also owners receive a substantial proportion of their incomes in share-price and dividend-related benefits then their interests as owners may override any conflicting interest they might have as managers. The spread of share option schemes and similar profit-linked incentives may therefore have the effect of bringing the objectives of a significant group of managers into line with the objectives of the owners.

Even if managers and owners were entirely different groups of individuals, having powerfully conflicting objectives, the managers would only be able to pursue their own objectives if they have the discretion to do so. Chapter 3 considers this issue in more detail, noting that there are a number of potentially powerful forces limiting the amount of discretion which managers have. These forces include:

- the threat of take-over and the market for corporate control
- the influence of powerful institutional shareholders, dependent for their own success on the financial performance of their investments
- the operation of internal labour markets.

The sectoral distribution of business activity

Long-term trends in the structure of industry

As economic development takes place there is a general trend for the balance of economic activity, especially if measured by employment, to shift first from agriculture to manufacturing and then from manufacturing to services. Agricultural employment in the UK, for instance, made up around 20 per cent of the labour force in the 1850s, but accounted for only 1.6 per cent of employees in employment in 1985. As the first economy to become industrialised, the United Kingdom experienced this shift much earlier than many other nations so that in West Germany and France, for instance, 20 per cent of the labour force was still employed in agriculture as late as the mid-1960s (Kuznets (1971).

While the shift of employment away from agriculture has continued in the UK, with the number of employees falling by 50 per cent from 1961 to 1985, it is the development of the service sector which has been the major feature of the period since the Second World War. Table 2.2 shows the changes in the distribution of employees in employment over the period 1961 to 1985.

Table 2.2 The sectoral shift in UK employment 1961–1985

Sector	Employees in 1961	Employees in 1985	% change
Agriculture, forestry, fishing	710	341	−52%
Manufacturing	8,540	5,365	−37%
Construction	1,485	1,022	−31%
Services	10,382	14,192	+37%
Total employees	22,233	21,509	−3%

Source: Social Trends

As the table shows, employment in the service sector grew by almost 40 per cent over the period, so that by 1985 approximately two-thirds of all employees were working in services. These long-term shifts in the balance of economic activity may be attributed to two major factors. On the demand side, the income elasticity of demand (see Chapters 6 and 7) is higher for manufactures than for agricultural products, so that as economies begin to grow wealthier the demand for manufactures increases much more rapidly than the demand for agricultural products. On the supply side, technological change in agriculture has led to more rapid productivity growth than in manufacturing so that supply and demand factors reinforce each other in reducing the size of the agricultural labour force which produces a relatively static level of output with far fewer workers. In manufacturing, during the period of industrialisation, growing demand coupled with slower rates of productivity growth means that employment in manufacturing takes up a larger proportion of the total.

In the later stages of development a similar shift takes place between manufacturing and the service sector, for similar reasons. The income elasticity of demand for services becomes increasingly large at higher levels of income so that the demand for services grows as fast, if not faster than the demand for manufactures. As productivity in the service sector has grown less rapidly than in manufacturing in this later period, the result is the shift in employment shown in Table 2.2.

The scale of the shift from manufacturing employment to service sector employment has led to speculation that a new era of economic development is about to begin, characterised as the *post-industrial* society in which service activities will dominate employment to an even greater extent, where leisure will occupy a greater proportion of the population's time and where attitudes to work will have to change dramatically if workless individuals are to retain a sense of respect for their own identities and play a meaningful and accepted role in society. Views on the accuracy of this forecast, and the desirability of the 'post-industrial' society vary widely. (Lewis (1973), Gershuny (1977)).

De-industrialisation in the United Kingdom

The shift towards services and away from manufacturing is clearly part of a very long-term trend common to many different economies. Its eventual outcome is difficult to predict but might lead to the realisation of a wealthy and comfortable post-industrial society or to the kind of frightening future depicted in science fiction novels, where a small very highly paid elite of workers co-exists unhappily with a mass of increasingly desperate unemployed.

In the shorter term, there has been particular concern in the United Kingdom over the very rapid decline in manufacturing employment which has taken place in the 1970s and 1980s. Out of the 3.2 million manufacturing jobs lost over the 24-year period 1961 to 1985, one quarter (812,000) were lost between 1971 and 1979 but this rose to a staggering 1.9 million (60 per cent of the total) in the six years between 1979 and 1985. While other advanced industrial nations have seen manufacturing account for a smaller proportion of total employment, many of them, including the United States and Japan, have continued to experience growth in the absolute number of manufacturing jobs. Some others, like Germany and France, have seen the absolute number of jobs in manufacturing fall, but not to the very great extent experienced in the United Kingdom.

In the face of this experience there has been concern in Britain over the issue of **de-industrialisation**, a term which has been used by different observers to mean different things.

1 The term *de-industrialisation* might be defined as a decline in manufacturing employment *as a proportion of total employment*. However, as noted above, such a shift is probably an inevitable part of economic development which has been experienced by many different economies, and may be accompanied by a rising *absolute number* of jobs in manufacturing. Such a definition of de-industrialisation does not capture the phenomenon which has been of concern in the United Kingdom, where there has been an acceleration of the long-term process and where absolute job losses have taken place in manufacturing.

2 Following the interpretation of Singh (1977), the 'Cambridge definition' of de-industrialisation is: 'the failure of industry to sell enough exports to pay for the full employment level of imports at a socially acceptable exchange rate'. While this is useful in drawing attention to the problems which can be caused by failing to produce enough manufactures for export, it is not satisfactory to define a phenomenon in terms of one particular explanation for it (the failure to compete on exports).

3 Similar objections apply to the thesis put forward by Bacon and Eltis in 1976, in a highly controversial book entitled *Britain's Economic Problem: Too Few Producers*. This saw the phenomenon of de-industrialisation as part of a process

in which the expansion of the public sector (described as the 'non-marketed' output of the economy) diverted resources away from the private sector, and from manufacturing in particular, leading to the fall in manufacturing employment. Like the Cambridge definition this approach involves identifying the problem with one particular explanation and is therefore unsatisfactory.

4 A fourth definition of de-industrialisation, put forward by Thirlwall (1982) is simply: 'a decline in the absolute number of jobs in the manufacturing sector'. This has the advantage of not tying the definition to any particular explanation and is therefore to be preferred.

Having defined the phenomenon it is then possible to consider *what are the causes of the very rapid and substantial de-industrialisation in Britain?*.

A number of different hypotheses may be offered. In the first place, it is conceivable that technological progress may have reduced the demand for labour by increasing labour productivity very rapidly. While it is certainly the case that over the very long term, increasing productivity in manufacturing is part of the process which shifts the balance of employment towards services, this explanation is not convincing in the case of Britain's experience in the 1970s and 1980s. Throughout that period productivity increases in UK manufacturing were very modest, both in absolute terms and in comparison with the productivity gains being achieved in other major economies. Those economies which did experience rapid technological change over the period, most notably Japan, saw increases rather than decreases in the industrial labour force.

The second explanation for de-industrialisation in the UK stems from the Eltis and Bacon hypothesis that growth in the public sector attracted resources away from manufacturing, thereby 'crowding-out' manufacturing activity. With respect to labour it is certainly true that the process of de-industrialisation was accompanied by rising public sector employment. However, it is difficult to sustain the argument that this drew labour away from manufacturing because there is little evidence that the manufacturing sector ever experienced difficulties in recruiting labour. Furthermore, the jobs which were lost in manufacturing were predominantly full-time jobs, usually carried out by men, while the growth in public sector employment involved a substantial proportion of part-time jobs for women.

The 'crowding-out' hypothesis may carry more weight with respect to financial resources, where it could be argued that large public sector borrowing requirements, which were common until the late 1980s, absorbed too large a proportion of the nation's savings, thereby reducing the funds available for investment in the private sector. On the other hand, observers of the British financial scene, including the Wilson Committee (1980) have concluded that shortages of finance have not been a major constraint on industrial investment, which would suggest that 'crowding-out' has not been important.

A third explanation for de-industrialisation in Britain concerns British industry's declining ability to compete with industry in other countries, both in the home market and abroad. In the home market import penetration has increased rapidly and the UK's share of world manufactured exports has declined rapidly.

This loss of competitiveness may be attributed to a number of factors. In the first place, there is the question of the **price-competitiveness** of UK products. If the level of costs in the UK, and the level of wages in particular, taken in combination with the exchange rate, raises the relative prices of British goods delivered abroad, and lowers the relative price of imports, British firms will be at a competitive disadvantage with respect to price.

In the second place, there is the broader question of **non-price competitiveness**, which refers to the quality of the products produced, their technological level, the speed and reliability with which they are delivered, and the effectiveness of the marketing and promotion effort associated with them. Some authors have suggested (Posner and Steer (1979), Freeman (1979)) that in major industrial markets, which have become very much more wealthy over the last few decades, non-price factors are more important than price factors in determining the ability of a nation's industry to sell its products.

While price and non-price factors provide a general explanation for the loss of competitiveness in UK manufacturing, there are also special circumstances arising from the discovery and exploitation of North Sea oil. As the United Kingdom became a major oil producer, exporting around half of the North Sea's output, and importing only one third of Britain's oil needs, so the current account on the balance of payments moved into a very strong surplus, mainly accounted for by the trade in oil. That very strong positive contribution to the balance of payments meant that the price of the pound was very much higher than it would otherwise have been, which effectively 'squeezed' manufacturers' ability to export by weakening their price competitiveness. Fig. 2.1 provides a graphical illustration of this point, showing the changes in the structure of the UK's trade balances over the period 1979–83.

As the figure shows, the development of very large surpluses in the oil sector was accompanied by a simultaneous and dramatic decline in the trading performance of manufacturing industry. This had been predicted by a number of economists (Kay and Forsyth (1980)) who noted that if the economy produced a huge increase in the value of goods traded internationally, but did not itself purchase those goods, then there would have to be a structural shift in the economy to accommodate the changing balance of output and trade. The burden of this adjustment process fell on the manufacturing sector in the late 1970s and 1980s.

The level of industrial concentration

The importance of concentration

The term 'concentration' refers to the extent to which industrial activity is concentrated in the hands of a small number of firms. While concentration is only one aspect of industrial structure it is probably the single most important determinant of competitive behaviour and performance and therefore merits close attention. If an industry is highly concentrated, the firms within it may be able to exert some degree of market power, resulting in a misallocation of resources to the detriment of consumers and

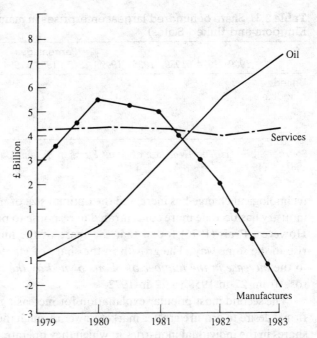

Fig. 2.1 The changing structure of UK trade balances 1979–1983
Source: Treasury and Civil Service Committee 1985, p. 100

a less efficient price system. On the other hand, a high level of concentration may be needed if firms are to operate at minimum cost by exploiting all of the available economies of scale and economies of scope (see Chapter 8).

The degree of concentration may be examined at two different levels. First, there is the **overall level of concentration** which refers to the extent to which the largest firms in an economy dominate total employment and output. Second, there is the level of **market concentration** which refers to the level of concentration in an individual industry or market. Each of these may be considered in turn.

The importance of the very largest firms

One of the major features of the business environment in the twentieth century has been the long-term trend towards a concentration of activity within the very largest firms. Table 2.3 shows the changes in the share of manufacturing net output accounted for by the hundred largest enterprises in the United Kingdom and the United States over the period 1909–1970.

As the table shows, both of these major economies experienced an increase in concentration over the period, although the shift has been more marked in the United Kingdom than in the United States.

Various suggestions have been put forward in explanation of the apparent secular trend towards larger enterprises. The most obvious such explanation is that

Table 2.3 Share of hundred largest enterprises in manufacturing net output (United Kingdom and United States)

	1909	1924	1929	1935	1947	1949	1953	1954	1958	1963	1967	1968	1970
						Percentages							
United Kingdom	16	22		24		22	27		32	37		41	40
United States	22		25	26	23			30	30	33	33		33

Source: S.J. Prais, *The Evolution of Giant Firms in Britain*, Cambridge University Press, 1981, p.140

technological change has increased the optimal size of manufacturing plants, so that industry has become more concentrated in response to plant-level economies of scale. However, Prais (1976) found that the share of the hundred largest *plants* did not rise in the same way. The growth in the share of giant enterprises was attributable to the *increase in the number of plants owned by the typical very large firm* which rose from 27 in 1958 to 72 in 1972.

The second most popular explanation for increasing overall concentration lies in firms' desire to acquire greater market power through the acquisition of larger market shares in the individual industries in which they operate. However, the evidence from the Prais study again suggested that this was not borne out by the facts in that there was very little correlation between the degree of multi-plant working in an industry and its level of concentration. If giant firms had increased the number of plants they operated in order to secure greater market power it would be expected that the two variables would be significantly positively correlated.

If neither scale economies nor the search for market power can explain the increasing level of overall concentration in industry other explanations need to be sought. One possibility is that large firms have advantages over smaller ones in respect of **economies of scope**, as opposed to plant-level **economies of scale**. Economies of scope arise when it is more efficient to carry out a number of different activities within the same firm, than to carry them out independently (see Chapter 8). Alternatively, as Prais argued, it might be the case that large firms have no inherent advantages over small ones, but that a random process of growth, referred to as **spontaneous drift** could produce the increasing levels of concentration. The details of such a process are too complex to examine in detail but it can readily be seen that if growth rates are variable and there is no correlation between growth rates and firm size then over time there will emerge a proportion of firms of ever-increasing size. Only the existence of **firm life cycles**, where older and larger firms eventually begin to fail, would prevent this from happening.

This random process of firm growth leading to increasing concentration may have been reinforced by the increasing importance of the financial institutions as major shareholders. If these institutions prefer to invest in large firms, financial pressures will encourage the formation of large industrial groups and the process of mergers (see Chapter 18).

Whatever its cause, the trend towards increasing overall concentration in the United

Kingdom has caused concern over its possible impact on the competitiveness and flexibility of the economy and upon the existence of an *enterprise culture*, which is often seen as being dependent upon the continuing health of the small business sector. Both governments and some academic economists have called for measures which shift the balance of advantage away from the very largest enterprises and towards smaller firms, in order to enhance the economy's ability to respond quickly and effectively to changes in the business environment.

The measurement of market concentration

Overall concentration is a highly aggregated phenomenon which may mask wide variations across individual industrial sectors. For the purposes of managerial economics, it is market concentration which is of the greatest interest, as it is concentration at that level which forms a major determinant of the environment in which individual firms operate.

Market concentration may be measured in a number of different ways. A useful starting point is with the **concentration curve**, which traces out the cumulative percentage of market output (or sales or employment or assets) against the cumulative number of firms, ranked from largest to smallest. Fig. 2.2 shows a number of such curves.

The advantage of the concentration curve is that it provides a graphical summary of the information relating to every firm in the industry. However, such a complete

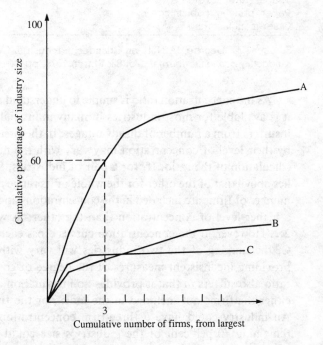

Fig. 2.2 Concentration curves

set of information is very expensive to collect and if empirical work is to be carried out some form of quantitative empirical measure needs to derived from it.

The most commonly used measure of concentration is the **concentration ratio**, which is the proportion of an industry's size accounted for by a group of the very largest firms. The three-firm concentration ratio, for instance, often denoted CR_3, shows the proportion of industry size accounted for by the three largest firms, shown for industry A in Fig. 2.2 as 60 per cent.

Table 2.4 shows the results of calculating five-firm concentration ratios for a large number of products in the UK in 1968 and then summarising the results for each major industrial sector by taking a weighted average of the results within each sector.

Table 2.4 Concentration in UK industry in 1968

Sector	Weighted average CR_5 %
Food, drink and tobacco	82
Chemicals and allied	79
Metals manufacture	75
Plant, machinery and instrument engineering	54
Electrical engineering	76
Vehicles	93
Other metals	58
Textiles	53
Leather, clothing, footwear	32
Bricks, pottery, glass, cement	65
Timber, furniture	23
Paper, printing, publishing	52
Other manufacturing	61

Source: K.D. George, 'A Note on Changes in Industrial Concentration in the United Kingdom', *Economic Journal*, Vol 85, March 1975, pp. 124–8

As the concentration ratio is simple to understand and relatively cheap to construct it is available for most industries in many industrialised economies. Unfortunately it suffers from a number of disadvantages. In the first place, the ranking of industries by their level of concentration may vary with the number of firms included in the calculation of the ratio. If, for a pair of industries, the concentration curve for one lies above that of the other for the whole of its range there is no difficulty. Whichever number of firms are included in the concentration ratio one industry will always record a higher level of concentration than the other, as with industries A and B in Fig. 2.2. However, if the concentration curves cross each other, as for industries B and C, the ranking of the two industries will vary with the number of firms chosen, providing inconsistent measures of the degree of concentration. The concentration ratio also suffers in that it provides no information at all about the relative sizes of either the firms not included in the index, or the firms which have been counted. An industry could have a three-firm concentration ratio of 60 per cent and the remaining 40 per cent of the industry's size could be distributed across just two additional firms having 20 per cent each, thereby being a five-firm oligopoly. On the other hand, the remaining 40 per cent could be quite evenly distributed across hundreds of other firms. Within the 60 per cent accounted for by the largest three firms there could be either an even distribution of around 20 per cent each, or a single firm could have 50 per cent with the two second largest having only 10 per cent between them. Such differences in market structure are likely to have important implications for the behaviour and performance of the firms but they will be hidden within the summary index.

A further difficulty with concentration ratios is that there is no theoretical reason for preferring a three-firm ratio to a five-firm or an n-firm ratio. The choice of the number of firms to include is entirely arbitrary.

An alternative measure of concentration, which does take into account the role played by all firms in the market, and yet still provides a single summary measure, is the **Herfindahl Index**. This is defined as the sum of the squares of the market shares of all firms, so that:

$$\text{Herfindahl Index} = \sum_1 s_i^2 \qquad \text{where } s_i^2 = \text{share of the i'th firm}$$

This index reflects both the number of firms in the industry and their relative size. It also has the intuitively useful property of providing a *numbers equivalent*. If an industry contained two firms of equal size the Herfindahl index would have a value of 0.5. If an industry had four firms the index would be equal to 0.25. If an industry has a Herfindahl index calculated as *n* then it has the same index value as an industry containing *1/n* firms of equal size, which helps to provide an intuitive 'feel' for the meaning of the measure. On the other hand, this could be misleading because there is no reason to suppose that an industry having index *n* actually contains *1/n* firms of the same size.

A different approach to the measurement of concentration is provided by measures of *inequality of firm size*. The best known such measure is the **Gini co-efficient**, which is derived from a **Lorenz curve**, as shown in Fig. 2.3.

The Lorenz curve shows the cumulative percentage of industry size set against the percentage of firms cumulated from the smallest. If the firms are all of equal size then the smallest 10 per cent will account for 10 per cent of the total industry and the smallest *x* per cent will account for *x* per cent of the total industry, so that the Lorenz curve will be a straight line from O to A, known as the *line of absolute equality*. If firms are of unequal size the Lorenz curve will lie below the line of absolute equality, with the extent of the divergence representing the extent of the inequality. That divergence can be quantified through the use of the Gini co-efficient which is equal to the shaded area divided by the area OAB. The Gini co-efficient has a maximum value of one and a minimum value of zero.

Although the Gini co-efficient takes account of all firms in the industry it has the disadvantage of being solely concerned with the relative size of firms, providing no information about their number. As a result, an industry containing only one firm, where there is no inequality of firm size, would take the same value of zero as an industry containing five or even 500 firms of the same size! Clearly there can be little

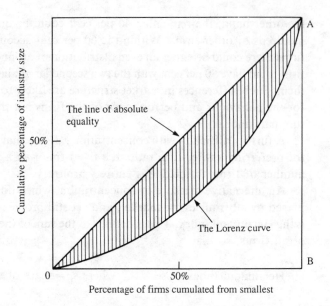

Fig. 2.3 Lorenz curves and Gini co-efficients

justification for using the Gini co-efficient as a measure of concentration, unless it is supplemented by other measures.

The determinants of market concentration

The level of concentration in an individual industry, and changes in that level, may be determined by a number of factors. The most obvious one is **economies of scale** in production or in advertising and promotion. It has been noted above, in the discussion on the overall level of concentration, that scale economies were dismissed in one major study as the prime determinant of the increase in overall concentration on the grounds that the level of concentration in plants had not increased to the same extent as concentration in firms. However, the evidence on the overall level of concentration does not preclude the possibility of market concentration being determined in many cases by scale economies. If technological change alters the extent of scale economies by changing the optimal scale of operations, the level of concentration may change as firms adjust to the new technology. It is also important to remember that scale economies are not limited to production alone. In consumer goods in particular, firms which can afford high levels of advertising may be able to secure discounts from the advertising media and the impact of advertising and promotion may be cumulative so that heavy spending on advertising secures consumer loyalty to a much greater extent than lower levels.

If concentration were solely determined by economies of scale firms would not expand beyond the size needed to reap all of the known scale economies. However, there is evidence that in some industries concentration is greater than is needed to secure the scale economies available. In this case the most important determinant of concentration lies in firms' attempts to secure the profits arising from having market power, by erecting entry barriers to limit new firms' access to the market or by merging with other firms in order to secure larger market shares. It is certainly the case that mergers have played a very important role in the process of concentration in both the UK and the US and one study of increasing concentration in UK manufacturing (Hannah and Kay (1977)) found that in the post-war period mergers actually accounted for more than 100 per cent of the increase in concentration, a result which implies that in the absence of mergers, concentration would have actually declined.

The links between concentration and the possibility of harmful abuse of market power are complex and causality may run in both directions. Concentration may provide firms with the monopoly power to exploit consumers, or it may be the drive to secure monopoly power which causes higher levels of concentration. Whichever way the relationship operates there is clearly a risk that in concentrated industries the beneficial forces of competition may be weakened. For that reason many countries, including the UK and the US, have policies which are designed to guard against that possibility, either by preventing firms from gaining a dominant position or by making illegal the abuse of a dominant position.

Illustration

R&D spending: Britain's lost opportunity

One of the most important issues which has been raised in the context of the UK's 'de-industrialisation' concerns the relationship between an economy's ability to innovate and its ability to compete in export markets. Freeman (1979) provides a useful and sobering commentary on that relationship in the UK.

Until the 1960s, economic theory explained trade patterns in terms of cost advantages based upon factor endowments. If a country had abundant labour then labour would be relatively cheap. That economy would have a price advantage in labour-intensive goods, and would export them.

Such traditional theories of trade assumed that the same technologies were available in all countries and that technological effort was not a determinant of trading success. That explanation, however, was increasingly challenged by theorists who developed 'technology gap' theories of trade, arguing that for some goods at least, a country's ability to export was not based upon factor endowments and costs, but on the possession of superior technology.

Various studies have suggested that trade performance is indeed linked to technological performance. Freeman points in particular to a study which used patent statistics as a measure of innovative effort and which examined the statistical relationship between export competitiveness and innovative effort. Exports per capita were regressed against US patents per capita for 40 industries, across 22 member countries of the OECD. The results suggested that there were two different categories of industry. First, there were those in which export performance is directly related to technological effort. That group included most types of machinery, metal products and chemicals. Secondly, there were industries which displayed no significant relationship between innovation and exporting, which included consumer goods and basic materials.

Examination of the UK's post-war technological effort in the light of that evidence shows that it had two outstanding features in comparison with most other industrialised countries. In the first place, throughout the 1950s and 1960s, Britain ranked much higher than Germany and Japan in terms of the absolute level of resources devoted to R&D. The country had an opportunity to secure a technological lead. Unfortunately, those resources were very highly concentrated in a very narrow range of applications. The aircraft industry and military applications absorbed a large proportion of the total spending and manpower. As a result, the technical effort was particularly weak in exactly those sectors where the evidence suggests that innovation was important to export performance.

The concentration of UK innovative effort in a narrow range of sectors had a very high opportunity cost. The country's limited technical manpower was used in projects, like Concorde, nuclear power stations and military hardware, which involved huge investments with very limited commercial returns. At the same time manufacturing industry in general employed far fewer graduate level engineers than its counterparts in Germany and Japan, weakening its capacity to compete. Market share was lost, and continued to be lost, as the technological content of UK goods fell behind that of its competitors.

In summary, then, the very substantial resources which were put into British research and development in the two decades after the Second World War were effectively wasted and the British economy has been paying the price for that mistake ever since.

References and further reading

A.A. Berle and G.C. Means, *The Modern Corporation and Private Property*, (New York, Macmillan, 1932, reprinted 1948)

R. Bacon and W. Eltis, *Britain's Economic Problem: Too Few Producers*, (London, Macmillan, 1976)

Committee to Review the Functioning of Financial Institutions (the Wilson Committee), *Report*, Cmnd 7937, HMSO 1980

C. Freeman, 'Technical Innovation and British Trade Performance' in Blackaby, F. *De-industrialisation*, (London, Heinemann, 1979)

J. Gershuny, 'The Fallacy of the Service Economy', *Futures*, April 1977

R.A. Gordon, *Business Leadership in the Large Corporation*, (Los Angeles, California UP, 1961)

L. Hannah and J. Kay, *Concentration in Modern Industry* (London, Macmillan, 1977)

J. Kay and P. Forsyth, 'The Economic Implications of North Sea Oil Reserves', *Fiscal Studies*, 1980

S. Kuznets, *Economic Growth of Nations*, (Cambridge, Mass., Harvard UP, 1971)

R. Lewis, *The New Service Society*, (London, Longman, 1973)

M.V. Posner and A. Steer, in Blackaby, F., *De-industrialisation*, op. cit.

S.J. Prais, *The Evolution of Giant Firms in Britain*, (London, Cambridge UP, 1976)

A. Singh, 'UK Industry and the World Economy: A Case of De-industrialisation', *Cambridge Journal of Economics*, 1977

A.P. Thirlwall, 'De-industrialisation in the United Kingdom', *Lloyds Bank Review*, 1982

Self-test questions

1 **Which of the following statements are correct?**

(a) sole proprietorship involves unlimited liability on the part of the owner.

(b) the concentration of share ownership in the hands of financial institutions is likely to give managers more discretion in setting the objectives of their companies.

(c) holders of preference shares usually have more significant voting rights than holders of ordinary shares

(d) the development of the joint stock company means that no one is liable for such a company's losses.

(e) Articles of Association are concerned with a company's external relations

2 **Which of the following aspects of *de-industrialisation*, have been experienced by the British economy?**

(a) declining manufacturing output

(b) increasing employment in the service sector

(c) declining absolute employment in manufacturing

(d) failure to export sufficient manufactures to pay for manufactured imports

3 **Which of the following are absolute measures of concentration?**

(a) concentration ratios

(b) Herfindahl index

(c) Gini co-efficient

4 **If an industry contains four firms of equal size what will be the value of**

(a) the Herfindahl Index

(b) The Gini co-efficient

(c) the three-firm concentration ratio

5 **According to the major study by Prais, which of the following factors appears to provide the best explanation for the increasing importance of the very largest firms?**

(a) increasing economies of scale at plant level

(b) the desire for greater market power

(c) a random process of spontaneous drift

Exercise

Explain and account for the shifting balance of employment between the manufacturing and service sectors in the United Kingdom.

Answers on page 397.

3 Business objectives and models of the firm

This chapter considers a variety of different models of the firm, based upon different assumptions about the firm's basic objective. The neo-classical economic model of the firm is developed first and then the chapter goes on to examine some of the criticisms which have been directed at that model, and some of the alternatives which have been put forward in its place.

The neo-classical economic model of the firm

There are many different models of the firm, embodying many different assumptions, which could be described as 'economic' models. However, there is one particular version which forms the mainstream orthodox treatment of the firm, to be found in every introductory textbook. This centres around three basic sets of assumptions concerning the aim of the firm, and its knowledge of the cost and demand conditions facing it.

The assumption of profit-maximisation

The first component of the neo-classical model of the firm is the assumption that the objective of the firm is to maximise profits, defined as the difference between the firm's revenues and its costs. In this simple form the assumption is too vague, because it makes no reference to the period of time over which profits are to be maximised. This may be resolved in one of two ways. The simplest is to see the model as a one-period or short-run model, where the firm's assumed aim is to make as much profit as possible in the short run. The short run, it will be remembered, is defined by economists as the period in which the firm is restricted to a given set of plant and equipment, and has some fixed costs which cannot be avoided even by ceasing production.

A slightly more complex version, which establishes a multi-period setting for the model, is to assume that the objective of the firm is to maximise the wealth of its shareholders, which in turn is equal to the discounted value of the expected future net cash flows into the firm. In this case, the firm can be thought of as facing two interrelated kinds of decision. First, it has to take long-run or investment decisions on the level of capacity and the type of plant it wishes to install. Second, it has to decide upon the most profitable use of that set of plant and equipment. These short-run, capacity utilisation, decisions are essentially the same as those facing the firm maximising profits in the short run, and the same analysis applies. If the profits made in each period are independent of each other, the single-period and multi-period models will be consistent with each other. However, there is a more difficult problem if the profits made in the current period could have an influence on the profits made in the future, because in that case it is possible that shareholders' wealth could be maximised by sacrificing profits in the current period.

For instance, if a firm has a monopoly position, the maximum profit possible in the current period may be very large. However, if the firm uses its monopoly power to make that maximum profit, other firms may be attracted into the industry, or it might draw the attention of the anti-trust authorities. In either case, it is possible that the maximisation of shareholders' wealth will be better achieved by not taking the maximum profit available in the short run. The simple neo-classical model of the firm does not consider such complications, being essentially concerned with the maximisation of short-run or single period profits.

The assumption of profit-maximisation gives the basic model of the firm a number of characteristics which distinguish it from other models. In the first place, it identifies a model which is 'holistic' in the sense that, however large and complex, the firm is seen as a single entity which can be said to have objectives of its own and which can be said to take decisions. This is in marked contrast to the 'behavioural' model of the firm, where it is argued that 'only people can have objectives, organisations cannot', and to the 'managerialist' model where it is argued that managers and shareholders have different and conflicting objectives.

The second characteristic of the model, which also stems from the assumption of profit-maximisation is that it is an 'optimising' model, where the firm is seen as attempting to achieve the best possible performance, rather than simply seeking 'feasible' performance which meets some set of minimum criteria. Again, this is in contrast to the behavioural model and to many quantitative techniques in operational research or operations management which seek merely to identify feasible, rather than optimal solutions to problems.

Costs and output

The second component of the textbook model of the firm concerns the nature of the firm's production and the behaviour of costs, considered in more detail in Chapter 8. The firm is assumed to produce a single, perfectly divisible, standardised product for which the cost of production is known with certainty. In the short run, when some costs are fixed, the average cost curve will be U-shaped, as shown in Fig. 3.1.

Cost per unit falls over the range A to B, as the fixed costs are spread over a

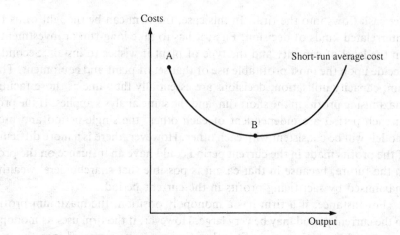

Fig. 3.1 The short-run cost curve

larger number of units, but begins to rise beyond B as the principle of diminishing returns leads to increasing variable costs per unit.

As the textbook model is essentially concerned with the short-run situation, it is short-run cost curves which are most relevant, and which are shown in the diagrams. The model depicts a firm which is attempting to maximise its profit with respect to a particular set of plant and equipment which has a particular short-run cost curve. If we also wish to consider long-run decisions then attention needs to be paid to the behaviour of costs in the long run, considered in more detail in Chapter 8.

Demand conditions

The third component of the orthodox model of the firm is the assumption that the firm has certain knowledge of the volume of output which can be sold at each price. These 'demand conditions' are considered in more detail in Chapters 4 to 6. For the purposes of this chapter it is sufficient to note that demand depends upon two sets of factors. First, it depends upon the behaviour of consumers, which determines the total demand for the product. Second, it depends upon the structure of the industry in which the firm is operating, and the behaviour of rival sellers. The simplest example to consider is that of the monopolist, where there is only one supplier of the product in question. In that case, consumer demand for the product can only be met by the single firm in the industry and there is no distinction between the total demand for the product and the demand for the individual firm. There is only one demand curve for the firm and the industry. The precise shape of that curve depends upon the nature of the product in question, the number of consumers in the market concerned and their incomes, wealth and tastes. However, as the analysis in Chapter 5 shows, it can generally be assumed that the demand curve will slope downwards from left to right, indicating that more of the product can be sold at lower prices.

Equilibrium in the profit-maximising monopoly model

Having assumed profit-maximisation, and certain knowledge of cost and demand conditions, it is possible to move on to the second stage of model building, which is to draw out the implications, or predictions, which follow from the assumptions. The method of reasoning used to do this is essentially that of the mathematician. It is assumed that the problem has been solved, and then the conditions which must therefore hold are examined. The mathematical formulation of the model can be simply set out as follows:

Maximise $(q)

Where $(q) = R(q) − C(q)   where

$(q) = profit
R(q) = revenue
C(q) = costs
q   = units of output sold

Translated into words, this formulation simply means 'maximise profit where profit is equal to revenue minus costs, and where costs and revenue each depend upon the amount of output which is sold.' Elementary calculus shows that if profit is to be maximised, the following conditions have to hold.

Condition 1: $d\$/dq = dR/dq - dC/dq = 0$
or $dR/dq = dC/dq$

Condition 2: $d^2R/dq^2 > d^2C/dq^2$

Again, restating these equations verbally, profit will be a maximum if the firm produces the level of output such that **marginal revenue** (dR/dq) equals **marginal cost** (dC/dq) and when the slope of the marginal cost curve exceeds the slope of the marginal revenue curve. This rather formal presentation of the model can be expanded upon using a diagrammatic version, shown in Fig. 3.2.

In Fig. 3.2, the profit-maximising level of output is X and the profit-maximising price is P. The reason for this is simply explained without resort to mathematics. The decision which the firm is facing concerns the level of output which should be produced and sold using the set of plant and equipment which it has installed. (The simple model always assumes that sales volume and output are equal, taking no account of the possibility of producing to stock or selling from stock.) It will pay the firm to produce any unit of output for which the extra revenue earned (marginal revenue) exceeds the extra cost (marginal cost). At level of output X all such units are being produced. If output is increased further, the additional units produced will add more to costs than to the revenues, and the level of profit will fall.

The diagram and the equations set out above identify the profit-maximising **equilibrium** for the firm. In the short run, under the assumptions made, the firm will produce the indicated level of output and sell it at the indicated price. If cost and demand conditions remain the same, the firm has no incentive to alter its price or output, and the firm is said to be in equilibrium.

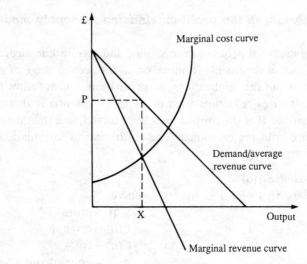

Fig. 3.2 Profit-maximising equilibrium

Applications of the simple model

The model which has been developed above may be used in a number of ways. Its purpose in mainstream economic theory is essentially to predict how a firm will respond to changes in its environment. If some aspect of the environment changes, the model indicates the ways in which the firm will respond in order to move to a new equilibrium. For instance, if demand increases, both price and output will increase. If costs rise, price will rise but output will fall. Fig. 3.3 shows the **comparative static properties** of the profit-maximising model.

Change	Impact on	
	Price	Output
Demand increase	+	+
Demand fall	−	−
Increase in variable cost	+	−
Lump sum tax or cost increase	0	0

Fig. 3.3 Comparative static properties of the profit-maximising model

In addition to these 'positive' uses of the model, it is sometimes also used for 'normative' purposes, providing prescriptions telling managers what they 'ought to do' in certain circumstances. For instance, the finding that a firm seeking maximum profit should produce every unit of output for which the marginal revenue exceeds marginal cost is often presented as just such a prescription, and extended in the management accounting literature into the similar finding that firms should always agree to accept business which brings in greater **incremental revenue** than **incremental cost**. Such prescriptions are valid, provided that the firm is attempting to maximise profit, and the assumptions of the model are completely fulfilled. If they are not, however, it could be extremely dangerous to adopt the prescriptions without further thought.

Profits in the long run: the maximisation of shareholders' wealth

The profit-maximising model set out above is concerned with capacity utilisation and the short run. The firm has some fixed costs, arising from a given set of plant and equipment, and is concerned to make as much profit as possible, given the constraints set by that equipment. However, the firm also has to take investment decisions, which are concerned with the long run, in which no costs are fixed and when the firm is free to choose whichever set of plant and equipment it prefers.

When considering these long-run decisions it is not sufficient to characterise the firm's objective as 'profit-maximisation' because profit is defined as revenue minus opportunity cost in a single period, without reference to the pattern of returns over time. It might be argued very simplistically that long-run profit-maximisation consists of maximising the simple sum of profits over a number of short periods, but that would leave the unanswered question 'over how long should profits be added up?'. More significantly, such a simple addition would give the same weighting to returns occurring at different times, thereby ignoring the time-value of money (see Chapter 15 for a fuller explanation).

In order to avoid this difficulty, the long-run objective of the profit-maximising firm is said to be the maximisation of shareholders' wealth, which is achieved by maximising the value of the firm. This in turn is measured by the present value of the stream of expected future net cash flows accruing to the firm. The restatement of the firm's profit objective in this way allows the short run and the long run to be properly integrated. In the long run, as shown in Chapter 15, the firm decides upon the set of capital equipment to purchase by using investment appraisal techniques based upon the calculation of present values. However, these calculations themselves require estimates of the revenues and costs which are associated with each investment project, on the assumption that the equipment, once purchased, will be used to secure maximum profit. Choosing a set of capital equipment in the long run therefore requires the solution of the short-run questions concerning revenues, costs and profits in the short run.

If the profits earned in each period, or each short run, are independent of each other, then the maximisation of profit in each period will lead to the maximisation of shareholders' wealth. However, as noted in the section on the assumption of profit-maximisation earlier in this chapter, if profits in one period depend upon profits in another, there may be a conflict between the two objectives. A firm with a monopoly position might make maximum profit in the short run by exploiting that position to the full, but in doing so it might attract entry to the industry, or anti-trust action from government, which would reduce profit in future periods. Maximising shareholders' wealth could require the sacrifice of immediate profits in order to protect their value in the longer term, depending upon the shape of the time-stream of profits, and the discount rate used to calculate present values. As the long-run objective, formulated in present value terms, takes account of the relative weighting to be given to profits accruing at different times, it should be given priority if such a conflict between objectives arises.

Managerial discretion models of the firm

'Managerial' criticisms of the profit-maximising model

The textbook model of the profit-maximising firm has been criticised on a number of different grounds. Perhaps the best known of these centres around the claim that it is unrealistic to assume that firms aim for maximum profits in a modern economy where ownership and control of firms lie with different groups of individuals. The pioneering work of Berle and Means (1932) in the United States demonstrated clearly that the modern corporation was not simply a larger version of the owner-managed firm, but that ownership and control had become separated. Control lay in the hands of professional managers while ownership rested with shareholders. If the interests of shareholders and managers differ, if shareholders have relatively limited information about the performance of the firms they own, and if shareholders take relatively little interest in the firms' operations, provided a satisfactory dividend is paid, then managers may have a good deal of 'discretion' to pursue their own objectives. This will be particularly true where firms have some degree of monopoly power and do not have to compete keenly in order to make a satisfactory level of profit. It has been suggested, therefore, that in oligopolistic markets, firms do not pursue profit as their major objective.

The suggestion that profit is not the objective of modern corporations has led to the search for alternative models based upon different assumptions about the firm's objective. There are many such models, but the best-known are:

- the sales-revenue-maximising model, developed by Baumol (1958)
- the managerial-utility-maximising model (Williamson (1963))
- the multi-period profit-maximising rate of growth model (Baumol (1967))
- the Marris model (Marris(1964))
- J.Williamson's integrative model (1966)

Each of these merits some attention.

Baumol's sales revenue-maximising model

Baumol's model stems from the observation that the salaries of managers, their status and other rewards often appear to be more closely linked to the size of the companies in which they work, measured by sales revenue, than to their profitability. In that case, managers may be more concerned to increase size than to increase profits, and the firm's objective will be to maximise sales revenue rather than profits.

If the assumption of profit-maximisation is replaced by that of sales-revenue-maximisation, then a different model results. In many respects, it shares fundamental characteristics with the standard model, as it is also an optimising model in which a single product firm aims for a single objective, having perfect information about its cost and demand conditions. Nevertheless, the details are different, as illustrated in Fig. 3.4, which sets out the basic version of the model, using total revenue, total cost, and profit curves.

In Fig. 3.4, the firm will choose to produce level of output A, giving total revenue B and profit C. Note that this implies a higher level of output, and therefore a lower price, than the equivalent profit-maximiser, which would produce output D and earn revenue E. A straightforward revenue- maximiser will always produce more and charge less than a profit-maximising firm facing the same cost and demand conditions for the following reason:

- for revenue-maximisation marginal revenue = 0
- for profit-maximisation marginal revenue = Marginal cost
- as marginal cost must be greater than 0, then for a profit-maximiser: marginal revenue must be greater than 0
- therefore marginal revenue for a profit-maximiser must be greater than marginal revenue for a revenue-maximiser
- as marginal revenue slopes downwards to the right, equilibrium output must be higher for a revenue maximiser than for the profit-maximiser.

As it happens, in Fig. 3.4, the sales-maximiser also makes some profit. However, this may not be enough to satisfy the shareholders, and in many cases maximising

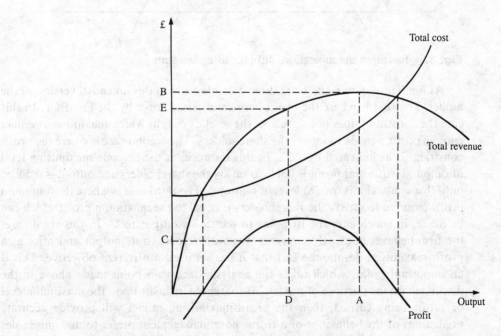

Fig. 3.4 Baumol's revenue-maximising model

revenue may imply making losses. As a result the simple revenue-maximising model is implausible, and the model needs to be amended to include a profit constraint. Instead of simply assuming that the firm aims for maximum revenue, without regard to the implications for profit, it is assumed that the objective is the maximisation of sales revenue, *subject to meeting a minimum profit constraint*. This version is shown in Fig. 3.5.

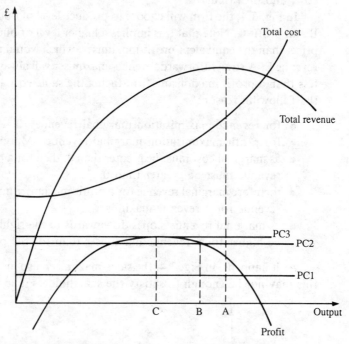

Fig. 3.5 Revenue-maximisation, subject to constraints

As the figure shows, there are three possible cases in this amended version of the model. The first is where the profit constraint is as shown by the line PC1. In this case the constraint does not 'bite'. At the level of output which maximises revenue, enough profit is made to satisfy the shareholders. The second case is where the profit constraint is as indicated by PC2. In this instance, at the revenue maximising level of output, insufficient profit is made to satisfy the shareholders and output is reduced until that constraint is met, at level of output B. The third case is where the minimum profit required to satisfy the shareholders is equal to the maximum profit which can be made, in which case the firm has to reduce its output to C. In this third case, the firm behaves in exactly the same way with respect to its output and price as a profit-maximiser, despite the fact that it has set itself a different objective. This is an important point, which takes the analysis back to a point made above in the discussion on the purpose of models. If shareholders insist upon the maximum level of profit being earned, then the profit-maximising model will provide accurate predictions of the behaviour of a firm whose management prefer to maximise sales revenue. If the purpose of the model is to predict the firm's behaviour the fact that managers see their aim as maximising sales revenue, and not profit, is irrelevant. The firm behaves 'as if' it were a profit-maximiser.

The revenue-maximising model can be compared to the profit-maximising model with respect to its comparative static properties, which reveals both similarities and differences. If demand increases, both types of firm respond in the same way, with an increase in output and price. On the other hand it has been shown above for a profit-maximiser that if fixed costs increase, or a lump-sum tax is imposed, price and output will not change. However, for a revenue-maximiser whose profit constraint is already biting, a lump-sum tax will reduce profits and will force the firm to lower its output and raise its price.

The managerial utility-maximising model

In Baumol's sales-revenue-maximising model, managers' interests are tied to a single variable, with the addition of a profit constraint. Williamson's managerial-utility-maximising model takes account of a wider range of variables by introducing the concept of **'expense preferences'** and beginning with the assumption that managers attempt to maximise their own utility. The term 'expense preference' simply means that managers get satisfaction from using some of the firm's potential profits for unnecessary spending on items from which they personally benefit. Williamson identifies three major types of expense from which managers derive utility. These are:

1. **The amount which managers can spend on staff, over and above those needed to run the firm's operations (S).** This variable captures the power, prestige, status and satisfaction which managers' experience from having control over larger numbers of people.
2. **Additions to managers' salaries and benefits in the form of 'perks' (M).** These include unnecessarily luxurious company cars, extravagant entertainment and clothing allowances, club subscriptions, palatial offices and similar items of expenditure. Such items may also be thought of as 'managerial slack' or 'X-inefficiency' (see below). They appear as costs to the firm, but are not necessary for the efficient conduct of its activities and are in effect coming out of profits.
3. **Discretionary profits (D).** These are after-tax profits over and above the minimum required to satisfy the shareholders. They are therefore available to the managers as a source of finance for 'pet projects' and allow the managers to invest in developing the firm in directions which suit them, enhancing their power, status and satisfaction.

Clearly there are conflicts and trade-offs between the different objectives in this model, and it is considerably more complex than those considered thus far. The detailed workings of the model go beyond the requirements of this text. Nevertheless, the main outlines are reasonably accessible. The basic form of the model is as follows;

$U = f(S,M,D)$ – managerial utility (U) depends upon the levels of S, M and D available to the managers.

In common with the utility theory of consumer behaviour it is also assumed that the principle of diminishing marginal utility applies, so that additional increments to each of S, M and D yield smaller increments of utility to the management.

If R = Revenue, C = Costs and T = Taxes then
Actual profit = R − C − S
Reported profit = R − C − S − M

If the minimum post-tax profit required by the shareholders is Z, then:

D = R − C − S − M − T − Z

The solution to the model requires a fairly complex use of calculus in order to maximise the utility function (see Reekie and Crook (1982) for an attempt at a geometrical exposition). However, it is possible to set out a simplified version.

If managerial utility is to be maximised, the last pound spent on S, M and D must yield the same marginal utility, i.e.:

$$MU_S = MU_M = MU_D(1 − t)$$ Where t is the rate of tax on profits.

This can be used to examine some of the comparative static properties of the model.

If demand declines, then at every level of output D will decline. On the assumption of diminishing marginal utility, MU_D will rise, so that the equilibrium condition is no longer fulfilled. To regain equilibrium the available profits will be redistributed towards D and away from S and M. The level of output will fall. Similarly for a rise in fixed costs, or a lump-sum tax.

If the tax on profits increases then $MU_D(1 − t)$ will fall and so there will be a shift towards S and M, accompanied by increasing output.

The complexity of the Williamson model can make it difficult to examine in every detail. However, it does have an interesting application in explaining how take-overs are often followed very quickly by increases in reported profits. If the new management team exhibits a weaker preference for S and M, both of which entail unnecessary costs, they will prune these in line with their own preferences and will be able to very quickly report higher profits without too much difficulty and before altering any of the fundamentals of the business.

As in the case of the Baumol model, it should always be remembered that the usefulness of the model depends upon the management team having the discretion to earn less than maximum profits. If the minimum profit required by the shareholders is equal to the maximum possible, the managers will not have the discretion to indulge their taste for 'perks' and unnecessary staff.

The profit-maximising rate of growth model

Both of the models set out above are **static** in that they contain no reference to developments over time and the equilibria identified involve sales, profits and utilities remaining constant unless preferences or outside circumstances change. In addition to such static models there are a range of **dynamic** models which consider growth over time in a multi-period setting.

One such model is the **profit-maximising rate of sales growth** model, developed by Baumol (1967). In this analysis the aim of the firm is to maximise the present value of expected future profits, which is simply the difference between the present value of expected future revenues and the present value of expected future costs, as shown in Fig. 3.6.

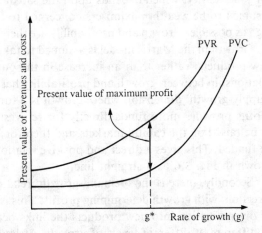

Fig. 3.6 Profit-maximising rate of growth

The present value of costs (PVC in Fig. 3.6) is made up of two components. First there are the costs of producing output, including both the fixed and variable costs of operation (see Chapter 8 for further details). Secondly, there are the costs associated with expansion, especially those concerning the development of a management team capable of controlling a larger organisation, and those involving the raising of finance. While the costs of production may rise proportionately with growth it is assumed that expansion costs will rise more than proportionately as the growth rate rises, so that PVC has the shape shown in Fig. 3.6, becoming increasingly steep.

The curve showing the present value of expected future revenues will also tend to be upward sloping, with an increasing slope. Whatever the discount rate used to calculate present values, the present value of future revenues will be larger as the growth rate of sales volume is larger. A relatively simple mathematical manipulation (see Reekie and Crook (1982) pp.61-62) shows that the slope of the line increases with the growth rate.

In this model the decision variable is not the level of output, but the growth rate of output, selected in order to maximise the present value of future profits, given by rate of growth g*, where the vertical distance between the revenue and cost curves is at its greatest.

The Marris model

The Marris model (Marris(1964)) is also dynamic in that it concerns growth rates, but it shares the basic assumption of the Williamson model that managers aim to maximise their utility. However, instead of managers gaining utility from expense preference, in this case it is assumed that their utility depends upon the rate of growth of the firm. While growth is their main aim, managers are also motivated by the need for job security, which depends upon the satisfaction of the shareholders, who are assumed to be wealth-maximisers concerned to keep share prices and dividends as high as possible. Growth and profitability are therefore the key variables in this model.

Growth in the Marris model is assumed to take place through diversification into new products, rather than an increase in the output of existing products, and the relationship between growth and profitability has two dimensions. First, there is the 'supply-growth' dimension where growth is a function of profits. A higher level of profits provides more funds directly for reinvestment and also allows more funds to be raised on the capital markets and therefore allows a higher rate of growth to be funded. This gives a direct and positive relationship between growth and profits, shown in Fig. 3.6 as a straight line.

Secondly, there is the **'demand-growth'** relationship which operates in the other direction, with growth determining profits. This is more complex. As growth consists of diversification into new products the links between profits and growth are seen as different at different levels of growth. At low levels of growth it is argued that the relationship is a positive one, with more growth providing more profits. At these levels it is argued that the firm will be introducing the most profitable new products from those which are possible and managers will be motivated to be more efficient by more growth. However, as the growth rate increases, with ever greater diversification, the relationship changes and becomes negative. The management team has to cope with increasing burdens, including the development of a larger management team, the higher rate of diversification can only be maintained by proportionately higher expenditures on advertising and research and development. As a result, beyond a certain growth rate, higher growth leads to lower profitability. The resulting relationship is shown in Fig. 3.7.

As both the 'supply-growth' and 'demand-growth' relationship must be satisfied, the combination of growth and profitability which the firm achieves must be where the two curves intersect, at point X.

In the example shown in Fig. 3.7 the combination of profitability and growth chosen is not one where profits are maximised. The managers' desire for growth, from which they gain utility, has encouraged them to seek more growth than is consistent with profit-maximisation. However, the extent to which they do this depends upon the strength of their desire for job security, which may be threatened if the shareholders feel that their wealth is not being maximised and if there is an active threat of take-over by other firms. This will affect the position of the 'supply-growth' relationship, through the retention ratio and the price of the firm's shares.

If the retention ratio is very low, so that nearly all profits are distributed to the shareholders, then at every level of profitability, growth will be low, as there is limited

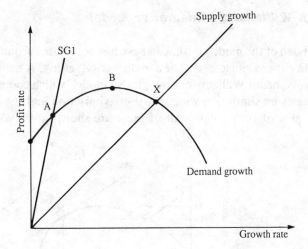

Fig. 3.7 The Marris model

finance for expansion. The supply-growth curve will be very steep, as shown by SG1 in Fig. 3.7. The equilibrium of the firm will be at a point like A, where less than maximum profit is earned and growth is relatively low. As the retention ratio rises, the supply-growth curve becomes flatter as more growth can be financed from retained earnings at each level of profitability. As a result, as the retention ratio rises, so does the equilibrium combination of growth and profitability until it reaches point B where profits are maximised. Up to this point the managers need have no fears for their job security as the combination of higher profits and higher growth must meet with the approval of the shareholders. However, if the managers of the firm wish to adopt even higher retention ratios, giving even higher growth then they need to pay careful attention to the impact on the wealth of shareholders. A further increase in retentions will reduce dividends because profits will be lower and the proportion of those distributed in dividends will be lower. In so far as share prices are determined by both dividends and the firm's growth rate it will probably be possible to go some way beyond point B without the firm's share price beginning to fall. However, at some point the effect of still higher retentions, creating an even flatter supply-growth curve and yet lower profits and dividends will be to reduce the share price and the value of shareholders' wealth, rendering the firm vulnerable to take-over and threatening the job security of the incumbent management. The actual position of the supply-growth curve will depend upon how real the threat of take-over is perceived to be and the relative preferences of managers for job security and growth. If the threat of take-over is perceived to be very powerful, and managers place a high value on job security then they will not push the firm beyond the point where shareholders' wealth and the share price is maximised. However, if the threat of take-over is perceived to be weak, and managers place a high value on growth relative to job security, they will adopt retentions policies which give higher growth and lower profits than those which would be optimal for the shareholders.

J. Williamson's integrative model

Each of the models outlined above has been based around a single objective function, in either a single-period or a multi-period setting. A number of these may be brought together in Williamson's integrative model, which combines single period profit and sales-maximisation with growth-maximisation and the maximisation of the present value of future sales. All of these are shown in Fig. 3.8.

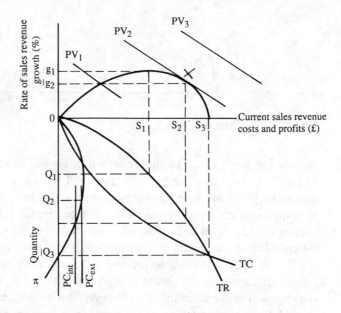

Fig. 3.8 An integrative model

The lower part of the diagram in Fig. 3.8 shows total cost, revenue and profit in a single period, along with the profit constraint required in the Baumol model. The upper quadrant shows the relationship between the rate of growth and current sales revenue. Growth of sales revenue is assumed to be directly related to profits, so that growth is maximised when profits are maximised and growth is zero when profits are zero. A single-period profit-maximiser and a sales-growth maximiser will therefore both produce level of output Q_1. A single-period revenue-maximiser, subjected to the externally imposed profit constraint, PC_{ext} will produce a higher level of output Q_2.

A firm which aims to maximise the present value of future sales will seek the combination of current revenue and growth rate which gives that maximum. This can be found in Fig. 3.8 by constructing 'iso-present-value' curves joining all points which have the same present value. As the present value increases with both the growth rate and the current sales value the maintenance of a constant present value requires that a higher growth rate be combined with a lower current value of sales and vice versa. The 'iso-present-value lines' must therefore be negatively sloped as shown in the diagram by the lines PV_1 to PV_3. Higher present values are given by lines which are further away from the origin and the present value of sales is maximised at point X. This must lie to the right of the profit-maximising position, by virtue of the downward slope of the 'iso-present-value' lines, so that a firm which aims to maximise the present value of sales will always choose a level of output which exceeds that of the profit-maximiser. If the firm is to achieve its maximisation target it must grow at rate 'g_2', which requires the level of current profit given by the profit constraint 'PC_{int}', which is an internally imposed profit constraint set by the management in recognition of the need to achieve growth rate 'g_2.

In the diagram shown, the internally generated profit constraint is lower than that imposed externally. Maximising the present value of sales requires an output level greater than Q_2 and there is a conflict between the firm's desire for a higher level of sales and the need to meet the profit constraint. The outcome of that conflict depends upon the extent to which the managers of the firm have the discretion to pursue their own objectives when they conflict with others.

In defence of the profit-maximising model

The methodological defence

The managerial models described above have their origins in dissatisfaction with the profit-maximising model arising from the claim that firms do not attempt to maximise profits in a world where ownership and control are separate and where the oligopolistic nature of markets gives firms a degree of monopoly power which cushions them from the need to maintain profits at their maximum level.

Supporters of the orthodox model put forward a number of arguments in its defence. In the first place, falling back on a methodological argument outlined above, it can be pointed out that the descriptive realism of an assumption is not a valid criterion on which to judge a model. If the purpose of a model is to predict, rather than simply to describe, then the criteria for evaluating a model are quite clear. First, the model must yield predictions, which the profit-maximising model does. Second, those predictions should be testable against the data, which is a test the model also passes. Third, the predictions should be supported by the data, which its supporters would claim is also the case. If this proposition is accepted, then the basic argument of the managerial school is ill-founded, as the realism of the profit-maximising assumption is quite irrelevant.

Links between ownership and control

Despite the apparent strength of the methodological argument, many economists continue to be uncomfortable with the prospect of depending upon a model based upon an unrealistic assumption. Other defences of the profit-maximising model have suggested that the basic assumption is in fact much more realistic than the managerialist arguments suggest.

In the first place it may be noted that the separation between ownership and control, upon which the managerialist argument depends very heavily, is by no means as great as it might appear. Although shareholders and managers are clearly not exactly the same set of people, there is considerable overlap between the two. In most companies, the directors own shares in the firm and a substantial part of their total remuneration package consists of the returns on those shares in the form of dividends and increases in share values. There is therefore a very important group of individuals who are both shareholders and senior managers, bridging the gap between ownership and control. As companies increasingly introduce profit-related bonus schemes, or give managers the option to purchase shares, managers have an increasing direct personal interest in the firm's profitability.

The power of institutional shareholders

A second strand in the managerialist argument is that shareholders are not well-informed about the activities of the firms they own, and exhibit only minor concern about their performance, being disinclined to criticise or displace the incumbent management provided a moderate level of dividend is paid. This allows the management of a firm to behave in ways which suit the managers, but are not in the interests of the shareholders. In so far as shareholders are private individuals, with small shareholdings and limited time to spend monitoring their performance, this is a valid argument. However, ownership of shares is not typically spread across private individuals alone, but is frequently concentrated in the hands of financial institutions like pension funds, investment trusts, insurance companies and other similar organisations. These institutions depend upon the financial performance of the firms in which they have invested in order to attract funds and to survive and make profits themselves. They employ professional managers to monitor their investments and use industry analysts (usually employed by their stockbrokers) to scrutinise the performance of the firms in which they have invested. Such shareholders are powerful, well-informed about the firms in which they own shares, and extremely concerned about their financial performance. As a result they may exert considerable pressure on managers to aim for maximum profit, removing the discretion they must have if the managerial models are to apply.

Such arguments are, of course, subject to a number of qualifications. If the financial institutions themselves are under little competitive pressure they may in turn make only limited efforts to monitor and control the firms in which they own shares. A financial institution may become 'locked into' a firm in which it has a major financial stake, being afraid to make public any doubts it has about the firm's policies and performance for fear of seeing a fall in the share price and a weakening of the performance of its own investment portfolio. The balance of the argument is not completely clear. Nevertheless, it is certain that in many circumstances pressure from shareholders may limit the extent to which managers have discretion.

The 'market for corporate control'

Shareholders may exert direct pressure on the management of a company if they believe it to be earning less profit than it could. The existence of a market for voting shares – the market for corporate control – provides a source of indirect pressure in the same direction, through the working of share prices.

Share prices are determined fundamentally by the amount which investors are willing to pay for them. For rational profit-seeking investors this amount will be equal to the present value of future profits. If a company's management is considered by the market to be using the firm's resources to make less than maximum profit, the share price will be lower than it would be if the management were more efficient. The firm and its assets will therefore be undervalued, and the company will present a very attractive target to 'take-over raiders', who may seek to buy up the relatively undervalued shares, shake-up or dispose of the existing management, and use the firm's resources more effectively in order to produce higher profits and a capital gain through an increase in the share price.

This form of discipline may work in two different ways. The most obvious one is where take-overs actually take place and lazy managements are displaced or disciplined by new owners with a greater concern for profits. Alternatively (see Holl (1977)) the threat of possible take-over may be enough in itself to act as a disciplinary force. In either case, the ability of managers to exercise discretion over the ways in which the firm's resources are used is severely restricted.

Agent/principal relationships

A recent development in the theoretical analysis of the firm, which also suggests that profit-maximisation may be a realistic assumption, is known as 'agency theory' (see Fama (1980) and Fox (1984)). In this approach the firm is seen as a network of contracts between the 'principal' and a group of 'agents'. The principal (who cannot have full knowledge of all factors affecting the business) hires a group of agents to carry out certain tasks (on which they will be better informed than the principal) and devises a contract, which may be partly unwritten and informal, to link the agent's performance to his reward. Different types of contract and different sets of information will give the agent incentives to behave in different ways, and if contracts are 'efficient' then the agents will choose to behave in ways which suit the principal. The conditions under which principal/agent relationships will be efficient are difficult to identify in detail, even at a theoretical level, but Fama suggests that contracts tend to be specified in ways which do force agents to direct their energies towards profit-maximising activities, because pressure from both above and below in a company tends to drive individuals in that direction. Pressure from above may link profit-maximising behaviour with rewards. Competition from below for seniority and position may also have a reinforcing effect.

A great deal of theoretical and empirical work needs to be done before the full implications of the agency model are clear. Nevertheless, the approach does suggest another avenue through which managers may be influenced in the direction of profit-maximisation.

The arguments for and against the assumption of profit-maximisation are difficult to balance in order to reach an unambiguous conclusion. Nevertheless, there are sufficient counter-arguments to the managerial criticisms for economists to be reasonably comfortable in maintaining that assumption as the foundation for their model of the firm.

The behavioural model of the firm

'Behavioural' criticisms of models of the firm

The 'managerial' models of the firm stem from criticism of the profit-maximising assumption, on the grounds that in an era when ownership and control are separate, and many firms compete in relatively comfortable oligopolistic market structures, managers are able to direct the resources of companies towards their own ends. In many other respects the managerial models share similar characteristics with the orthodox textbook model of the firm. It is assumed that the firm is a single entity, being capable of having objectives, even if these are held by a group of managers, and the firm is seen as taking and implementing decisions. The models outlined above are all optimising models and it is also assumed that the firm has certain knowledge of the cost and demand conditions facing it. In many respects the managerial models differ from the orthodox only in that they begin with a different assumption with respect to the firm's objective.

A much more radical attack on the orthodox model of the firm, which also implies criticism of the managerial models, has been made by a group of theorists referred to as the 'behavioural school', building on seminal work by Simon (1959) and Cyert and March (1963). In this approach attention focuses on behaviour within the firm, which is not seen as a single entity, but as a set of shifting coalitions amongst individuals, each of which has their own set of objectives. The fundamental argument is that organisations cannot have objectives, only people can, and that to perceive a firm as having an objective is an example of 'reification', confusing an abstract concept with a real entity.

In addition to rejecting the notion that a firm can have objectives, the behavioural theorists also reject the assumption that those taking decisions are perfectly informed. The assumption of certainty is abandoned and emphasis is placed on the idea that most organisations are so complex that the individuals within them have only limited information with respect to both internal and external developments.

The behavioural alternative

The behavioural model of the firm is therefore very different from either the orthodox model or the managerial models. It is not a 'holistic' model in that the firm is not seen as a single entity. It is not an optimising model where the firm achieves the best possible performance with respect to its objective, and it is not based upon the assumption of certainty. In place of these features of the other models it contains a number of key elements.

First, **the 'firm'** hardly exists, consisting as it does of a group of individuals who form coalitions and alliances amongst themselves based upon common interests or characteristics, departmental loyalties or simple personal affinity. As a result **the firm has multiple objectives which are in conflict with each other** and which cannot be reconciled through a concept like the utility function, which gives a weight to each objective and allows an overall 'score' to be achieved. The accountants in a firm may wish to keep the level of stocks down in order to reduce the costs of holding them. At the same time the sales force may wish to hold a high level of stocks in order to be able to meet orders quickly. The research department may wish to employ a large number of qualified scientists, while the marketing department would prefer to spend more on advertising. Longer established employees may wish to avoid interruptions to their routine while newly employed executives may be anxious for change. Each individual will themselves have multiple objectives, arising from their personal histories, preferences and position within the firm and these multiple sets of objectives cannot be reduced to any simple overall statement which explains what the organisation as a whole is attempting to achieve.

The second major feature of the behavioural model, which distinguishes it from those outlined above, is that **decision-makers exhibit 'satisficing' behaviour**, rather than 'optimising' behaviour. Neither the firm nor its component coalitions, nor individuals, are seen as attempting to maximise or minimise anything. Instead, each person or group has a 'satisficing' level for each of its objectives. If these levels are reached, they will not seek for more, in the short term at least, but if they are not met action will be taken in order to remedy the problem.

An important consequence of satisficing behaviour is that firms acting in this way will not keep costs down to a minimum. Instead they will exhibit 'organisational slack', incurring higher costs than are absolutely necessary.

A third feature of the behavioural model is that action within the firm takes the form of **'problem-oriented search using rules of thumb'**. If one of the multiple objectives is not met, so that someone within the firm is dissatisfied, a search will take place for a means of meeting that objective. However, the search will be fairly narrow, relating solely to the objective which is not being met, and the firm will use rules-of-thumb to attempt to put the problem right. These rules-of-thumb are not arrived at through any detailed analysis, but are a function of the past experience of the firm and the people within it. For instance, if revenue falls, the firm may automatically raise its price, because that has been tried in the past, and appeared to be successful.

Fourthly, the aspirations of the individuals within the firm, which determine the levels of each objective with which they will be satisfied, change over time as a result of **'organisational learning'**. If a firm succeeds in meeting all of its objectives for a period of time then eventually the individuals and groups will raise their aspiration levels, demanding more of whatever it is they care about. Eventually a situation will be reached where not everyone achieves 'satisficing' levels with respect to all of their objectives, at which point a problem-oriented search will take place to seek a solution to the problem. If one is found, the process of gradually increasing aspirations can continue. On the other hand, if a solution is not found despite a number of searches aspiration levels with respect to the particular variable concerned will have to be reduced.

Clearly, the behavioural model is very different to the others which have been considered, and describes a number of very familiar features of organisational life. In many respects it is descriptively more realistic than either the orthodox or the managerial models and is very attractive for that reason. However, it also has to be recognised that it has relatively limited use-value in addressing the questions with which managerial economics is concerned. If we consider the positive question of 'how do firms respond to changes in their environment?' the model offers little assistance, as it focusses entirely within the firm. If we consider the normative question 'can we identify the decision-rules which firms should follow in order to meet their objectives?' that question is not addressed either by the behavioural model. On the other hand, a firm which conforms well to the description set out by the behavioural theorists could behave in exactly the same way with respect to price and output decisions as the profit-maximising firm, or the firm described by one of the managerial models. If the shareholders are a powerful group within the firm and will only be satisfied with maximum profit, and if employees and managers are concerned for the firm's survival, the process of organisational learning may lead the firm towards profit-maximisation. For the purposes of managerial economics, then, the behavioural model is of relatively limited usefulness.

The concept of X-inefficiency

A useful concept which links the behavioural model, and the managerial utility model, is that of '**X-inefficiency**'. In the standard, neo-classical, profit-maximising model it is assumed that the firm incurs the minimum cost achievable for the level of output being produced, given the set of plant and equipment which has been installed. In terms of the diagram, the firm is on its cost curve. Such a firm may be described as being 'X-efficient' or 'operationally-efficient'. However, this may not be the case. A firm which is maximising managerial-utility, for instance, will tend to spend more on staff and on 'perks' for the management than is necessary, in which case it may be said to be 'X-inefficient'. In terms of a diagram, it will be above its cost curve, as shown in Fig. 3.9. Similarly, a firm which conforms to the behavioural model will incur higher costs than are strictly necessary and be X-inefficient, or have '**organisational slack**'. Liebenstein (1966) emphasises the importance of X-inefficiency and considers the factors which are likely to encourage or discourage it. This analysis draws together a number of issues already considered above.

In the first place, the degree of X-inefficiency will be partly determined by factors which are internal to the firm. If contracts between principals and agents (the owners, managers and workers) are not as efficient as has been suggested above then workers

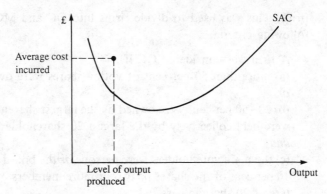

Fig. 3.9 An 'X-inefficient' firm

and managers will not be motivated to keep costs down, and the firm will be X-inefficient. If larger firms are more difficult to control, with a greater degree of bureaucratic rigidity, then they will also tend to be more X-inefficient.

The second set of factors which determine the degree of X-inefficiency is to be found in the external environment in which the firm operates. If the firm is forced by its environment to aim for maximum profit, it must eliminate X-inefficiency. On the other hand, if the management has the discretion to avoid profit-maximisation it will allow its costs to rise above the level which is strictly necessary. The environmental factors which lead to X-inefficiency are therefore the converse of the factors which force the firm to aim for maximum profits. If shareholdings are diffused amongst a large number of relatively ill-informed small shareholders there will be little pressure from that direction. If the threat of take-over is limited, perhaps because the firm is too large to be under serious threat, or because anti-trust legislation prevents take-over, then the likelihood of X-inefficiency is correspondingly higher.

Similarly, the degree of X-inefficiency will tend to be higher as the market structure in which the firm operates is less competitive. If there are a small number of competitive rivals who are able to avoid direct competition with each other, and they are protected by barriers to entry into the industry, then there will be few penalties for slackness and X-inefficiency is correspondingly more likely to result.

Illustration

Ownership, control and performance in UK firms

Ever since Berle and Means drew attention to the separation between ownership and control it has been recognised that firms which are owner-controlled (OC) may behave in ways which differ from firms which are manager-controlled (MC). Holl (1975) provides an interesting example of an empirical study which attempted to identify the links between the type of control and the performance of firms.

The starting point for the analysis lay in two sources of data. The first was a study by Florence (1961) which provided data on ownership patterns for nearly 300 UK firms. This was used to divide firms into OC and MC firms on the basis of the following criteria:

> A firm was considered OC if
> (a) more than 50 per cent of voting shares were owned by one person
> *or*
> (b) 20–50 per cent were owned by the largest shareholder, *or* at least 20 per cent were held collectively by the largest 20 shareholders
> *and*
> (c) the main vote holders were persons *or* the board of directors own more than 10 per cent of the shares *or* two or more members of the board are amongst the largest 20 shareholders

All other firms were considered MC.

The second source of data was a data bank in Cambridge (UK) which provided information on company performance, which was measured with respect to profitability, growth, the distribution of profitability over time, and the firms' distribution ratio.

Holl then used a variety of 'managerial models' to develop hypotheses about the differences in performance to be expected between OC and MC firms. First, the Marris model is invoked to suggest that MC firms would tend to have higher growth rates and lower profits than OC firms. Secondly, it is argued on the basis of models developed by Baumol (1959) and Monsen and Downes (1965) that MC firms will exhibit less variation in profit from year to year and less skewness in their distribution over time than OC firms. (The argument is essentially that in MC firms there is an asymmetry between the punishments and rewards arising from poor or good performance. Poor performance is punished but good performance is not well rewarded. As a result, the managers of MC firms attempt to maintain steady profits over time, thus avoiding punishment while not sacrificing rewards.)

Thirdly, following Florence's argument, it is suggested that MC firms will tend to plough back profits, while OC firms favour the distribution of dividends.

Having developed a series of hypotheses, Holl then used a relatively sophisticated statistical technique known as discriminant analysis, in order to test them. This essentially consists of dividing the data set into two groups, OC and MC, and then measuring the statistical 'distance' between them.

The results suggested a number of conclusions. For OC firms the profit rate was higher and the growth rate lower, as suggested by the Marris model, while both the variance and skewness of their profits were greater, which was also as predicted. Those results were statistically different from zero, which is one measure of success, but if the equations fitted were used with the original data to predict which class of firm each of the observations would fit into, almost 40 per cent of firms would have been mis-classified. The discrimination achieved was not, therefore, very sharp.

Holl's first set of results were arrived at by examining the full sample of firms available. However, that approach could involve the introduction of biases arising from variables like firm size and market structures. In order to control for that possibility the results were re-calculated for matched samples. First, OC firms were matched with MC firms of equal size, which led to very little change in the results. Secondly OC firms were matched with MC firms in the same industry, which gave statistically insignificant results. The results with respect to profitability and the growth rate therefore suggest that control type has no significant impact on firm performance. Similar calculations were carried out with respect to the distribution ratio and similar results emerged.

These findings are significant for the debate on the importance of managerial theories of the firm. The evidence suggests that MC firms are in fact forced to behave in the same way as OC firms, in which case the managerial models are redundant. Managers might have different personal objectives from the shareholders but they do not have the indiscretion to indulge themselves in the pursuit of those objectives to the neglect of the company's owners.

References and further reading

W. Baumol,'On the Theory of Oligopoly', *Economica*, 1958

W. Baumol, *Business Behaviour, Value and Growth*, (New York, Harcourt, Brace and World, 1967)

A.A. Berle and G. Means, *The Modern Corporation and Private Property*, (New York, Macmillan, 1932)

R. Cyert and J. March, *Behavioural Theories of the Firm*, (Englewood Cliffs, Prentice-Hall 1963)

E. Fama, 'Agency Problems and the Theory of the Firm', *Journal of Political Economy*, 1980

P.S. Florence, *Ownership Control and Success of Larger Companies*, (London, 1961)

R. Fox,'Agency Theory: A New Perspective', *Management Accounting*, 1984

P. Holl, 'Control Type and the Market for Corporate Control in Large US Corporations', *Journal of Industrial Economics*, 1977

H. Liebenstein, 'Allocative Efficiency *vs* X-Efficiency', *American Economic Review*, 1966

R. Marris, *The Economic Theory of 'Managerial Capitalism'*, (London, Macmillan, 1964)

R.J. Monsen and A. Downs, 'A Theory of Large Managerial Firms', *Journal of Political Economy*, June 1985

H. Simon, 'Theories of Decision-Making in Economics and Behavioural Science', *American Economic Review*, 1959

J. Williamson, 'Profit, Growth and Sales Maximisation', *Economica*, 1966

O. Williamson, 'Managerial Discretion and Business Behaviour', *American Economic Review*, 1963

Self-test questions

1 In which of the following models will the firm incur higher costs than are necessary?

(a) Baumol's revenue-maximising model
(b) Williamson's managerial utility model
(c) Marris's model
(d) the behavioural model

2 Explain whether each of the following will make firms more likely or less likely to adopt profit-maximisation as their objective.

(a) an anti-trust policy which forbids take-overs
(b) powerful, well-informed shareholders
(c) an efficient stock market

(d) oligopolistic market conditions
(e) stock option schemes for managers

3   Which of the following concepts are compatible with the behavioural model of the firm?

(a) optimising
(b) satisficing
(c) certainty
(d) aspiration levels
(e) rules of thumb

4   If fixed costs rise, what will happen to the level of output in each of the following models?

(a) profit-maximising
(b) revenue-maximising, with a profit constraint
(c) managerial utility maximising

5   Which firm would you expect to have the highest share price?

(a) a profit-maximiser
(b) a revenue-maximiser
(c) a managerial utility maximiser

Exercise

Explain the differences between the neo-classical theory and the X-inefficiency theory of the firm.

Answers on page 399.

4 The importance of risk and uncertainty

This chapter introduces the problem of imperfect information. Techniques for decision-making in the presence of risk and uncertainty are outlined and the chapter then goes on to consider the broader implications of uncertainty for the analysis of the firm.

Alternative states of information

Three alternative 'states of information' may be identified. The first is **certainty**, where the decision-maker is perfectly informed in advance about the outcome of his decisions. For each decision there is only one possible outcome, which is known to the decision-maker. Realistic examples are difficult to find, but it is important to remember that the simple model of the firm, outlined in Chapter 2, is based on the assumption that the firm has certain knowledge of its cost and demand conditions.

The second state of information is known as **risk**. In this situation a decision may have more than one possible outcome, so that certainty no longer exists. However, the decision-maker is aware of all possible outcomes and knows the probability of each one occurring.

The third state of information is that of **uncertainty**. In this situation a decision may have more than one outcome and the decision-maker does not know the precise nature of these outcomes, nor can he objectively assign a probability to the outcomes.

Various techniques exist to assist decision-making in conditions of risk or uncertainty, which may be considered in turn.

Techniques for decision-making in risky conditions

The use of expected monetary values

If a decision-maker knows the possible outcomes which may result from a decision, and can assign probabilities to each of those outcomes, then **expected monetary values** may be substituted for certain values in choosing between alternative courses of action.

The expected monetary value (EMV) of a particular course of action may be defined as:

$EMV = \Sigma p_i V_i$ where:

p_i = the probability of the i'th outcome
V_i = the value of the i'th outcome
and $\Sigma p_i = 1$

Expressed in words, the EMV is equal to the weighted sum of the possible outcomes, when each outcome is weighted by its probability, and *all possible outcomes are taken into account.*

To take an example, an ice-cream shop may know that its takings vary with the weather, which may be sunny (with a probability (p) of .2) or cloudy (p = .4), or raining (p = .4). In this case, the EMV is calculated as shown below:

Weather conditions	Probability	Takings
Sunny	.2	£500
Cloudy	.4	£300
Raining	.4	£100

Expected monetary value = £500(.2) + £300(.4) + £100(.4) = £260

In the example given here there are only three possible weather conditions and three probabilities, which sum to 1. This is known as a **discrete probability distribution**, shown diagrammatically in Fig. 4.1.

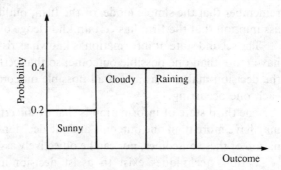

Fig. 4.1 A discrete probability distribution

As the figure indicates, there are no weather conditions which come in between those specified, and no level of takings possible apart from those given. A slightly more difficult case is where there is a **continuous probability distribution**, as shown in Fig. 4.2.

If the takings of the ice-cream shop can take a very wide range of values, the graph of takings against probabilities will be a smooth curve, rather than a set of discrete points. There are a wide variety of such distributions, and a detailed analysis of them lies outside the scope of this chapter. However, if the distribution of ice-cream

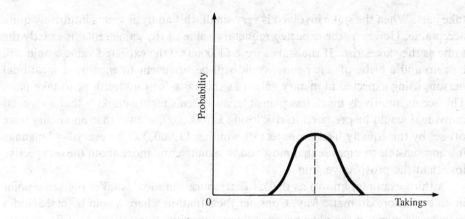

Fig. 4.2 A continuous probability distribution

shop takings is characterised by the **normal distribution**, then the expected monetary value of the takings is given by the **mean** of the distribution.

The limitations of expected values

If expected monetary values are used as the decision criterion, then a rational decision-maker deciding between two alternatives will always choose the course of action which yields the highest expected monetary value. However, while this may appear an intuitively sensible way in which to take decisions, a number of examples show that its application can lead to a number of quite clearly non-sensical conclusions. Consider first a person's decision to insure their house against destruction by fire. If the house has a value of £100,000 and the probability of it burning down in a year is one in ten thousand (.0001) then the expected value of the loss is £10. A decision-maker employing the expected value approach would be willing to pay £10 for insurance, but no more. However, it seems intuitively quite clear that many rational people would be willing to pay much more than £10, in order to be absolutely certain that they will never be faced with the prospect of having to lose their house without recompense. In some sense, people 'care' more about the possible loss of £100,000 than they do about the certain insurance cost of £10. The same point can be made through another example. Imagine that a rational person is asked to take part in a game with another player which consists of tossing a coin for a stake of £1. If the coin lands with 'heads' up the there is a gain of £1. If it lands 'tails' up, there is a loss of £1. Provided that the coin is a fair one, so that 'heads' and 'tails' are equally likely, the expected value of this game is equal to:

$$.5(£1) - .5(£1) = 0$$

A person using the expected monetary value criterion would be absolutely indifferent to whether or not he played the game or not. The slightest inducement to play (a bribe of one penny for instance) would be sufficient to encourage him to take part. When the stake involved is very small, this analysis seems intuitively quite acceptable. However, the expected monetary value of the game remains exactly the same as the stakes rise. If the stakes were £1,000,000 the expected value would still be zero and a bribe of one penny would still be sufficient to encourage a rational person, using expected monetary values as the basis for the decision, to take part. This seems intuitively much less plausible, as it seems highly unlikely that a rational individual would be prepared to risk losing £1,000,000, even if that possibility were off-set by the equally likely prospect of winning £1,000,000. In everyday language it seems sensible to suppose that most people would 'care' more about the prospective loss than the prospective gain.

A third example, known as the 'St Petersburg Paradox', makes the same point in an even more dramatic way. Consider the situation where a coin is tossed and a payment is made to the player, depending upon which toss of the coin first comes up 'heads'. If it comes up the first time, the payment is £2. If it does not come up until the second toss, the payment is £2^2 = £4, and if it does not come up until the nth toss, the payment is £2^n. How much would a rational person be willing to pay to take part in this game? The expected monetary value of the game is given by:

$$EMV = .5(2) + .5^2(2^2) + .5^3(2^3) + \ldots\ldots + .5^n(2^n) + \ldots\ldots$$
$$= 1 + 1 + 1 + \ldots\ldots + 1\ldots\ldots\ldots$$
$$= \text{infinity}$$

In other words, the expected monetary value is infinity, and a person using the EMV as a means of decision-making would be willing to pay everything they have to take part in the game!

These examples illustrate a major problem with expected monetary values as a means of taking decisions. Individuals will not accept fair bets involving large amounts of money because they 'care' more about the possibility of loss than they do about the possibility of an equal gain. In the language of economic analysis, the 'utility' lost as a result of losing £100 may be more than the utility gained by winning £100.

Utility and attitudes to risk

The analysis above suggests that expected monetary value has serious limitations as a criterion on which to base decisions. It seems intuitively likely that the value, or 'utility', placed on a loss of £100 by a rational individual may well exceed the utility arising from a gain of £100. This suggests that an explicit examination of the links between utility and income may help to provide an alternative means of assessing decisions in situations of risk. Fig. 4.3 shows three different possible relationships between an individual's level of income, and the utility they experience as a result of having that income. Each can be seen to illustrate different attitudes to risk on the part of the individual concerned.

In Fig. 4.3(a), the curve linking utility and income becomes less and less steep at higher levels of income, indicating decreasing marginal utility of income. If such an individual is at level of income A, which gives him utility X, and is considering

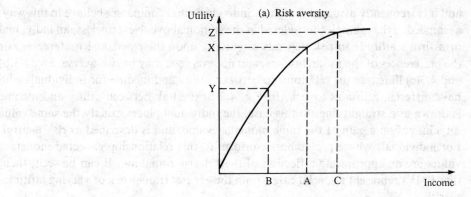

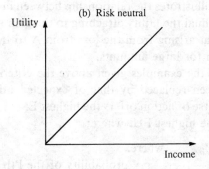

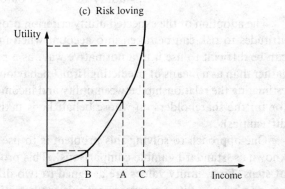

Fig. 4.3 Utility and income

whether or not to accept a fair bet with a 50/50 probability of either increasing his income to C or reducing it by an equal amount to B, he will consider the impact on his utility. If his income is reduced to B, his utility falls to Y. On the other hand, if his income is increased to C, his utility rises to Z. However, as Fig. 4.3(a) clearly shows, the decrease from X to Y is substantially larger than the increase from X to Z. If these are equally likely, as in the example given, the individual in question will not accept the bet offered.

The type of behaviour illustrated in Fig. 4.3 (a) is known as **risk averse** behaviour, and it is frequently assumed that most individuals and companies behave in this way, as implied in the examples considered in the section above. Nevertheless, an individual or a firm's **attitude to risk** depends essentially upon their personal preferences, or the preferences of their shareholders, and not everyone may be risk-averse. Fig. 4.3(b) and 4.3(c) illustrate the relationship between utility and income for individuals who have different attitudes to risk. In Fig. 4.3(b) the link between utility and income is drawn as a straight line. In this case, the individual places exactly the same value on a loss as on a gain of the same monetary value, and is described as **risk neutral**. For individuals whose preferences conform to this relationship expected monetary values are an appropriate reflection of their decision-making. It can be seen, then, that EMVs represent a special case within the general framework of varying attitudes to risk.

Fig. 4.3(c) illustrates the relationship between income and utility for a **risk lover**. For this individual the utility attaching to the gain in income from A to C is clearly larger than that arising from the loss from A to B. Such an individual will accept fair bets, even for large amounts.

In each of the examples given above the criterion of expected monetary value (EMV) has been replaced by that of **expected utility** (EU). Instead of choosing whichever course of action offers the highest EMV, the decision-maker chooses that which gives the highest EU, where:

$$EU = \Sigma \; p_i U_i$$

where:

p_i = probability of the i'th outcome
U_i = utility of the i'th outcome

The adoption of the expected utility criterion provides a means by which different attitudes to risk can be taken into account when modelling decisions. However, it can be difficult to use it in a normative way, as a prescription and a practical tool, rather than as a means of predicting firms' behaviour in a general way, as it involves estimating the relationship between utility and income for a particular decision-maker (or for the shareholders on whose behalf he is taking decisions, which adds to the difficulties).

One approach to solving this problem is to use a technique involving what are known as 'standard gamble comparisons'. This procedure can be set out as a series of steps. First, utility values are assigned to two different money values. As utility has no obvious unit of measurement this can be entirely arbitrary, provided that the larger money value is assigned the higher utility value. For example, let a money value of £0 yield a utility of 0 and a money value of £100,000 yield a utility value of 1.

The aim is now to find the utility values of monetary amounts between £0 and £100,000 for a particular decision-maker. Imagine that the aim is to find a utility value for £50,000. In this case, the decision-maker is asked to consider the choice between:

(a) receiving a certain £50,000
(b) taking part in a lottery whose outcome will be either a gain of £100,000, with probability P, or a gain of zero, with probability (1 − P).

At very low values of P, the decision-maker will prefer the certain £50,000, but at some higher value he will change his view and will prefer to take part in the lottery. Clearly a knowledge of that value sheds light on the individual's attitude to risk, which can be used to solve the problem in hand. If, for instance, the decision-maker in question becomes indifferent between the two alternatives at a probability of .6 then it can be inferred that at that value the utilities attaching to the certain £50,000 and the risky '£100,000 or £0' are the same. Therefore:

$$U(£50,000) = .6(U(£100,000)) + .4(U(£0))$$

But we have assigned values to the utility arising from £100,000 and £0, and can therefore evaluate the equation given, on the same scale.

$$U(£50,000) = .6(1) + .4(0) = .6$$

This exercise could be repeated to find the value of utility attaching to any amount between £0 and £100,000.

If the aim is to identify the value of utility (or dis-utility) attaching to losses, rather than gains, the technique can be used in a similar way. In order to evaluate the utility loss arising from a monetary loss of £60,000 the decision-maker is asked to choose between a certain pay-off of £0 (whose utility has been assigned a value of zero) and a lottery involving probability P of losing £60,000 and probability (1 − P) of gaining £100,000 (whose utility has been assigned a value of 1). Once the value of P, at which the decision-maker is indifferent is known, then the utility value of losing £60,000 is the only unknown remaining in the equation, which can therefore be solved. For example, if the decision-maker declares himself to be indifferent between £0 and the lottery when P = .1, then:

$$U(£0) = .1(U(-£60,000)) + .9(U(£100,000))$$
or
$$0 = .1(U(-£60,000)) + .9(1)$$
therefore
$$U(-£60,000) = -9$$

This method of estimating utilities suffers from the fact that it relies upon the decision-maker's ability to answer hypothetical questions in the same way in which he would answer real ones. Nevertheless, it offers a means of making the analysis operational.

Indifference curves and attitudes to risk

The analysis above shows how attitudes to risk are reflected in different relationships between utility and income. However, it does not provide a direct measure of the riskiness of any particular course of action. The most common measure of the riskiness of an action, or the risk associated with a particular financial asset (a share, a portfolio of shares, or a foreign currency, for instance) is the **standard deviation** of the returns accruing to it. This is simply a measure of the variability of the returns, and is defined as:

$$SD = P_i(X_i - X)^2$$ where:

P_i = probability of outcome i

X_i = value of outcome i

n = number of possible outcomes

X = mean value of all outcomes

When considering choices between alternative courses of action, decision-makers may be thought of as deciding on different combinations of return on the one hand, measured by the expected value of the returns, and risk on the other, measured by the standard deviation of those returns. In this case, indifference curves can be drawn up, showing the different combinations of risk and return which will leave an individual equally satisfied. If individuals are assumed to be risk-averse, which is the assumption generally made, then the indifference curves will be as shown in Fig. 4.4 below, rising from left to right, with the more desirable combinations being as indicated by the arrow, having higher returns and lower risk.

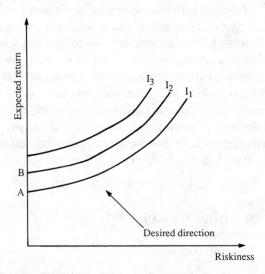

Fig. 4.4 Indifference curve for risk and return (risk averters)

The extent of an individual's risk aversion will be reflected in the slopes of the indifference curves. An individual who is very highly risk averse will be prepared to sacrifice a large amount of return in order to secure a small reduction in risk and will therefore have relatively steep indifference curves, relative to one who is only slightly risk averse. (A risk neutral individual will have horizontal indifference curves. For a risk lover, for whom both risk and return are desirable characteristics, the curves will slope downwards from left to right, rather than in the other direction.)

The concept of the certainty-equivalent

The most important applications of the 'risk versus return' (or mean/variance) indifference analysis concern the construction of portfolios of financial assets and therefore lie beyond the scope of this chapter or this book. However, there is one useful concept which should be noted, which is that of the **certainty-equivalent** of a course of action involving risk. This is defined as the sum of money, available with certainty, which would leave the decision-maker as satisfied as if he had undertaken the risky action. This may be interpreted, in terms of the indifference curves, as the vertical intercept of the curve which includes the course of action concerned. In Fig. 4.4, for instance, £A is the certainty equivalent of any combination of risk and return in the indifference curve I_1 and £B is the certainty-equivalent of any combination on curve I_2.

The use of decision trees

Another well-known technique which can be helpful in analysing situations involving risk is the use of '**decision trees**'. These are particularly useful when a number of related decisions need to be made in sequence and where the outcome of each decision depends upon the response of the environment. Fig. 4.5 shows the decision tree concerning the possible development and launch of a new product, which entails two decisions. The first is whether or not to spend £1m on research and development (R&D) in pursuit of the new product. The second, which only arises if the new product

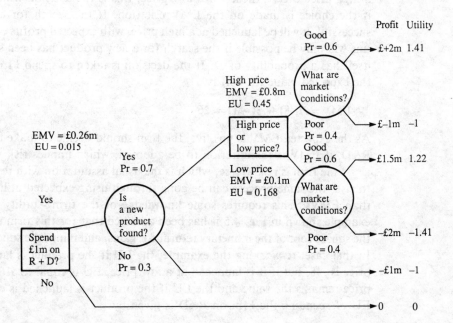

Fig. 4.5 A decision tree

is successfully developed, concerns the choice between a product launch at a high price or a low price. Decisions, or choices, are represented by square boxes, or '**decision nodes**', while outcomes determined by the environment, or '**chance nodes**', are represented by circles.

Working from the left, in order to set out the decision process, the first decision which has to be taken is whether to spend £1m on R&D. If the answer to this question is no, the monetary value of the exercise is zero, as shown in the lowest branch of the decision tree. If the answer is yes, the next question is whether a new product is found or not, which depends upon factors in the environment outside the control of the firm. The chance node shows that there is a probability of .7 that a new product is found, .3 that it is not. If no new product is found, the £1m has been wasted and the monetary value of the activity is -£1m. On the other hand, if a new product is found, the firm then has to decide whether to launch it with a high price or a low price. Whichever decision is taken, there is a range of possible outcomes, depending upon the economic circumstances of the time. Each of these is shown as an eventual profit, and the probability of that profit.

Decision trees of this kind may be used in conjunction with either the *expected monetary value* (EMV) or *expected utility* (EU) *criteria*. In either case, the basic method involves working backwards through the decision tree from right to left. For each of the possible routes through the tree a monetary value, or utility, is calculated, as shown. Each of these is then worked back to the next chance node, and an EMV or EU calculated at that point. In the example shown, for instance, if the product is launched at a high price, the expected profits are equal to £.8m. If it is launched at a low price, the expected profits are £.1m. As the expected profits arising from a high price exceed those for a low price, this is the decision which will be taken, if the choice is made on the EMV criterion. If the search for a new product is successful, it will be launched at a high price, with expected profits of £8m. However, this will only be possible if the search for a new product has been successful, which itself has a probability of .7. If the decision is taken to spend £1m on R&D, then, the expected value (in £m) is:

$$EMV = .7(.8) + .3(-1) = .26$$

As the expected EMV is positive, the firm should decide to make the investment in R&D, if EMV is the criterion to be adopted, which implies risk neutrality.

If the firm is risk averse, which is the usual assumption with respect to attitudes to risk, the same process can be gone through using expected utilities (EUs) rather than EMVs. This requires some knowledge of the firm's utility function. In the example shown in Fig. 4.5 it has been assumed that for this firm utility is equal to the square root of the monetary return, for gains, and minus the square root of losses. In that case, re-working the example, the EU if the product is launched at a high price is .45, but if it is launched at a low price, EU is equal to .168. The choice of price remains the same and the EU if the product is launched is equal to .45. The EU of spending the £1m on R&D is given by:

$$EU = .7(.45) - .3(1) = .015$$

In the example given the EU criterion yields the same decision as EMV. However, it can be seen that if the degree of risk aversion were higher then both the decision on price and the decision on whether to proceed with the R&D project could alter.

Alternative types of probabilities

A situation of risk is one where the probabilities of different outcomes are known to the decision-maker. There are a number of different ways in which such probabilities might be arrived at.

A first useful distinction is between probabilities which are calculated or known **'a priori'** and those which are only known **'a posteriori'**. An 'a priori' probability is one which can be calculated through prior knowledge. For instance, if a coin has two sides and is fair it is known that the probability of it landing on either side is .5. 'A posteriori' probabilities are only known after a sample of events has occurred and the frequency of each outcome is known. For instance, if it has rained on 10 out of every 30 days in June for the past 20 years, the 'a posteriori' probability of it raining on a day in June may be said to be .333.

Both 'a priori' and 'a posteriori' probabilities may also be described as **'objective'** probabilities in that they arise from an agreed analysis of fundamental principles or from observation of past events. The effective use of many statistical techniques depends upon such probabilities being available. However, many business decisions are non-repetitive and unique, so that objective probabilities are not available. If the environment is changing then a probability drawn from past experience may no longer be applicable. In that case, resort has to be made to **'subjective'** probabilities, based upon the decision-maker's own expectations, preferences, experience and judgment about the future. Such preferences may be quantified by asking the decision-maker to make comparisons between the real world problem being considered and a hypothetical gamble whose objective probabilities are known. This can provide some assistance in allowing a probability to be estimated but it is clear that different individuals in an organisation may ascribe different probabilities to the same outcome, or that the same individual may arrive at different probabilities for the same outcome if asked at different times. As different individuals in a firm will all have slightly different information relevant to the decision, and as it is possible that no single individual has all the relevant information, the use of subjective probabilities can be a dangerous guide to decision-making.

If satisfactory probabilities cannot be ascribed to outcomes, or if the possible outcomes are not even known, then the situation is not one of risk, but of uncertainty.

The expected value of information

It is clear from the discussion above that information is valuable and that a firm may wish to improve its knowledge of a particular situation by gathering additional information. However, in order to do so cost-effectively decision-makers need to know the value of acquiring additional information, in order to judge how much additional expenditure is worthwhile. Two different cases may be identified. The first is where it is possible to acquire perfect information about the future and the second is the more general case where it is only possible to secure imperfect revelation of which future states of nature will occur.

If it were possible to acquire perfect **advance state revelation** then the expected value of that perfect information could be measured as the difference between the expected value of future actions, given the information currently available, and the expected value of future actions given that perfect advance state revelation had been acquired. Foster (1978) uses the example of a bank which is deciding whether to make a $1 million loan at 10 per cent to a company which might default, or whether to use the same funds to purchase risk-free government securities at 7 per cent. If the loan is made to the firm, and it does not default, the bank's wealth in respect of the action is valued at $1.1 million. If the firm defaults, the bank's wealth is reduced to $900,000. If risk-free government securities are purchased, the bank's wealth is valued at $1.07 million with certainty. It is estimated that the probability of the firm defaulting is equal to .2.

Fig. 4.6 sets out this basic information in tabular form.

Alternative	Alternative outcomes	
	Firm defaults (Pr = .2)	No default (Pr = .8)
Lend to firm	$900,000	$1,100,000
Buy government stock	$1,070,000	$1,070,000

Fig. 4.6 A bank lending decision
Source: G. Foster, Financial Statement Analysis, p.6

If a decision is made on the basis of the information currently available, the bank will compare the expected monetary values of the two alternative courses of action, using the method outlined above. This gives the following calculation:

Expected value if the loan is made to the firm:
$$EV = (.8)(\$1,100,000) + (.2)(\$900,000) = \$1,060,000$$
Expected value of a risk-free investment in government stock:
$$EV = \$1,070,000$$

As the action with the highest expected value is investment in government stock, this is the option which will be taken up and the expected value of the action, with the information currently available is equal to $1,070,000.

If it now proves possible for the bank to acquire '**perfect state revelation**' so that it will know for certain whether the firm will default or not, the situation changes. In this case, whichever outcome occurs, the bank will have been able to choose the optimal action. If it is discovered that the firm will default, the bank will choose to invest in government stock. If it is discovered that the firm will not default, the bank will choose to make the loan.

In order to calculate the expected value in this case, it is noted that the probability of default is .2 and that if default takes place, the bank will have invested in government stock. The probability of the firm not defaulting is .8, in which case the firm will have made the loan. This gives the expected value of the bank's wealth as:

$$EV = .8(\$1.1m) + .2(\$1.07m) = \$1.094m$$

This can be compared with the expected value of the optimal action in the situation where the bank has not acquired perfect information about the future, which has been calculated above as $1.07 million. The difference between the two values, $24,000, is the **expected value of perfect information (EVPI)**.

The circumstances under which perfect information about the future is available are very rare indeed and in most cases the purchase of additional information will not provide absolutely certain advance state revelation. Nevertheless, the calculation of EVPI is still a useful tool in such situations because it provides an upper limit to the value of additional information which might be collected. The first step which should be taken when considering the purchase of additional information is to consider whether the cost of acquiring it exceeds the EVPI. If it does, the information should not be acquired as its expected value could not possibly exceed that of perfect information.

If the cost of acquiring additional information is less than the EVPI then it may be worth acquiring that information. The basic principle involved in placing a value on the extra information is essentially the same as that involved in calculating EVPI. The value of the information is equal to the difference between the expected value given currently available information and the expected value with the additional information which has been acquired. This can be difficult to calculate in practice (see Foster (1978), pp.8–13, for an example which is a continuation of the bank loan problem considered here), but the principle is clear enough.

Techniques for coping with uncertainty

The problems considered above have all related to situations of **risk**, where the probabilities of different outcomes are known. If probabilities are not known, the situation is one of **uncertainty**, rather than risk, and the techniques outlined above cannot be applied. Nevertheless, there are a number of different strategies which may be adopted in order to make decisions on rational criteria.

The maximin criterion

A firm making a decision may be characterised as choosing between alternative courses of action, whose outcomes depend upon which 'state of nature' happens to be in force at the time of the action. In a situation of uncertainty the probabilities of the different states of nature are not known. In order to begin analysing the problem a 'pay-off matrix' may be constructed, as shown in Fig. 4.7 below.

States of nature

Actions	A	B	C
1	20	40	180
2	−40	100	220
3	60	70	90

Fig. 4.7 A pay-off matrix

Each cell in the matrix shows the pay-off, which could be in terms of monetary values or utilities, for the given course of action, given the state of nature indicated.

If the maximin criterion is adopted, the decision-maker examines the worst pay-off for each action and then chooses the action for which the worst pay-off is highest. In the example given in Fig. 4.7 the worst pay-offs are:

- Action 1: 20
- Action 2: -40
- Action 3: 60

In this example, Action 3 is selected, guaranteeing that the lowest pay-off which will be received is 60.

The maximin rule ensures that the worst possible outcomes are avoided and may be described as a pessimistic, conservative, or highly risk averse strategy. The obvious difficulty with it is that it ignores the higher value pay-offs which may imply foregoing some possibly very large gains.

The minimax regret criterion

In the case of the minimax regret criterion the decision-maker considers the extent of the sacrifice made if a particular state of nature occurred but the best action for that state of nature was not chosen. In the example shown in Fig. 4.7 for state of nature A, Action 1 involves a 'regret' of 40, Action 2 a 'regret' of 100 and Action 3 a 'regret' of 0. Fig. 4.8 shows a complete 'regret matrix' for all actions and states of nature.

States of nature

Actions	A	B	C	Largest regret
1	40	60	40	60
2	100	0	0	100
3	0	30	130	130

Fig. 4.8 Regret matrix

Having set out the regret matrix, the action is chosen for which the largest regret is a minimum, leading to the choice of Action 1. Such a strategy ensures that the maximum regret is not experienced, and is also a relatively pessimistic basis on which to make a decision.

As in the case of the maximin criterion a major criticism of this technique is that it only makes use of a very limited amount of the information which is available, ignoring everything else. Actions which are rejected may have much smaller regrets than the one which is chosen, apart from their largest regrets. It is also possible that use of this approach could lead to inconsistent decisions in that if an action is chosen from a group of alternatives and then one of the rejected actions is deleted from the options, a different action may now be chosen, despite the fact that the original 'best' option is still available.

The maximax criterion

This criterion is the opposite of the maximin criterion in that the best outcomes of each action are identified, and then the action is selected for which the best outcome is largest. In the case set out in Fig. 4.6, this would lead to the choice of Action 2. This is clearly an 'optimistic' criterion to use in that it selects the action which provides a possibility of making the highest possible return. As in the case of the other criteria considered, its main failing is that it only takes a limited amount of the available information into account. The action which offers a prospect of the highest possible return may also be the one which offers the prospect of the largest possible loss (as in the example shown), but this is ignored.

The Hurwicz 'alpha'-criterion

The Hurwicz approach is an attempt to use more of the information available by constructing an index (the 'alpha-index') for each action, which takes into account both the best and worst outcomes and the extent to which the decision-maker wishes to adopt a pessimistic or optimistic posture.

The index is defined in the following way for each action:

$$I_i = al_i + (1 - a)L_i$$ where:

I_i = the index for action i
a = an optimism/pessimism index
l_i = the lowest pay-off for action i
L_i = the highest pay-off for action i

The action which has the largest alpha-index is the one selected. The optimism/pessimism index may vary from between 0 and 1 and may be estimated by increasing the value of x in the situation shown in Fig. 4.9 until the decision-maker is indifferent between the two actions.

States of nature

Actions	A	B
1	0	1
2	x	x

Fig. 4.9 Estimating the optimism/pessimism index

A very pessimistic decision-maker will be indifferent between the two actions at a very low value for x (he will be quite happy with a small certain gain compared with the prospect of either 0 or 1, because his pessimism leads him to suspect that the outcome of Action 1 would be zero). On the other hand a very optimistic decision-maker, who suspects that the outcome of Action 1 is likely to be 1, will only be equally content with a certain amount which is almost as large as 1.

Once the value of x has been estimated, through direct questioning of the decision-maker, it is assumed that as the decision-maker is indifferent between Action 1 and Action 2 they both have the same alpha-index. From the formula given, Action 1 has an index of $(1 - a)$ and Action 2 has an index of x. It follows, therefore, that:

$$(1 - a) = x$$

and the value of a can be calculated from the known value of x, arrived at by experiment.

It should be noted that if x has a value of 1, so that a takes the value of 0, this indicates that the decision-maker is very highly optimistic, and the alpha-index criterion is exactly the same as the maximax criterion. Similarly, if the decision-maker is highly pessimistic, so that a takes the value of 1, the alpha-index criterion is equivalent to using the maximin approach. The Hurwicz technique therefore has the rather elegant property of encompassing maximin and maximax as special cases, each at a different end of a spectrum of decision-making attitudes which may vary from highly optimistic to highly pessimistic. As the technique also makes use of more information than either maximin or minimax it may be said to be superior to either of them in that respect, but nevertheless, like them, it also wastes some of the available information concerning the possible outcomes of actions, using only that for the best and the worst outcomes.

Combinations of different strategies

There is no reason to suppose, of course, that firms do, or must, adopt any single criterion in taking decisions under uncertainty. They may adopt different strategies on different occasions, or may consciously combine different strategies in order to 'spread the risk' associated with any single approach.

The broader implications of uncertainty for the theory of the firm

While techniques to assist decision-making under uncertainty are potentially useful they are clearly very limited and there is a danger that they may obscure the fact that the existence of uncertainty has very profound implications for the theory of the firm. In a situation of uncertainty firms and the individuals within them cannot calculate the probabilities of the outcomes of their actions. In many situations their ignorance may extend even further than this and they may not even be aware of what the possible outcomes are for any particular action. Recognition of this important limitation on firms and individuals has led to a number of significant insights into the workings of the firm.

Uncertainty and 'bounded rationality'

If a firm is operating in a situation of uncertainty its ability to act rationally is limited because of its lack of information. The 'hyper-rational' firm represented by the neo-classical model, in which the firm has perfectly accurate knowledge of its cost and demand conditions, has to be replaced by a model in which decision-makers exhibit 'bounded rationality'. That is not to imply that they are simply irrational, they are 'intendedly rational, but only limitedly so', to quote Simon's phrase (Simon (1959)). Each decision-maker attempts to seek rational answers to his problems in the context of his limited knowledge and experience. Instead of 'optimising', as in the neo-classical model, decision-makers 'satisfice' as in the behavioural model of the firm. Instead of immediately identifying the appropriate course of action, or solution to a problem, actions and solutions are arrived at through a process of searching through sequences of possible alternatives, using past experience and rules-of-thumb as guidelines.

Clearly, the concept of 'bounded rationality', which is important in situations of uncertainty, leads away from the orthodox picture of the firm as a fully-informed optimiser, and suggests the usefulness of a much more behavioural approach.

Uncertainty and transactions costs

Another implication of uncertainty is that it makes it difficult and expensive to draw up complete contracts between individuals. If all future contingencies are known, then a contract between two individuals could specify how each should behave in the event of each contingency, and that contract could be enforced by law. However, as Williamson (1986) points out, if the future possibilities are not all known, contracts will have to be incomplete and there is a difficulty in deciding how to resolve any conflicts which may arise in an unforeseen situation. This need not matter if all parties to all contracts behave without guile towards each other, because in that situation a contract may be thought of as 'a promise, rather than a plan' and each party could agree not to take advantage of the other in unforeseen situations. Unfortunately, in a situation of uncertainty some parties to incomplete contracts may behave 'opportunistically', taking advantage of circumstances to the disadvantage of their partners to the contract.

This is a much more fundamentally important issue than it might appear at first sight, because it reaches to the heart of the question 'what is the firm?', and is important for the understanding of such apparently different phenomena as vertical integration, licensing agreements, and the existence of the multinational enterprise. If contracts between individuals could always effectively and cheaply bring about transactions there would be no need for firms to even exist. All economic activity could be organised through contracts between individuals or households. Only when some transactions are organised by management authority, instead of the market mechanism, does a firm come into being. If there were complete certainty, or even just risk, then market transactions organised through complete contracts could cheaply co-ordinate economic activity. Only when there is uncertainty is a substitute for market transactions required and the firm has a role to play.

Kay (1984) makes a similar point in a particularly graphic way by noting that most 'real world' firms are organised into functional departments, usually including production, marketing, finance, and research and development. However, if perfect knowledge were actually available, and there were no information problems, none of these departments would be needed. Marketing departments only exist because consumers are not perfectly informed of the firm's products, their characteristics and their prices. Finance departments are only needed because the firm does not have perfect access to financial information. Research and development (R&D) is only required because perfect technological information is not available. Production departments would continue to exist, but they would only need capital and direct labour because the functions of foremen, managers, clerks and typists would not be needed. Furthermore, only one category of labour would exist, because the basic difference between different types of labour is *informational* in that each type of labour – manager, welder, fitter, electrician – is distinguished from the others by the information that each has with respect to their own specialist function. In a world of perfect information where everyone has access to the all the knowledge required every worker would be able to fulfil any function!

Uncertainty, entrepreneurship and innovation

Textbook models of the firm, which assume certainty or risk, present the firm as a relatively passive entity, having an objective and responding to an environment which is given and over which it has no control. Cost conditions are determined by factor prices and the state of technology and demand conditions are determined by consumers' preferences, which are internal to themselves. The firm has no capacity to change the world in which it operates. A very different way in which to characterise the firm, often associated with the 'Austrian view' on competition (see Chapter 14), is as a much more active participant in the world, changing and creating its own environment through its actions. In this view of the firm, uncertainty is the most important characteristic of the environment, and innovation is the means by which dynamic firms are constantly producing new technologies and developing new consumer needs in order to give themselves at least temporary monopoly positions, which other firms then proceed to attempt to break down by either entering the market or themselves producing hitherto unknown substitutes. In this view of the world profit is essentially a reward for taking the risks associated with innovation, which provides a (temporary) monopoly position. The entrepreneur plays a significant role in creating and changing the environment in which he operates, going far beyond the optimal responses to exogenous changes in the environment which are depicted in textbook economic models. Innovation is the key feature of firms' behaviour and that process of technological change (see Chapter 13) is both a cause of, and a response to, uncertainty.

Illustration

Betting on butter: an example of a risky decision

Bunn and Thomas (1977) provide an excellent example of the way in which technique can be combined with flair to help a company think its way through a real-life decision involving uncertainty.

At the time in question, butter imports were subject to a quota system, which provided substantial incentives to butter smuggling. Smugglers would attempt to disguise a load of butter as 'sweetfat', which has a similar density by mis-representing it in the paperwork and including some sweetfat in the load, in case of inspection.

The customs authorities intercepted such a load and then offered it for sale to retailers, one of which was J. Sainsbury Ltd. The sale was to be made by tender, with each prospective purchaser making a confidential bid, the sale being made to the highest bidder.

The problem for Sainsbury's was to decide how much to offer for the load, given that its butter content was unknown, the prices of butter and sweetfat at the time of delivery were unknown, and the prices which would be offered by the competition were unknown.

The starting point was to estimate the value of the consignment, which depended on the future prices of butter and sweetfat, and the ratio of butter to sweetfat in the load. For the prices of butter and sweetfat, the company used its 'market experience' to estimate subjective probability distributions, shown in Fig. 4.10.

A similar approach was used to estimate the proportion of butter in the load. The customs authorities provided Sainsbury's with a random selection of 10 cases from the freezer, eight of which contained butter. That random sample could have

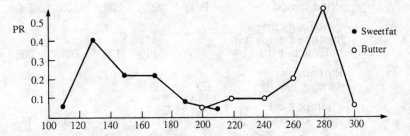

Fig. 4.10 Probability distributions for butter and sweetfat prices

been used in conjunction with the Binomial distribution, in order to find a probability distribution for the proportion of butter in the load, and such a distribution was calculated. However, Sainsbury's buyer preferred to adjust that distribution in the light of a subjective 'hunch', based on 'second-guessing' the way in which the smugglers would have packed sweetfat around the butter in the hold of the ship. Having arrived at this adjusted probability distribution for the ratio of butter to sweetfat Sainsbury's were able to calculate the probability distribution of value per ton, and the expected value per ton, which was estimated at £233. Subtracting £8 per ton for administrative expenses left £225 per ton as the net value per ton. The buyer then had to decide how much to bid, given that other firms had also been invited to tender. The starting point in this respect was the assumption that other firms would place the same value on the load as Sainsbury's had. Then it was assumed that competitors would expect to make a margin of around 20 per cent, which provided a base-line estimate of other companies' bids of £185.

This base-line figure needed adjustment in two respects. First, other firms may have placed a different value on the load and secondly, other firms may have tried to 'second-guess' Sainsbury's by making their own estimate of what Sainsbury's would bid, and then raising their own bid slightly above that estimate. Sainsbury's buyer made subjective estimates of the probability distribution for each of these factors. Combining them gave a probability distribution for the average competitor's bid, shown in Table 4.1 below.

Table 4.1 Probability distribution for the average competitors' bid

Bid price (x)	180	185	190	195	200	205	210	215
Probability (Pr)	.025	.110	.300	.245	.185	.100	.030	.005
Cumulative Pr that competitors' bid is less than x	.025	.135	.435	.680	.865	.965	.995	1.000

If Sainsbury's were to win the tender they had to make a bid which did not simply beat the average bid, but beat all offers made. As the number of competitors was expected to be around three, the probability of that happening was calculated, using the Poisson distribution, to be $e^{(-3p)}$, where 'p' is the probability of an average

Table 4.2 Expected profit at each price bid

Price bid (x)	190	195	200	205	210
Probability that an average competitor bids higher (p)	.565	.320	.135	.035	.005
Probability of winning ($e^{(-3p)}$)	.19	.39	.77	.90	.99
Profit per ton (225 − x)	35	30	25	20	15
Expected profit per ton	6.6	11.7	19.2	18.0	14.8

competitor bidding higher. That in turn is given for each bid price in Table 4.1 by subtracting the cumulative probability in the bottom row from 1.

Taking this information together, it is possible to construct a table showing the expected profit per ton at each price bid by Sainsbury's. This is shown in Table 4.2. In the light of the figures given, Sainsbury's bid of £203 per ton, won the contract, and made an actual profit of £40 per ton. By combining market experience with simple statistical reasoning the firm was able to structure its thinking through a complex problem in order to provide a reasoned solution to its dilemma.

References and further reading

D. Bunn and H. Thomas, 'J. Sainsbury and the Haul of Contraband Butter' in G. Kaufman and H. Thomas (eds.) *Modern Decision Analysis*, (Harmsworth, Penguin, 1977)

G. Foster, *Financial Statement Analysis*, (Englewood Cliffs, Prentice-Hall, 1978)

N. Kay, *The Emergent Firm*, (London, Macmillan, 1984)

R.D. Luce and H. Raiffa, *Games and Decisions*, (London, Wiley, 1957)

W.D. Reekie and J.N. Crook, *Managerial Economics*, (Oxford, Philip Allan, 1982)

H. Simon, 'Theories of Decision-Making in Economics and Behavioural Science', *American Economic Review*, 1959

O. Williamson, *Economic Organisation*, (Brighton, Wheatsheaf, 1986)

Self-test questions

1 Which of the following is a situation of risk?

(a) gambling on the toss of a coin
(b) launching a wholly new product
(c) lending to a firm with an established record

2 Mr. X knows that the probability of his house burning down is one in a thousand. His house is worth £100,000 and he willingly pays an insurance premium of £200 per year. Which of the following best describes his attitude to risk?

(a) risk neutral
(b) risk loving
(c) risk averse

3 Draw a graph with risk on the horizontal axis and return on the vertical axis. What shape will the indifference curves for a risk neutral individual be?

(a) vertical lines
(b) horizontal lines
(c) downward sloping

4 Which of the following strategies for decision-making under uncertainty would be adopted by a very optimistic decision-maker?

(a) maximin
(b) maximax
(c) minimax regret

5 Which of the following best describes the phenomenon of 'bounded rationality'?

(a) decision-makers evaluate all possible options
(b) decision-makers evaluate those options of which they are aware
(c) decision-makers consider only one possible option

Exercise

Distinguish between certainty, risk and uncertainty and explain how utility theory might be used to assist decision-making in the presence of risk.

Answers on page 401.

5 Consumer behaviour and market behaviour

This chapter sets out the principal economic theories of consumer behaviour and examines their links with the demand curve for an industry's product.

Economic theories of consumer behaviour

Models of the firm, and models of markets, make extensive use of the concept of *the demand curve*, showing the amounts of a commodity which consumers are able and willing to purchase at different prices. In an elementary treatment of the issues it is sufficient to adopt a relatively simple approach to the demand curve, noting that commonsense seems to suggest that it slopes downwards, with more of a commodity being purchased at lower prices, looking no more deeply at the behaviour of the individuals and households who are responsible for the purchasing. However, 'commonsense' can be a dangerous guide and such an approach leaves the demand curve without any theoretical underpinning. There is a need to model the behaviour of consumers with respect to their purchasing decisions, in order to predict how they will respond to changes in price and other variables. As in the case of the model of the firm, there are a number of different models of consumer behaviour which offer insights into the decision-making process and which provide a theoretical underpinning for the central concept of the demand curve. The simplest of these is **utility theory**, outlined in Ross and Shackleton(1988, pp.35−38). More sophisticated approaches, covered in this text, include:

- indifference analysis
- revealed preference theory
- the characteristics approach

Each of these models may be examined in turn.

Indifference analysis

The limitations of utility analysis

In the 'utility theory' approach to consumer behaviour it is assumed that every consumer aims to maximise their 'utility', which is a cardinally measurable concept, often denominated in some imaginary unit such as 'utils'. As a consumer obtains more and more units of a commodity, the number of utils gained from each successive unit declines according to the 'principle of diminishing marginal utility'. In order for the household to reach its objective of maximum utility it has to select amounts of different commodities such that, for any pair, the ratios of the marginal utilities are equal to the ratios of the prices. This analysis provides an underpinning for the demand curve and helps to predict how consumers will react to changes in prices. However, it relies upon a concept of utility which is cardinally measurable, like height, weight or temperature and which can be directly compared with prices. This is a rather restrictive assumption to make and economists have attempted to consider whether it is possible to build a model of consumer behaviour which embodies the basic insights of the utility theory without having to assume that utility is cardinally measurable. The theory which results is known as **indifference analysis**. In many respects it is similar to utility theory although it also allows for a more detailed analysis of the changes which arise from an alteration in prices.

Indifference curves and the indifference map

The starting point for indifference analysis is the assumption that although consumers cannot assign a precise utility value to different amounts of a commodity, they are able to decide which combinations of commodities they prefer to others. The consumer's aim is not to maximise cardinally measurable 'utility' but to achieve the highest possible level of ordinally measurable 'satisfaction'. In this case consumers will not be able to count the number of utils arising from the consumption of different units of a commodity but they will be able to decide which combinations of goods they prefer to others. Consumers know which combinations of goods give them most satisfaction. They also know when they are indifferent between two different combinations of commodities. It will be possible, therefore, for any pair of commodities, to draw a set of **indifference curves** which show the combinations of different amounts of the two goods which consumers are indifferent between. Fig. 5.1, for instance, has been arrived at by first randomly selecting a combination of apples and oranges, at point A, then considering which other combinations of apples and oranges would leave the consumer feeling equally satisfied.

The shape of an indifference curve will depend upon a number of different factors. If both commodities in question are 'goods', rather than 'bads', in other words they are both commodities which consumers get satisfaction from, the indifference curves will slope downwards from left to right, showing that if a consumer has less of one they will require more of the other in order to remain equally satisfied.

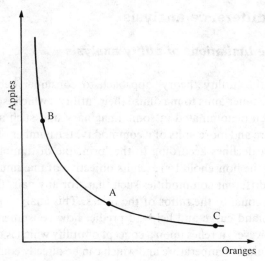

Fig. 5.1 An indifference curve

If the basic principle behind the concept of diminishing marginal utility also holds true, so that consumers experience successively less additional satisfaction from each additional unit of a good, the indifference curves will be concave upwards, as shown in Fig. 5.1.

If the consumer has a large number of apples and a small number of oranges, as at point B, then they will be prepared to sacrifice quite a large number of apples (which are giving them relatively little satisfaction at the margin) for a small number of oranges (which give them a high level of satisfaction). The indifference curve will therefore be relatively steep at a point like B. On the other hand, at a point like C, where the converse is the case and the consumer has a large number of oranges and few apples, the curve will be relatively flat, showing that if they gave up a large number of oranges they would need relatively few apples in order to compensate. This is very much the same idea as the principle of diminishing marginal utility, known in the context of indifference analysis as **diminishing marginal rate of substitution.**

Indifference analysis generally assumes that indifference curves are concave upwards like this, and also that they are smooth and continuous, implying that the goods in question are very highly divisible and that levels of satisfaction also change in a continuous fashion.

If the consumer is being faced with a choice between two 'goods', and increasing amounts of a commodity yield diminishing marginal satisfaction, indifference curves will take the general shape shown in Fig. 5.1, falling from left to right and concave upwards. Their precise shape depends upon the strength of the consumer's relative preferences for the two commodities in question. If the consumer is an 'apple-lover', with a great liking for apples and a lesser liking for oranges, the curve will be relatively flat, as shown in Fig. 5.2(a), because the consumer would be willing to sacrifice a large number of oranges in return for a small number of additional apples. On the other hand, if the consumer is an 'orange-lover' the curve will be relatively steep as in Fig. 5.2(b).

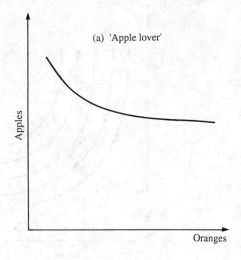

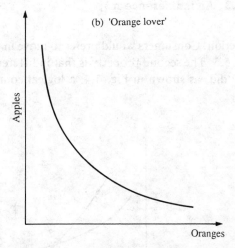

Fig. 5.2 Indifference curves and consumer preferences

A single indifference curve clearly embodies a great deal of information about a consumer's preferences for the commodities concerned. However, it concerns only one level of satisfaction, showing as it does all the different combinations of apples and oranges for which the consumer is indifferent to the combination at point A. As point A was chosen at random it is clear that there are an infinite number of indifference curves, one for every point in the space on the diagram. Fig. 5.3 shows a number of indifference curves, each conforming to the general shape identified above. Clearly this can only be a selection of the total number of curves as to draw them all would involve millions of curves, completely blacking out the space.

A diagram like Fig. 5.3 is known as an **indifference map** as it is a close analogy to a conventional contour map showing the height of the land above sea-level.

There are two properties of an indifference map which warrant attention. The first is that curves which are further away from the origin represent higher levels of

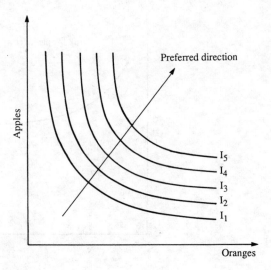

Fig. 5.3 An indifference map

satisfaction. Consumers would prefer to move in the direction indicated by the arrow in Fig. 5.3. The second property is that indifference curves cannot cross each other. If they did, as shown in Fig. 5.4, a logical contradiction would be implied. Point

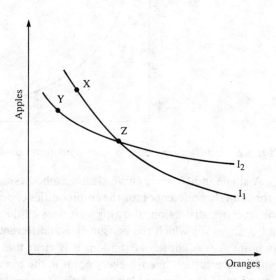

Fig. 5.4 Indifference curves cannot cross

X on indifference curve I_1 must indicate a higher level of satisfaction than point Y on indifference curve I_2, as it lies further from the origin. But point Z, which lies on both indifference curves, yields the same level of satisfaction as both Y and X. Clearly this cannot be the case and indifference curves cannot cross.

Consumer equilibrium

Having established the concept of the indifference map it is then possible to analyse the consumer's choice between alternative combinations of commodities. As the aim of the consumer is to reach the highest possible level of satisfaction, this can be represented in the analysis by noting that the consumer will choose the combination of commodities which is located on the highest possible indifference curve. However, the consumers are restricted in their choice of combinations of commodities by their income, which only allows them to purchase a limited amount of goods. The combinations of goods which consumers are able to purchase depends upon their income and the price of goods and can be represented in the diagrammatic analysis by a **budget line**, as shown in Fig. 5.5.

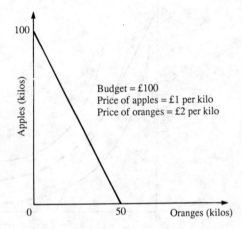

Fig. 5.5 The budget line

If the consumer has an income of £100, apples cost £1 per kilo and oranges cost £2 per kilo, then the combinations of apples and oranges which the consumer can buy are given by the straight line shown in Fig. 5.5. If all of the consumer's income were spent on apples, they could consume 100 kilos of apples and no oranges. Conversely, by spending all of the available income on oranges the consumer could have 50 kilos of oranges and no apples. Intermediate combinations of apples and oranges which the consumer is able to purchase are given by the straight line joining the two intercepts, which is simply the line given by the equation:

$$Y = P_A.A + P_O.O$$ where:

Y = consumer's income
P_A = price of apples
P_O = price of oranges
A = amount of apples
O = amount of oranges

The slope of this line, it may be noted, is equal to the ratio of the prices of the two commodities.

It is assumed that all of the consumer's income must be spent on the two goods in question, which are the only commodities available. The analysis can easily be extended to cover a larger number of goods but in that case diagrams have to be replaced by mathematical workings.

The budget line shows the combinations of goods which the consumer is able to purchase and the indifference map shows the combinations which give the highest level of satisfaction. Bringing the two together makes it possible to identify the equilibrium combination of goods, which gives the highest level of satisfaction. This is shown in Fig. 5.6 at point X.

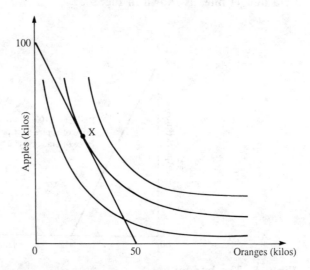

Fig. 5.6 Consumer equilibrium

As the figure shows, at the equilibrium position the slope of the budget line, which is equal to the ratio of the prices of the two commodities, is equal to the slope of the indifference curve to which it is a tangent, which may be interpreted as the marginal rate of substitution between the two commodities in question.

Income and substitution effects

Having identified the equilibrium position for the consumer it is possible to consider how changes in prices will affect consumer behaviour and the implications of the analysis for the shape of the demand curve for commodities. Fig. 5.7 shows the same initial equilibrium position as in Fig. 5.6, but also illustrates the change which takes place if the price of oranges falls from £2 to £1.

The most obvious effect of the change in the price of oranges is to shift the budget line from BB to BB₁. As a result of that change, the optimal combination of apples and oranges shifts from X to Y.

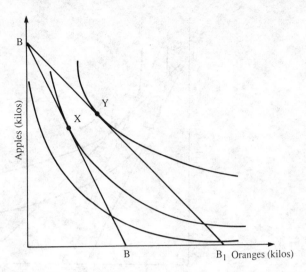

Fig. 5.7 The impact of a price change

In the example shown, more oranges are bought when their price falls (indicating a downward-sloping demand curve for oranges) and more apples are also bought. This is clear enough in the specific example given, but it remains to consider whether this is a general result which must always hold, or whether it is simply a function of the particular circumstances indicated in the diagram. In order to analyse this issue effectively it is necessary to carry out a careful examination of the factors involved in the shift from the original equilibrium X to the new position Y.

When the price of a good falls, leading to a change in the optimal basket of goods chosen by a rational consumer, two separate events may be said to have taken place. First, the fall in price has led to an increase in the real income of the consumer and this change in income will alter the goods which the consumer chooses to purchase. That change is known as 'the income effect.' Second, the relative prices of apples and oranges have changed, which will also alter the choice of purchases. That change is known as 'the substitution effect.' These two phenomena may be examined separately, by extending the diagram set out in Fig. 5.7, as shown in Fig. 5.8.

The overall change induced by the fall in the price of oranges is indicated by the shift from X to Y, which is known as 'the price effect.' This can be subdivided into two separate components, as indicated. In order to isolate the income effect it is necessary to ask 'how would the basket of goods purchased change if the consumer's real income rose by the amount which it has, but relative prices stayed the same?' The answer can be found by recognising that the change in the consumer's real income is represented by the shift from the lower indifference curve I_1 to the higher one I_2 and that relative prices are represented by the slope of the budget line. In terms of the diagram the answer can be found by examining how the basket of goods would change if the consumer were on indifference curve I_2, enjoying the higher level of income, but relative prices were as given by the original budget line BB. This can be found simply by shifting the line BB outwards, parallel to its original position,

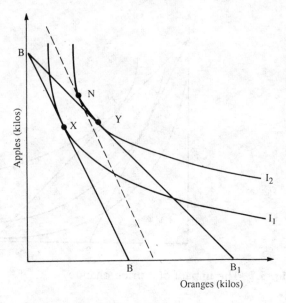

Fig. 5.8 The income and substitution effects

thereby indicating the same relative prices, until it is tangential to the higher indifference curve I_2. Point N, where the two lines meet, shows the combination of goods which the consumer would purchase if their income rose sufficiently to place them on I_2 but relative prices remained unchanged. The shift from the initial equilibrium position X to N is the income effect.

The substitution effect may be found by a similar process. It may be defined as the change in the basket of goods which would be purchased if relative prices changed, at a constant real income. This may be interpreted as the movement around the indifference curve I_2 from N to Y. The total 'price effect', then, may be disaggregated into its two components, the income effect changing the basket of goods from X to N and the substitution effect taking it from N to Y. Each of these may then be examined separately in order to illuminate the links between price changes and the level of demand for a good.

If the substitution effect is taken first, it is clear that its impact must always be to increase the demand for a good whose price has fallen. As indifference curves slope from left to right, with the slope decreasing to the right, then a fall in price of the commodity measured on the horizontal axis, which makes the budget line flatter, must mean that the point of equilibrium shifts to the right, as illustrated in Fig. 5.9.

While the direction of the substitution effect is unambiguous and supports the notion of a downward-sloping demand curve, the income effect is much more uncertain. It is feasible that for some goods increases in income lead to less, rather than more, being bought. Such commodities are known technically as 'inferior goods', possible examples in the United Kingdom include paraffin, some types of margarine and long-distance bus travel.

In the case of inferior goods, the consumer's overall response to a fall in price

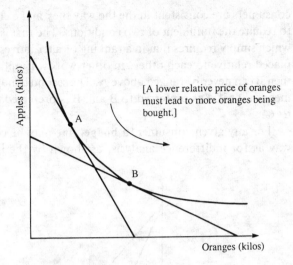

[A lower relative price of oranges must lead to more oranges being bought.]

Fig. 5.9 The impact of the substitution effect

depends upon the balance between the income effect and the substitution effect. If the substitution effect is larger than the negative income effect then a lower price will lead to more of the good being bought, as in the case of normal goods. However, in the extreme case where the negative income effect is larger than the substitution effect a fall in price will actually lead to less of the commodity being bought, rather than more, in contradiction to the downward-sloping form of the demand curve. Such goods are known as 'Giffen goods' after Sir Robert Giffen who suggested that amongst the very poor in the nineteenth century the demand for staple foods like bread behaved in this way. If consumers were spending a very high proportion of their income on the very cheapest foodstuffs then a fall in their price would lead to a very substantial increase in their real income. That increase in real income could lead them to substitute other types of food for the bread which they previously relied upon, thereby reducing the demand for bread as its price fell.

Revealed preference theory

The major advantage of indifference analysis over utility theory is that it involves making a much less restrictive set of assumptions about consumers' decision processes. Instead of assuming that every consumer can assign a cardinally measurable utility score to every unit of every commodity consumed, it assumes that they have a consistent set of preferences and know which combinations of commodities they prefer to others. Nevertheless, it has been argued that this is still a very restrictive set of assumptions to make, and theorists have sought alternative means by which a theory of consumer behaviour may be constructed. One such alternative approach is known as **revealed preference theory**.

The starting point for revealed preference theory is the assumption that the consumers are consistent in the the way they make choices. Consistency may be said to require the fulfilment of two conditions. The first is known as **two term consistency**, which simply requires that in a ranking of alternatives any two are always consistently placed relative to each other. In other words, if option A is placed above option B, then B can never be ranked above A. The second condition is **transitivity**, which simply means that if A is preferred to B and B is preferred to C, then A must be preferred to C.

For any given consumer, a **budget line** may be constructed, in exactly the same way as for indifference analysis, as shown by the line AO in Fig. 5.10.

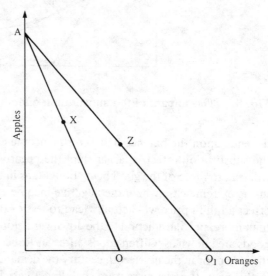

Fig. 5.10 Revealed preference I

The line shows all the different consumption possibilities facing the consumer in question. In the case of revealed preference theory no knowledge of indifference curves is assumed, so there is no way of predicting where exactly the consumer will choose to be on the line AO. Instead the consumers' behaviour is simply observed as a means of revealing their preferences. Imagine that the consumers in question chooses the combination of goods indicated by point X. Now imagine that the price of oranges falls, so that there is a new budget line AO_1. As the consumers will now choose to be somewhere on the new budget line, they will choose a new combination of apples and oranges, perhaps point Z. In the example shown, point Z involves the purchase of more oranges than before, and the lower price of oranges has led to increased demand for them. The demand curve slopes downwards. However, the analysis thus far has offered no reason to suppose that this must necessarily be the case. Point Z was chosen arbitrarily, in order to illustrate the point. In the case of indifference analysis the move from one consumer's equilibrium to another was explained in terms of an income effect and a substitution effect, each of which could be seen to have certain characteristics. A similar procedure can be carried out using the assumptions of revealed preference theory, without having to assume detailed knowledge of preferences.

The example has shown a consumer moving from point X to point Z as a result of a change in price. This is the 'price effect', which may be divided into an income effect and a substitution effect. In the case of indifference analysis it was possible to isolate the substitution effect by defining 'a constant level of real income' to mean 'being on the same indifference curve', so that a movement around an indifference curve could be seen to represent a pure substitution effect, with changes in real income having been cancelled out. Clearly, this cannot be done within the framework of revealed preference theory, because no knowledge of indifference curves is assumed. However, there is an alternative way forward, which can be explained with the help of Fig. 5.11.

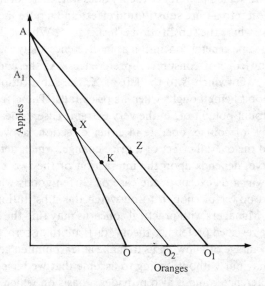

Fig. 5.11 Revealed preference II

In Fig. 5.11 the thick lines and the points X and Z simply repeat the situation already described in Fig. 5.10. The thin line A_1O_2 is drawn parallel to line AO_1, in order to represent the relative prices which hold after the fall in the price of oranges. It also passes through the original choice of goods at X. This line therefore shows the choices available to the consumer if his income remained at the level required to buy the original basket of goods, but the relative prices of apples and oranges were those which hold after the reduction in the price of oranges. If the consumers found themselves in this position they would choose a new combination of goods, like K for example. Without detailed knowledge of the consumer's preferences it is not possible to predict exactly where K will be. However, on the very limited assumptions made about the consistency of consumers' choices it is possible to be certain that the point K must lie on or to the right of point X, between X and O_2. This is because the consumer's initial choice of point X indicates that it is considered superior to all the other combinations between A and X. As the combinations between A_1 and X are all inferior to those between A and X, consistency ensures that the consumer must choose to be either at X or to the right of it.

If the consumer selects point K such that it coincides with X then it could be said that there is no substitution effect. The change in relative prices leads to no change in the basket of goods selected. In this case, the whole of the shift from point X to point Z must be an income effect. On the other hand, if point K lies to the right of X (as shown) it is more difficult to unravel income and substitution effects. Certainly the move from K to Z is entirely due to the income effect, because it takes place without any change in relative prices. However, the move from X to K is a combination of substitution effect arising from changing relative prices and income effect arising from the fact that the consumer now faces a higher real income.

Revealed preference theory does not, therefore, allow a clear division of the price effect into a pure substitution effect and a pure income effect, except in the extreme case where the substitution effect is zero. What it does achieve, though, is essentially the same general conclusion as indifference analysis, without having to claim a detailed knowledge of consumers' preferences. As the consumer will never choose a point on A_1O_2 which is to the left of X, the substitution effect can never lead to less of a good being bought when its price falls. The effect must always be to increase the amount bought or, in the very extreme case, to leave it constant. The income effect may, of course, operate in either direction, as was shown in indifference analysis and the overall effect of a price change, which determines the shape of the demand curve, depends upon the interaction of the two effects. Demand curves will slope downwards except in the case of Giffen goods where the income effect is negative and powerful enough to outweigh the substitution effect.

Managers with practical concerns may find the usefulness of an abstract exercise, like revealed preference theory, difficult to discern. Nevertheless, it has the theoretical advantage of allowing us to make at least limited general predictions about consumer behaviour without having to assume that we have detailed knowledge of consumer preferences, and it also provides a basis on which statisticians and econometricians can build empirical models of demand behaviour which could provide estimates of consumers' responses to price and income changes which would be of practical help to decision-makers.

The characteristics approach to demand

Utility theory, indifference analysis and revealed preference are all couched in terms of consumers' demand for individual commodities. An alternative approach, developed by Lancaster (1966), is to suggest that instead of demanding products, consumers demand certain 'characteristics' and that products are composed of bundles of characteristics. To take the example of motor cars, for instance, the relevant characteristics may include speed, acceleration, safety, fuel consumption, and comfort. Different models of car will be composed of different amounts of each characteristic. In the case of the oranges used in previous examples, the most important characteristics may be sweetness and juiciness. If each brand of oranges possesses these qualities in different ratios, then a consumer who purchases only one brand of oranges will only be able to consume the characteristics of sweetness and juiciness in the proportions embodied in that brand. This is illustrated in Table 5.1 and Fig. 5.12.

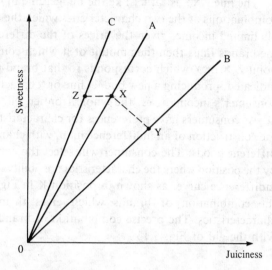

Fig. 5.12 The characteristics approach I

Table 5.1 The characteristics of different brands of oranges

Brand	Sweetness index	Juiciness index	Sweetness/Juiciness ratio	Price
A	2	1	2.0	10
B	3	3	1.0	20
C	6	2	3.0	30

If each brand of orange has the characteristics shown then buying more and more oranges of a single brand will give the consumer the combinations of characteristics shown in the straight lines OA, OB and OC in Fig. 5.12.

If the consumer has an income of £1000 then he could buy 100 kilos of brand A, (at point X) or 50 kilos of B (at point Y), or 33.3 kilos of C (at point Z), as shown in the diagram.

By combining different amounts of the different brands the consumer can acquire different mixes of the two characteristics as given by the lines joining the points Z and X and X and Y. Points on the line ZX show the combinations of characteristics which a consumer can achieve by spending all of his income on different mixes of brand A and brand C, while the line XY shows the combinations which can be had by spending all the available income on different mixes of brand A and brand B. (There is also a line between Z and Y which shows the combinations of characteristics which the consumer could acquire by spending all of their income on combinations of brand C and brand B. However, as this line lies inside the frontier set by ZXY it gives smaller amounts of both characteristics than can be had by spending the same income on the other combinations and will not therefore be chosen by a rational consumer who wants more, rather than less, of each characteristic.)

The line ZXY is rather like the budget line in indifference analysis, showing the combinations of the two characteristics which the consumer is able to purchase with his limited income, given the prices of the different brands. If the price of one of the brands falls, then the amount of it which could be purchased will rise, and the point Z,X or Y which corresponds to that brand will move outwards along the ray indicated, producing a new budget line or 'characteristics possibility frontier.' If the consumer's income rises, the whole frontier will move outwards.

As consumers have preferences for characteristics, the analysis can progress with the construction of an indifference map, with characteristics on the axes, rather than different goods. The consumer will select the combination of characteristics given by the position where the characteristics possibility frontier touches the highest possible indifference curve, as shown in position K in Fig. 5.13. The consumer will choose the combination of brands which gives them the indicated combination of characteristics. The precise combination of brands which achieves this can be seen with the aid of Fig. 5.13.

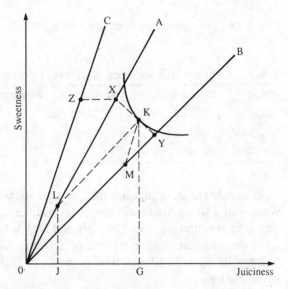

Fig. 5.13 The characteristics approach II

First, a line is drawn from the point K to the ray OA, parallel to the ray OB, meeting it at point L, and a similar line is drawn from K to the ray OB, parallel to OA, meeting OB at point M as indicated by the dotted lines in Fig. 5.13. The optimal brand mix at point K can then be seen to be arrived at by purchasing more and more units of A, moving along the ray OA from O to L, and then purchasing units of B, moving from L to K.

Alternatively, the brand mix can be arrived at by moving from O to M and then from M to K. It can be seen from the diagram that this is equivalent to moving from O to L, purchasing brand A and from O to M purchasing brand B. In the example shown it is apparent that the consumer will gain OJ units of juiciness from brand A and JG units of juiciness from brand B.

This framework can be used to examine the impact of changing prices upon the consumer's choice of brands, in much the same way as indifference analysis. If the price of brand A falls, the point X will move further out along the ray OA, there is a new characteristics possibility frontier and a new equilibrium position, giving the consumer higher levels of both of the characteristics which they seek. The new combination of brands can be found as before and the impact of the price change on the demand for each brand depends upon the shapes of the indifference curves. If the price of A rises then the point X will move towards O and the characteristics frontier will move inwards until at some point the new frontier consists of a line from Z to Y, omitting X, showing that from that price onwards only combinations of C and B are efficient and brand A will not be bought at all.

Watkins (1986) suggests that the characteristics approach comes close to providing a practical tool for market researchers and for companies concerned to identify the characteristics needed for new brands. In Fig. 5.13, for instance, the consumer buys a combination of two brands in order to consume sweetness and juiciness in the desired ratio available at point K. However, if a new brand were introduced having the characteristics in that desired ratio the consumer would spend all of his income on that brand.

If this approach is to be made practically useful it requires a number of extensions, as Watkins notes. In the first place, the characteristics of a brand, as seen by consumers, are not always perceived objectively. Market research may be required in order to identify the characteristics which consumers attribute to different brands. Secondly, different consumers may perceive the same brand as embodying characteristics in different ratios, so that the rays from the origin in Fig. 5.13 have different slopes for different consumers and further research is required to measure those variations in perception. Thirdly, if the technique is to be practically useful, consumers' preferences need to be measured, in order to provide information on their indifference curves and their preferred combinations of the subjectively perceived characteristics. Certainly, there are market research techniques which attempt to provide information on each of these issues and they might be brought together to make the characteristics approach operational. On the other hand, there is no evidence to suggest that such an approach has actually been taken up by marketing departments and it is probably more realistic simply to note its similarities with more practical aspects of market research.

Becker's revision of demand theory

Each of the analytical approaches outlined above has assumed that consumers are rational in their behaviour. The meaning of rational behaviour has been defined in each case and the implications of that behaviour explored, providing a theoretical underpinning for the demand curve. Becker (1962) provides a different framework in support of the notion that the demand curve slopes downwards, which does not rely on the assumption of rational behaviour on the part of individual consumers. Instead it rests upon statistical expectations of consumer behaviour in the aggregate. This approach can be explained with the assistance of Fig. 5.14.

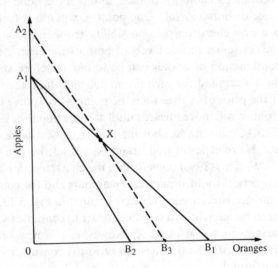

Fig. 5.14 Becker's approach to demand theory

In Fig. 5.14 the line A_1B_1 shows the original budget line facing a consumer, and point X shows the original combination of goods chosen. If the price of oranges rises, the budget line shifts to become A_1B_2. If we now consider what the position would be if the consumers experienced the price change, but suffered no decrease in their real income, this can be represented by shifting the new budget line outwards, keeping the same slope, until it just passes through the original choice point X. This gives the new line A_2B_3, which illustrates the combinations of goods available to the consumers if the new relative prices prevailed but their income were still sufficient to buy the original basket of goods. It is now possible to consider the 'consumption opportunity set' available to the consumer in each situation. In the original situation, the consumer is able to consume any combination of the two goods in the triangle OA_1B_1. When the price of oranges rises but the consumer's income remains high enough to purchase the original basket of goods, the consumption opportunity set is given by the triangle OA_2B_3. Clearly the second set involves a greater opportunity to consume apples and a smaller opportunity to consume oranges than the original one. If rational consumers relate their decisions to the 'availability' of different products in any way, they will choose to consume more apples and less oranges than in the original situation, and the demand curve will be downward sloping.

Some of the most interesting applications of Becker's analysis are not to the rational consumers considered thus far, but to irrational consumers who buy on impulse, or inert consumers who are generally unresponsive to prices. In the case of the impulse buyer, who has no particular preferences but buys at random, it is impossible to predict where any individual consumer will choose to be. However, if a large number of independent consumers are averaged out, the average consumption will be at the mid-point of the line showing the different combinations available. In the original situation, with the combinations A_1B_1 available, the chosen point will be the mid-point of the line, which is X. Clearly, the mid-point of the new line A_2B_3 is to the left of the point X and the analysis shows that when the price of oranges rises, the average consumer will purchase less oranges, thus indicating a downward sloping demand curve.

In the case of the inert consumer, who tends to buy the goods he has always bought, a similar argument may be employed. Such consumers who began somewhere along the line segment A_1X will remain where they are after an income-compensated change in prices, ignoring the greater opportunities offered. However, consumers who were originally on the line segment XB_1 no longer have their original choices available to them and are forced to move leftwards, consuming less of the good whose price has risen. Again the analysis leads to the conclusion that demand curves will be downward sloping.

Limited information and conspicuous consumption

Each of the analyses above has tended to confirm the original commonsense notion that demand curves slope downwards, except in some identifiable and extreme cases. As a result the remainder of this book will use such downward sloping curves whenever a demand curve is needed. However, it is worth noting that there may be some situations where this will not be the case. If consumers are ill-informed about the performance characteristics of a product they are purchasing, which may be the case for goods which they buy infrequently, or for goods where quality may vary in an unobservable way from batch to batch, it is possible that they may use the price as an indicator of quality, in which case consumers concerned to buy high quality merchandise may buy more of the same product at a higher price than at a lower price, mistakenly presuming that they are receiving a better quality product. Anecdotal evidence, at least, suggests that this may sometimes be the case. (Colleges offering short courses for industry, for instance, commonly report more demand for the same product at higher prices than at lower prices.) However, for consumers to continue to behave in this way implies that they never learn and can always be seduced into parting with more of their hard-earned income than they need. If there is active competition between firms and easy entry into the industry, if there are consumer organisations and standard setting bodies, or if consumers simply share their experiences with each other, it is difficult to argue that such behaviour will be common or long-lasting. It is certainly not a sufficiently important phenomenon to suggest that the analysis of the firm should rest upon upward sloping demand curves, or that firms seeking profits should raise their prices in order to generate a greater volume of sales.

In addition to the case where consumers mistakenly interpret high prices as indicators of high quality, there is another situation where the demand curve for a product may slope upwards. This is where consumers take satisfaction in 'conspicuous consumption', enjoying the fact that the goods they purchase have a high price, and deriving less satisfaction from the same goods if they are available at a lower price. In this case consumers are not simply deriving utility or satisfaction from the performance characteristics of the commodity in question, and seeing the price as the sacrifice they have to make, but seeing the price itself as one of the characteristics which directly gives them satisfaction. For some types of luxury goods this is a phenomenon which should not be ignored.

The practical application of demand theory

The main purpose of the analyses set out above are to provide economists with a theoretical underpinning for their models of the firm and markets, and it would be inappropriate to expect them to have very direct practical applications for managers. Nevertheless, they do provide a starting point for the statistical analysis of demand functions which is one way in which practically useful data on the behaviour of consumers may be discovered. This, and other means of estimating demand, are considered in Chapter 7.

Illustration

Housing in Hong Kong: prices, characteristics and 'feng shui'

The 'characteristics' approach to demand can be particularly useful when examining the demand for commodities which are not homogeneous. Wong (1989) provides a good example, with an analysis of the relationships between the prices of apartments in Hong Kong and their characteristics.

In order to examine the factors at work, Wong collected data on nearly three hundred recently purchased apartments in Hong Kong. For each apartment he collected data on two types of characteristics. The first concerned the attributes of the apartments themselves, which included the following variables:

age of apartment/net floor area/number of bedrooms/
door facing South/door facing North/sunlight into bedrooms/
view of hills or greenery/view of the sea/households per floor/
management fees/per cent windows facing West/per cent windows facing South-East/
floors above ground/subjective noise pollution.

The second type of characteristics concerned the neighbourhood in which the apartments were located. These included:

mean age of buildings/complaints on air pollution/

recreational facilities/entertainment facilities/
school enrolments/crime rate.

The prices of the apartments and their characteristics were examined by fitting 'hedonic' price equations. A computer package was used to carry out stepwise calculations of a series of multiple regression equations which had the price of the apartments as the dependent variable and their characteristics as the independent variables. As the functional form of an 'hedonic' price equation cannot be predicted from theory, various such forms were fitted including linear, log-linear and squared terms.

Examination of the results showed a number of interesting features. By far the most important explanatory variable was the net floor area of the apartments. (Newcomers to Hong Kong from the UK are often surprised by the way in which accommodation is almost universally described in terms of square footage, rather than the number of bedrooms and bathrooms, as is the practice in Britain.) This explained almost 70 per cent of the variance in housing prices. Other variables, like the age of the property, were statistically significant, but accounted for only a very small proportion of the variances. This included variables like sea-views and south-facing doors which might have captured the impact of the mysterious Chinese art of 'feng shui' (wind/water) which is supposed to determine the luck of those inhabiting the property. According to Wong's simplification of the immensely complicated rules of 'feng shui' a view of water should raise the value of a property and a south-facing door should reduce it, as indeed the results confirmed. On the other hand the results confirmed that a north-facing door also reduced property values! Clearly, the subtleties of Chinese geomancy cannot be captured by step-wise regression.

Further examination of the equations fitted suggested that 'neighbourhood characteristics' had a statistically significant impact on prices. Property values were positively related to the mean age of buildings in the district and negatively associated with measures of noise and air pollution and the number of households per floor. However, all of these variables accounted for tiny proportions of the variance. Other neighbourhood variables, like the crime rate, were not even significant.

The evidence suggests, then, that the prices of property in Hong Kong are very largely a question of floor area, which is perhaps not surprising in a city which is said to contain some of the most densely populated areas on Earth. Such econometric analysis requires careful interpretation as the author makes clear, because 'hedonic' price equations are not direct measures of demand but 'reduced-forms' which reflect the influence of both supply and demand. Nevertheless, they do provide a useful pointer to the characteristics which consumers value most and a tool for the property valuer. It is interesting to note that when Hong Kong people have emigrated to Canada they have sometimes offended their Canadian neighbours by completely covering building plots with their dwellings. That is hardly surprising in the light of Wong's findings and suggests that the high valuation placed on floor space in Hong Kong travels with emigrants from that city to their new locations.

References and further reading

G. Becker, 'Irrational Behaviour and Economic Theory', *Journal of Political Economy*, 1962.

K. Lancaster, 'Change and Innovation in the Technology of Consumption', *American Economic Review*, 1966.

L.W. Ross and J.R. Shackleton, *Economics*, (London, Longmans/ACCA, 1988)

T. Watkins, *The Economics of the Brand*, (London, McGraw-Hill, 1986)

K.-F. Wong, 'An Economic Analysis of Demand for Residential Housing in Hong Kong', MPhil Dissertation, Chinese University of Hong Kong

Self-test questions

1 Which of the following statements are correct?

(a) the substitution effect always leads more of a good to be bought at lower prices.

(b) the income effect always leads more to be bought at lower prices

(c) inferior goods have upward-sloping demand curves

(d) indifference analysis involves ordinal, rather than cardinal measurement

(e) revealed preference avoids the need for a concept of 'utility' or 'satisfaction'.

2 Draw indifference maps for beer and cigarettes for consumers with the following preferences.

(a) likes both beer and cigarettes

(b) gets no enjoyment (or discomfort) from cigarettes, likes beer

(c) the opposite of (b)

(d) is made ill by both beer and cigarettes

3 Use the information in Fig. 5.13 and Table 5.1 to identify:

(a) the amount of sweetness and juiciness the consumer receives

(b) the amount of each brand of oranges purchased

4 In Becker's approach, why will impulse buyers still tend to have downward sloping demand curves?

(a) because they prefer lower prices

(b) because on the average they will tend to cluster round the mid-point of the consumption opportunity set available

(c) because the income effect leads them to buy more

5 What assumptions are needed as a basis for the revealed preference approach?

(a) consumers are consistent in their choices

(b) the income and substitution effects can be separated

(c) consumer preferences are known

Exercise

Explain why economic analysis assumes that demand curves slope downwards, using either indifference analysis or revealed preference analysis in support of your argument.

Answers on page 403.

6   Demand and elasticity

This chapter examines in detail the concepts of the demand curve and elasticity of demand, linking them to the behaviour of revenues and to the structure of the industry in question.

The market demand curve

The determinants of demand

Economic theories of consumer behaviour suggest that in general the demand curve for an industry's product will slope downwards, indicating that as the price of the product falls, consumers will choose to purchase more of it. However, the price of the product itself is only one determinant of the volume of demand. A more complete listing of the factors which may affect the demand for an individual final product includes:

- the price of the product itself (P_o)
- the price of other products, especially complements and substitutes (P_c, P_s)
- consumers' disposable incomes (Y_d)
- consumers' tastes and preferences (T)
- the level of advertising for this product (A_o)
- the level of advertising for other products, especially complements and substitutes (A_c, A_s)
- rates of interest (i)
- the availability of credit (C)
- consumers' expectations of future prices and supplies (E).

These factors may all be drawn together into a demand function, which can be written:

$$Q_d = f(P_o, P_c, P_s, Y_d, T, A_o, A_c, A_s, I, C, E)$$

As 'own-price' (P_o) is likely to be one of the most powerful influences upon demand, attention is most often focused upon the **demand curve**, showing the

95

relationship between own-price and the quantity demanded. Nevertheless, it is important to remember that own-price is only one of many factors influencing demand.

The demand curve

The demand curve, like the example shown in Fig. 6.1, shows the quantities of a product which will be bought at different prices, *for some fixed combination of the other factors which affect demand.*

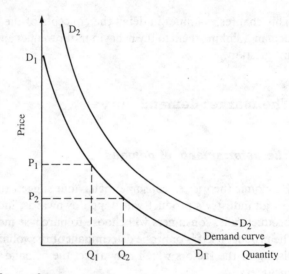

Fig. 6.1 The demand curve

The requirement that all other factors remain constant is sometimes referred to as the '*ceteris paribus*' assumption, that phrase being the Latin for 'other things being equal.' This is sometimes misunderstood to mean that economists believe that other things are always equal, when in reality they are clearly not. In fact, of course, the assumption implies no such thing. As the demand function shows clearly, economists are well aware that other factors like incomes, advertising and tastes may all change, affecting the level of demand. However, a diagram on a flat surface can only represent two dimensions at a time, so that a demand curve shows the links between own price and demand, *for a fixed combination of other factors.* If any of those other factors should change, the demand curve will shift.

This simple distinction between movements along a demand curve and shifts of the whole curve is an important one. If not fully understood it is possible to make nonsensical, but apparently correct statements, like the following: demand rose, therefore prices rose which led demand to fall, then because demand fell prices fell, so that demand rose, so that prices rose . . . and so on . . .

The mistake in this endless sentence arises from a confusion between two different types of change in demand, one involving a shift in the demand curve, and the other involving a movement along it. If the initial statement that 'demand rose' referred to an upward shift in the demand curve, then the result in a simple supply and demand type market would be for price to rise and a new equilibrium to be reached at the higher price. No further changes would take place. The higher price would not lead to a fall in demand because that refers to a movement along the demand curve.

In order to avoid such confusions it is only necessary to keep in mind that when own-price changes, the result is a *movement along the demand curve*. When any other determinant of demand changes, *the demand curve shifts*. In Fig. 6.1, for example, the demand curve is initially as given by the line D_1D_1, the price is initially P_1 and quantity Q_1 is demanded. If the price of the product falls to P_2, demand rises to Q_2 in a movement along the curve. If, on the other hand, consumers' income increases or the price of a substitute rises, the whole curve will shift, as given by the line D_2D_2.

Concepts of elasticity

Own price elasticity of demand

While the demand curve will generally be downward sloping, the precise extent of the slope will vary from commodity to commodity. It would be possible to use the slope of the demand curve as a measure of the responsiveness of demand to price. However, such a measure would vary with the scales being used on the price and volume axes, which is obviously unsatisfactory. A better way to measure the responsiveness of demand to changes in price is by using the concept of **own price elasticity of demand**, which may be defined as:

$$\frac{\text{percentage change in quantity demanded}}{\text{percentage change in the price of the good}}$$

or

$$\frac{\text{change in quantity}}{\text{change in price}} \times \frac{\text{price}}{\text{quantity}}$$

For a downward-sloping demand curve own price elasticity will always take negative values, as prices and quantities change in opposite directions.

Arc and point elasticities

There are two different types of own-price elasticity, known as **arc elasticity** and **point elasticity**. The term 'arc elasticity' refers to elasticity over a measurable interval along the demand curve, as in the case of the shift from point A to point B in Fig. 6.2.

Referring back to the definition given above shows that there is a possible ambiguity in the calculation of elasticity of demand along the arc AB. The change

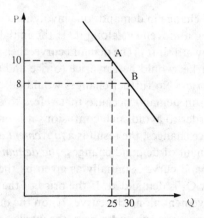

Fig. 6.2 Arc elasticity of demand

in price is 2, with a plus or minus sign depending upon its direction, and the change in quantity demanded is correspondingly minus or plus 5. However, the base against which the percentage change in price and quantity is calculated differs in size with the direction of the change. If the price was originally 10 then the original price/quantity combination is 10/25 and the value of elasticity is calculated as:

$$E_d = \frac{+5}{-2} \cdot \frac{10}{25} = -1$$

On the other hand, if the price rose from 8 to 10, moving along the curve from B to A, the calculation reads:

$$E_d = \frac{-5}{+2} \cdot \frac{8}{30} = -.66666$$

An arc elasticity of demand takes different values for the same arc of the demand curve, depending upon the direction of the change in price and quantity. It is possible to re-define an arc elasticity as a form of average of the two different values, but that is not particularly helpful as the meaning of the result is unclear. It is easier to simply note that the implication of the basic definition of elasticity is that arc elasticities can take two values, depending upon the direction of the changes under consideration.

It is intuitively clear that as points A and B in Fig. 6.2 come closer together, the difference between the two values for the arc elasticity will become smaller. If the distance AB is negligible then the arc has become a point and the arc elasticity is replaced by a **point elasticity**. This can be defined with the help of elementary calculus as:

$$E_d = \frac{dQ}{dP} \cdot \frac{P}{Q}$$

In the case of point elasticities the ambiguity with respect to the value of elasticity disappears, and it is this concept which is most frequently used in economic analysis.

Figures 6.3(a) to 6.3(d) illustrate a number of different demand curves and their elasticities.

In Fig. 6.3(a) the demand curve is a vertical line, illustrating that when price changes, quantity remains the same. In this example, elasticity is equal to zero at every point on the demand curve. In Fig. 6.3(b), where the demand curve is a horizontal line, any amount of the commodity can be sold at the price of P_1, but none can be sold at a higher price, indicating an elasticity equal to infinity, at every point on the demand curve. In Fig. 6.3(c) the demand curve takes the form of a

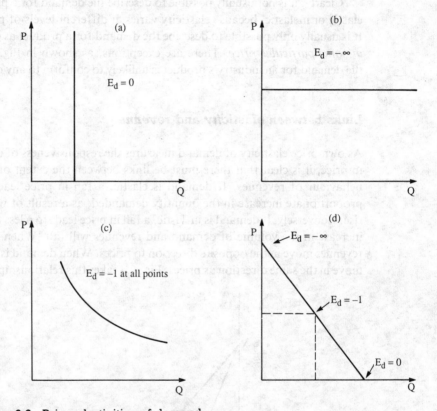

Fig. 6.3 Price elasticities of demand

rectangular hyperbola, which has the unusual property that at every point the price multiplied by the quantity is equal to the same constant. If the demand curve were this shape, elasticity of demand would be equal to minus one at every point.

Each of these three examples is unlikely to be met in practice, and it is correspondingly unlikely that elasticity of demand for a product always takes the same value. Fig. 6.3(d) shows a straight line demand curve, cutting both axes, which has more in common with most 'real-life' demand curves. As the diagram shows, and reference to the definitions confirms, elasticity of demand on this curve takes every value from zero to minus infinity along its length. At point X, where the curve meets the price axis, elasticity is equal to (minus) infinity. At point Y, where it cuts the quantity axis, elasticity is equal to zero. At the mid-point Z, elasticity takes the value minus 1.

The terms **elastic demand** and **inelastic demand** are used to describe different degrees of elasticity. If elasticity has an absolute value of less than 1, demand is said to be inelastic. If the absolute value of elasticity is greater than one, demand is said to be elastic. In the extreme cases of elasticity being equal to zero or (minus) infinity, demand is said to be respectively **infinitely inelastic** or **infinitely elastic**. If elasticity is equal to minus one, demand is said to have **unitary elasticity**.

Clearly, it is not usually possible to describe the demand for a product as generally elastic or inelastic, because elasticity varies at different levels of price and quantity. It is usually only possible to describe the demand for a product as elastic or inelastic, *at some particular price*. There are exceptions, as shown in Fig. 6.3(a) to (c), but the demand for an industry's product is unlikely to conform to any of these in practice.

Links between elasticity and revenue

As own-price elasticity of demand measures the responsiveness of demand to changes in price, it is clear that there must be links between the extent of elasticity and the behaviour of revenues. If demand is elastic, a fall in price leads to a more than proportionate increase in the quantity demanded, as a result of which revenues will rise. Conversely, if demand is inelastic, a fall in price leads to a less than proportionate increase in the volume of demand and revenues will fall. When demand is elastic, revenues move in the opposite direction to prices. When demand is inelastic, revenues move in the same direction as prices. Fig. 6.4 takes this relationship one stage further,

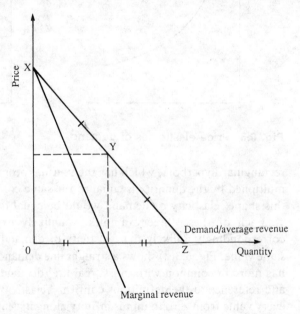

Fig. 6.4 Elasticity and marginal revenue

using a straight-line demand curve to illustrate the links between own-price elasticity and **marginal revenue**, defined as the change in revenue which takes place when one additional unit of output is sold.

The figure shows that when demand is elastic, between points X and Y, marginal revenue is positive, indicating that in order to sell one more unit of the commodity the price only has to fall by a very small proportion, so that total revenue increases. At the point Y where elasticity is equal to (minus) one, marginal revenue is zero, reflecting the fact that revenue remains the same when price changes. Where demand is inelastic, between Y and Z, marginal revenue is negative, showing that in order to sell one additional unit of output the proportionate change in price is so large that revenue falls.

The determinants of own-price elasticity

The extent of own-price elasticity of demand for a product depends upon a number of factors. The most obvious of these is the existence or otherwise of other commodities with similar price and performance characteristics which can act as substitutes. The closer the substitutes available are, the more elastic the demand for the product will be. This also implies that the extent of elasticity will depend upon how broadly the good in question is defined. If the commodity is very broadly defined ('meat', for instance) then the closest substitutes have rather different characteristics and the demand for 'meat' will be relatively inelastic. On the other hand, if the commodity is very narrowly defined ('belly of pork', for instance) there will be a number of quite close substitutes and demand will be much more elastic.

A second factor which will determine elasticity is the proportion of the consumers' total income which is spent on the commodity in question. If a commodity absorbs a large proportion of consumers' income then a change in its price will produce a substantial income effect, which in turn will have a pronounced effect upon the level of demand. On the other hand, if a commodity absorbs only a tiny fraction of consumers' income they will be much less sensitive to changes in its price and demand for it will tend to be inelastic.

A third factor determining own-price elasticity is the period of time being taken into account. In the long run demand will tend to be more elastic than in the short run, as consumers gradually learn about price changes and devise alternative ways of meeting their needs. In the case of heating fuels, for instance, a change from coal-fired heating to gas-fired heating involves time and expense. As a result, if the relative prices of the fuels change, customers with heating systems already installed will not immediately switch energy sources but will delay the changeover until they next replace their systems. This will mean that demand is much more elastic in the long run than in the short run.

Income elasticity of demand

Own-price elasticity is the type of elasticity of demand most commonly encountered in economic theory. However, demand is also responsive to other factors and the extent of that responsiveness is measured by other variants of the elasticity concept.

Income elasticity of demand is defined as:

$$E_I = \frac{\text{percentage change in quantity demanded}}{\text{percentage change in consumers' incomes}}$$

The **arc income elasticity** is given by:

$$E_I = \frac{\text{change in quantity demanded}}{\text{change in consumers' incomes}} \times \frac{\text{consumers' incomes}}{\text{quantity demanded}}$$

The **point income elasticity** is correspondingly given by:

$$e_I = \frac{dQ}{dY} \cdot \frac{Y}{Q} \qquad \text{where:}$$
$$Q = \text{quantity demanded}$$
$$Y = \text{consumers' income}$$

The size and sign of the income elasticity of demand for a product depends to a great extent upon the nature of the product in question and the level of income which consumers have reached. In the case of *necessities*, consumers will purchase a certain amount even at very low levels of income, but they will not increase their spending on these goods as their income rises. The **Engel curve** showing the relationship between income and demand for the product will be relatively flat, as shown in Fig. 6.5(a) and income elasticity of demand will be positive but less than 1, indicating income inelasticity of demand.

In the case of *luxury goods*, little or nothing will be spent at very low levels of income, but once a threshold level has been passed, as at Y_1 in Fig. 6.5(b) consumption of such goods will increase rapidly, indicating that demand is income elastic, having an income elasticity greater than 1.

For *normal goods*, including both necessities and luxuries, income elasticity is positive, as consumption increases with income. For *inferior goods*, which have been discussed in Chapter 5, income elasticity is negative as consumers choose to purchase less of such commodities as they have higher incomes, as shown in the Engel curve in Fig. 6.5(c).

Cross-price elasticities of demand

The third major category of demand elasticity is **cross-price elasticity of demand**, which indicates the responsiveness of the demand for a commodity to changes in the prices of other goods, the most important other goods to consider being close **substitutes** and **complements**. Cross-price elasticity between good A and good B is defined as:

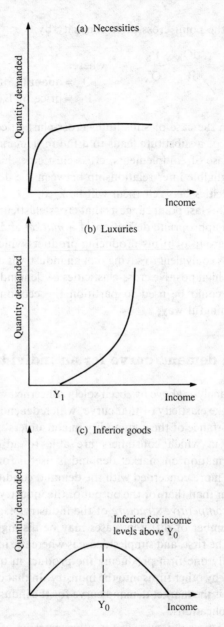

Fig. 6.5 Engel curves

$$E_x = \frac{\text{percentage change in the quantity of good A demanded}}{\text{percentage change in the price of good B}}$$

The *arc cross-price elasticity* is given by:

$$E_x = \frac{\text{change in quantity of A demanded}}{\text{change in price of B}} \times \frac{\text{price of B}}{\text{quantity of A}}$$

and the point cross-price elasticity by:

$$e_x = \frac{dQ_A}{dP_B} \cdot \frac{P_B}{Q_A}$$

where:

Q_A = quantity of A
P_B = price of B

In the case of substitutes cross-elasticities have a positive sign, as a fall in the price of a substitute leads to a fall in demand for the product being considered. In the case of complements, cross-elasticities have a negative sign. Clearly, if there is a negligible inter-relationship between the demand for two commodities the cross-elasticities between them will be zero.

This last point suggests that cross-elasticities of demand may be useful in arriving at an appropriate definition of a *market* and/or *industry*. If an industry is defined as a group of firms producing products which are close substitutes for each other, that is equivalent to saying that an industry is a group of firms producing goods which have high positive cross-elasticities of demand. If cross-elasticities could be estimated they could be used to partition the economy into industries in an economically meaningful way.

The demand curve for an individual firm

The analysis above has been solely concerned with the market demand curve for goods, and the elasticity of that curve, which depends upon the existence of substitutes, the importance of the commodity in consumers' total spending, and upon the length of time in which consumers are able to adjust their purchasing patterns. While information on market demand is useful for individual firms they will tend to be even more concerned with the demand conditions for their own individual product, rather than that for the output of the industry as a whole. This in turn depends upon the *competitive structure* of the industry, examined in detail in Chapters 9 and 10. A number of different cases may be distinguished.

The first, and simplest, case is where the industry is a **pure monopoly** in that there is only one firm producing the product in question, and there is no possibility of entry by other firms into the industry. In that case the demand curve for the individual firm is the market demand curve for the industry as a whole, and there are no further complications.

The second case, at the other extreme of the spectrum of market structures, is **perfect competition**, where there are a large number of firms in the industry, all producing identical variants of the product. In this case, the price will be set by the interaction of supply and demand and each individual firm will be able to sell as much as it wishes at that price, but none at higher prices. The demand curve for the individual firm will be a horizontal straight line, as shown in Fig. 6.3(b).

In the case of market structures which are neither pure monopolies nor perfectly competitive, demand conditions for the individual firm will depend upon a number of factors.

The first is the **elasticity of market demand** for the product as a whole. Clearly, if demand for the product as a whole is perfectly elastic, individual firms will be unable to sell their product at anything apart from the indicated price.

The second determinant of the elasticity of demand for an individual firm is the **degree of product differentiation or brand loyalty** on the part of purchasers. If products are highly differentiated and purchasers are extremely loyal to a particular firm, the demand curve will be downward-sloping, rather than horizontal. Each firm is essentially a 'mini-monopolist', producing a product for which there are no very close substitutes. On the other hand, if products are identical, and consumers exhibit no brand loyalty, demand curves will be horizontal lines, as no consumer will be prepared to pay more for the product of one firm than for the product of another.

The third factor which will determine the elasticity of demand for the individual firm's output will be **its share of the market**. If a firm has a very large market share, a reduction in its price will need to attract a substantial proportion of other firms' customers if the proportionate increase in its demand is to be large. On the other hand, a firm with a very small market share will be able to induce a large proportionate increase in its sales by attracting a relatively small proportion of its rivals' customers.

Fourthly, the elasticity of demand for an individual firm's product will depend upon **its rivals' reactions** to its changes in price. If rivals react to a price reduction by increasing their output (and reducing their own prices) then clearly demand will be less responsive than if rivals maintain or even reduce their output.

For the case of undifferentiated products, Needham (1978, p.59) identifies the following simple equation linking the various different determinants of the demand for an individual firm's product:

$$E_f = \frac{(E_m + E_s . S_r)}{S_f}$$

where:

E_f = elasticity of demand for the firm's product

E_m = market elasticity

E_s = elasticity of rivals' supply with respect to changes in the firm's price

S_f = the firm's market share

S_r = rivals' market share

As the formula confirms, elasticity of demand for the firm's product is partly determined by rivals' reactions to its own actions, which cannot be known for certain, and which are therefore sometimes referred to as '**conjectural variation**'.

A diagrammatic approach to the demand curve for a firm having rivals is known as the '**kinky demand curve**' model, covered in more depth in Chapter 9. If such a firm knows that it can sell quantity Q_o at price P, as shown in Fig. 6.6, then point A is one point on the firm's demand curve.

The difficult problem for the firm lies in evaluating the volume of sales at other prices, as that depends upon the reactions of its rivals. However, if the firm conjectures that its rivals will not match an increase in its price, but will match any price decreases, then demand will be highly elastic for price rises, but relatively inelastic for price reductions. The result is a kinked demand curve as shown in Fig. 6.6.

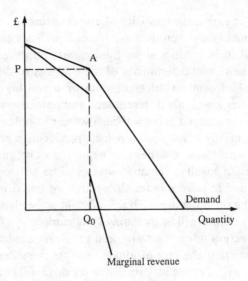

Fig. 6.6 The kinky demand curve

If the demand curve has such a kink, the associated marginal revenue curve will have a 'dog-leg' shape, as illustrated. If the firm were to attempt to sell output greater than Q_0, it would have to reduce its price. This would lead rival firms to follow suit and even a small increase in volume sold would require a relatively substantial fall in price. As a result, marginal revenue falls dramatically for increases in volume beyond Q_0. The implications of this are followed through in detail in Chapter 9, but it is clear enough from the analysis thus far that firms will be reluctant to lower prices in this situation.

Elasticity of demand and the power of buyers

Chapter 10 introduces the method used by Porter (1980 and 1985) for carrying out **structural analysis** of the state of competition in an industry. One of the **'five-forces'** described as determining competition in that framework is the **power of buyers**. That power is in itself determined by two sets of factors, which determine:

- the price sensitivity of buyers
- their bargaining power

Neither of these concepts are quantifiable in the Porter approach, but clearly, the price sensitivity of buyers is a concept very close to that of elasticity of demand. Porter identifies the following factors as the main determinants of price sensitivity:

- **Purchases of the product as a proportion of total purchases.** If purchases of the product are an unimportant proportion of buyers' total purchases, they will tend to be relatively insensitive to price.
- **Product differences and brand identity**, which will reduce price sensitivity.

- **The impact of the product on the quality of the buyers' product or service.** If the product being sold is a key element in maintaining the quality or low cost of buyers' own product, they are unlikely to be price-sensitive.
- **Customers' own profitability.** Profitable customers are said to be less price sensitive.
- **Decision-makers' incentives.** Purchasing managers within customer companies face a variety of incentives, some of which encourage them to be more price-sensitive, others of which reduce the emphasis on price.

The first two of these factors have already been referred to in the section on the determinants of own-price elasticity above. The others illustrate the importance of industrial customers, as opposed to consumers. It is useful to remember that while most economic analysis focuses on the consumer as the customer, the consumer is only one type of buyer. For many firms it is the behaviour of industrial buyers which is most important.

Illustration

Finding the demand curve: the case of Jaguar

Harrison and Wilkes (1973) provide a good example of the losses which may be incurred by a firm which fails to give adequate consideration to the link between price and the quantity of the product which can be sold.

In July 1972, Jaguar launched the XJ12 luxury sports car, having developed a product which was acknowledged to be of excellent quality and performance. The price had been set at £3,726, compared with at least £6,000 for comparable vehicles.

As might be expected, demand exceeded supply, a situation which was made worse by industrial action at the factory. By the end of 1972 there was a two-year waiting list for the product, and second-hand cars were being sold for prices which exceeded the list price by more than 40 per cent.

Critics argued that by setting such a low price, which had been arrived at by estimating the cost per car at full capacity, and then adding a 'satisfactory' margin, the company was sacrificing revenue at a time when it could not afford it. Harrison and Wilkes attempted to quantify that loss, using Fig. 6.7.

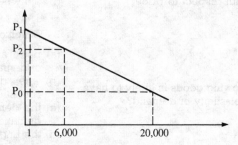

Fig. 6.7 Harrison and Wilkes' analysis

In Fig. 6.7, the straight line shows the [unknown] demand curve for the XJ12. The price set by the company is P_0 at which price it is believed that the planned output of 20,000 units could be sold. The actual quantity sold is 6,000 units. That combination of price and quantity is below the demand curve, because it is known that more cars could be sold at the current price. It is also known that one car has been sold at the higher price, P_1. The objective of the exercise is to estimate the price P_2 at which the current output of 6,000 units could be sold, in order to estimate the lost revenue arising from the pricing policy adopted.

The first stage is to make the assumption that the demand curve is linear, with intercept 'a' and slope 'b'. In that case,

$$P = a - bQ$$

As P_1 is the price at which a single unit was sold it provides an estimate for 'a', which is therefore equal to £5,226. The slope 'b' is equal to $(P_1 - P_0/(20,000))$, which equals .075.

The price at which 6,000 units could be sold is therefore given by the equation:

$$P_2 = 5,226 - (.075)(6,000) = 4,776$$

This is £1,050 more than the price which the firm actually charged, suggesting that on 6,000 units an opportunity loss of more than six million pounds was made.

References and further reading

R. Harrison and F.M. Wilkes, 'A Note on Jaguar's Pricing Policy, *European Journal of Marketing*, 1973

D. Needham, *The Economics of Industrial Structure, Conduct and Performance*, (London, Holt, Rinehart and Winston, 1978)

M. Porter, *Competitive Strategy*, (New York, Free Press, 1980)

M. Porter, *Competitive Advantage*, (New York, Free Press, 1986)

Self-test questions

1 Which of the following goods is likely to have inelastic demand with respect to price?

(a) table salt
(b) domestic gas
(c) small family cars
(d) daily newspapers

2 Which of the following goods is likely to have a negative income elasticity of demand?

(a) bus travel
(b) cheap margarine
(c) expensive margarine
(d) petrol

(e) car accessories
(f) daily newspapers

3 Which of the following statements are correct?

(a) petrol and tyres have positive cross-elasticities of demand
(b) when demand is own-price elastic, marginal revenue is negative
(c) the demand for food is less elastic than the demand for rice
(d) the Engel curve for bread is vertical for most of its range
(e) the price sensitivity of buyers is positively

related to the importance of the product in their total purchases

4 If the demand curve for a product is a straight line, cutting both axes, which of the following statements are correct?

(a) there is a price above which none of the product will be purchased
(b) an infinite amount of the product could be given away
(c) elasticity of demand is lower as price is higher
(d) a rise in price above the mid-point of the curve will increase revenue

(e) elasticity of demand is zero at the point where the curve crosses the horizontal axis

5 In an oligopolistic industry, does elasticity of demand for an individual firm's product rise or fall with:

(a) increasing market share for the firm
(b) decreasing market elasticity of demand
(c) increasing rivals' cross-elasticity of supply with respect to changes in the firm's price

Exercise

'Elasticity of demand for an individual firm's product is largely determined by the structure of the industry in which the firm is operating.' Discuss.

Answers on page 406.

7 Estimating and forecasting demand

This chapter examines the estimation and forecasting of demand. Alternative methods of estimation are considered and the problems associated with each one examined. Attention is then directed to forecasting methods, including time-series analysis and market research techniques.

Alternative methods of estimation

It is clear that in principle the concepts of the demand curve and elasticity of demand are potentially of great significance for the process of business decision-making. However, the theoretical concepts can only be of practical application if reliable quantitative estimates can be made of the level of demand and of elasticity. This is a difficult task which may be approached in a number of ways. The most fundamental distinction is between **estimation**, which attempts to quantify the links between the level of demand and the other variables which determine it, and **forecasting** which simply attempts to predict the level of demand at some future date.

Simple estimation of arc elasticity

One of the crudest ways in which the market elasticity of demand could be estimated is by observing the quantity of a product sold before and after a price change and assuming that the two known combinations of price and quantity are points on the same demand curve. In Fig. 7.1, for example, if 100 units of output were sold at a price of 8 (point A) and 120 units were sold when the price fell to 6 (point B), then elasticity of demand can be directly estimated from the standard formula.

A more sophisticated version of this technique was used in a well-known study by Simon (1966) which attempted to measure the price elasticity of demand for liquor in the United States. Its advantage lies in the fact that it is very simple and estimates can be made on the basis of a single price change. The disadvantages are that adjustments have to be made to compensate for speculative building up or running down of stocks in anticipation of a price change, and there is no guarantee that the

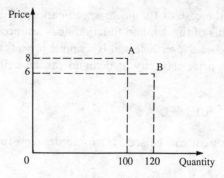

Fig. 7.1 Direct estimation of arc elasticity

two price/output combinations which are observed lie on the same demand curve. It could quite easily be the case that both supply and demand curves shifted in the movement from A to B.

Econometric estimation of demand curves

The second, more sophisticated approach to demand estimation is through 'econometrics', the statistical analysis of economic data using techniques like multiple regression, which allow empirical data on demand and its determinants to be used to estimate the co-efficients of a demand function. The general form of the demand function has been set out above as:

$$Q_d = f(P_o, \ P_c, \ P_s, \ Y_d, \ T, \ A_o, \ A_c, \ A_s, \ I, \ C, \ E)$$

In this form the equation simply states that the quantity demanded is a function of each of the determinants, without specifying any particular functional form for the relationship between the dependent variable (Q_d) and the independent variables ($P_o, P_c, P_s, Y_d, T, A_o, A_c, A_s, I, C, E$).

If the size of the co-efficients linking the various independent variables with the level of demand are to be estimated a particular functional form needs to be chosen. The two most common forms are the **linear demand function** and the **exponential demand function**.

The linear demand function can be written:

$$Q_d = a + b_1 P_o + b_2 P_c + b_3 P_s + b_4 Y_d + b_5 T + b_6 A_o + b_7 A_c + b_8 A_s + b_9 I + b_{10} C + b_{11} E$$

If data is available on each of the variables, and there are sufficient observations to apply the statistical technique of multiple regression then the co-efficient for the intercept (a) and the co-efficients showing the impact of each determinant upon the quantity demanded (b_1 to b_{11}) can be estimated. Once they have been estimated it is possible to predict the level of demand for any set of values for each of the determinants by simply inserting these values into the equation.

In the case of the linear specification of the demand curve, estimating the co-efficients of the demand function does not provide a direct estimate of the elasticity of demand. Nevertheless, it is a simple process to calculate elasticities. The definition of own-price elasticity of demand can be written as:

$$e_d = \frac{dQ}{dP_o} \cdot \frac{P_o}{Q}$$

However, it can be seen from the demand function that:

$$\frac{dQ}{dP_o} = b_1$$

So that:

$$e_d = b_1 \cdot \frac{P_o}{Q}$$

Other elasticities, including income elasticity, cross-price elasticity and advertising elasticity can be calculated in the same way.

The linear specification of the demand function allows the estimation of elasticity, and the own-price elasticity which is calculated as a result does change with different combinations of price and quantity, as is to be expected. However, the linear form embodies the assumption that a given change in price always has the same effect on volume, regardless of the level of price. That assumption conflicts with most economic reasoning, including theories of consumer behaviour, so that alternative specifications are often used in attempting to estimate demand.

The most popular alternative to the linear form is the **exponential form**, which may be written:

$$Q_d = P_o^a . P_s^b . P_c^c . A_o^d . A_s^e . A_c^f . Y_d^g . I^h . C^i . E^j$$

In this form the elasticities are the exponents (the co-efficients a to j) and the equation can be rewritten in a linear form by taking logarithms. This gives the equation:

$$\log Q_d = a\log P_o + b\log P_s + c\log P_c + d\log A_o + e\log A_s + f\log A_c + g\log Y_d + h\log I +$$

$$i\log C + j\log E$$

This equation can be estimated using the methods of multiple regression, giving direct estimates of the various different elasticities of demand. This is the most commonly used form of the demand function for the purposes of estimation, although it should be noted that it embodies an assumption that elasticities are constant, in place of the assumption in the linear form that the marginal impact of price (and the other factors) on volume is constant.

The basic principles involved in estimating the demand function are simple enough, but there are a number of very substantial statistical problems involved in arriving at estimates which cannot be held to with any confidence. A detailed treatment of them lies beyond the scope of this book, but it is useful to note them briefly.

In the first place, the method of multiple regression does not provide an exact relationship between the level of demand and each of its determinants. It simply shows the relationship which has the 'best fit' to the data. In some cases that 'best fit' may be very poor, in which case the equation specified explains only a small proportion of the variation in the level of demand. If this is the case, the equation will have little value in estimating and predicting the level of demand.

In the second place, the estimated values of the individual co-efficients in the demand function are only good estimates (known as best linear unbiased estimators (BLUES)) if a number of quite restrictive assumptions about the behaviour of the error term (the difference between the estimate of the level of demand given by the equation and the actual value) are valid. If they are not then various corrections will need to be made, none of which are entirely satisfactory.

Thirdly, there is what is known as the **identification problem**. If statisticians have collected a number of observations on the price of a commodity, over time, and the level of demand at each price, it is tempting to conclude that the line which provides the best fit to this set of observations is the demand curve. In Fig. 7.2(a) such a line is shown as ABC.

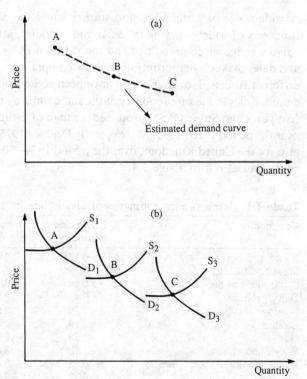

Fig. 7.2 The identification problem

However, such a set of observations could have arisen in a number of different ways. Certainly, if it is known that the demand curve remained in the same position (indicating that none of the factors other than price changed over the period of observation) but the supply curve shifted, then the points traced out would identify the demand curve. On the other hand, the same set of points could have been generated by both the demand curve and the supply curve shifting, as in Fig. 7.2(b), in which case the line AB does not represent the demand curve at all. It is helpful when considering this point to appreciate that if neither the demand curve nor the supply curve shifted over the period of observation, the set of data recorded would consist of multiple observations of a single point on the diagram, price and quantity remaining the same at every observation.

The identification problem can be solved, subject to a range of qualifications, but the solution is quite complex and requires the estimation of a model made up of a number of simultaneous equations, rather than a single equation for demand. Despite their limitations, many of the attempts to statistically estimate demand and elasticities have used methods based on a single equation.

Some estimates of elasticity

A wide range of economists and statisticians have attempted to estimate demand functions of widely varying types. In most studies, attention has focused on a very narrow range of commodities and the differences in methods used, areas covered and dates makes it inappropriate to draw comparisons of the estimated values across different studies. However, there have been some studies which examine a range of commodities in the same country at the same time, using the same methods. Twenty-five years ago Stone (1953) produced a range of estimates for the United Kingdom over the period 1920–1938. More recently Deaton (1975) carried out a similar exercise, also for the United Kingdom, over the period 1954–70. The estimates from this latter study are set out in Table 7.1.

Table 7.1 Some recent estimates of elasticities in the UK

Commodity	Own-price elasticity	Income elasticity
Bread and cereals	−0.12*	0.72
Meat and bacon	−0.27*	1.36
Sugar and sweets	−0.48	−0.17*
Dairy produce	−0.41	0.86
Potatoes and vegetables	−0.20	0.99*
Clothing	−0.99	2.68
Gas	−1.65	−3.53
Wines and spirits	−1.12	3.55
Running costs of motor vehicles	−0.63	3.81
Rail travel	−0.73	−2.52
Newspapers	−0.43	−0.73
Recreational goods	0.33*	4.28

* indicates that the result is not significantly different from zero

Source: A. Deaton, Models and Projections of Demand in Post-War Britain, London, Chapman and Hall 1975

In many respects the figures presented in Table 7.1 accord with expectations, in that the own-price elasticities have negative signs and luxury goods like recreational goods, wines and spirits and the running of motor vehicles all have large positive income elasticities. Most of the own-price elasticities indicate inelastic demand which is to be expected for the relatively broad product categories identified. Nevertheless, some of the results seem implausible enough to raise doubts. The highly negative income elasticity of demand for gas, identifying it as an inferior good, seems intuitively unlikely, as does the negative value for the income elasticity of demand for newspapers.

Estimates such as these provide useful broad indicators of demand conditions, but the difficulties of estimation and the possibly outdated nature of the data on which they are based require that they be treated with great caution. The very broad product categories to which many such estimates relate, and the fact that they measure market elasticity rather than firm elasticity, also tend to reduce their direct usefulness to companies.

Forecasting demand

The methods discussed above build upon a theoretical model of the market and the demand curve in order to estimate the way in which demand will respond to changes in price. The aim of such procedures is to quantify the causal links between the level of demand and its determinants. If the aim is more limited, being restricted to simply predicting the future volume of sales, without quantifying responsiveness to the various different determinants of demand, then a variety of other forecasting techniques may be employed.

Extrapolation and time series analysis

One of the simplest techniques is to assume that some aspect of the past behaviour of the variable being forecast will continue to be true in the future, thereby providing the basis for the prediction. At its most elementary this includes 'naive methods' of forecasting such as the assumption that next year's volume of sales will be equal to this year's figure, or that next year's growth of sales will be equal to this year's. A slightly more sophisticated version is to identify any trends over the recent past and then to extrapolate those trends forward into the future. Fig. 7.3 illustrates the procedure.

The scatter of points in Fig. 7.3 shows the level of sales in recent time-periods, and the solid line is that which provides the 'best fit' to those points, fitted either by eye or by simple linear regression. The extension of that relationship into the future, marked by the dotted line, provides the forecast of sales levels for future periods. The major weakness of such methods is that they make no reference to the causal factors which determine the volume of demand, in effect assuming that time is the only determining factor which needs to be taken into account. They also assume that

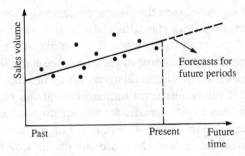

Fig. 7.3 Forecasting by extrapolation

the relationship between time and the variable being forecast is a very simple one consisting only of a long-term trend.

A more sophisticated type of extrapolation is **time series analysis**, which includes a wide range of different techniques (see Makridakis, et al (1983) for a full exposition). Perhaps the best-known of these techniques is the **decomposition method**. In this approach it is assumed that any time series is made up of a series of components. The first component is the **trend (T)** showing long run changes in the variable being considered. The second component is **seasonal movement(s)** within each year, and the third component is **irregular movement (I)**, which consists of non-recurring and essentially unpredictable changes. Forecasting textbooks usually also include a fourth component consisting of **cyclical movement** made up of regular contractions and expansions over periods of a few years, but the practical value of this component is much more doubtful. It is not at all clear whether industries really are subject to regular cyclical movements and isolating such movements from the data can involve making arbitrary judgments. Whichever model is adopted, each individual observation is assumed to be made up of these components, which may be linked additively, in which case:

$$X_t = T_t + C_t + S_t + I_t$$ where:

X_t = the observation for period t
T_t = the trend value for period t
C_t = the cyclical component for period t
S_t = the seasonal component for period t
I_t = the irregular component for period t

Alternatively the relationship between the components could be multiplicative, in which case:

$$X_t = T_t . C_t . S_t . I_t$$

In order to use time-series analysis for forecasting, the raw data is divided up into its constituent components in a number of stages. This can be done in many different ways but a simple example can illustrate the basic features. In this example a cyclical component is not included, for the reasons outlined above.

First, the trend factor in the data is isolated, either by taking a moving average of the raw data or by fitting a straight line to the raw data using regression analysis.

The new time series which results represents the effects of the *trend*. If the resulting value for each time period is subtracted from the actual observation, the differences represent the *seasonal* and *irregular* components taken together. In order to separate out the seasonal component alone, an average is taken of these 'seasonal-plus-irregular' components for each season of the year, across the full period for which data is available. As the irregular component for each season is thereby averaged out, the results provide the *seasonal component*, giving a value for each season. As the seasonal components should add to zero, some adjustment of the result may be needed (see the worked example below).

Once the trend and seasonal components have been identified, the construction of a forecast for any future period consists of using the regression equation to calculate the trend value for the future period in question and adding in the seasonal component for the season in question. This procedure may be made more clear by working through an example.

Table 7.2 Time series analysis of sales volume

Stage 1: Calculate the 'trend factor'

The following set of figures shows the sales of bicycles for each season over the period 1980–1985

Time period	t	Actual observation
1980		
Spring	1	2419
Summer	2	2947
Autumn	3	3396
Winter	4	3515
1981		
Spring	5	2742
Summer	6	3127
Autumn	7	3978
Winter	8	2439
1982		
Spring	9	2686
Summer	10	3493
Autumn	11	4185
Winter	12	3920
1983		
Spring	13	2690
Summer	14	3598
Autumn	15	4317
Winter	16	4035
1984		
Spring	17	3069
Summer	18	3337
Autumn	19	4439
Winter	20	4242
1985		
Spring	21	2910
Summer	22	3923
Autumn	23	4809
Winter	24	4570

A simple regression of sales volume against time gives:

$$T_t = 2926.2 + 18.16t \qquad \text{where}$$

$$T_t = \text{trend value of sales}$$
$$t \;\; = \text{time period}$$

Stage 2: Separate out 'seasonal plus irregular'

t	Actual observation (Col 1)	Trend values (Col 2)	Seasonal plus irregular (Col 1 – Col 2)
1	2419	2944.36	−525.36
2	2947	2962.52	−15.52
3	3396	2980.68	415.32
4	3515	2998.84	516.16
5	2742	3017.00	−275.00
6	3127	3035.16	91.84
7	3978	3053.32	924.68
8	2439	3071.48	−632.48
9	2686	3089.64	−403.64
10	3493	3107.80	385.20
11	4185	3125.96	1059.04
12	3920	3144.12	775.88
13	2690	3162.28	−472.28
14	3598	3180.44	417.56
15	4317	3198.60	1118.40
16	4035	3216.76	818.24
17	3069	3234.92	−165.92
18	3337	3253.08	83.92
19	4439	3271.24	1167.76
20	4242	3289.40	952.60
21	2910	3307.56	−397.56
22	3923	3325.72	597.28
23	4809	3343.88	1465.12
24	4570	3362.04	1207.96

Stage 3: Identify the seasonal component for each season

Season	Values of 'seasonal plus irregular' (Col 1)	Average of Col 1
Spring		
	−525.36	
	−275.00	
	−403.64	−373.3
	−472.28	
	−165.92	
	−397.56	
Summer		
	−15.52	
	91.84	
	385.20	260.0
	417.56	
	83.92	
	597.28	

Autumn

	415.32	
	924.68	
	1059.04	1025.1
	1118.40	
	1167.76	
	1465.12	

Winter

	516.16	
	−632.48	
	775.88	606.4
	818.24	
	952.60	
	1207.96	

If these seasonal values are added together, they sum to 1518.2. However, the total of seasonal factors over a year should sum to zero, so the factors as calculated require adjustment. This can be done in a number of ways but the simplest is to add the *absolute values* of the components together, giving a total of 2264.8 and then to *scale* each of the seasonal factors in proportion to their size so that their total sums to zero. In the case of the seasonal component for summer the scaling factor is given by:

$$\frac{260.6}{2264.8} \times 1518.2 = 174.7$$

This scaling factor is then subtracted from the seasonal component as originally calculated. Repeating this for each season gives the following results.

Stage 4: Scaling the seasonal factors

Season	Seasonal factor as originally calculated	Scaling factor	Adjusted seasonal factor
Spring	−373.3	250.2	−623.5
Summer	260.6	174.7	85.9
Autumn	1025.1	687.2	337.8
Winter	606.4	406.5	199.8
Total			0.0

A forecast for any future period can now be made by calculating the trend value for that period and adding in the seasonal factor. For instance, if we wish to forecast sales volume for Winter 1986, it is first noted that Winter 1986 is period 28. The Trend Value is given by the regression equation:

$$T_t = 2926.2 + 18.16\, t \qquad \text{As } t = 28 \qquad T_t = 3434.7$$

The seasonal factor for Winter is 199.8, so that the forecast value is:

Forecast for Winter 1986 = 3434.7 + 199.8 = 3634.5

It should be noted that this example adopts the simplest possible approach, which may not be the most appropriate one for the particular set of data in question. A multiplicative model, the inclusion of a cyclical factor or alternative methods of scaling might all improve the quality of the forecast. A number of different approaches could be attempted, and their accuracy measured by '**back-forecasting**' which simply involves using the model to forecast within the period for which data is available and measuring the accuracy of the forecasts arrived at by using different techniques.

Barometric forecasting techniques

Time series analysis uses information about the past in order to make forecasts of the future. Barometric forecasting uses indicators of current activity in order to provide forecasts of the future. Perhaps the most common barometric technique is the use of **leading indicators**. A leading indicator is a variable which is known, or believed, to be correlated with the future behaviour of the variable for which a forecast is required. For instance, to take a simple example, if we wish to forecast the number of children who will be entering school for the first time in five years time in the UK, the number of children born this year will provide a very useful leading indicator. In that example the connection between the leading indicator and the variable being forecast is very close indeed. In other cases there may be no obvious causal link between the indicator and the variable being forecast. It has been suggested, for instance, that sunspot activity is closely correlated with the business cycle (another reason perhaps for being suspicious about the value of the cyclical component)!

Given the importance to businessmen of being able to predict general movements in the level of economic activity, there are a large number of leading indicators which are used in the attempt to identify changes in total spending, income and employment. These include new orders for machine tools, which often rise in advance of an increase in economic activity, the length of the working week, and the performance of the Stock Exchange. A number of such general leading indicators used in the United Kingdom or the United States are:

- new orders for machine tools
- average hours worked in manufacturing
- index of new business formation
- new orders for durable goods
- orders for plant and equipment
- new building starts
- changes in manufacturing inventories
- industrial materials prices
- Stock Exchange indices
- profit figures
- price to unit labour cost ratios
- increases in consumer debt.

The marketing approach to demand measurement

In the simple economic model of the firm, the business being modelled produces a single product for a single market, and the amount of information required on the level of demand is relatively limited. Real companies are much more complex and require a great deal more information concerning the markets they operate in.

Different categories of market

In the first place, distinctions may be drawn between a number of different concepts of 'the market' for a product (see Kotler (1984) for a typical marketing treatment of these concepts). The **potential market** for a product is that group of households and organisations who indicate some interest in the product on offer. However, not all of these potential purchasers will have the income needed to turn their interest into an actual purchase, and some of those who have both an interest and the necessary income will not have access to the product. The **available market** is the group of consumers who have the interest, the necessary income, and access to the product. Very few companies make sales to every possible purchaser in the available market, and the **served market** is the group of households and organisations which the company decides to focus on. Finally, the **penetrated market** is those customers who actually buy the product.

This categorisation of 'the' market suggests that firms may need information on four different aspects of the market for their product. Furthermore, the firm's 'product' may also be defined at a number of different levels. Most obviously there is the distinction between the **market for the industry** as a whole, and the **market for the individual firm**. However, very few firms produce a single product so that information will also be needed on the **market for a product line**, within that the **market for a product form**, and within that the **market for an individual product item**.

When it is also recognised that a firm needs information on different geographical markets, including *local*, *regional*, *national*, *continental* and *global*, and for different time periods, perhaps simply *short term*, *medium term* and *long term*, then it becomes very clear that an enormous amount of information is potentially required if a firm is to be fully informed about its markets. This information may be collected in a number of different ways.

Market surveys

Perhaps the best known form of market research is the market survey. This is not only used to forecast the level of demand for a product, but may be used for a wide range of other purposes as well, including testing buyers' reactions to different product configurations and packaging, and identifying links between purchasing behaviour and other variables, like buyers' age, sex, social status and income. If the aim is to estimate the level of demand a sample of buyers are asked direct questions about their intentions with respect to purchasing the product within a specified future period. That information is used in conjunction with other evidence about the potential market to construct an estimate of the total volume of sales. The effectiveness of this technique depends upon a number of variables.

First, it depends upon **the number of potential buyers**. If the number is very large, only a small sample can be reached for a reasonable cost. It may be possible to construct a truly representative sample, in which case the results from that sample can be extrapolated in order to reach a forecast for the market as a whole. However, if the sample should contain an unknown bias, which can be difficult to avoid, the results will also be biased and could give misleading estimates. Market surveys are therefore of most use when the number of potential buyers is small so that a very high proportion of them can be questioned.

The second variable which determines the usefulness of market surveys is **the clarity of buyers' intentions**. If buyers themselves are vague about their own intentions they will be unable to provide useful information to the market researcher.

Other factors which will affect the cost-effectiveness of market surveys are:

- the cost of identifying and contacting buyers
- buyers' willingness to disclose their intentions
- buyers' propensity to carry out their intentions.

This analysis suggests that market surveys will be of most value for industrial products, for consumer durables and for other products where buyers plan their purchases in advance. Market surveys may also be useful for new products where there is no past data on sales, so that time-series analysis or estimation is not possible.

Sales force opinion

If market surveys are inappropriate, an indirect method of forecasting buyers' intentions is to survey the sales force, asking them to provide estimates of the future volume of sales. Clearly, this approach is fraught with problems as the sales force may not be fully aware of changes in the economy which may affect sales, or changes in the firm's marketing strategy. Furthermore, the sales force may have an incentive to provide biased forecasts in pursuit of their own interests. They may provide deliberate under-estimates of sales in order to be given low sales quotas which they will be able to exceed without effort, or over-estimates in order to justify their continued employment. This is an example of the principal/agent problem referred to in Chapter 3. It may be possible for the firm to devise methods which bring the interests of the firm and the interests of the sales force together, so that the sales force has an incentive to provide accurate forecasts. Bonuses could be linked to the accuracy of forecasts, for instance, or the amount spent on advertising and promotion could be linked to the forecast level of sales in order to avoid deliberate under-estimation. (This last approach could, of course, prove counter-productive if salesmen deliberately over-estimate sales in order to secure greater advertising and promotion in their territories.)

While sales force opinion clearly has its drawbacks as a forecasting tool there are advantages in the method, both as a means of collecting data and as a more general instrument of good management. The sales force are closer to customers than most other groups within the firm, and may be able to spot trends first. Their knowledge is at a very detailed level with respect to different products, markets, distribution channels and individual customers, which may allow a more accurate forecast than a more aggregated approach. If the sales force is directly involved in the construction of forecasts and the setting of sales quotas they will have a better understanding of that process and will tend to exhibit greater commitment and motivation as a result.

Expert opinion

A third approach to demand forecasting is to ask experts in the field to provide their own estimates of future sales volume. Experts may include executives directly involved in the market, such as dealers, distributors and suppliers, or others whose major interest is in the forecast itself, such as stockbrokers' industry analysts, specialist marketing consultants or officers of the trade association. Various mechanisms exist for the construction of such forecasts. Most obviously, each expert could be asked independently to provide a confidential estimate and the results could be averaged. The advantage of that approach is that there is no danger that the group of experts develop a **group-think** mentality where their independent judgment is impaired by their desire to be seen as loyal and conforming members of the group. On the other hand, if estimates are produced entirely independently the experts have no opportunity to weigh the opinions of others or to take into account factors known to the others but not to themselves.

One well-known approach which seeks to avoid 'group-think' while allowing the experts to pool their knowledge is the **Delphi technique**. Each participant is asked independently to produce a forecast. Each of these forecasts, with the reasoning behind it, is then presented as feedback to each of the participants, with anonymity being maintained so that none of the experts know who is responsible for the other forecasts. Each of the experts is then asked to revise his own forecasts in the light of the forecasts and reasoning of the others, and this process is repeated until a consensus is reached. This may not always be possible if the experts disagree and will not allow their opinions to be shifted, but experience with the method suggests that the process of iteration does often lead to the convergence of the different forecasts around an agreed value.

Market testing

If a product is new, or an established product is being sold in a new market or through a new distribution channel, there will be no past data to analyse. Direct questioning of buyers will be difficult as they will have only hypothetical information about the product's characteristics and neither the sales force nor the experts will have any solid basis of experience on which to base estimates of the likely demand. In this situation market testing may be the most appropriate method of collecting information. Kotler (1984) identifies a number of different methods which may be employed.

Sales-wave research involves selecting a group of consumers, supplying them with the product at no cost and then re-offering them the product and/or competitors' products at reduced prices a number of times. This allows the market researchers to measure the repeat purchase rate and to estimate the impact of different competing brands. Different groups of buyers may also be exposed to different packaging and different advertising concepts, in order to evaluate their differential effect.

Simulated store techniques involve establishing a group of shoppers, showing them a number of advertising commercials, including those relating to the new product, and then giving them small amounts of money which they may spend or keep. The amounts spent on the product being investigated are noted as is spending on competing brands. The group of shoppers are brought together to discuss their immediate reactions to the products and the reasons for their purchasing behaviour and follow-up telephone interviews are carried out later, to establish consumers' more lasting responses.

Test marketing involves actually selling the product in a limited number of locations, while providing different marketing mixes (see Chapter 12) or different packaging, advertising or promotional concepts in order to test their effectiveness. The scale of test marketing may vary from a limited exercise in a small number of participating stores, independent of the firm's usual distribution channels, to a full-scale exercise involving whole regions.

While test marketing can provide a realistic simulation of an actual product launch and may allow the company to identify any product faults that have been overlooked, it can be expensive and may not prove an accurate means of forecasting total sales volume. The markets in which the tests take place may not be representative of the market as a whole, and general economic conditions may vary between the test marketing and the actual product launch. Perhaps most important of all, test marketing reveals the company's intentions to competitors and they may well take counter-measures, in which case the environment into which the product is launched will be substantially different to that in which the test took place, invalidating its results.

Clearly, there are no perfect solutions to the problem of demand forecasting. The choice of technique depends to a very great extent upon the particular circumstances, the cost of acquiring better information and the value of the investment put at risk if a venture should fail. If the price of failure is low there is little point in spending substantial sums on improving demand forecasts. On the other hand, if the cost of failure is high, spending on the acquisition of additional information will be well worthwhile.

Illustration

Measuring the elasticity of demand for liquor: a US example

Taxes on alcohol are a major revenue earner in many economies, which implies that the elasticity of demand for liquor is of considerable practicable importance. If elasticity is low, a tax increase will lead to large increases in tax revenue, and the tax will be largely passed on to consumers. If elasticity is high, tax revenue will be much smaller as consumers forego consumption of the product and most of the tax is absorbed by the producers.

J L Simon (1966) attempted to measure this important parameter, using a method which he described as 'quasi-experimental'. This consisted of a number of steps. First, monthly data was collected for the price of liquor in each of the American states. If the price changed by more than 2 per cent, then a 'price change event' was said to have taken place. (States where the production of illicit 'moonshine' liquor was important were excluded.) Secondly, per capita consumption of liquor was calculated for the 12-month period which began three months before the 'price change event', and the 12-month period which began three months after it. This gave a figure for consumption 'before' and 'after' the price change. The gap of six months was introduced in order to avoid the changes in demand that arise from consumers attempts to stock up before a price change, and to use up those stored purchases in the period after the price change. Thirdly, the change in consumption for the state in which the price change event took place was compared with the change in consumption in other states, taking care to exclude other states which themselves experienced price changes or sales tax changes. This provided a measure of the proportionate change in demand given by the following formula:

$$\frac{\text{Change in per capita consumption, following the price change}}{\text{Per capita consumption in comparison states, before the price change}}$$

minus

$$\frac{\text{Change in per capita consumption in comparison states}}{\text{Per capita consumption in comparison states, before the price change}}$$

Fourthly, the proportionate relative change in price was estimated by calculating the actual change and comparing it with the actual change in the price of popular 'benchmark' brands. Finally, the change in quantity, as calculated above, was divided by the change in price as calculated, giving an estimate for elasticity of demand.

This process produced estimates for the different states which had a median value of − .79, corresponding to the theoretical expectation that the demand for liquor is inelastic. The median was used as a measure of central tendency in preference to the mean in order to eliminate the influence of 'outliers' (i.e. extreme observations), and in order to avoid the conceptual problem associated with the fact that for six states elasticity was estimated to be positive, implying an upward-sloping demand curve. Indeed, the estimates for individual states varied from $+.97$ to -4.35, which is a very substantial variation.

Simon's central conclusion with respect to the price elasticity of demand for liquor was that:

we may say with .965 probability that the mean of the population from which this sample of elasticity estimates was drawn is between $-.03$ and $-.97$.

If the exact value of elasticity were of crucial importance, this could hardly be said to be a very useful result. On the other hand, the key issue for policy is whether demand is elastic or inelastic. As the result suggests quite strongly that demand is inelastic, policy-makers can perhaps rest assured that liquor taxes are indeed a useful way to raise revenue, whose immediate burden falls largely on consumers.

References and further reading

A. Deaton, *Models and Projections of Demand in Post-War Britain*, (London, Chapman and Hall, 1975)

P. Kotler, *Marketing Management: Analysis, Planning and Control*, (London, Prentice-Hall, 1984)

S. Makridakis, S.C. Wheelright and V.E. McGee, *Forecasting: Methods and Applications* (New York, John Wiley, 1983)

J.L. Simon, 'The Price Elasticity of Liquor in the US and a Simple Method of Determination', *Econometrica*, 1966

R. Stone, *Measurement of Consumers' Expenditure and Behaviour in the United Kingdom, 1920–38* (Cambridge, Cambridge UP, 1954)

Self-test questions

1 Which of the following goods would you expect to have very low price and income elasticities of demand?

(a) table salt
(b) brandy
(c) golf club membership
(d) designer clothing
(e) telephone calls

2 Of the goods listed in 1. above, which would you expect to have very high income elasticities of demand?

3 Which of the following best describes a leading indicator?

(a) a variable in which changes follow changes in a variable we are trying to forecast
(b) a variable which changes in advance of a variable we are trying to forecast.

(c) a variable which changes at the same time as one we are trying to forecast.

4 The list below shows a number of goods and a number of forecasting techniques. Which technique is best suited to which good?

1 An industrial product with a limited potential market
2 A consumer good which has been on sale for many years
3 A new product whose full-scale launch will be very expensive
4 A technically very complex new product, to be sold in a very wide market.
A Time-series analysis
B Expert opinion
C Market testing
D Survey of buyer' intentions

5   In which of the following situations will there be no identification problem?

(a) if it is known that neither supply nor demand curves have shifted.

(b) if it is known that both supply and demand-conditions have shifted.

(c) if it is known that only the supply curve has shifted.

(d) if it is known that only the demand curve has shifted.

Exercise

Explain the difference between estimation and forecasting and outline the difficulties associated with *one* method of each.

Answers on page 408.

Production and the determination of costs

This chapter begins by setting out the basic relationships between inputs and outputs, as represented by the production function. Isoquants are then used to identify the cost-minimising combinations of inputs in both the short run and the long run, and this analysis is linked to the concept of the cost curve. The sources of scale economies and diseconomies are then analysed, paying particular attention to the problems of empirical estimation through statistical analysis, the engineering approach and the survivor technique. Having completed the conventional economic analysis of costs, attention is then given to linear cost functions and break-even analysis before completing the chapter with a brief outline of the other 'cost drivers' which firms may need to take into account.

Production functions and isoquants

The production function and its properties

The starting point for the economic analysis of production and costs is to be found in the production function, which is simply a mathematical statement of the relationship between inputs and outputs. In its simplest and most general form the production function is usually written as follows:

$Q = f(K,L)$ where:
Q = level of output
K = a measure of the capital input
L = a measure of the labour input

There are various more specific functional forms which could be taken by the production function, but one of the most useful and best-known is the **Cobb–Douglas production function,** which is written:

$Q = AK^aL^b$ where:
A = a constant
a,b = positive fractions

The production function is assumed to have a number of properties. In the first place, both K and L are assumed to be infinitely divisible and independently variable and the function is continuous, so that output increases smoothly as either the capital input, the labour input, or both, are increased. If the level of one input, capital for instance, is kept constant and the level of the other input (labour) altered, the rate at which output changes is known as the **marginal product of labour**. In accordance with the **principle of diminishing returns** it is assumed that as more and more of one factor of production is combined with fixed quantities of another the point must eventually be reached where marginal product begins to decline, as in Fig. 8.1.

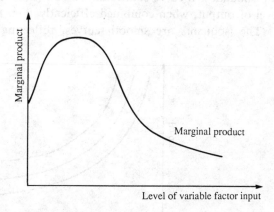

Fig. 8.1 The marginal product of a factor of production

For the specific case of the Cobb–Douglas function, simple calculus can be used to calculate the marginal product of a factor, and the slope of the marginal product curve.

marginal product of labour $(MP_L) = \dfrac{dQ}{dL} = bAK^aL^{b-1}$

slope of the marginal product curve $= \dfrac{dMP_L}{dL} = (b-1)(b)AK^aL^{b-2}$

As $0<b<1$ the slope of the marginal product curve is always negative, and it can be seen that the Cobb–Douglas function has the simple property of a marginal product curve which always slopes downwards.

If both factors of production are increased together, the impact on the level of output depends upon the **returns to scale** exhibited by the production function. In the case of the Cobb–Douglas example, if both capital and labour are increased by the factor 'k' it is relatively easy to calculate the increase in output:

Initial output $Q_1 = AK^aL^b$
Increased output $Q^* = A(kK)^a(kL)^b = AK^aL^bk^{a+b} = Q_1k^{a+b}$

As the equation shows, if the level of inputs increases by the factor k the level of output increases by k^{a+b}. If $(a+b)>1$, there are *increasing returns to scale*, as the increase in output is larger than the increase in inputs. If $(a+b)=1$ there are *constant returns to scale*, with outputs increasing at the same rate as inputs, and if $(a+b)<1$ there are *decreasing returns to scale*.

Isoquants

A production function can be represented graphically through the use of **isoquants**. An isoquant is a curve connecting all combinations of inputs which give the same level of output, when combined efficiently. Fig. 8.2 provides some examples.

The isoquants are smooth curves, reflecting the assumption that there are

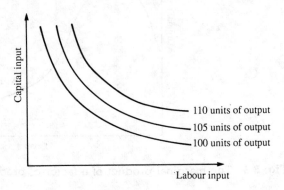

Fig. 8.2 Isoquants

continuous possibilities for substitution between one factor of production and another. They are convex to the origin or concave upwards, (like indifference curves, to which they are formally equivalent) and their slope shows the rate at which one factor has to be substituted for another in order to maintain a constant level of output. This is known as the **marginal rate of technical substitution**. There is an isoquant for every possible level of output, and isoquants can never cross each other.

If a set of isoquants were drawn for equal increments of output, the distances between the isoquants would reflect the returns to scale embodied in the production function, as shown in Fig. 8.3(a) to (c).

In Fig. 8.3(a), the isoquants are evenly spaced, illustrating constant returns to scale. In 8.3(b) they are closer together as the distance from the origin increases, showing that there are increasing returns to scale, and in 8.3(c) they are further apart indicating decreasing returns to scale.

In the language of economic theory, a production function represents a **technology**, which encompasses all known methods of producing the commodity in question. Each point on an isoquant represents a **technique**, embodying a particular method of production, using a particular ratio of capital to labour. It is worth noting that this terminology differs from the layman's usage of the term 'technology', where it is

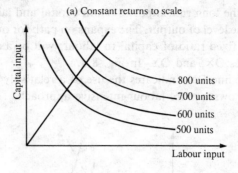

(a) Constant returns to scale

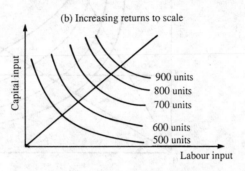

(b) Increasing returns to scale

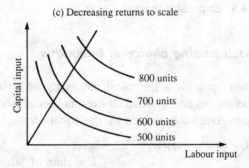

(c) Decreasing returns to scale

Fig. 8.3 Isoquants and scale economies

quite in order to refer to 'a labour-intensive technology', or a 'capital-intensive technology.' In economic theory a given state of technology is deemed to encompass knowledge of a virtually infinite range of techniques.

<u>Isoquants may be used to illustrate the way in which a firm can increase its output in the long run and the short run.</u> In the short run, there are some fixed factors of production, represented by the capital input, and output can only be increased by using more of the variable factor, which is labour. If, in Fig. 8.4, the level of capital input is fixed at K*, the short-run expansion path for output is given by the line K*B. For equal increments in output, shown by the isoquants, increasingly large increments of labour input are required, as the diagram shows, illustrating the **principle of diminishing returns**.

In the long run, inputs of both capital and labour can be increased in order to raise the level of output. The expansion path for output, given the use of a technique with a fixed ratio of capital to labour, will be a ray from the origin, as shown by the lines OX_1 and OX_2 in Fig. 8.4.

The line OX_1 indicates the use of a relatively capital-intensive technique, while OX_2 shows a more labour-intensive approach.

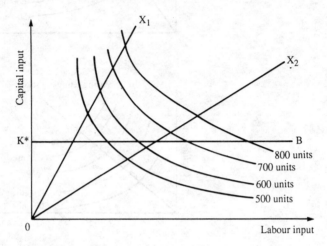

Fig. 8.4 Expansion paths

Cost-minimising choice of technique

Isoquants provide a graphical means by which the cost-minimising technique of production can be identified. If the unit cost of labour is w and the unit cost of capital is r then total cost is given by the equation:

$$TC = (w)(L) + (r)(K)$$ where:

L = units of labour hired
K = units of capital hired

If the cost-minimising method of producing Q* units of output is to be found, the problem can be stated in terms of the equations as:

Minimise $TC = (w)(L) + (r)(K)$
subject to $Q* = f(K,L)$

In terms of the diagrams, the equation for total cost is simply a straight line, whose slope reflects the price ratio of capital and labour. For a given amount of expenditure, combinations of capital and labour which may be purchased are given by a straight line, known as an **isocost** line. Higher levels of spending have isocost lines which are further away from the origin, as shown in Fig. 8.5. If level of output Q* is to be produced at minimum cost, it is necessary to find the lowest cost at which the firm can purchase a combination of capital and labour which is sufficient to produce output

Q*. This can be seen in Fig. 8.5, as the point where an isocost line is a tangent to the isoquant for output Q*.

It is clear from Fig. 8.5 that the cost-minimising technique of production depends upon the relative prices of capital and labour. If labour is relatively expensive, the isocost lines will be relatively steep and the chosen production technique will be capital-intensive. In the opposite case, if labour is cheap, the isocost lines will be relatively flat and the cost-minimising technique will be relatively labour-intensive.

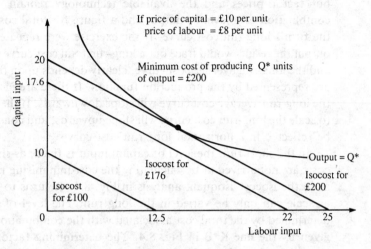

Fig. 8.5 Cost-minimising technique of production

The diagrammatic version of the analysis can also be used to examine the condition for cost-minimisation in more detail.

The condition for optimality is that the slope of the isocost line should be equal to the slope of the isoquant. It can readily be seen from the diagram that the slope of the isocost line is equal to the ratio of the factor prices (w/r). The slope of the isoquant is equal to the marginal rate of substitution which is in turn equal to the ratio of the marginal product of labour to the marginal product of capital. The equilibrium condition, then, could also be written:

$$\frac{w}{r} = \frac{MP_L}{MP_K}$$

This is turn could be rewritten to give:

$$\frac{MP_L}{w} = \frac{MP_K}{r}$$

The last equation provides the intuitively plausible result that cost-minimisation requires that the marginal productivity of the last £1 spent on labour should equal the marginal productivity of the last £1 spent on capital, without which it would be possible to shift spending from one factor to another and increase output without increasing cost.

Cost curves in the short run and the long run

From production functions to cost curves

The analysis set out above shows the amounts of each factor of production which will be employed in order to achieve cost-minimisation for one particular level of output, on the assumptions that the amounts of both capital and labour can be varied, but factor prices and the available technology remain constant. The resulting combination of a level of output and a figure for total cost provides one point on the firm's long-run cost curve. If the exercise were repeated for different levels of output the results would trace out a long-run total cost curve. The shape of this curve, and the long-run average cost curve, clearly depends upon the returns to scale which are represented by the production function. If there are increasing returns to scale, the long-run average cost curve will slope downwards. If there are decreasing returns to scale the long-run cost curve will slope upwards, and constant returns to scale will be reflected in a horizontal long-run cost curve.

In the short run, the level of capital input is fixed, as shown in Fig. 8.4, so that costs are not arrived at by calculating the cost-minimising ratio of capital to labour as in the isocost/isoquant analysis in Fig. 8.5. Returns to scale are also irrelevant as scale can only be varied in the long run. The level of cost in the short run is determined by the total cost associated with the combinations of capital and labour given by the line K*B in Fig. 8.4. The determining factors for cost here are the spreading of the fixed costs across a larger number of units of output, on the one hand, and the principle of diminishing returns on the other. Fixed costs per unit fall as the level of output rises, but variable costs per unit tend to rise beyond a certain point.

Short-run cost curves

The total and average short-run cost curves implied by this analysis are shown in Fig. 8.6(a) and 8.6(b).

As the figure shows, fixed cost (FC) is constant, at an amount equal to K*r (the cost of using K* units of capital), yielding a downward-sloping curve for average fixed cost (AFC). Variable cost (VC) increases with a slope that first decreases (indicating decreasing marginal cost) and then increases (indicating increasing marginal cost) giving an average variable cost (AVC) curve which falls and then rises.

The combination of fixed and variable costs yields an average total cost curve (ATC) which is u-shaped and which is intersected by the marginal cost curve (MC) at its lowest point.

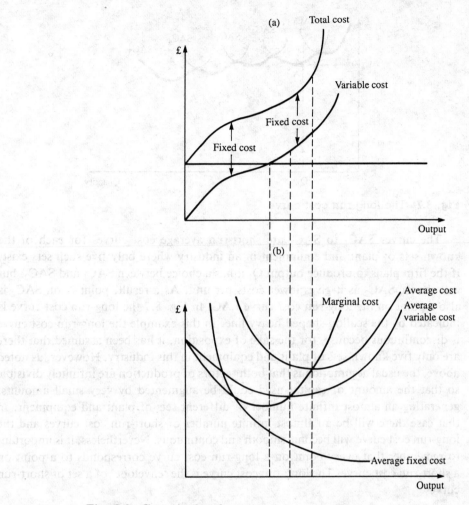

Fig. 8.6 Costs in the short run

Long-run cost curves

In the long run the firm is free to choose whichever combination of inputs it expects to be most profitable, and in the long run the firm is essentially concerned with investment decisions. The behaviour of costs in this period depends fundamentally upon the extent to which there are **economies of scale** to be had from the construction of larger sets of plant and equipment.

Long-run cost curves can be constructed from a set of short-run curves. As each short-run curve shows how costs will behave when the firm has a fixed level of capital input (or is restricted to a given set of plant and equipment), the long run may be thought of as the period in which the firm chooses which short-run cost curve to locate itself on. The implication is that the long-run average cost curve is simply made up of segments of short-run cost curves. This is illustrated in Fig. 8.7.

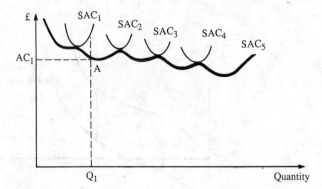

Fig. 8.7 The long-run cost curve

The curves SAC_1 to SAC_5 are short-run average cost curves for each of the known sets of plant and equipment in an industry where only five such sets exist. If the firm plans to produce output Q_1 it has a choice between SAC_1 and SAC_2, but will choose SAC_2 as it gives lower costs per unit. As a result, point A on SAC_2 is also a point on the long-run cost curve LAC. In Fig. 8.7 the long-run cost curve is indicated by the scallop-shaped heavy line. In this example the long-run cost curve is discontinuous because, for the sake of exposition, it has been assumed that there are only five known sets of plant and equipment in this industry. However, as noted above, the usual assumption is that both factors of production are infinitely divisible so that the amount of capital used could be augmented by very small amounts, generating an almost infinite number of different sets of plant and equipment. In that case there will be an almost infinite number of short-run cost curves and the long-run cost curve will become smooth and continuous. Nevertheless, it is important to remember that every point on a long-run cost curve corresponds to a point on a short-run cost curve. The long-run cost curve is the 'envelope' of a set of short-run curves.

Economies and diseconomies of scale

The sources of scale economies

The shape of the long-run cost curve is a matter of great significance for the structure and performance of an industry and has been the object of considerable debate, both in terms of theoretical analysis and in terms of attempts to provide empirical measurements of scale effects.

Theoretical analysis of scale effects suggests that both costs of production and distribution and costs of managing and controlling the enterprise need to be taken into account when considering the impact of higher levels of output on unit costs. If attention is first focused on the factors which reduce costs then it is possible to identify a number of general sources of scale economies. The first of these arises from the simple mathematics of many **production engineering relationships**. If, for example, an industrial process requires mixing or some similar activity to take place, the surface area of the tank in which the mixing is to take place increases much less rapidly than its volume. If cost depends upon the surface area but output depends upon the volume, scale economies will result as larger volumes can be processed with less than proportionate increases in cost. Some observers (Haldi and Whitcomb (1967)) have suggested that such relationships lead to an exponential relationship between total costs and the level of output of the form:

$$TC = aQ^b$$

where:

TC = total cost
Q = output
a,b = constants

In this equation b is the scale co-efficient which is estimated to take a value around .6, indicating that a 100 per cent increase in output can be had for a 60 per cent increase in costs.

The second source of scale economies lies in the existence of **indivisibilities**. If some items of equipment, or some activities, have a minimum size and cannot be divided up into smaller units, operating them at less than capacity will involve a cost penalty. If a series of processes, each involving indivisibilities, are linked vertically, this effect will be magnified as efficient production will require balancing the processes against each other. For example, if a simple industrial process consists of mixing, heating and then pouring the raw material and mixing machines only work efficiently at three units of output per day, heating machines at five units of output per day and pouring machines at seven units per day, the plant will not reach minimum cost until output is equal to $(3 \times 5 \times 7) = 105$ units per day.

Indivisibilities are not restricted solely to aspects of production engineering, but extend into administration and management as well. The production of an invoice is an indivisible activity that may cost as much for a transaction of £1,000,000 as for one involving £10,000. A manager may be capable of overseeing a section of 100 people and the input of management may be indivisible in the sense that it is not possible to more cheaply acquire smaller 'units of management', taking full responsibility for smaller groupings of personnel.

A third source of scale economies lies in **specialisation** and the **division of labour**. Ever since Adam Smith's observation of the pin factory in the eighteenth century it has been recognised that greater specialisation on the part of workers and machines can improve the efficiency of production as they focus on a narrower task. At smaller outputs a firm will not be able to achieve the same degree of specialisation as its volume of output will not be sufficient to fully utilise workers or machines dedicated to a relatively narrowly defined task.

Fourthly, there are **stochastic economies of scale**, associated in particular with levels of inventory held and with the amounts of 'back-up' equipment which need to be provided in the event of failure. If a firm has a production process which would involve very heavy costs in the event of breakdown, it will need to have a second set of equipment on stand-by. However, if a second production line were to be installed, doubling the level of output, it would not be necessary to also provide another set of back-up equipment, provided that the chance of both systems failing simultaneously is low enough to be an acceptable risk.

Sources of diseconomies

It is not in dispute that virtually every industry is subject to some degree of scale economies. It is almost impossible to think of any activity which can be carried out as cheaply at the minimum conceivable scale as at a larger one. It is also indisputable that in some industries, including motor vehicles and many parts of the chemical industry, the cost reductions attributable to larger scales of output are very substantial indeed. What is much more difficult to determine with any certainty is whether or not firms also face diseconomies of scale once their level of output expands beyond a certain size.

If attention is restricted to technological factors there is little reason to suppose that diseconomies of scale exist. There may come a level of output beyond which no further economies can be had, in which case the long-run cost curve will become flat, but none of the forces which lead to scale economies are likely to work in reverse at very high levels of output. If diseconomies of scale do exist they are attributable to **managerial factors** rather than technological factors. As a firm produces a higher level of output it also becomes a larger organisation, which may become more difficult to control. Whether or not this is inevitable is the subject of debate. On the one hand, it may be argued that as an organisation becomes larger 'control loss' inevitably begins to set in. If firms are organised in a hierarchical fashion and each individual can only function efficiently with a limited **'span of control'** (the number of individuals reporting directly to him) then a larger organisation implies more layers in the hierarchy. As information travelling from the bottom of the hierarchy to its apex, and instructions passing in the other direction, have to pass through an increasing number of individuals, the opportunities for distortion, either deliberate or unintended, are increased. As the volume of detail involved in the firm's operations increases, it becomes impossible for it all to be absorbed fully by one person, and the sharing and communicating of details by a broader group is often less efficient.

If these arguments generally hold true there will be **managerial diseconomies of scale** which become more severe as the level of output increases and which may eventually outweigh the **technological economies**. Whether this is in fact the case remains theoretically unresolved. There clearly must be some limit to the size of firms, because otherwise the economy would consist of one single company. However, whether these limits arise as a result of diseconomies of scale, as opposed to other factors, is difficult to judge. Firms need not be organised hierarchically, in which case the arguments concerning control loss lose much of their force. On the other hand it is difficult to imagine how a firm, or part of a firm, producing a single product on a large scale could be organised in any other way. Non-hierarchical or 'organic' methods of organising firms usually require the different groupings of individuals to be involved in technologically unrelated activities, rather than co-ordinating the production of a single product.

Empirical evidence on scale economies

The need for empirical resolution of the theoretical problem

As the theoretical debate on the existence of diseconomies of scale remains unresolved there are a number of different shapes which the long-run cost curve might take, as set out in Fig. 8.8(a) to (c).

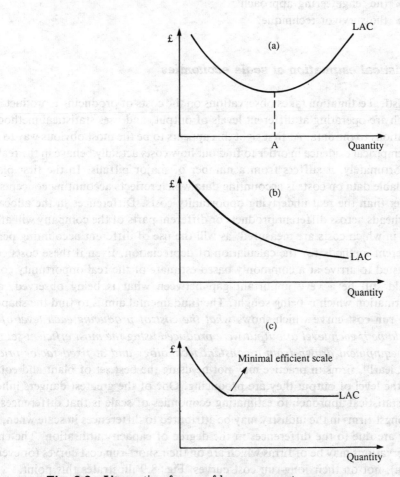

Fig. 8.8 Alternative forms of long-run cost curve

Fig. 8.8(a) shows a u-shaped long-run cost curve exhibiting diseconomies of scale beyond level of output A. Fig. 8.8(b) shows a curve where economies of scale are never exhausted, so that the curve always has a downward slope. Fig. 8.8(c) shows a third, commonly used form, which exhibits a downward slope to a point known as the **'minimum efficient scale'** (MES), beyond which no further scale economies are known to exist.

As theory has failed to discriminate between these alternative forms of the long-run cost function it is natural to turn to the empirical evidence in an attempt to resolve the issue. Unfortunately, the difficulties of estimating the extent of scale economies in a satisfactory way are so great that it is not possible to reach an unambiguous conclusion. There are three basic ways by which empirical evidence may be sought on the shape of the long-run cost function. These are:

- statistical estimation
- the 'engineering approach'
- the survivor technique.

Statistical estimation of scale economies

Statistical estimation takes observations on the costs of producing a product in firms which are operating at different levels of output, and uses statistical methods to fit equations to the data. At first sight this appears to be the most obvious way to address the empirical evidence in order to find out how costs actually behave in the real world. Unfortunately, it suffers from a number of major pitfalls. In the first place, the available data on costs is accounting data which reflects accounting concepts of cost rather than the real underlying opportunity costs. Differences in the allocation of overheads across different products or different parts of the company will affect the way in which costs are measured, as will the use of different accounting periods or different methods for the calculation of depreciation. Even if these costs could be adjusted to arrive at a commonly based estimate of the real opportunity cost there would still be a very important gap between what is being observed, and the information which is being sought. The fundamental aim is to find the shape of the long-run cost curve which shows *what the cost of producing each level of output would be if each level of output were produced using the most efficient set of plant and equipment drawn from a constant technology and at fixed factor prices.*

Clearly, firms in practice may not be using the best set of plant and equipment for the level of output they are producing. One of the greatest dangers inherent in the statistical approach to estimating economies of scale is that differences in cost amongst firms in the industry may be attributed to differences in scale when, in fact, they are due to the differences in the degree of capacity utilisation. The empirical observations may be of firms which are on their short-run cost curves (or even above them), not on their long-run cost curves. Fig. 8.9 illustrates this point.

In Fig. 8.9 the curve LAC is the long-run cost curve whose shape is being sought. The points A, B and C are observations on actual combinations of output and cost being experienced by three firms. The statistical approach would estimate a line of best-fit to these observations on the assumption that this is an estimate of the long-run cost function. However, as the diagram shows, it is no such thing. In the example given, there are very few scale economies in truth, the curve LAC being relatively flat. Firm A has a low level of output Q_1 and high costs because it is X-inefficient and is operating above its short-run cost curve for the level of output it is producing. Firm B has a higher output Q_2 and lower costs, but these are not attributable to scale

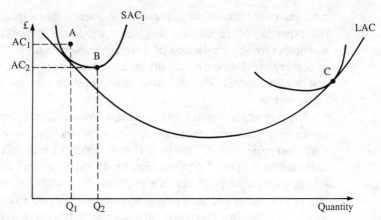

Fig. 8.9 Problems in estimating the long-run cost curve

economies as it is using the same set of plant as firm A. It is using that set of plant efficiently in the short run but has not built the most appropriate set of plant for the long run production of Q_2. Only firm C is actually on the long-run cost curve. Clearly, any attempt to interpret the line from A to B to C as the LAC curve is wholly misleading.

There are many other problems with statistical cost analysis of this type. The cost curve which is sought refers to different levels of output for exactly the same product, but real firms will rarely be producing identical products. Different firms will have set up their existing capacity at different times, thereby drawing upon different states of technology, and different firms may be paying different prices for their factors of production as a result of imperfections in the markets for inputs. All of these factors reduce the usefulness of the statistical approach to the measurement of scale economies and illustrate just how difficult it can be to appeal directly to empirical evidence in an attempt to discriminate between different theories.

There is a further problem with the statistical cost approach, which is worth noting in view of the dispute over the existence or otherwise of diseconomies of scale. If there are such diseconomies it would be hoped that the evidence would show that beyond a certain scale of output, costs begin to rise. However, to find such evidence would imply that firms had actually built sets of plant and equipment which had higher costs than smaller and more cost-effective plants. But why should firms ever do so? It could happen by mistake but, under competitive conditions at least, a firm would never deliberately choose such a set of plant. If there are diseconomies of scale and competitive conditions it is not to be expected that firms could be observed on the rising part of the cost curve, as to operate on that part of the cost curve in the long run would mean that the firm could not survive.

The engineering approach

The **technological studies method** or the **engineering approach**, to scale economies offers an alternative means of measurement, which avoids many of the problems inherent in the statistical approach. In essence this approach involves drawing on the expertise of production engineers to design hypothetical sets of plant and equipment for the production of different levels of output. The fact that the estimates of cost are hypothetical is actually an advantage of this approach because the engineers will be able to work with the same technology for each level of output and the same factor prices.

The advantages of the engineering approach mean that the most often quoted estimates of scale economies are arrived at in this way. Nevertheless, they do embody a number of serious difficulties. The problems of reconciling accounting data with economic concepts of cost remain, as do the problems of apportioning total cost amongst different products in a multi-product setting. Perhaps most important of all, such estimates are clearly most accurate with respect to engineering and production aspects of cost, but much less satisfactory with respect to the costs of distribution, administration and management. Unfortunately, the whole debate about the existence or otherwise of diseconomies of scale hangs around the onset and impact of 'control loss' as the firm expands its scale of output. The engineering approach is therefore particularly weak on a key aspect of the evidence.

As might be expected, the long-run cost curves derived from the engineering approach generally have the shape shown in Fig. 8.8(c), indicating a fall in costs down to the minimum efficient scale after which costs are assumed to be constant as all known technical scale economies have been exploited and managerial diseconomies are not taken into account. In practice it would be very expensive to calculate costs for a large number of different outputs in order to draw a smooth curve and many attempts to measure scale economies in this way confine themselves to estimating just two points on the curve, the minimum efficient scale (MES), and a point corresponding to an output level at (say) 50 per cent of the MES, in order to estimate the slope of the curve and the extent of the cost penalty incurred by firms producing at below the optimal scale.

It is important to note that while economies of scale may be measured in absolute terms, showing the levels of output which constitute the minimum efficient scale, it is the relationship between MES and the size of the market which is important. If it is said that there are substantial scale economies in an industry what is meant is that the MES is large relative to the size of the market in which firms are operating. Table 8.1 shows some empirical results on MES for British industry, expressed in this way.

As the table shows, there are some industries, including dyestuffs and machine tools, where the MES is larger than the total size of a domestic market like the United Kingdom. The implication for industrial structure, of course, is that for efficiency the domestic market can only accommodate a single producer, but if that producer faced no competition it would be in possession of substantial undesirable monopoly power. The only resolution to that difficulty is either to control the monopolist in the domestic market or to widen the scope of the market in which competition takes place, so that there is room for more than one firm operating at minimum efficient scale.

Table 8.1 Some estimates of scale economies relative to the size of the UK market

Product	MES as % of UK market	% increase in cost at 50% of MES
Oil refining	10	5
Dyestuffs	>100	22
Beer	3	9
Bread	1	15
Steel production	33	5–10
Cars: one model	25	6
Cars: a range	50	6
Aircraft: one type	>100	20
Machine tools: one model	>100	5
Diesel engines: one model	10	4
Footwear	0.2	2
Newspapers	30	20

Source: Reproduced by permission of the Department of Applied Economics, Cambridge from C.F. Pratten, *Economies of Scale in Manufacturing Industry*, CUP 1971.

The survivor technique

The third approach to the estimation of scale economies is known as **'the survivor technique'**, developed by Stigler (1958). In this method it is assumed that market forces work efficiently so that firms in the most efficient size category take an increasing share of the market, while firms in less efficient size categories take smaller market shares. The firms in an industry (or plants in some applications) are divided into size categories and the market share of each size category is observed over time in order to estimate an implied shape for the long-run cost curve. In Stigler's study of the American steel industry, the shares of the largest and smallest categories of firm both declined over time, while the shares of firms in a range of medium-sized categories grew, apparently implying a U-shaped long-run cost curve with a considerable flat range, as shown in Fig. 8.10.

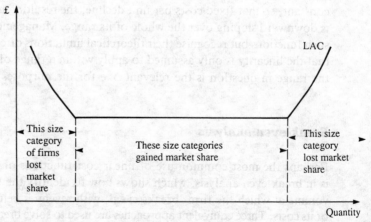

Fig. 8.10 The findings of the survivor technique in the US steel industry

Unfortunately, too many assumptions have to be fulfilled if the survivor technique is to adequately estimate the cost curve. All firms have to be pursuing the same set of objectives, all firms have to be operating in similar environments, factor prices and technology must remain unchanged over the period of observation and market forces have to work effectively, unimpeded by collusive arrangements or barriers to entry. It seems very unlikely that these conditions ever hold for a period of time long enough for differences in the market share performance of different size categories of firm to become apparent. As a result, the survivor technique has not been used extensively in the estimation of scale economies.

Linear cost functions and break-even analysis

Linear cost functions

The cost functions considered above are all curvilinear in form, following the underlying economic principles embodied in the production function and economic concepts like the principle of diminishing returns. Many, perhaps most, economists would argue that these are the most appropriate forms for cost curves to take. However, many decision-making techniques for business, including many used by management accountants, are set out in terms of cost functions which are linear with respect to average variable costs. The theoretical foundations for such cost functions are somewhat shaky as they must imply an underlying production function which has some rather unlikely characteristics (see Dorward (1987) for an explanation of this point). Nevertheless, as they are often used in standard costing and in break-even analysis it is useful to examine them.

The typical form of a linear cost function is set out in Fig. 8.11, which shows both total costs and costs per unit, in the short run.

As the figure shows, average variable costs are assumed to be constant, which implies that marginal cost is equal to average variable cost. As total fixed costs are constant, so that fixed costs per unit decline, the resulting unit cost function (ATC) is downward sloping over the whole of its range. Management accountants who use such functions but recognise their theoretical limitations often qualify them by noting that the linearity is only assumed to apply within a range of the cost curve, but that the range in question is the relevant one for the purposes on hand.

Break-even analysis

Perhaps the most common use of linear cost functions of the type outlined above is in break-even analysis, which shows how to identify the level of output and sales volume at which the firm 'breaks even', with revenues being sufficient to cover all of its costs. Three equivalent approaches are used to solve break-even problems, known as:

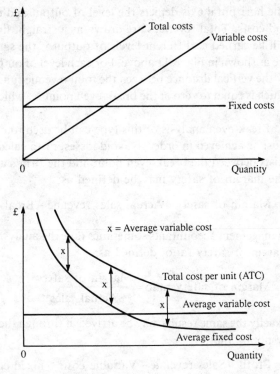

Fig. 8.11 A linear cost function

- the graphical method
- the equation method
- the contribution margin method.

The graphical method is set out in in Fig. 8.12.

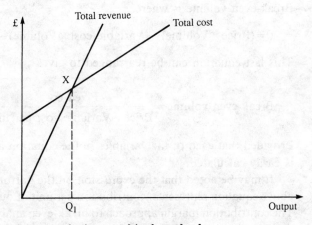

Fig. 8.12 Break-even analysis: graphical method

The horizontal axis depicts the level of output and the vertical axis shows revenues and costs. Total revenues are drawn as a straight line, showing the revenues which will be earned at different levels of output if the same price is charged. Total costs are as shown in Fig. 8.11 above. For each level of output profits or losses are indicated by the vertical distance between the total revenue function and the total cost function, which is equal to zero at the break-even point X, which corresponds to level of output Q_1.

Break-even analysis of this type can be used to calculate the level of sales which must be achieved in order to avoid losses, or to calculate the margin of safety which exists between the break-even point and the firm's actual or expected level of sales. The margin of safety may be defined as:

Margin of safety = Actual sales revenue − Break-even sales revenue

Management accountants sometimes take the analysis a stage further to calculate the margin of safety ratio, defined as:

$$\text{Margin of safety ratio} = \frac{\text{Margin of safety}}{\text{Actual sales}}$$

Exactly the same results may be arrived at through the **equation method**, which begins by noting that:

Profit = Sales revenue − Variable costs − Fixed costs

As, in this model:

Sales revenue = Price × Volume
Variable cost = Variable cost per unit × volume
Fixed cost   = a constant

And break-even volume is where:

Profit = 0

Break-even volume is where:

0 = (Price × Volume) − (Variable cost × Volume) − Fixed cost

This last equation can be rearranged to give:

$$\text{Break-even volume} = \frac{\text{Fixed cost}}{\text{Price} - \text{Variable cost per unit}}$$

Provided that each of the variables in the equation are known, break-even volume is easily calculated.

It may be noted that the expression on the bottom of the right hand side of the above equation represents 'contribution per unit of output' or **'contribution margin.'** The contribution margin approach to break-even analysis consists simply of rewriting the equation in the following form:

$$\text{Break even volume} = \frac{\text{Fixed costs}}{\text{Contribution margin}}$$

In addition to calculating break-even volumes, the method may be used to calculate the sales volume required to generate a target level of profit. All that is required is to add the target level of profit to fixed costs in the last equation, to give:

$$\text{Volume required to give target profit} = \frac{\text{Fixed costs} + \text{Target profit}}{\text{Contribution margin}}$$

A comparison of the break-even model and the standard economic model

Having set out the standard economic model of the firm in Chapter 3, and the break-even model above, it is useful to briefly compare the two, shown together in Fig. 8.13(a) and (b).

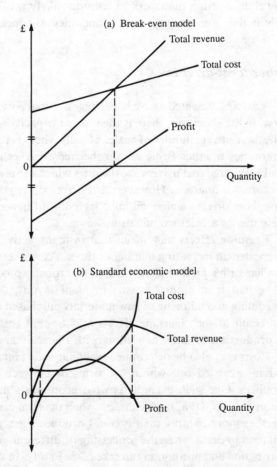

Fig. 8.13 Comparing the break-even model with the standard model of the firm

A number of differences become immediately apparent. In the first place, the economic model is an optimising model, which identifies the profit- and contribution-maximising level of output and price. The break-even model shows no optimum as the levels of profit and contribution simply increase with the level of output. That does not imply that accountants using the break-even model believe that higher levels of sales always imply greater profits. The purposes of the model are different. The aim of the economic model is to predict the levels of output and price which profit-maximising firms will choose to produce. The aim of the break-even analysis is to examine cost and revenue relationships within a narrow range of output in order to assist in the planning and control of business activity and in particular with short-term profit planning.

In the break-even model price is an exogenous variable, rather than one for which the analysis provides a solution. Clearly, if the price of the good is increased, the break-even level of output will be reduced. However, that cannot be taken as a recommendation that prices should always be increased because at higher prices the level of output which can be sold will tend to be lower. Break-even analysis can be useful in assisting managers to consider likely profit levels at different prices, but only if they are sensitive to the fundamental concept of elasticity of demand.

Other 'cost-drivers'

The analyses presented above have suggested that costs are determined by three factors. First, in the short run, there is the level of **capacity utilisation**. Secondly, in the long run, there are **economies of scale**. Thirdly, there is the degree of **X-efficiency**, which determines whether firms are on their cost curves or above them.

These three **cost drivers** are the ones which are given the most extensive treatment in economic analysis. However, as Porter (1985) points out, there are a number of other cost drivers which will also have an influence on the level of costs. Each of these merits a brief examination.

Learning effects may mean that in many activities costs decline as the activity is repeated an increasing number of times. As workers and management become more familiar with a production process or a particular product there will be cost reductions to be had from improvements in plant layout, design modifications, improved scheduling and tailoring of raw materials purchased to the process and product. The end result of such learning effects may be that costs reduce with the **total volume of production to date**, as well as with the scale and rate of output.

Costs may also be determined by **linkages** and **interrelationships** between different activities carried out within the firm, or between the firm and its customers or suppliers. One such example is what economists have called **economies of scope**, (Baumol, *et al.* (1982)) which occur when the firm can produce a number of products together more cheaply than it could produce them independently. Such economies will tend to occur when the processing of different goods can share inputs, or where distribution and promotion can take place jointly. In this case, costs will be determined by the **breadth of the product range** as well as the other factors discussed above.

Linkages and interrelationships are not restricted to those which lead to economies of scope. There may be cost reductions to be had by co-ordinating other activities taking place within the firm, like advertising and direct sales, or production and maintenance. There may be gains to be had by increasing **the degree of vertical integration** within the firm, moving closer to the final customer (forward vertical integration) or to sources of supply (backwards vertical integration). Alternatively some of these gains could be had by co-operation with suppliers and distribution channels, rather than by undertaking these activities within the firm. Porter cites the example, for instance, of a confectioner arranging with his supplier to have chocolate delivered in bulk as liquid, rather than in solid blocks, thereby reducing costs for both the confectioner and the supplier.

Costs will also be affected by **timing** within the business cycle or timing with respect to other firms' actions. The purchase of major items of capital equipment may be heavily influenced by the level of demand and capacity utilisation in the supplying industries, where highly advantageous deals may be had if suppliers are suffering from a lack of orders and over-capacity. There may be **first-mover advantages** to be had by being the first to undertake an activity, especially if there are substantial learning effects, which a first-mover will begin to gain from before late-comers. On the other hand, in some situations there may be **late-mover advantages,** as in situations where the technology is developing very rapidly and first-movers may have invested heavily in technology which has become out-dated.

Costs may also be affected by **geographical location** when factor prices, tax regimes and government incentives vary from place to place, and by **institutional factors** like unionisation, tariffs and local content rules.

Finally, it should be noted that costs will also depend upon a very wide range of the firm's **discretionary policies,** like the nature and design of the product being produced, the level of service provided to customers, delivery dates achieved, the form of distribution, the nature of the technology and raw materials produced and the full package of human resources policies adopted on pay, training, incentive schemes and employee benefits.

This last section has made it clear that a full listing of the determinants of cost would be very long indeed and that the most important factors will vary from industry to industry and firm to firm. A business which hopes to be successful will need to think very carefully about which cost drivers are the most important in its own particular case in order to concentrate its efforts on keeping cost as low as possible, commensurate with implementing its overall company strategy (see Chapter 11 for details).

Illustration

Scale economies in industrial plants: their sources and extent

Haldi and Whitcomb (1967) use data from the engineering literature in North America and Europe to estimate the extent of scale economies in production. They collected data on three different sources of cost, which were:

- individual units of industrial equipment
- initial investment in plant and equipment
- operating costs, made up of labour, raw materials and utilities.

In respect of units of industrial equipment they used data on cost and capacity to fit a least-squares line derived from the following equation:

$$C = aX^b \qquad \text{where:}$$
$$C = \text{cost}$$
$$X = \text{capacity}$$

Fitting the equation for nearly 700 types of equipment, including containers, pipes, reaction vessels and mining machinery, gave estimates of 'b' for each type, which are summarised in Table 8.2.

Table 8.2 Estimates of 'b' for industrial equipment*

Range of values	Number of estimates	% of estimates
0–.49	176	25.6
.50–.79	442	64.3
.80–.99	90	13.1
1.00+	39	5.7

* *Adapted from:* J. Haldi and D. Whitcomb, 'Economies of Scale in Industrial Plants', *Journal of Political Economy*, Vol. 75, No. 4, 1967, pp. 376, 380 and 382.

As Table 8.2 shows, 94.3 per cent of the estimates had a value of less than one, implying that as capacity increased, costs rose less than proportionately and there were economies of scale.

The evidence that there are economies of scale for individual items of equipment suggests strongly that there are scale economies for complete systems, but it is not conclusive proof. In order to investigate further, Haldi and Whitcomb took data on construction costs and capacity for the plants required to produce 221 products calculated by cost engineers, and summarised the findings with respect to the estimates of 'b'. The results are set in Table 8.3.

Again, the evidence in support of scale economies in production is substantial, with a median value of 'b' equal to .73 and only 6.8 per cent of the estimates being in excess of 1.00.

The third aspect of cost investigated in this study was operating costs, defined as in-plant production costs, excluding depreciation and payments on capital. The results are shown in Table 8.4, using the same approach, and distinguishing between total operating cost and labour cost only.

Table 8.3 Estimates of 'b' for plant investment costs*

Products	<.4	.4–.59	.6–.9	1.00+	Total estimates
Cement			2	1	3
Fertiliser			5	1	6
Gases	4	9	29	3	45
Industrial chemicals		5	36	1	42
Plastics			3		3
Rubber			6	2	8
Misc. chemicals	3		4	1	8
Desalination			5	1	6
Electric power		8	7		15
Petroleum products		11	45	1	57
Aluminium			12	3	15
Pulp and paper			5	1	6
Shipping			1		1
Other	2	1	3		6
Totals	9	34	163	15	221
%	4.1	15.4	73.7	6.8	100.0

Table 8.4 Estimates of 'b' for operating and labour costs*

Value of 'b'	Total operating cost		Labour cost only	
	Number of estimates	%	Number of estimates	%
0–.4	4	12.5	37	71.2
.4–.69	9	28.1	14	26.9
.7–.99	19	59.4	1	1.9
1.00+	0	0.0	0	0.0
Total	32	100.0	52	100.0

These results very strongly suggest that it is labour costs in particular which exhibit substantial scale economies. More detailed examination of the individual studies from which Table 8.4 was drawn point to limited scale economies in respect of the usage of raw materials and utilities, but significantly increasing returns to scale in respect of operating labour, supervision and management costs, and maintenance.

The major conclusions of the Haldi and Whitcomb study are that initial investment costs exhibit scale economies up to the largest plants observed in industrial countries, that operating expenses for labour, supervision and maintenance also show increasing returns to scale, but that usage of raw materials and utilities offer few opportunities for the exploitation of economies.

References and further reading

W.J. Baumol, J.C. Panzar and R.D. Willig, *Contestable Markets and the Theory of Industry Structure*, (New York, Harcourt, Brace Jovanovich, 1982)

J. Haldi and D. Whitcomb, 'Economies of Scale in Industrial Plants', *Journal of Political Economy*, 1967

M. Porter, *Competitive Advantage*, (New York, Free Press, 1985)

C.F. Pratten, *Economies of Scale in Manufacturing Industry*, University of Cambridge, Department of Applied Economics, Occasional Papers, No.28 (Cambridge, Cambridge UP, 1971)

G.J. Stigler, 'The Economies of Scale', *Journal of Law and Economics*, 1958

Self-test questions

1 Which of the following statements are correct?

(a) an isoquant shows economies of scale
(b) an isoquant shows the different techniques which can be used to produce a fixed quantity of a product
(c) a technology may be described as 'labour-intensive' or 'capital-intensive'.
(d) a given set of plant and equipment may exhibit economies of scale
(e) if a large firm is experiencing higher costs per unit than a small firm, this means that there are diseconomies of scale

2 If a firm has selected the cost-minimising technique of production, which of the following conditions must hold?

(a) the isocost line is a tangent to the isoquant
(b) the extra output per extra dollar spent on labour must equal the extra output per extra dollar spent on capital
(c) the ratio of the factor prices must equal the ratio of the marginal products of the factors
(d) a higher level of spending cannot lead to a higher level of output
(e) the same output cannot be produced with less labour or less capital

3 Which of the following factors leads the short-run cost curve to rise beyond a certain level of output?

(a) diseconomies of scale
(b) diseconomies of capacity utilisation
(c) the principle of diminishing returns
(d) reduced availability of inputs
(e) higher input prices

4 What exactly does a long-run average cost curve show?

5 Humberside Business School is organising a conference, at a fee of £50 per delegate. Speakers will cost £500 and the cost of catering and conference materials is £10 per delegate. It is anticipated that 40 delegates will attend.

(a) use the contribution margin approach to calculate the break-even number of delegates.
(b) if the management of the Business School demands that at least £500 profit be made on any conference, calculate the required number of delegates.

Exercise

'Accountants' use of break-even models ignores the important factors of diminishing returns and elasticity of demand.'' Explain this statement and consider the uses to which break-even analysis may legitimately be put.

Answers on page 410.

9 Formal models of competitive structure

This chapter examines a number of formal economic models of market structure, covering the cases of perfect competition, monopoly, monopolistic competition and oligopoly.

The analysis of competitive structure

Once a firm has established its objectives, as discussed in Chapter 3, and identified the demand and cost conditions facing it, outlined in Chapters 5 to 8, it can begin to consider how these objectives are to be achieved. This cannot be done without reference to the structure of the industry in which it is operating, because that structure determines the relationship between a firm and its competitors. An important starting point for the development of a competitive strategy is a careful appraisal of the competitive structure of each industry in which the firm is involved.

This analysis can be approached in a number of ways. In the first place, formal textbook economic analysis identifies a number of different 'ideal-types' of market structure for which rigorous models can be developed. These market structures are known as:

- perfect competition
- monopoly
- monopolistic competition
- oligopoly.

Careful examination of these models illustrates the importance of a number of economic forces which shape the competitive environment in which firms operate. However, they are restricted to a number of relatively simple market structures, and they do not cover every dimension of competitive structure. As a result, it is useful to go beyond these to a less rigorous, but much more complete, approach to the analysis of competitive structure, known as the 'five forces' approach, developed at the Harvard Business School by Professor Michael Porter.

This chapter examines the formal textbook models of market structure. Chapter 10 introduces the 'five forces' approach.

153

Perfect competition

The conditions for perfect competition

Perfect competition is a relatively simple form of market structure in which a number of conditions are met. These are:

- a large number of small buyers and sellers, none of whom are large enough to affect the market price by their actions
- free entry to the industry, so that any firms wishing to compete with the existing firms can do so on equal terms
- identical products
- profit-maximising behaviour on the part of all firms
- perfect mobility of factors of production
- perfect knowledge of market opportunities.

Short-run equilibrium in perfect competition

In the perfectly competitive situation, the price at which every firm must sell its output will be set by the market forces of supply and demand. Each individual firm will be able to sell as much as it chooses at that price, but it will not be able to sell anything at all at a higher price, because its competitors are producing identical products and selling them at the market price to consumers who are well-informed of the prices being asked by every firm.

Fig. 9.1 shows the short-run situation for both an individual firm and for the industry as a whole.

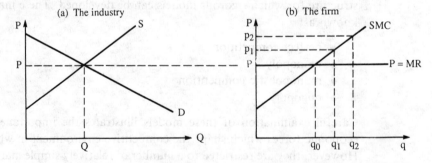

Fig. 9.1 The firm and the industry in perfect competition

As the diagram shows, the forces of supply and demand determine a price of P and a total industry output of Q. Each individual firm has a demand curve which is a horizontal line PP, showing that it can sell any amount at the price P, but none at higher prices.

Because the demand curve is horizontal the **marginal revenue** curve, which shows the additional revenue earned when one more unit of output is sold, is given by the same horizontal line. When the firm sells one more unit of output, the amount it receives for it is the price P, which is also the addition to revenue.

As each firm is a profit-maximiser it will produce the level of output given by q_0 in the diagram, which is the output at which the marginal revenue is just equal to marginal cost. If the firm were to produce more than q_0 then it would be producing units of output for which the marginal cost is more than the marginal revenue, which would reduce profit. On the other hand, if it produces less than q_0 then it is failing to produce some units of output for which the marginal revenue exceeds the marginal cost, which would add to profit.

As the industry is no more than the sum of the individual firms, it is clear that the industry's output Q must equal the sum of the outputs of the individual firms. This simple point also helps in understanding the nature of the supply curve. It can be seen from the diagram for the firm that at price P the firm chooses to supply output q_0 because that is the ouput which yields most profit. If the price rose to P_1 the firm would choose to increase its output to q_1, and if the price rose further to P_2 the firm would increase output to q_2. The firm's marginal cost curve traces out the levels of output which the firm would choose to supply at each price. In other words, the marginal cost curve for the firm is the same thing as the firm's supply curve! The supply curve for the industry as a whole is simply the horizontal sum of the marginal cost curves for the individual firms.

Fig. 9.1 shows only the marginal cost curve for the individual firm, in order to be as clear as possible. However, a more complete picture requires the inclusion of the average cost curve, in order to examine the level of profits being made. This is shown in Fig. 9.2.

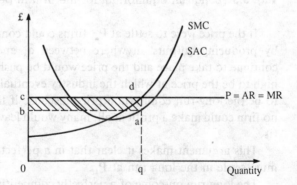

Fig. 9.2 The perfectly competitive firm in short-run equilibrium

In the diagram as shown, the individual firms are making '**economic profits**' or '**supernormal profits**', because the average cost of producing output q is less than the price P, set by the market. The amount of profit earned is shown by the shaded area abcd and consists of the profit margin bc multiplied by the number of units sold.

Equilibrium in the long run

Up to this point the analysis has been of short-run behaviour. Each firm has a given set of plant and equipment, involving it in some fixed costs. New firms cannot enter the industry because to do so would require them to set up new plants, which is not possible in the short run. In the long run, however, such profits would attract new firms into the industry. In that case, the additional competition would push the price downwards and eventually eliminate the profits being made. In terms of Fig. 9.1 new entry will move the supply curve to the right as more firms set up and their marginal cost curves contribute to the supply curve.

In order to identify where the industry's price must settle in the long run, it is necessary to examine the long-run cost curves for the individual firms. Each firm must have the same long-run cost curve, because they all have access to the same technology and the same prices of inputs. Fig. 9.3 shows such a curve.

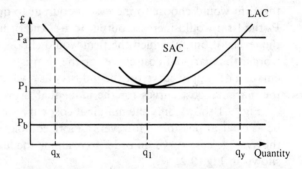

Fig. 9.3 Long-run equilibrium for the firm in perfect competition

If the price were to settle at P_a, firms could continue to make supernormal profits by producing outputs anywhere between q_x and q_y. In that case, entry would continue to take place and the price would be pushed downwards. Clearly, P_a is too high to be the price at which the industry eventually settles. Similarly, P_b is too low to be the long-run equilibrium price, because if the price should fall to that level, no firm could make a profit at all, many would leave the industry and the price would rise.

This argument makes it clear that in a perfectly competitive industry, the price must settle in the long run at P_L.

The long-run outcome of a perfectly competitive industry, then, is that the price is forced down to the level of the lowest possible average cost. Each firm uses the set of plant and equipment which gives least cost production and operates it at the most efficient level of output.

The working of a perfectly competitive industry is determined by its structure. The production of identical products by a large number of small firms, coupled with perfect knowledge on the part of consumers, ensures that each firm has a horizontal demand curve. Freedom of entry ensures that if supernormal profits are made in the short run they will be competed away in the long run by new entry. Provided economies of scale are limited, so that the industry contains a large number of small firms, all producing at the bottom point on their long-run cost curve, a long-run equlibrium will be established and maintained until the external environment changes.

Perfect competition and 'rivalry'

In this type of market structure, the firm has very little opportunity to act for itself, and very few decisions to make. The price is set by the market, and the firm is a 'price-taker'. There is no reason to advertise because the firms are all producing exactly the same product and customers know them to be identical. The only decision the firm has to take in the short run is on the level of output. In the long run it has also to ensure that it has built the lowest cost plant, or it cannot survive. The firm is not even able to determine its own objectives because unless it makes maximum profit it will make a loss and will cease to survive.

In perfect competition the industry is **'competitive'** in the sense that its structure drives prices down to the level of lowest cost, not in the sense that firms are intense rivals for each other. Indeed, in such an industry there is no rivalry at all between individual firms because each firm is very small, being faced by anonymous market forces, rather than by identifiable rival firms. In perfect competition firms could not be said to have strategies. They simply take limited decisions under very powerful pressure from market forces.

Perfect competition and social optimality

Perfect competition is often regarded as a socially optimal form of market structure, for a number of reasons. In the first place, every firm is forced by market pressures to build the least cost set of plant and equipment and to operate it at its optimal level of output, so that cost per unit is at the lowest possible level. Secondly, no supernormal profits can be earned, except in the short run. Thirdly, and most important from an economic point of view, price is equal to marginal cost. This is most important because price equal to marginal cost is the condition required for the maximisation of social welfare. This can be seen using the diagram set out in Fig. 9.4.

'Maximisation of social welfare' requires that the level of output produced is that which gives the greatest **'net benefit to the economy'**. Net benefit consists of the difference between the benefits consumers receive from having the commodity and the costs incurred in its production. If this apparently vague idea is to be given meaning, some method has to be found to measure the benefits received by consumers. This can be done quite simply if we accept three basic axioms about consumer behaviour. These are:

- consumers are rational
- consumers are self-interested

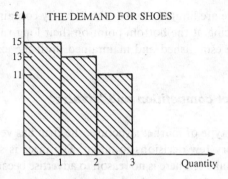

Fig. 9.4 Measuring 'benefit to consumers'

- each individual consumer is the only valid judge of his own welfare.

If these axioms are adopted then the benefit which a consumer receives from having different amounts of a commodity may be measured by the amount he is willing to pay for them. If a consumer is willing to pay a maximum of £10 for a pair of shoes, and he is rational and self-interested, that £10 is a direct measure of the sacrifice he is prepared to make in return for the shoes and an indirect measure of the benefit he expects to get from having the shoes.

Once this idea has been established it becomes relatively easy to measure the benefit to consumers from having different amounts of a commodity, because the demand curve shows how much individuals are prepared to pay for those different amounts. Fig. 9.4 shows, for instance, that someone is willing to pay £15 for the first pair of shoes on the market. The total benefit from having one pair of shoes, then, is equal to £15. If the second pair of shoes will only be sold when the price falls to £13, and the third pair when the price has fallen to £11, then the total benefit of three pairs of shoes is equal to £15 + £13 + £11 = £39.

In general, the benefit to consumers from producing quantity Q of a commodity is given by the area under the demand curve at Q, as shown in Fig. 9.5(a).

In a similar way, the costs of producing a commodity can be calculated by adding up the marginal costs of producing each successive unit, thereby measuring the costs of producing quantity Q by the area under the marginal cost curve, as shown in Fig. 9.5(b).

Bringing the measure of the benefits and the costs together, in a simple form of cost/benefit analysis, it can be readily seen that the maximum net benefit is received at output Q_0 and price P. However, it has already been noted that under perfect competition the marginal cost curve for the industry and the supply curve are the same. In other words, in perfect competition, the industry automatically produces the level of output which maximises social welfare.

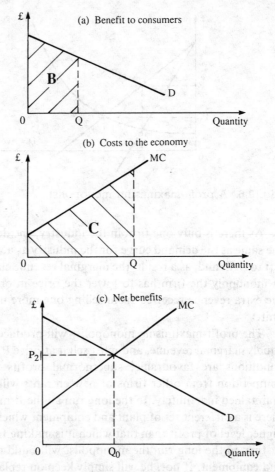

Fig. 9.5 Maximising net benefit to the economy

Monopoly

Profit-maximising equilibrium in 'pure monopoly'

Monopoly is a form of market structure in which the pressures imposed on the perfectly competitive firm are absent. For a firm to be a **'pure monopoly'** it has to contain just one firm and there must be no possibility of entry.

In this type of market structure the firm and its management have very much more discretion to decide on both their objectives and their actions. They may decide to opt for an objective other than profit-maximisation, as discussed in Chapter 3. However, textbook models of monopoly assume as a starting point that the aim of the monopolist, like the perfect competitor, is to make maximum profit.

For the pure monopoly, the analysis is relatively simple. Fig. 9.6 shows the diagram for a profit-maximising monopolist in the short run.

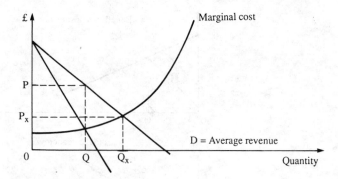

Fig. 9.6 A profit-maximising monopolist

As there is only one firm in the industry, the demand curve for a monopolist is the same as the demand curve for the industry as a whole. It slopes downwards from left to right and, as a result, the marginal revenue curve lies below it. (This is because in monopoly the firm has to lower the price in order to sell more output, so that the extra revenue received from selling one more unit is less than the price for that unit.)

The profit-maximising monopolist will produce output Q, where marginal cost equals marginal revenue, and must sell it at price P. Provided that cost and demand conditions are favourable, supernormal profits will be made and the lack of competition from other firms or new entrants will mean that those profits can be maintained indefinitely. In the long run all the firm has to do is to consider whether there is a different set of plant and equipment which would allow it to make an even higher level of profit than that which it is making from its current capacity. If there is, then in the long run the monopolist will build that more profitable set of plant and equipment. If not, he will simply keep on replacing the current set of plant and equipment when it becomes worn out.

It is worth noting that a monopolist does not necessarily make supernormal profits. If a firm has a monopoly in a product which consumers do not want at all, or which is so expensive to produce that consumers are not willing to pay a price which is high enough to cover the cost, then it will not be able to make profits. What is important about monopoly is that if the firm is in a position to make profits those profits will not be eroded away by competition.

Monopoly and the misallocation of resources

Although a firm and its shareholders will find a monopoly position highly attractive the existence of monopoly is often regarded as socially undesirable, for a number of reasons. In the first place, the firm is not forced to set up the configuration of plant and equipment which has the lowest possible cost. In the second place, earning monopoly profit is often regarded as an 'unfair' and undesirable outcome which should be prevented. Thirdly, and most important from an economic point of view, price in a monopoly is not equal to marginal cost. It can be seen from Fig. 9.6 that the optimal level of output from society's point of view is Q_x, sold at P_x. However, the monopolist produces less than that at output Q and sells it at a higher price P. If an industry is a monopoly, there is said to be a **misallocation of resources**.

This problem of resource misallocation under monopoly forms an important aspect of the rationale for **anti-monopoly** or **anti-trust** policy, discussed in more detail in Chapter 16.

Monopolistic competition

Equilibrum in monopolistic competition

A third form of market structure is known as '**monopolistic competition**'. This type of industry resembles perfect competition in that it contains a large number of small firms and there is free entry to the industry in the long run. However, in monopolistic competition,there is some degree of **product differentiation** in that each firm produces a slightly different product, each of which is preferred to the others by some consumers. In this type of market structure each firm will have a downward-sloping demand curve, being a '**mini-monopolist**' with respect to its own particular variant of the industry's product. The diagram which shows the firm's price and output in the short run will look exactly like Fig. 9.6, illustrating monopoly, with the qualification that there is no longer an industry demand curve.

In the short run, as in perfect competition, firms may make supernormal profits. However, if they do, new entrants will be attracted into the industry, each firm will lose some of its customers to the new entrants and eventually the supernormal profits will be competed away. Fig. 9.7 shows the position which firms in the industry will reach in the long run.

This result is sometimes known as the '**tangency solution**', because the individual firm reaches a position where its demand curve is at a tangent to its long-run average

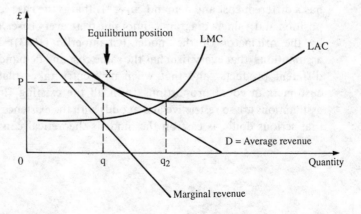

Fig. 9.7 Monopolistic competition in the long run

cost curve. The firm must find itself in this position because if the demand curve were any higher supernormal profits could be made and further entry would take place. On the other hand, if the curve were any lower losses would be made and firms would leave the industry, moving the remaining firms' demand curves upwards.

Monopolistic competition and the allocation of resources

Just as the outcome of perfect competition and monopoly can be evaluated from a social point of view, so it is possible to consider the outcome of monopolistic competition. In the long run, supernormal profits are not earned so that the charge of 'unfairness' does not arise. On the other hand, price does not equal marginal cost so that there is a misallocation of resources in that sense. Furthermore, as Fig. 9.7 makes clear, each firm will not use the lowest cost set of plant and equipment. As the equilibrium is established where a sloping demand curve is tangential to the long-run average cost curve, the equilibrium level of output is one where not all economies of scale have been exploited. If each firm set up the plant and equipment designed to produce level of output q_2 costs per unit would be considerably lower. A major effect of introducing product differentiation is to reduce efficiency as each firm fails to take the maximum advantage of economies of scale. This finding is sometimes referred to as the '**excess capacity theorem**'. On the other hand it has to be remembered that consumers are able to choose from a wide variety of different product variations. If consumers value these differences there will be compensating gains.

While the analysis set out above outlines the basic features of monopolistic competition it is also important to point out some difficulties with the model. In particular it is difficult to be clear on the question of 'which firm is illustrated in the diagram?' In the case of perfect competition there is no difficulty in showing a diagram for 'the' individual firm, because all firms are producing the same products, using the same technology and facing the same prices of inputs. As a result, firms all have the same cost curves in the long run. In monopolistic competition, however, each firm is producing a different product which would seem to imply that each firm has a different cost and demand curve. If that is the case, every firm is in a different position and a single diagram cannot illustrate every case. This problem was avoided by the originator of the model (Chamberlin (1933)) by adopting the '**heroic assumptions**' that every firm has the same cost and demand curve, despite producing different products, and that when new entry takes place the new firms attract customers in equal proportions from all the existing firms. Unfortunately these assumptions are so restrictive and at odds with the existence of product differentiation that serious doubt is cast on the model's theoretical consistency.

Oligopoly

Alternative forms of oligopoly

The term **oligopoly** refers to an industry in which there are only a few firms. The important characteristic of an oligopolistic industry is that the firms within it are interdependent upon each other, so that the actions of one company have a noticeable impact on the others. The existence of that interdependence means that the oligopoly situation is much more complex than the other market structures and much more difficult to model. It also means that in oligopoly firms are centrally concerned with their competitive strategies and may be seen as rival players in a very complex game.

Unlike perfect competition and pure monopoly, which are tightly defined market structures, in which outcomes can be easily modelled, oligopolies may vary in a number of ways.

First, they may differ with respect to the **number of firms**, which may vary from two in a **duopoly** up to a dozen or more.

Second, oligopolies may vary with respect to the **extent of product differentiation**. At one extreme, sometimes referred to as 'pure oligopoly', the firms may all produce identical products. At the other extreme they may produce highly differentiated products.

Thirdly, oligopolies vary with respect to the **'condition of entry'**. At one extreme, entry to an oligopoly may be completely **'blockaded'** so that competition concerns only the incumbent firms. At the other extreme, entry may be completely free so that potential competition from new entrants is a key determinant of the incumbent firms' behaviour.

As there is such a wide variety of different types of oligopoly it is not possible to set out a single rigorous analysis which will cover all possible cases. What can be done is to examine a number of different possible outcomes and to consider the factors which make each one more or less likely to occur.

Explicit collusion or cartelisation

If firms are interdependent upon each other, and recognise that interdependence, one possible outcome of the situation is that they join together and behave as a monopolist. In that way they are able to make the maximum profit possible and avoid the costs of competing with each other. Price and quantity will be set as illustrated in Fig. 9.6 above.

The formation of a cartel in this way is such an obvious strategy for firms to adopt, and the advantages to them so substantial, that it is tempting to conclude that this is the usual outcome of oligopoly. Fortunately for consumers there are a number of other factors which have to be taken into account. The first of these is the law on competition (see Chapter 16). The governments of most industrial nations subscribe to the view that monopoly is harmful and have legislation which makes cartels illegal.

Even if cartels were not illegal there are a number of forces at work which make their establishment and maintenance difficult to achieve. In the first place, a group of rivals who set out to cartelise their industry have to come to an agreement on the price to be set in order to make maximum profit. Having taken a decision on the price to be set the members of the cartel have to decide how much output can be sold at that price and to allocate production quotas for each member. If this is not done the cartel may produce more output than can be sold at the agreed price. Output will remain unsold and stocks will pile up, exerting downward pressure on the price. The negotiation of quotas is an extremely difficult issue because precise information about demand conditions is rarely available so that the level of output which corresponds to the profit-maximising price is not known with certainty. Once an estimate has been made of the total amount to be produced that total has to be divided amongst the members. This is particularly sensitive because the division of output determines the distribution of profit. It may be the case that the members are simply unable to agree on quotas and the cartel collapses before it can be put into effect.

Even if a cartel is able to negotiate production quotas there continues to be a tendency for the arrangements to collapse as a result of **cheating** or suspected cheating on the part of members. Every member of a cartel faces a very powerful incentive to cheat on the others by charging a price which is a little way below that agreed, thereby attracting a very high level of demand. As every member is in the same position, and every member knows it, there will tend to be a high level of suspicion among the firms who make up the cartel. If one firm is suspected of cheating the others will follow suit by cutting their prices and the cartel will have collapsed.

The key factor in this situation is the extent to which the rival firms are well-informed about each other (Fraas and Greer (1977)). If they are very well-informed, cheating will be identified immediately, the response will be immediate, and the gains to cheating will be non-existent. As a result, it is likely that in this situation the cartel will hold together as none of the members think it worthwhile to cheat. On the other hand if firms are poorly informed about each other, cheating will be difficult to identify, the incentive to cheat will be greater and the cartel is more likely to collapse.

This analysis suggests a number of variables which will determine the likely success of a cartel, each of which affects the extent to which firms are well-informed about each other.

- **The number of firms.** If an industry contains a very small number of firms they will be able to monitor each other's activities at relatively low cost, thereby deterring cheating.
- **Product differentiation.** If firms produce very similar products they will be well-informed about their rivals' cost and demand conditions, simply by being well-informed about themselves. Cheating will be deterred. If there is a high degree of product differentiation, or if products are non-standardised, it will be much more difficult for firms to keep themselves in touch with the activities of others, and the differences between products will make it extremely difficult to set monopoly prices, taking into account the cost variation between different firms' brands.

- **Publication of prices.** If prices are published, firms will find it much easier to monitor each others' activities than if prices are kept confidential.
- **Slow rates of technological progress.** If technological progress is rapid, the industry will experience a much greater degree of uncertainty and instability than if companies are all using an established, mature set of techniques which develop only slowly. As a result, cartelisation is much more difficult in conditions of rapid technological change.
- **The existence of a trade association.** If there is an active trade association in an industry, this can provide an effective channel of communication between firms, thereby assisting in the process of cartelisation. Trade associations may also be able to exert some degree of discipline over firms who do not conform by denying them access to the association's facilities, or by more subtle means such as failing to elect them to prestigious posts or even social ostracism.

If the conditions are favourable, firms in an industry may be able to establish a cartel, negotiate prices and output quotas, and maintain orderly behaviour. In that case it will be possible for supernormal profits to be earned, in the short run at least. In the longer term there are a number of other forces which will tend to break down the cartel's power.

The first of these forces is the **threat of new entry**. If a cartel is successful in raising the price and increasing profits for its members this immediately creates an incentive for other firms to enter the industry. This need not matter if entry is '**blockaded**', so that new firms are absolutely unable to enter. However, totally blockaded entry is a relatively rare phenomenon and cartels in most industries are subject to breakdown in the long run as a result of the cartel's success leading to new entry. It is possible, of course, that new entrants join the cartel but that would increase the number of firms and reduce the cartel's manageability. As long as a cartel uses its power to earn supernormal profits there will be market forces working to break down that cartel.

The second factor which works to eliminate the power of a cartel in the long-run is the **search for substitutes**. If the price of the product produced by the cartel increases, this creates an incentive for users of the product to seek alternatives, and for other firms to invent and produce such substitutes. While this may take some time its eventual effect will be to reduce the demand for the cartel's product and make it more elastic, thereby reducing the cartel's ability to charge high prices and make large profits.

Perhaps the most important example of a cartel is the Organisation of Petroleum Exporting Countries (OPEC), whose history provides a graphic illustration of the issues raised by cartels. When OPEC raised the price of oil in the early 1970s this immediately encouraged other countries to begin searching for their own sources. At the oil prices which held in the 1960s it was not commercially sensible to search for oil in difficult environments like the North Sea, because the cost of exploration and recovery could not be justified by the value of any oil which might be found. However, once the oil price rose, the economics of oil exploration changed dramatically, so that it became worthwhile for a number of countries to begin searching for oil in order to enter the industry themselves. As a result, OPEC members' share of the oil industry declined, reducing its capacity to act effectively as a cartel.

In addition to the pressures caused by new entry, the oil industry has been affected by the drive to find substitutes for its products. In some cases these substitutes are relatively direct, as in the use of ethyl alcohol as a fuel for cars. In other cases the substitutes may involve quite different products from those produced by the cartel. Better insulation for housing, for instance, or car engines with improved fuel consumption both provide indirect substitutes for oil.

To summarise with respect to cartels, then, there are a variety of market forces which tend to break them down, especially in the long run. These forces may take a considerable time to have their full effect, allowing a cartel to make substantial profit for that time, but unless governments place legal barriers in the way of potential entrants, it is to be expected that in most cases cartels contain the seeds of their own destruction.

'Price leadership' and tacit collusion

A cartel is an example of **explicit** collusion, where the firms involved are parties to an agreement to reduce output and raise prices to the monopoly level, in order to make maximum joint profits. In many countries such arrangements are illegal and firms risk the penalties set by law if they become involved in them. As a result, firms may not wish to become involved in explicitly collusive arrangements like cartels. However, there are other forms of unspoken or **tacit** collusion which firms may develop. These do not necessarily involve any form of conspiracy on the part of the firms involved, they simply stem from the recognition of interdependence amongst rivals and of the costs which may be involved if rivalry becomes too intense.

One of the most important forms of tacit collusion is known as **price leadership** (Markham (1951)). In this situation, one of the firms in the industry adopts the role of **price leader**, setting a price which is followed by the others. If the firms are all producing identical products then the followers set the same price as the leader. If products are differentiated the followers use the leader's price as a benchmark and adjust their own prices upwards or downwards according to the different quality and cost of production of their particular product variants. In this way the firms in the industry can establish what is sometimes termed 'orderly' competition amongst themselves. In the language of the corporate strategists (Porter (1985)) they behave as **'good competitors'** for each other.

If price leadership is to be established, the leader must have a powerful position in the industry, in order to be able to offer an unspoken threat of punishment to any firm which fails to act as a follower. The most obvious such punishment would be to push the price down so far that the offending firm cannot survive. That implies that the price leader needs to be the lowest cost producer in the industry, and to have substantial market share and production capacity in order for the threat to be credible.

Price wars and the theory of games

While cartels and tacit collusion are two possible outcomes in the oligopoly situation, competition between rivals is not always so comfortable. There are situations in which rivalry between the firms in a concentrated industry becomes so intense that a 'price war' breaks out, with prices being cut until they may even fall below marginal cost as each firm strives desperately to keep its market share. Clearly, such an outcome is not in the interests of any firm, but the structure of an oligopoly may create incentives which lead to the outbreak of price wars.

In order to understand how such a situation can arise it is useful to introduce some elementary elements of a mathematical technique known as **game theory**. This technique was originally developed during the Second World War in order to assist military strategists. Nevertheless, it is also particularly relevant to oligopoly because it concerns the behaviour of interdependent rival players, each of which has a choice of moves, the outcomes of which depend heavily upon the actions of the others.

The basic application of game theory to oligopoly can be shown in a simplified example. If we consider an industry which contains only two firms, both producing an identical product, and both firms are trying to decide between setting a high price or a low price. The results of the alternative pricing policies can be set out in a simple **pay-off matrix**, illustrated in Fig. 9.8.

FIRM A's ACTIONS

	HIGH PRICE	LOW PRICE
HIGH PRICE	A's profit £10m / B's profit £10m	A's profit £5m / B's profit −£2m
LOW PRICE	A's profit −£2m / B's profit £5m	A's profit £1m / B's profit £1m

FIRM B's ACTIONS

Fig. 9.8 A pay-off matrix

The matrix shows the profits made by each firm, for each combination of its own decision on price and that of the other firm. As the matrix shows, if both firms decided together to opt for a high price, that would give them both very substantial profits. However, if one firm sets a high price and the other one a low price, the high price firm loses all of its customers to the other firm. In that event the high price firm makes substantial losses and may even go out of business, while the low price firm makes substantial profits.

Consider the decision facing each firm trying to decide upon its price. Each has a choice between a high price and a low price, but the outcome depends upon what the other firm does. How can the firm decide? Each firm is in a situation of uncertainty, with the results of its decisions depending upon the 'state of nature' which prevails after the decision has been taken. One possible strategy in that situation is to adopt the **maximin** decision criterion, choosing between a high price and a low price by selecting the option which guarantees that the worst possible outcome is avoided. In that case, each firm will consider the alternatives and will then opt for the low price, in order to avoid the possibility of being undercut by its rival. However, both firms face the same situation and will tend to apply the same logic to it. As a result, both firms select a low price, the opportunity to make a higher level of profit is lost, and a price war has broken out.

Just as in the case of collusion, the key to the rivals' problem lies in the information they have about each other and the degree of trust they share. If they are well-informed about each other, and trust each other not to cheat, then the price war situation can be avoided by both firms charging the joint monopoly price. On the other hand, if they do not trust each other then fear of rivals' reactions will drive both firms to a very low price.

The example given above illustrates that, in the language of game theory, oligopoly is not generally a **zero-sum game**. A zero-sum game is a situation where the winner's gains are exactly equal to the loser's losses. If two gamblers bet each other £1000 on the toss of a coin, that constitutes a zero-sum game. No matter what the outcome the gains to one player are exactly equal to the losses incurred by the other. In the case of oligopoly it is possible for both players to gain (if they set a monopoly price) or both to lose (if they become involved in a price war).

Price stability and the kinky demand curve model

The analysis of oligopoly would be incomplete without reference to the **kinky demand curve model**. This is a simple model of the individual firm in oligopoly which brings together a number of issues already discussed, in the marginal cost and marginal revenue framework which has been used to analyse firms in other market structures. The model is set out in Fig. 9.9.

The starting point for this model is the assumption that firms in the industry have found some way of establishing a price (perhaps through collusion or price leadership) and each firm knows the level of output which it can sell at that price. This position is indicated in the diagram by P_{est} and Q_{est}.

While the firm in the diagram knows how much it can sell at the established price, the amounts which it can sell at higher or lower prices are less clear and depend upon the reaction of the firm's rivals. The firm cannot know these for certain, but can at least make guesses as to the likely responses. If the firm raises its price, it guesses that its rivals will not follow suit. As a result, price rises will imply the loss of a

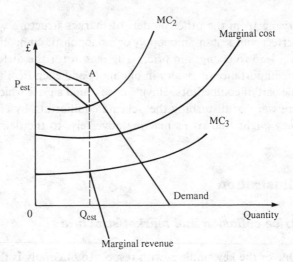

Fig. 9.9 The kinky demand curve

substantial proportion of the firm's customers, and the demand curve for prices above P_{est} will be highly elastic. On the other hand, if the firm lowers its price its guess with respect to its rivals reactions is that they will follow its example and also lower their prices. As a result the demand curve for price reductions is highly inelastic, as shown in the diagram.

The demand curve which results from this analysis has a 'kink' in it, as shown. Following from that, the marginal revenue curve has an even more pronounced discontinuity, taking the form of a 'dog-leg' shape, also as shown. This follows directly from the behaviour of demand. If the firm wishes to sell more than Q_{est} it has to lower the price, but if it does so then its rivals will also cut their prices so that a small increase in demand for the firm's product will require a proportionately large fall in price. As a result the additional revenue earned from an additional unit of output sold will be very small or even negative.

If the oligopolist is a profit-maximiser, it will operate at the point where marginal cost equals marginal revenue, which corresponds to output Q_{est} in the diagram. That provides very little useful information because the firm started from that position. What is useful and interesting about the model is that the same price and quantity will continue to be chosen by the firm, even if marginal costs vary quite substantially. In the example shown, marginal cost could rise as high as MC_2, or as low as MC_3 without the firm choosing to change its price.

Similar considerations apply to increases in demand. If the demand curve shifts to the right, the kink remaining at the same level of price, the firm will choose to increase its output, but the price chosen will remain the same for quite substantial changes in demand.

The kinky demand curve model does not provide a prediction about the level of price which will be reached in an oligopoly situation. What it does predict is that once a price has been established it will tend to be stable in the face of changing costs and demand conditions, within limits. That is a very different prediction from those arising from the other models of market structure which have been discussed. In perfect competition, monopoly or monopolistic competition changes in cost or demand will lead to changes in price. The reason for the difference, of course, stems from the importance of rivalry in oligopoly and each firm's fears of adverse reactions on the part of competitors. Having once found a price which can be sustained, oligopolists are wary of disturbing the delicate equilibrium by changing prices. If they do so, they might find rivals reacting adversely, to the detriment of their profitability.

Illustration

Price collusion and market structure

One of the key findings with respect to oligopoly is that when an industry's output is concentrated in the hands of a small number of firms there is a significant probability that the firms involved will join together to form a cartel. However, the theory does not indicate exactly how small the number of firms has to be for cartel formation to take place, nor does it identify the other factors which make price-fixing easier or more difficult. Fraas and Greer (1977) provide an empirical study of this issue.

The starting point for their analysis lay in data from the US Department of Justice over the period 1910 to 1972, which yielded a sample of 606 cases of price-fixing. Each case was assigned to an industrial category and a range of characteristics was identified.

The theoretical analysis which underlay the study's methodology began with the observation that explicit price collusion will only take place when it is both possible and necessary. When the conditions for collusion are highly adverse, price-fixing will be impossible and will not take place. At the other extreme, when conditions for collusion are very highly favourable, price-fixing can take place without the need for explicit collusion, which becomes unnecessary.

This basic idea can be used to establish a number of empirically testable hypotheses. For instance, if there is an inverse relationship between the ease of collusion and the number of firms involved, in all conspiracy cases (whether explicit or implicit) would have a lower central tendency (whether mean, median or mode) than the frequency distribution of the number of firms in industries in general. Furthermore, the distribution for explicit cases of collusion would have an inverted U-shape, not simply because the general distribution has such a shape but because the rising part of the curve reflects the changing trade-off between tacit and explicit collusion. When there are a very small number of firms in an industry, implicit collusion will be easily achieved, so that very few cases of explicit collusion will be identified. As the number of firms increases, it becomes more difficult to collude so that explicit, and hence observable, collusion is necessary and the curve is steeply positively sloped. Once the number of firms rises beyond a certain level, collusion becomes much more difficult and is rarely practised, so that the curve becomes negatively sloped and steeper than the distribution for firms in general. Fig. 9.10 illustrates this point in a simplified form.

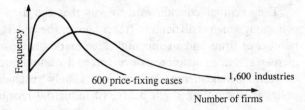

Fig. 9.10 Frequency distributions for 1,600 industries and 600 price-fixing cases

As Fig. 9.10 shows, the distribution for price-fixing cases bears the predicted relationship to the distribution for industries.

Having compared these two distributions, the basic method may be extended by making other comparisons. If some particular structural factor (like the existence of a trade association, for instance) is thought to make price-fixing easier then price-fixing arrangements will be able to take place when there are more firms, if that structural factor is present. Such hypotheses can therefore be tested by dividing the sample of price-fixing cases into a series of sub-samples, each associated with different structural characteristics, and examining their means, medians and modes.

Table 9.1 shows Fraas and Greer's main results.

Table 9.1 Median number of firms involved in price-fixing agreements having different characteristics

Sample	Median
All Price-Fixing Agreements	8
Trade Associations Involved	16
International Scope	5
Bid Rigging	6
Patents Involved	6
Resale Price Maintenance	12
Market Allocations	7
Single sales agent	16
Coercion	10

Adapted from: A.G. Fraas and D.F. Greer 'Market Structure and Price Collusion: An Empirical Analysis', *Journal of Industrial Economics*, Vol. XXVI, September 1977, p. 31 and p. 34

As Table 9.1 shows, the median number of firms involved in price-fixing arrangements was higher in the presence of trade associations, resale price maintenance agreements, single sales agents and coercion, indicating that these factors make collusion easier to arrange, while the involvement of international scope, bid rigging or patents make collusion more difficult.

Table 9.1 offers only a crude test of the various hypotheses because each of the sub-samples contains agreements having a number of different characteristics. Within the sub-sample of collusions involving trade associations, for instance, there are also agreements which involve patents. Fraas and Greer therefore devise a series of more sophisticated tests, using more homogeneous sub-samples and different reference groups, in order to use the same basic empirical technique.

The eventual conclusion drawn is that the data supports the belief that tacit collusion, which is difficult to 'reach' under the law, is only possible with a very small number of firms and an uncomplicated market environment. As the number of firms increases, price-conspiracies are forced to adopt more elaborate and explicit co-operative arrangements which are increasingly 'reachable'. The implication for public policy is that only a slight degree of industrial reorganisation would be needed to secure an industrial structure in which tacit collusion was extremely difficult. To be more specific, Fraas and Greer suggest that competition, rather than collusion, will be the norm, provided that there are 12 or more firms in a sector and the law against explicit price-fixing arrangements is enforced.

References and further reading

E. Chamberlin, '*The Theory of Monopolistic Competition*', (Cambridge, Harvard UP, 1933)

A.G. Fraas and D.F. Greer, 'Market Structure and Price Collusion: An Empirical Analysis,' *Journal of Industrial Economics*, 1977

J.W. Markham, 'The Nature and Significance of Price Leadership', *American Economic Review*, 1951

M. Porter, *Competitive Advantage*, (New York, Free Press, 1985)

Self-test questions

1 Which of the following characteristics are shared by perfect competition and monopolistic competition?

(a) large number of small firms
(b) free entry to the industry
(c) identical products
(d) perfect knowledge of market opportunities

2 Which of the following statements are correct?

(a) a profit-maximising monopolist will always produce on the elastic portion of its demand curve.
(b) a monopolist will always make supernormal profits
(c) oligopolists frequently alter their prices
(d) monopolistic competition gives economic efficiency
(e) perfect competitors are 'price-makers'.

3 Which of the following factors will make the maintenance of a cartel more difficult?

(a) rapid technical progress

(b) production of identical products
(c) a relatively large number of firms
(d) the invention of substitutes for the cartel's product
(e) a well-organised trade association

4 Which of the following statements are correct?

(a) in long-run equilibrium in monopolistic competition, price equals average cost.
(b) in monopoly, price is greater than marginal cost.
(c) in oligopoly, entry cannot take place
(d) in perfect competition, there cannot be substantial economies of scale.
(e) free entry ensures that price cannot remain above average cost in the long run.

5 What would be the value of the Gini co-efficient for:

(a) a perfectly competitive industry
(b) a monopoly
(c) a duopoly with both firms of equal size

Exercise

Explain the statement that perfect competition gives an optimal allocation of resources but that the existence of scale economies may make perfect competition impossible.

Answers on page 412.

10 The five forces approach to competitive structure

This chapter builds upon the formal models of competitive structure, outlined in Chapter 9, to introduce the more general 'five forces' approach to the structural analysis of industries. Each of the five forces is considered in turn and the analysis is applied to two very different industries, in order to illustrate its use in practice.

The structural analysis of competition

The limits of standard economic models of market structure

The relatively formal textbook analysis of market structures points to the importance of some dimensions of market structure. In perfect competition and monopolistic competition, for instance, freedom of entry is the major force which eliminates supernormal profits in the long run. On the other hand, in the case of pure monopoly, the impossibility of entry ensures that superprofits can be made for ever. Clearly, the condition of entry is a key variable in deciding how attractive an industry is for the firms in it.

The textbook models also illustrate the importance of rivalry between existing firms, the extent of product differentiation and the threat of substitutes. However, there are a number of important gaps in the textbook analyses. The first is that they pay no attention at all to the possibility of market power on the part of the firm's customers or their suppliers, which are important features in many industries. The second is that they pay no attention to the factors which determine the key dimensions of market structure. Entry, for instance, is said to be entirely free or entirely blockaded without any consideration of the factors which make it so. Rivalry exists in oligopoly, but not in any of the other market structures, and the models pay no attention to the factors which determine the intensity of that rivalry.

In order to fill these gaps left by the textbook analyses of market structure, corporate strategists have developed more thorough approaches to the characterisation of market structures, which recognise many more types of structure than the four considered in Chapter 9, and which attempt to identify the determining factors for each dimension of competitive structure.

An outline of the five forces model

Perhaps the best known approach of this type is known as the 'five forces' approach to the structural analysis of industries, developed by Professor Michael Porter at the Harvard Business School. (Porter (1980)). This approach is set out schematically in Fig. 10.1.

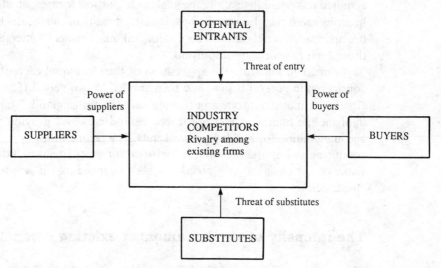

Fig. 10.1 The five forces model
From *Competitive Strategy: Techniques for Analysing Industries and Competitors* by Michael E. Porter. Copyright © 1980 by The Free Press, a Division of Macmillan Inc. Reprinted by permission of the publisher.

According to the 'five forces' approach, the structure of competition in an industry can be described in terms of five major 'forces'. These are:

- the intensity of rivalry amongst existing firms
- the threat of entry
- the threat of substitutes
- the power of buyers
- the power of suppliers.

Each of the five forces is in turn determined by a number of different factors, which themselves need to be considered in order to build up a full picture of competition in an individual industry. The interaction of the five forces taken together determine how attractive the industry is to the firms within it.

The five forces model is much more complete than the set of textbook models, but it is also much less rigorous. It allows for dozens of different types of market structure but does not provide absolutely clear predictions with regard to the outcome of those structures. Indeed, its value lies not in providing predictions for every conceivable type of industry, but rather in giving executives a thorough checklist which they can use to identify the most important features of competition in their industry. These salient features provide a starting point from which firms can begin to develop a competitive strategy (see Chapter 11).

A clear understanding of the five forces model requires a brief explanation of the factors which determine each of the five forces. When carried out in the abstract this can be a relatively laborious process, as there are more than 30 different factors which have to be taken into account. Nevertheless, they all require some preliminary consideration if they are to be understood. Once that basic understanding has been acquired it is possible to apply the analysis to particular cases, at which point its value becomes more clear because in most industries many of the factors listed are relatively unimportant. Once these have been identified, management's attention can focus upon those factors which are important.

In order to illustrate the application of the technique, each of the five forces is considered in general below, and then applied to two very different industries. The first is the industry producing touring caravans in England. Touring caravans are light mobile homes, which are towed behind cars and provide a mobile form of accommodation for holidays or weekends. The second industry is the global industry producing an important chemical feedstock for other chemical industries. The actual name of the chemical concerned has been changed and it is referred to simply as 'feedstock'.

The intensity of rivalry amongst existing competitors

The intensity of rivalry amongst firms is not a variable which can easily be measured in a quantitative way. Nevertheless, in some industries rivalry is said to be intense, even 'cut-throat', while in others relations between firms are said to be 'gentlemanly', or 'polite' or 'orderly'. The Porter analysis identifies the factors which determine the **degree of rivalry**.

Industry growth

Industry growth is a key factor. If growth of the industry as a whole is rapid, each firm will be able to grow without needing to take market share away from its rivals and managerial time will be devoted to keeping up with industry growth, rather than attacking rivals. As a result, rivalry will be less intense in rapidly growing industries. On the other hand, if an industry is growing slowly or declining, growth for one firm can only be at the expense of others and rivalry will be intense.

In touring caravans, the industry has seen a decline in output during the 1980s, leading to intense rivalry. In feedstock production, industry growth has been positive, but less than the growth in world GNP, indicating substantial rivalry.

High fixed costs or storage costs

If these costs are high, failure to maintain the volume of sales may cause a dramatic increase in costs and loss of profits. As a result firms will be very concerned to maintain the volume of sales and will tend to cut prices if they feel there is any danger of reducing sales volume. Rivalry will therefore tend to be directly related to the importance of these costs.

In touring caravans fixed costs are not very large, but storage costs can become prohibitive if production is not sold. In feedstock production the fixed costs of plant are enormous, running into tens of millions of pounds.

Intermittent over-capacity

If an industry experiences periods of over-capacity, either because demand fluctuates or because economies of scale require that additions to capacity are very large, rivalry will tend to become more intense. In touring caravans volatile demand often causes over-capacity. In feedstock production additions to capacity have to be very large indeed, which can cause similar problems though for different reasons.

Product differences, brand identity and switching costs for customers

If an industry's products are identical and there is no brand identity and customers can change from one supplier to another without incurring costs then customers will be very sensitive to price and the demand for each firm's product will be very highly elastic, as in perfect competition. A firm which charges a low price will gain customers very substantially, and a firm which charges a high price will lose heavily. In this situation rivalry will tend to be intense. At the other extreme, if all firms produce substantially different products, with strong brand identities, and customers incur high costs in switching from one supplier to another then demand for each firm's output will be much less elastic as customers have preferences and brand loyalties and rivalry will be much less intense.

Feedstock is a 'commodity chemical', being produced to an international standard, so that every firm's output is identical, provided it meets that standard. In touring caravans there are product differences and a degree of brand identity which firms attempt to reinforce. However, it is not clear how far this allows firms to create buyer loyalty.

The number of firms and their relative size

If the number of firms producing close substitutes is relatively large, it will be difficult for them to monitor each others' activities and there will be the danger that some firms believe that they can make competitive moves without being noticed. As a result rivalry will tend to be intense. A smaller number of firms will lead to less rivalry. However, if firms in an industry are of the same size that too will tend to intensify rivalry as the outcome of a competitive contest will be unclear and bold managements may be tempted to embark upon aggressive moves towards their rivals. The intensity of rivalry is likely to be lowest in an industry with a relatively small number of firms, one of which is more powerful than the others, and therefore able to ensure 'orderly' competition through mechanisms like price-leadership.

In touring caravans there is a market leader which is substantially bigger than the other firms, a second tier of five or six medium-sized firms and several dozen smaller firms. 'Orderly' competition is very difficult to maintain. In feedstock production there are only about six producers world-wide. One of these has more 'free capacity' than the others (i.e. capacity whose output is not directly committed to its own plants) and it is able to exert price leadership.

Diversity of competitors

If rivals within an industry share objectives and goals and have similar 'corporate cultures' and relationships with their parent companies, then they will tend to think in similar ways, be able to predict how each other will respond and agree on an implicit set of 'rules of the game'. On the other hand, if they do not, rivalry will tend to be more intense. An industry which contains foreign competitors, or both large corporations and owner-managers, will therefore tend to have a higher intensity of rivalry.

This variable can be difficult to assess for different industries. In both caravans and feedstock the rivals seem to be similar companies, though of very different types. In caravans executives move from firm to firm, and many are located in the same part of the country, creating a common outlook. In feedstock, the players are all global chemical companies.

Corporate stakes

Rivalry will tend to be more intense if success in the industry is of particular importance for the firms involved, either because of its potential contribution to their profits, or because it has some strategic value to them. Caravan companies are generally single product independent firms, totally dependent upon the caravan industry for their survival. Feedstock producers are all involved in a much wider range of products, although in some cases, feedstock is a major contributor to group profits.

High exit barriers

If leaving the industry entails incurring high costs then firms will be anxious to remain in the industry and rivalry will tend to be intense. The costs of leaving may include financial costs like redundancy payments or the loss in value of highly specialised assets, but may also include **psychic** costs like executives' unwillingness to abandon a business, or loss of goodwill from government if unemployment is caused.

The caravan industry is one in which exit barriers are very low, and exit is common.

In feedstock production, exit would render tens of millions of pounds worth of capacity valueless.

Summarising the intensity of rivalry

Taken together, the factors listed above determine the extent of rivalry. As many of them can only be measured qualitatively, it is not possible to simply add them together to give an overall 'index of rivalry'. However, it is possible to consider whether the impact of each factor will tend to lead to relatively high or relatively low intensity of rivalry and then to attempt an overall aggregation. Fig. 10.2 summarises the position for the touring caravan and feedstock industries.

(a) Touring caravans in the UK

Determinant	Low rivalry	High rivalry
Industry growth		*
Fixed/storage costs	*	
Intermittent over-capacity		*
Product differences	*	
Brand identity	*	
Switching costs for consumers		*
Concentration/balance		*
Diversity of competitors	*	
Corporate stakes		*
Exit barriers		*

Overall judgment on the intensity of rivalry: *Very intense rivalry*

(b) Feedstock production

Determinant	Low rivalry	High rivalry
Industry growth	*	
Fixed/storage costs		*
Intermittent over-capacity		*
Product differences		*
Brand identity		*
Switching costs for consumers		*
Concentration/balance	*	
Diversity of competitors	*	
Corporate stakes	*	
Exit barriers		*

Overall judgment on the intensity of rivalry: *Very intense rivalry but the importance of market leadership as a stabilising factor should be noted*

Fig. 10.2 The intensity of rivalry in two industries

The threat of new entrants

The second of the five forces is the threat of new entrants, whose importance is determined by the height of '**barriers to entry**' . If entry barriers are very high, the existing firms in the industry do not need to concern themselves unduly with the possibility that high prices and profits may attract competition from new entrants. On the other hand, if entry barriers are low, entry may take place with ease whenever the incumbent firms in an industry make substantial profits. The pioneering work on entry barriers is that of Bain (1956). Chapter 12 considers ways in which firms may set prices in order to deter entrants. The determinants of entry barriers may be considered in turn.

Economies of scale

If there are substantial economies of scale, a firm which is considering entering the industry must either build a large market share immediately, in order to achieve the scale required to keep costs down, or suffer higher costs than the incumbent firms. As a result, scale economies are an important source of entry barriers. It is important to remember that such economies are not limited to production activities. There may be important scale effects in almost any business activity, including research and development, marketing and distribution.

In the feedstock industry, economies of scale in both production and research and development are an absolutely key feature of the industry's economics. In touring caravans, by contrast, scale economies are relatively insignificant, as indicated by the continued survival of some very small firms.

Product differentiation and brand loyalty

If existing firms have successfully developed buyer loyalty to their products a new entrant may have to make expensive and risky investments in advertising and promotion in order to overcome that loyalty. If entry should fail, those investments become worthless.

In feedstock there is no product differentiation at all. In caravans there is some differentiation but the real extent of consumer loyalty to individual brands is not clear.

Capital requirements

In some industries, very large amounts of capital have to be acquired if entry is to take place. While these may be available if capital markets work well, entry will often be regarded as a risky venture and investors will require high returns in order to persuade them to take that risk.

In feedstock production capital requirements are very high indeed and form a major entry barrier. In caravans they are insignificant.

Switching costs for buyers

If customers have to face additional costs in switching from one supplier to another, they will be unwilling to change suppliers and it will be difficult for a new entrant to be successful, without a heavy investment to help customers overcome those switching costs.

Switching costs are not significant for either caravan or feedstock buyers.

Access to distribution channels

A new entrant must establish its own distribution channels, persuading wholesalers and retailers to stock and display its product alongside, or in preference to, the products of existing firms. If the incumbent firms have well-established relationships with the distribution channels it may be difficult or expensive for a new entrant to gain access to them.

This factor is of some significance in the caravan industry, but is not relevant for feedstock.

Absolute cost advantages

One of the most general sources of entry barriers is the existence of absolute cost advantages, whereby incumbent firms have lower costs than entrants. If there are such advantages, existing firms will always have the ability to cut their prices to a level at which new entrants cannot survive, which will provide a major disincentive to entry (see Chapter 12 for details). The possible sources of absolute cost advantages include:

- **Proprietary technology.** If a firm has a product or a process which is protected by a patent, or by secrecy, new entrants will not be able to copy that product or process and will be at a disadvantage.
- **Access to inputs.** Existing firms may have access to inputs on favourable terms.
- **Proprietary learning effects.** As firms gain experience in an industry, they are usually able to reduce their costs as a result of 'learning effects'. If these effects are 'proprietary' and a new firm cannot acquire them simply by hiring executives from the existing firms, then an entrant will be at a disadvantage until it has had time to learn for itself, by which time the longer-established firms may have benefitted from additional learning, staying one step ahead of the entrant.
- **Favourable locations.** For some activities there are only a limited number of

suitable locations. If these are all occupied by existing firms, new entry will be extremely difficult.

In feedstock production absolute cost advantages are a crucial aspect of the industry's competitive structure. The market leader has a proprietary technology which it controls, learning effects are continuous and important and are consciously pursued through research and development. Locations next to sources of raw materials, which are relatively few, are important in securing low costs. In touring caravans existing firms have few, if any cost advantages over entrants.

Expected retaliation

In many industries the reaction of the established firms to new entry is a key factor determining the entrant's success. If they are accommodating, an entrant has a greater chance of success. On the other hand, if they retaliate aggressively through price-cutting or promotional campaigns, the entrant will only be able to survive if it has some very strong advantages to compensate for its inexperience in the industry. As a result the threat of retaliation will in itself present an important barrier to entry.

In caravans the threat of retaliation is relatively empty. In feedstock production it is very important indeed.

Government policy

In some industries, in some countries, government policy sets up barriers to entry. At the extreme these involve industrial licensing, where a firm has to have government permission before setting up in an industry. In other cases the barriers to entry established by government policy may be more subtle and are often unintended. For instance, if a government imposes strict health and safety legislation on an industry this may increase the capital requirements needed to enter and thereby raise entry barriers.

Summarising the threat of entry

In common with the intensity of rivalry, the threat of entry is not a variable which can be measured quantitatively. However, it is possible to attach qualitative values to each of the determining factors, and to summarise the overall position. Fig. 10.3 shows the results for the two industries under consideration.

The threat of substitutes

If substitutes are available for the industry's products customers will be able to switch to those substitutes if the existing firms attempt to charge high prices. The threat

(a) Touring caravans in the UK

Determinant	Low threat	High threat
Economies of scale		*
Product differentiation		*
Switching costs for buyers		*
Capital requirements		*
Access to distribution	*	
Absolute cost advantages		
Proprietary products/processes		*
Access to inputs		*
Proprietary learning effects		*
Government policy		*
Expected retaliation		*

Overall estimate of the threat of entry: **Very high threat of entry**

(b) Feedstock in the global market

Determinant	Low threat	High threat
Economies of scale	*	
Product differentiation		*
Switching costs for buyers	*	
Capital requirements	*	
Access to distribution	*	
Absolute cost advantages		
Proprietary products/processes	*	
Access to inputs	*	
Proprietary learning effects	*	
Government policy	*	
Expected retaliation	*	

Overall estimate of the threat of entry: **Very low threat of entry**

Fig. 10.3 The threat of entry

of substitutes is therefore an important market force setting limits upon the prices which firms are able to charge. The importance of this threat depends upon three factors, each of which can be considered briefly.

The relative price and performance of substitutes

If substitutes are available which offer similar performance at the same level of price, then the threat of substitution is very strong. On the other hand, if substitutes are more expensive and offer inferior performance, the threat is much weaker.

In the case of touring caravans the only threat of substitutes comes from tents on the one hand and motorised caravans on the other. Neither offer comparable price and performance. In the case of feedstock, a number of the products derived from feedstock could be substituted for, but the product is an input into such a wide range of production processes that outright substitution on any scale is unlikely and the threat from substitutes limited, given current price/performance characteristics.

Switching costs for customers

This factor has been referred to above as a source of entry barriers, and it also determines the threat of substitutes. In the case of feedstock, customers would incur little cost in switching from one supplier of feedstock to another. However, they would incur very substantial costs indeed if they should attempt to switch from a feedstock-based process to a different one. The threat of substitutes is therefore limited. Caravan users who decide to switch to tents or motor-homes face insignificant switching costs.

Buyers' propensity to substitute

If customers put relatively little effort into searching for substitutes and are disinclined to change suppliers, the threat of substitution is correspondingly reduced. Very little is known with certainty about this factor for either industry under consideration. However, both feedstock and caravans represent major purchases for the firms and families which buy them, which suggests that the propensity to substitute, given an incentive to do so, is likely to be high.

Summarising the threat of substitutes

Fig. 10.4 summarises the extent of the threat of substitutes for the feedstock and caravan industries.

(a) Touring caravans

Determinant	Low threat	High threat
Price/performance of substitutes	*	
Switching costs for buyers		*
Buyers' propensity to substitute		*?

Overall importance of the threat from substitutes: **Difficult to judge**

(b) Feedstock

Determinant	Low threat	High threat
Price/performance of substitutes		*
Switching costs for buyers	*	
Buyers propensity to substitute		*?

Overall importance of the threat from substitutes: **Important in the longer term for some end-uses but not all**

Fig. 10.4 Threat of substitutes

The power of buyers

The power of buyers depends upon two general factors. The first is the extent of their **price sensitivity** and the second is their **bargaining leverage**, each of which can be considered in turn.

Price sensitivity

Price sensitivity is essentially the same concept as **elasticity of demand**, although in the Porter analysis no attempt is made to quantify it. Price sensitivity is a function of:

- **Purchases from the industry as a proportion of total purchases.** If the industry's product makes up an unimportant proportion of users' total purchases, they will tend to be relatively insensitive to its price, as it will have little impact upon their costs. On the other hand, if a product makes up a considerable portion of buyers' total purchases they will be highly conscious of its price and concerned to see it as low as possible. In caravans, a purchase is a major investment for a customer, who is likely to be price sensitive. In feedstock there are wide variations from buyer to buyer which makes generalisation difficult.
- **Product differences and brand identity.** Both of these will reduce price sensitivity. There are no such differences in the case of feedstock. In caravans there are some, though not on the scale associated with motor cars, for example.
- **The impact of the industry's product on the quality of the customer's product or service.** If the industry's product is a key element in maintaining the quality of the customer's own product, they are unlikely to be price sensitive. This factor is irrelevant in caravans. In feedstock it varies with the end-use.
- **Customers' own profitability.** Highly profitable customers are likely to be less price sensitive, which will reduce the price sensitivity of feedstock. This factor is not directly relevant to caravans where the purchasers are consumers, rather than other firms.
- **Decision-makers' incentives.** Managers responsible for purchasing may face a variety of different incentives, some of which encourage them to be highly price sensitive, some of which encourage them to place a greater premium upon other factors like delivery and quality. For caravans this is not a relevant issue. In feedstock, managers responsible for purchasing need to be assured that deliveries will be guaranteed and that international quality standards are met, but are then likely to have an incentive to seek the lowest prices.

Bargaining leverage

The extent to which buyers can exert bargaining leverage also depends upon a fairly extensive list of factors, as listed below:

- **Buyer concentration and buyer volume.** The more concentrated buyers are, and the greater volume they purchase, the more leverage they will be able to exert. Caravan buyers are not concentrated and do not purchase in volume, giving them limited leverage. In feedstock, buyers are more concentrated and purchase in greater volumes but the very wide range of end-uses for the product limits buyers' power.

- **Buyer switching costs.** If switching costs for buyers are high, they will be less able to exert leverage over their suppliers, as the threat that they will take their business elsewhere will have limited credibility. Caravan buyers can easily switch to another supplier, as can users of feedstock.

- **Buyer information.** Well-informed buyers will be better able to exert leverage. Both caravan buyers and feedstock purchasers are well informed about product characteristics and prices.

- **Threat of backward vertical integration by buyers.** If buyers are able effectively to threaten to enter the industry, by backward integration, they will be able to exert powerful leverage. There is little threat of backward integration in either industry being considered. Caravan buyers are unlikely to set up in production. In the case of feedstock, users have become less, rather than more, vertically integrated in recent years.

- **The existence of substitutes.** If there are close substitutes for an industry's product, buyers will have substantial bargaining leverage. There are no close substitutes for either caravans or feedstock.

Summarising the power of buyers

Fig. 10.5 shows the summary diagram for the determinants of buyer power.

(a) Touring caravans

Determinant	Weak buyers		Strong buyers
Price sensitivity:			
Price/total purchases			*
Product differences		*	
Brand identity		*	
Impact on buyers' quality	not applicable		
Buyer profits	not applicable		
Decision-makers' incentives	not applicable		
Bargaining leverage:			
Buyer concentration	*		
Buyer volume	*		
Buyer switching costs			*
Buyer information			*
Ability to integrate backwards	*		
Existence of substitutes	*		

Overall judgment on buyer power: ***Buyers are price sensitive in some segments but have limited bargaining power***

(b) Feedstock

Determinant	Weak buyers	Strong buyers
Price sensitivity:		
Price/total purchases	*	
Product differences		*
Brand identity		*
Impact on buyers' quality		*
Buyer profits	*	
Decision-makers' incentives	?	
Bargaining leverage:		
Buyer concentration	*	
Buyer volume	*	
Buyer switching costs		*
Buyer information		*
Ability to integrate backwards	*	
Existence of substitutes	*	

Overall judgment on buyer power: **Buyers are price sensitive in some segments but have limited bargaining power**

Fig. 10.5 The power of buyers

The power of suppliers

The last of the five forces to be considered is the power of suppliers, determined by the following factors.

Differentiation of inputs

If firms in an industry are dependent upon the particular variants of an input produced by individual suppliers, those suppliers will be relatively powerful. Neither of these factors is significant in caravans or feedstocks.

Switching costs of transferring to alternative suppliers

If these are high, suppliers will be relatively powerful as firms face costs in transferring to competing suppliers. This is not a significant factor in the caravan industry but is very important indeed in the production of feedstock where the cost of switching to a different supplier of the raw materials (mainly natural gas) is prohibitively high.

Availability of substitute inputs

If substitute inputs are available, supplier power will be reduced. In caravans this can be easily done. In feedstock production the use of substitute inputs would require a completely new technique of production, involving very high levels of investment in new plant and equipment.

Supplier concentration

Higher levels of concentration amongst suppliers will tend to enhance their power, especially if suppliers are more concentrated than buyers. Suppliers to caravan firms are not concentrated. Suppliers of the major inputs to feedstock production are very highly concentrated, especially in the case of natural gas where there is only one supplier in each country.

The importance of volume to suppliers

If suppliers are dependent for their survival or profits on maintaining large volumes of sales, they will tend to have more limited bargaining power. Suppliers to the caravan and feedstock industries are not substantially dependent for their sales volume upon sales to those industries and are not thereby weakened.

Cost relative to the purchasing industry's total costs

If the cost of inputs purchased from a particular supplier industry is an important part of the industry's total costs, suppliers will find it harder to exert leverage. On the other hand, if a supplier industry supplies inputs which are only a small proportion of the users' total costs it will find it much easier to secure higher prices.

In caravans, purchases of inputs are spread across a wide range of supplying industries. In the production of feedstock purchases of gas and a small number of other bulk inputs account for a high proportion of total variable costs.

The impact of inputs on costs or differentiation

Supplier power will also depend upon the importance of inputs in the users' ability to maintain low costs or to differentiate the product. If the quality of inputs, or their cost, is an important determinant of the industry's ability to compete, then suppliers will have substantial bargaining power.

This factor is unimportant in caravans. In feedstock production companies need to have supplies at particular locations, which give suppliers at those locations considerable power.

The threat of forward integration by suppliers

If forward integration into the industry by suppliers is easy to achieve then suppliers will have considerable bargaining power. Any attempt on the part of firms in the industry to secure lower input prices could be met by suppliers establishing production facilities for themselves. In both caravans and feedstocks this is unlikely. In the case of caravans, input suppliers have very different skills and competences from those required to assemble caravans. In the case of feedstock, suppliers of gas and other bulk inputs might be able to integrate forwards but the barriers to entry are so substantial that this is not seen as an immediate threat.

Summarising the extent of suppliers' power

Fig. 10.6 summarises the determinants of supplier power in the two industries being examined.

(a) Touring caravans

Determinant	Low supplier power	High supplier power
Differentiation of inputs	*	
Switching costs	*	
Substitute inputs	*	
Supplier concentration		*
Importance of volume to supplier		*
Costs relative to total purchases	*	
Impact of inputs on cost/performance		*
Threat of forward integration	*	

Overall judgment on power of suppliers: **Limited**

(b) Feedstock

Determinant	Low supplier power	High supplier power
Differentiation of inputs	*	
Switching costs		*
Substitute inputs		*
Supplier concentration		* (gas)
Importance of volume to supplier	* (gas)	
Costs relative to total purchases	*	
Impact of inputs on cost/performance		*
Threat of forward integration	*	

Overall judgment on power of suppliers: **Gas suppliers have power, balanced by their need to maintain the volume of sales to feedstock producers**

Fig. 10.6 The power of suppliers

Conclusions to be drawn from the five forces approach

As this chapter has indicated, application of the five forces technique requires quite substantial research into the industry in question, the analysis of a wide range of factors and the exercise of judgment in attempting to aggregate the different determinants of each force. However, once the analysis is complete, it is possible to focus on the most important aspects of competition for the industry in question, paying less attention to less important features. It should also be possible to assess the overall 'attractiveness' of the industry from the point of view of a firm within it.

In the case of touring caravans in the United Kingdom the analysis suggests that the important forces are rivalry amongst incumbents, which is intense, and the threat of entry, which is very powerful. In that case, the industry can be seen to be rather unattractive, a judgment which seems to be confirmed by the number of bankruptcies in the industry, the relatively low level of profitability, and the lack of interest shown in the industry by large conglomerates.

In the case of feedstock the picture is very different. Rivalry amongst incumbents is judged to be high, but the existence of a market leader does much to generate orderly competition. The threat of entry is insignificant, as is the threat of substitution. Supplier power is balanced by the industry's importance as a customer. Buyers have limited power. Clearly, this industry is a much more attractive prospect, as witness the substantial profits made by the incumbents.

Having completed an outline of the five-forces approach to the structural analysis of industry it is possible to go on to consider the various different components which go to make up a competitive strategy. These are taken up in Chapter 11.

Illustration

Carrying out a structural analysis of an industry

If the five forces analysis is to be carried out effectively, a substantial volume of information on the industry must be collected. Porter (1980) offers some useful guidance on how to set about such analysis.

The first stage is to develop a framework for systematically collecting raw data by establishing a general overview. That consists of first identifying the leading firms in the industry, then searching for broadly-based industry studies which may already have been completed, and reading the Annual Reports from the leading companies. A rapid perusal of those reports for a ten or fifteen year period, paying particular attention to the President's letter, will often highlight key factors in the industry's development.

Porter then suggests that the researcher should quickly become involved in fieldwork, through interviews, before trying to exhaust the published information. Rapid engagement with the industry's practitioners allows field research and library research to feed on each other. Interviewees are often aware of obscure but useful published material on the industry and are able to comment on the value of other published material, much of which may have become out-dated and useless.

As the work proceeds, Porter argues that the researcher's morale tends to go through a U-shaped cycle. An initial euphoria at grasping the basics of the industry is followed by confusion and panic as mounds of information accumulate and the sector comes to seem impossibly complex, followed by growing confidence as at last the pieces come together to form a coherent whole.

Published sources for the analysis of an industry vary in quality and quantity. If the industry is large, long-established and is subject to little change, then it tends to be well-documented. In other cases, it may not be. In either case, two principles are important. The first is to comb published sources for other published sources, and for the names of key informants who should be interviewed. The second is to keep a careful bibliography, including the citation of sources for each item. The published material itself may be found in a number of sources, including:

- libraries
- trade associations
- market intelligence companies
- trade magazines
- business press
- company directories
- government censuses, samples and regular statistical series
- company documents, especially for publicly quoted companies.

Field data may be gathered from various sources and again it is useful to have a systematic framework within which to approach the various sources. In particular it is important to recognise that informants will exhibit varying degrees of sensitivity and nervousness about divulging their knowledge.

Porter identifies four basic categories of informant. The first are observers who have little direct stake in the industry and little reason to be sensitive about disclosing their knowledge and opinions. Such sources include international organisations, government bodies, consumer groups and the financial community, standard setting organisations, unions, Chambers of Commerce and the press. The second category of informant works within the service organisations associated with an industry. These include the trade associations, consultants, auditors, banks and advertising agencies. In so far as these organisations have a stake in the industry they may have a degree of sensitivity to the industrial researcher but as their stake is not usually identified with an individual firm, they can often provide fairly objective comment on the key players.

A similar group of observers may be found in the industry's suppliers, distributors and customers, some of whom may have had direct business dealings with a number of the industry's incumbents, providing them with some key insights.

Finally, and most obviously, there are the informants within the industry itself, whose direct stake may make them the most sensitive. Some of these sources will be best qualified to provide information on their own company alone, but others will also have information concerning their competitors. Market researchers and sales staff, R&D staff and engineers, servicing departments and purchasing departments

– all of these have day-to-day contact with a range of useful sources and can provide intelligence on a range of industry participants. This group of informants also includes former employees, although their testimony needs sensitive interpretation in the light of their reasons for leaving and their attitude towards their former company.

When approaching this mass of potential informants, it makes sense for the researcher to begin with those which do not have a direct stake in the industry, moving on to those who are more sensitive after a good general picture has been drawn up, and enough personal contacts made to give the researcher the credibility needed to secure trust. If the research process is to be successful, Porter recommends a number of practical hints.

- Make contact by phone, rather than by letter. A telephone request for an interview is more personal and more difficult to 'shelve' than a letter.
- Allow plenty of 'lead-time' when organising interview trips.
- Offer the interviewee some form of 'quid pro quo' in the form of sharing general observations, or providing a copy of the final report, where possible.
- Be clear and honest about the purpose of the research and the affiliation of the researcher.
- Persevere. Remember that an interview becomes a personal interaction and even the most unenthusiastic informant may become very helpful once the interview has begun.
- Display a good knowledge of the industry, in order to maintain credibility.
- Interview in teams of two, if possible, so that one person can keep good notes while the other engages the attention of the interviewee.
- Be careful not to ask questions in such a way as to prejudge the answer which will be given.
- Observe the informants' surroundings for clues, as well as the things they say.
- Build a relationship with the informant.
- Attempt to build-in some informal activity as part of the meeting. A trip around the plant, or having lunch, may lead to the disclosure of information which would not be forthcoming in the formal setting of an interview.
- Make it clear that proprietary information is not required. If some of the questions are quantitative in nature, and might be sensitive, phrase them in terms of 'ball-park' figures or relatively wide ranges.
- Get further leads from each interview.
- Remember that the telephone interview can be very productive, especially if the questions are tightly focused, and addressed to informants who are not likely to be sensitive with respect to their content.

If these 'practical tips' are followed, the process of carrying out an industry analysis is much more likely to be successful.

References and further reading

J.S. Bain, *Barriers to New Competition*, (Cambridge, Harvard UP, 1956)

C. Bowman and D. Asch, *Strategic Management*, (London, Macmillan, 1987)

M. Porter, *Competitive Strategy: Techniques for Analysing Industries and Competitors*, (New York, Free Press, 1980)

Self-test questions

1 Which of the following 'five-forces' analyses best fits a perfectly competitive industry?

(a) intense rivalry amongst existing firms, low threat of entry, low buyer power, low threat of substitutes, high supplier power

(b) limited rivalry amongst existing firms, high threat of entry, low buyer power, low supplier power, low threat of substitutes

(c) intense rivalry amongst existing firms, high threat of entry, high buyer power, high threat of substitutes, high supplier power

(d) no rivalry, no threat of entry, no buyer power, no supplier power, no threat of substitutes.

2 Which of the industries described in Question 1 above will be the most attractive to incumbent firms?

3 Which of the following factors is a determinant of both rivalry amongst incumbents and the threat of entry?

(a) absolute cost advantages

(b) product differences

(c) brand identity

(d) scale economies

(e) switching costs for customers

4 Which of the following would you expect to observe in the UK touring caravan industry, given the analysis of its structure set out in Chapter 10?

(a) high profits

(b) frequent entry and exit to and from the industry

(c) ownership in the hands of large enterprises

(d) rapid technological progress

5 Which of the following will tend to make rivalry amongst existing firms less intense?

(a) rapid growth in the industry

(b) a low ratio of fixed costs to value added

(c) high exit barriers

(d) existence of a price leader

Exercise

Compare the 'five forces' analysis of competitive structure with the textbook approach to perfect competition, monopoly and oligopoly. Pay particular attention to the aims of the different approaches and to their overlaps.

Answers on page 414.

11 Elements of business strategy

This chapter considers broad elements of business strategy, beginning with an outline of the strategy formulation process and going on to consider the setting of business objectives, internal and external appraisal, and the generation and selection of strategic options. For each stage of the process attention is paid to some of the best-known analytical tools available to assist managers in their strategic thinking. Brief coverage is also give to the means through which strategies may be implemented.

The links between managerial economics and corporate strategy

The greater part of this text is devoted to the economic analysis of decisions which managers have to take. These include tactical decisions like pricing (Chapters 12 and 13), advertising, promotion, and location (Chapter 14). They also include more strategic decisions like those involving investment decisions (Chapter 15) the **'scope'** of the firm with respect to the extent of vertical integration and diversification (Chapter 18) and the extent of multinationalisation (Chapter 19).

Before introducing the economic analysis of each of these issues it is useful to place them in the broader context of 'business strategy' by providing an introduction to the process of strategic management and to some of the best known techniques and concepts employed in that process.

The definition of 'strategy'

Various authors have attempted definitions of the term 'strategy', without satisfactory resolution (Hofer and Schendel (1978)), because the term may refer to both ends and means, or to ends only, and it may be interpreted at different levels within the organisation. Asch and Bowman (1987, p.36) attempt a broad definition of strategy as:

> 'the match an organisation makes between its own resources and the threats or risks and opportunities created by the external environment in which it operates'

The term is often used to refer to 'corporate strategy' where the major concern is with the 'scope' of the firm as a whole, including the industries in which it wishes to operate, the markets in which it wishes to compete, the extent of its vertical integration and diversification and its geographical spread.

At a lower level within the firm, the concern is with the 'business strategy' of a particular operating unit or **strategic business unit** (SBU). As the SBUs, taken together, make up the corporate body there are clearly very close links between their strategy and that of the corporation as a whole. However, such links may be highly complex, with influence running in both directions. It is possible that the business strategy of each SBU is simply 'handed down' from corporate management in a simple 'top-down' process. At the other extreme, the corporate strategy may be arrived at in the opposite way, through the aggregation of the strategies of the SBUs with little corporate level input. Neither of these simple 'top-down' or 'bottom-up' approaches are adequate representations of the strategic management process in most firms, where influence runs in both directions.

In addition to 'corporate strategy' and 'business strategy' it is also possible to refer to **functional strategies**, including:

- marketing strategy
- financial strategy
- manufacturing strategy
- human resource strategy
- information strategy

Clearly, the term strategy covers a very wide range of activities, and the essence of strategic management involves drawing together all of the different strands which go together in the operation of a group of businesses.

For the purposes of exposition, the process of strategic management may be divided into two distinct stages. The first of these is the **formulation** of strategy and the second is its **implementation**. As this text is concerned with those aspects of business strategy which relate most directly to managerial economics attention is limited to the process of formulation. Implementation is concerned with issues of organisation and management which lie outside the scope of this book.

The formulation of strategy

Fig. 11.1 shows a simple descriptive model of the strategy-formulation process. As the model shows, the logical starting point for the analysis lies in the establishment and clarification of the firm's objectives and its current strategy. Once these have been established it is then possible to identify the firm's current position, which is determined by both its internal strengths and weaknesses and the threats and opportunities offered by the external environment. This appraisal of the current position is one of the key components in the formulation of a strategy and there are a number of techniques available for the systematic representation of the firm's current position (see below for details).

Once the appraisal of the current position is complete, a range of **strategic options**

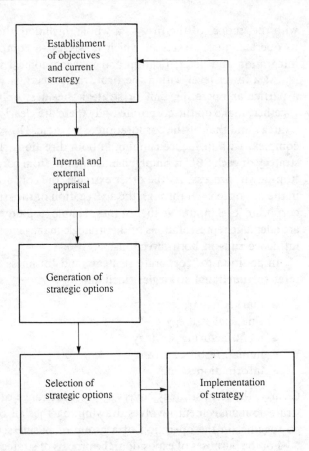

Fig. 11.1 The strategy formulation process

may be identified, followed by **strategic selection** from the options available, in the light of both the managers' values and aspirations and those of the other stakeholders, including shareholders, employees, government and society at large. Having selected from the strategic options available, the firm is then in a position to move on to implementation after which it may wish to return to the starting point, revising its objectives and strategy in a new round of strategy formulation.

When presented in this way, the process of strategy formulation appears explicit, simple and sequential. While this is useful for the purposes of exposition it does not represent the full complexity of the process. Other models of the formulation process (Ansoff (1965), Hofer (1977)) suggest a much more detailed set of stages. In many firms there is no explicit articulation or management of the formulation process. The stages outlined take place in some way, but the boundaries between them are frequently blurred and they may take place in a very different order to that shown in the diagram. In real life, each of the stages has interconnections with the others. Despite these complications, the model can be used to consider each aspect of strategy formulation in turn.

Setting strategic objectives

The first stage in the formulation of strategy is the **establishment of objectives**. These have been discussed in some detail in Chapter 3, where it was concluded that profit is the most important single objective, but that managements may also have aims which conflict with profit-making and a degree of discretion which allows them to pursue those aims. If competition, shareholder pressure and the market for corporate control do not impose perfect discipline on managers the aim of the firm will be an amalgam of profitability and 'managerial' objectives. Corporate strategists have considered other approaches to the fundamental objectives of the firm, including the suggestion that the objective may be **survival** (Asch and Bowman (1987)) or that **social responsibility** is a major feature (Galbraith (1967)). However, profitability is a necessary condition for the achievement of both of these other objectives and the general conclusion that firms seek to achieve some combination of profitability and more 'managerial' objectives, the balance between which varies with the individual circumstances, seems generally valid.

Appraisal of the current position

The second stage in the development of a strategy is **appraisal of the current position**, which in turn has two components. The first is the **internal appraisal** of the firm's strengths and weaknesses with respect to the market and the competition. The second is an **external appraisal** of the opportunities and threats in the business environment.

SWOT analysis

One of the simplest approaches to appraisal is known as **SWOT analysis**, consisting of an internal appraisal of the firms **strengths** and **weaknesses** and an external appraisal of the **opportunities** and **threats** offered by the firm's environment. The identification of strengths and weaknesses requires the development a profile of the firm's major skills and resources and then comparing these with the requirements of the marketplace and the skills and resources of the competition. Each of the firm's major functional areas can be examined, including marketing, production, finance, human resources, research and development and organisational structure in order to systematically identify strengths and weaknesses. Product ranges and geographical scope can also be examined.

For the external appraisal of opportunities and threats a wide range of factors needs to be taken into account. The current position may be analysed by using the five forces structural analysis of competition outlined in Chapter 9. In order to project the analysis into the future the firm may also attempt to forecast the broad changes which are expected to take place in the environment over the short, medium and long term. While this may include a range of relatively narrow forecasting exercises, like those involved in forecasting the level of demand, it should also include an attempt to develop a much broader vision by examining possible socio-political changes, developments in technology and developments in both the national and global economy at large. Some of these developments, most obviously short-term economic forecasting, may be susceptible to quantitative and relatively objective analysis. Others, like long-term global changes or socio-political developments, may only be accessible through qualitative and subjective techniques like the Delphi approach (see Chapter 7) or the generation of **scenarios** where a group of experts or managers discuss and analyse possible future developments and their implications for the firm's competitive position.

SWOT analysis is a generic term covering a very wide range of approaches which may vary from the very formal, thorough, and systematised to the relatively casual. One of its greatest difficulties is that the firm's perceptions of its strengths and weaknesses, opportunities and threats tend to be drawn from the experience and judgment of its managers so that 'objectivity' is lost. This might be avoided by having the analysis carried out by outside consultants but they have the disadvantage of lacking intimate knowledge of the firm and their judgments may not carry credibility with managers who feel that they know best about their own organisation.

Another problem which is commonly encountered in carrying out SWOT analysis (Stevenson (1976)) is that many of a firm's attributes may be simultaneously perceived as both strengths in one sense and weaknesses in others, which can make it extremely difficult to translate the analysis into action.

Portfolio analysis

As SWOT analysis can be complex, subjective and relatively unstructured, management consultants have sought to develop simpler and more objective techniques for the appraisal of a firm's position. Perhaps the best known set of such techniques is known as '**portfolio analysis**', used very extensively in the 1970s and 1980s by some of the world's largest firms (Haspeslagh (1982)). There are many different variants of this approach to appraisal, but the best known are:

- the Boston Consulting Group (BCG) growth/share matrix
- the General Electric business screen
- Hofer and Schendel's product/market evolution matrix

Each of these merits a brief outline.

The Boston Consulting Group growth/share matrix

The BCG matrix is the simplest and best-known of the various portfolio techniques available. In order to carry out the analysis, each of the firm's businesses or products is mapped on a diagram having two axes. The vertical axis represents the rate of growth of sales for that business or product. The horizontal axis shows relative market share, defined as the ratio of the firm's market share to that of its largest competitor. (In the usual presentation of the model, higher market shares are indicated rather eccentrically by a scale which gives a higher market share to the left of the diagram, and a lower share to the right.) Fig. 11.2 shows an example of a BCG matrix.

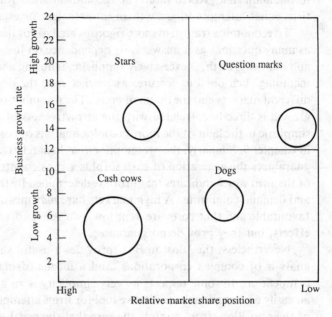

Fig. 11.2 The Boston Consulting Group growth/share matrix

Each business or product is represented by a circle whose size represents the level of sales associated with it. The vertical axis, representing the growth rate, is arbitrarily divided into 'low growth' and 'high growth' and the horizontal axis is similarly divided in a way which positions market leaders to the left and others to the right. This partition gives a matrix of four cells, each of which is said to represent a generic type of business or product, each of which is given a picturesque title.

Businesses or products located in the top left quadrant have high growth and high market share and are labelled **stars**. They are expected to be self-sustaining in terms of cash flow, offering further opportunities for growth and profit and should be supported with additional resources.

Businesses located in the bottom left quadrant have relatively low growth but high market share and are referred to as **cash cows**. These are an important resource for the firm because they are predicted to yield cash surpluses which can be used to support the further development of stars.

The bottom right quadrant of the BCG matrix represents businesses which have low growth and low market shares. These are labelled **dogs**. As they are predicted to be relatively unprofitable and a drain on resources the recommendation for such businesses is that the firm should attempt to dispose of them in whatever way produces the most cash.

The fourth category of business identified in the BCG matrix is that involving high growth but low market share. These are labelled **question marks** as their growth rate makes them a possibly attractive future prospect, but their low market share is taken to mean that they have a large requirement for cash injection if they are to maintain that growth rate. The recommendation for such businesses is that the firm either attempts to grow them into stars or divests itself of them.

To economists trained in more rigorous analysis of the firm, the BCG matrix raises as many questions as it answers. Its dependence on just two variables, market share and market growth, is excessively simplistic, ignoring a whole range of other factors, including such obvious features as market size, the degree of risk associated with different markets and the threat of entry. The presumption that a high rate of business growth is directly correlated with the attractiveness of a sector seems dubious and simplistic in the light of the more complex analysis of competitive structure examined in Chapter 9. Similarly, the presumption that high relative market share automatically guarantees the generation of cash surpluses runs counter to the elementary analysis of the firm which indicates that profit is determined by the relationship between costs and demand conditions. A high market share *may* mean that demand conditions are favourable and that costs are kept low as a result of scale economies and learning effects, but they provide no guarantee.

Nevertheless, the 'Boston Box' provides a useful shorthand vocabulary for the analysis of complex corporations, and a means of making comparisons with the competition. In some respects its very simplicity is an advantage in that it provides an easily understandable **qualitative** tool for firms attempting to take a broad overview of their position. It is certainly the case that the vocabulary of 'stars', 'cash cows', 'dogs' and 'question marks' has come to be very widely used in the business world.

The General Electric 'business screen'

An alternative approach to portfolio analysis, which avoids some of the shortcomings of the Boston Box is the matrix developed by General Electric (GE), known as the GE business screen. This has nine cells rather than four, as shown in Fig. 11.3.

In the GE approach, the horizontal axis represents the firm's **competitive position** and the vertical axis shows the extent of **industry attractiveness**. As each of these are composite variables this allows for a much less simplistic approach than the Boston Box (but also allows much more room for disagreement over interpretation). Industry attractiveness can be examined using an analysis very similar to the 'five forces' approach, with each of the factors being given a weighting and a score on a scale of one to five in order to arrive at a composite rating. Competitive position is also given a composite rating by considering factors such as market share, technological capability, quality of management and marketing skill.

Once ratings have been arrived at for each business they are placed in a nine-cell matrix, with each business represented by a circle whose size indicates the size of the industry and whose shaded segments indicate the firm's market share of each industry. Competitive position is rated on a threefold scale of 'strong', 'average' or 'weak' and industry attractiveness categorised as 'high', 'medium' or 'low'. Businesses

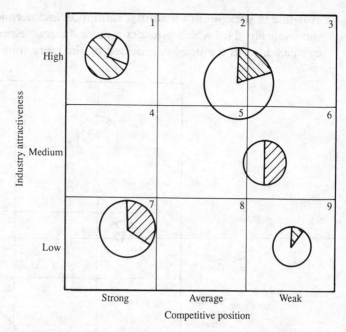

Fig. 11.3 The General Electric matrix

which are in the cells numbered one, two and four in Fig. 11.3 are picked out for priority in the allocation of resources and deemed to be suitable for growth and development. Businesses in the cells numbered six, eight and nine are singled out for divestment and businesses along the diagonal, in cells three, five and seven are subject to a policy of 'holding', taking a low priority in the allocation of resources and management time and effort.

Clearly, the GE business screen allows a much more sophisticated analysis than that put forward by the Boston Box, allowing for intermediate categorisations and the input of a much wider range of information. Its major disadvantage is the converse of the advantages of the Boston Box in that its complexity may make consensus on the composite variables difficult to reach and the information requirements may be difficult and expensive to meet. The other major criticism of the GE approach is that it can be difficult to carry out a meaningful analysis for new businesses in new industries.

Hofer and Schendel's product/market evolution matrix

Hofer and Schendel's approach follows that of the GE screen in so far as it considers the competitive position of businesses as one side of the matrix, and represents each business by a circle showing industry size containing a segment which shows the firm's market share of that sector. However, the other side of the matrix shows the stage of evolution of the industry or segment concerned, ranging from **development** through

growth and **shake-out** to **maturity, saturation** and **decline**. The resulting matrix is shown in Fig. 11.4 which provides a more dynamic element to the analysis which can be added to the insights provided by the more static approaches.

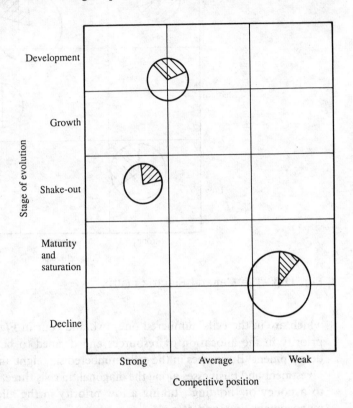

Fig. 11.4 The product/market evolution matrix

Such an approach can be useful, provided that the different stages in a market's development can be clearly distinguished. If they cannot, the technique suffers from some of the disadvantages of the product life cycle model (see Chapter 12) where an unjustified belief in the life cycle can lead managers to take inappropriate decisions which may shorten a product's profitable life span unnecessarily.

Appraisal of strategic business units and the 'value chain'

Portfolio analysis is centrally concerned with strategy at corporate level, and with describing and categorising the position of the different strategic business units (SBUs) which make up the firm as a whole. Individual SBUs also need to carry out appraisals of their current position, which may use some of the techniques already described, at a more disaggregated level. SWOT analysis may be carried out at SBU level, and portfolio analysis may also be used to characterise different product lines within an SBU, as opposed to the position of the SBU as a whole.

Another well-known technique for the appraisal of an SBU is the **'value chain'**, devised by Porter (1985) as a means of systematically examining all the activities a firm carries out within a particular industry. This is shown in Fig. 11.5.

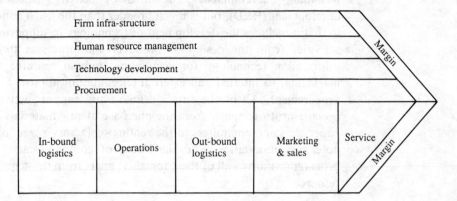

Fig. 11.5 The value chain
From *Competitive Advantage: Creating and Sustaining Superior Performance* by Michael E. Porter. Copyright © 1985 by Michael E. Porter. Reprinted by permission of The Free Press, a Division of Macmillan Inc.

In value-chain analysis the firm is divided into a total of nine different activities. Five of these are known as **primary activities**, which include:

- **in-bound logistics** – all activities associated with receiving, storing and handling inputs to the production process.
- **operations** – all activities concerned with the transformation of inputs into outputs, including machining, assembly, testing, maintenance and facilities management.
- **outbound logistics** – those activities associated with moving the product from the operations stage to buyers. This includes order processing and scheduling, the movement and storage of product within the firm, warehousing and vehicle scheduling.
- **marketing and sales** – activities which provide buyers with the opportunity to buy the product and the inducement to do so. This part of the value chain includes advertising and promotion, pricing and tendering, sales force management, the selection of distribution channels and the maintenance of links with those channels.
- **service** – activities involving the provision of service as a part of the package offered to buyers. This includes installation and maintenance of the product, repair facilities, customer training, spare parts supply and product up-grading.

The other four areas of the firm are referred to as **support activities** which provide services for all of the primary activities. These include:

- **firm infrastructure**, which takes into account planning, finance, accounting, legal services, government liaison, quality management and general management.

- **human resource management**, consisting of all activities concerned with the recruitment, hiring, training, appraisal, promotion, development and compensation of all types of personnel.
- **technology development**. This area of activity includes research and development (R&D), but is much broader than the usual conception of R&D in that it includes the development of technology in support of all the firm's activities from the design of products and processes through improved information technology for accounting, human resource management or marketing, to internal and external telecommunications.
- **procurement**. All of the firm's primary and support activities involve the procurement of inputs, from the purchase of raw materials and equipment, paper clips and computers to the renting of factory space, office space, and hotel accommodation, and the hiring of company cars. The activity of procurement draws all of these together, apart from the acquisition of human resources.

Having divided a firm's activities into these nine different types of activity, the process of appraisal can proceed by examining each of the activities in order to consider how effectively it is currently being carried out and whether there are improvements which could be made to it in order to develop the firm's competitive advantage. This is a potentially very complex and detailed process (see Porter (1985)). However, the basic method is for the firm to decide which of three **generic competitive strategies** it wishes to pursue (see below for details) and then to examine each primary and support activity in order to see how it currently contributes to the successful development of that type of competitive advantage, how it compares with the activities of the competition, and how it might be improved.

For example, the firm might choose to compete through **cost leadership** – keeping its costs below those of the competition. In that case (see Porter (1985) pp.62–119) the firm can develop a cost advantage either by having a value chain which is configured differently from that of its competitors, or by having a cost advantage on some or all of the activities which it carries out. The process of appraisal begins by allocating the firm's total costs and assets across the different activities, in order to identify where the most important and least important costs are incurred (a **first-cut analysis of costs**). Having done that, the **cost drivers** (outlined in Chapter 8) which determine the costs of each activity can be identified and opportunities for improvement can be sought by systematically considering how the cost drivers may be controlled and used to create cost leadership in each activity and in the value chain as a whole. Porter argues that such a systematic evaluation can often identify relatively simple steps which can substantially reduce costs. Alternatively, if ways cannot be found to use the cost drivers in order to reduce costs, the firm may need to **reconfigure the value chain** relative to its competitors, by carrying out the whole process of design, production, marketing and distribution in a different way.

Just as Porter's structural analysis of industry, and the terminology of the Boston Box have become accepted parts of the language of corporate strategy, so has the concept of the value chain begun to form a standard part of the conceptual framework within which business strategy can be analysed.

The generation and selection of strategic options

Once the process of internal and external appraisal is complete, the firm may consider the strategic options available to it. This may be approached in a wide variety of different ways and full coverage lies beyond the scope of this text. However, two analytical tools in particular have gained widespread acceptance and may be used together to map out the possible range of options available. These tools are:

- Ansoff's product/mission matrix
- Porter's concepts of 'generic strategy' and 'scope'.

Ansoff's product/mission matrix

The product/mission matrix put forward by Ansoff (1965) and adapted by Asch and Bowman (1987) is essentially concerned with strategies available at the level of the strategic business unit, rather than the corporate body as a whole. It has two dimensions, one concerning the business's products, where a distinction is made between **present** products and **new** products, and the other concerning the firm's mission, where a similar distinction is made between the present mission and a new mission. The concept of **'mission'** is quite a complex one, but it can be taken to mean the firm's overall strategic objectives and its **'scope'**, which essentially means the range of industries, markets and areas in which the business is involved (see below for further details.)

Fig. 11.6 sets out the matrix, as adapted by Asch and Bowman. Each of the four cells in the matrix represents a set of strategic options. In the top left cell, representing present products and the present mission, the firm may choose to increase its penetration of existing markets with existing products, or to consolidate its position, or to liquidate its activities. In the bottom right-hand cell, representing both new products and a new mission, the firm is faced with the option of diversification. At the top right, involving new products but no change in mission, the option involves product development and in the bottom left-hand cell the product range remains the same but the mission is different, leading to market development, as opposed to product development.

The Ansoff matrix, as amended, therefore produces a range of six basic strategic options, each of which merits further discussion below.

'Generic strategies' and 'scope'

Before considering each of the six basic strategic options it is useful to add two further concepts to the 'toolkit' for the generation of and selection of strategies. Both of

	Product	Present	New
Mission			
Present		Market penetration Consolidation Liquidation	Product development
New		Market development	Diversification

Fig. 11.6 The product/mission matrix

these stem from the work of Porter (1980, 1985) and can be linked into the 'five forces' structural analysis and the concept of the 'value-chain' which have been treated thus far as methods of appraisal.

The starting point for the analysis is the suggestion that the development of a corporate strategy involves two major strategic decisions. The first involves deciding on a **'generic strategy'** and the second involves deciding on the **'scope'** of the firm. Each of these concepts requires a brief explanation.

Porter argues that there are only two fundamental ways in which a firm can compete. The first of these, referred to briefly above, is **cost leadership** where the firm secures a cost advantage over its rivals, either by carrying out the activities in the value chain in less costly ways, or by re-configuring the value chain. The other approach is through **differentiation** where the firm seeks to be unique in its industry by offering a wide range of buyers some attributes which they value. In addition to these basic strategic options there is a third variant, referred to as **focus**, where the firm chooses to serve the needs of a relatively narrow group of users, with unusual needs, to the exclusion of others. This narrow group of users may be served either by developing a cost advantage in serving them, in which case the strategy is known as **cost focus**, or by seeking differentiation in meeting the particular needs of that group, in which case the strategy is known as **differentiation focus**, giving a total of four basic generic strategies.

A central aspect of the Porter thesis is that each of the generic strategies requires a fundamentally different approach to securing competitive advantage and that in most cases a company must make a firm choice between them. To attempt to sustain more than one such strategy within the same organisation is said to involve a major risk of becoming **'stuck in the middle'** and achieving no overall competitive advantage.

While cost leadership and differentiation require different approaches to the development of competitive advantage they are not entirely independent of each other in that whichever strategy is adopted the firm has to give considerable attention to the question of **proximity** to its competitors. A firm seeking cost leadership cannot produce a product which is so unappealing to buyers that it can only be sold at a price which is so low that it nullifies the firm's cost advantage. Similarly, a firm which seeks to compete through differentiation cannot ignore costs for fear of having to charge a price which is so high that it outweighs the advantage to buyers of the unique product being offered.

Porter's approach to the development of competitive advantage involves selecting a generic strategy and then examining the firm's value chain, that of its competitors and that of its buyers and suppliers, in order to identify ways in which each activity can be configured to support the generic strategy being implemented. However, for that to be done effectively, it also has to take into account the firm's 'scope'.

The determination of the firm's 'scope' is the second major aspect of corporate strategy in the Porter approach. Scope has four different dimensions. These are:

- **Segment scope**, which refers to the range of product varieties which the firm chooses to produce and the buyers who are to be served by these products.
- **Vertical scope** which concerns the degree to which the firm is vertically integrated, carrying out activities in-house as opposed to buying them in from independent firms.
- **Geographical scope** which is the range of countries or regions in which the firm intends to compete.
- **Industry scope**, which is the range of industries in which the corporation is aiming to develop a competitive advantage.

The firm's scope is of crucial importance in the development of a successful generic strategy because scope determines the configuration of the value chain, or value chains, for a group of strategic business units.

A complete summary of the Porter approach is difficult to achieve as it necessarily does an injustice to the complexities of the interrelationships involved. Nevertheless, the key components of the strategic process are clear enough. The firm has to develop competitive advantage by organising its scope in such a way that it has a value chain that can be managed in such a way as to enable the firm to achieve either cost leadership, differentiation or focus.

Having set out these basic analytical tools it is possible to return to the set of strategic options identified in the amended Ansoff matrix in Fig. 11.6, in order to consider each one briefly.

Market penetration, consolidation or liquidation

If the firm chooses to remain in the top left hand cell of the Ansoff matrix, with its present products and its present mission (which implies no change in scope) then it has three major sub-options — market penetration, consolidation or liquidation.

Market penetration involves gaining market share, and the feasibility of this option depends very much on market circumstances. If the market is in an early stage of development and growing, or generally 'attractive' in terms of the five forces structural analysis, then market penetration may be an attainable objective. In order to achieve it the firm may seek either cost leadership or differentiation by manipulating its value chain. On the other hand, if the market is saturated or declining, market penetration may be an inappropriate option to pursue.

Consolidation involves maintaining, rather than increasing, market share but this does not imply that the firm can proceed by making no changes to its activities. If the market is moving through different phases of development, then consolidation will require appropriate action to match the firm's resources to the changes in its environment. If the market is still growing, investment will be required in order to maintain cost leadership or differentiation. If the market has ceased to grow or has begun to decline then less new investment will be needed but the firm may need to think carefully about how to utilise its experience in order to meet buyers' needs in a more mature marketplace.

Liquidation or **divestment** is a strategy which may be appropriate if the industry has become unattractive or if the business has become a 'dog' in the vocabulary of the Boston Box. Two approaches to divestment can be identified. The first is early liquidation, where the firm sells the business as quickly as possible. The alternative is known as **harvesting** or **milking**. In this approach the business's demands on the firm's cash flow are reduced as far as possible, with no new investment and stringent programmes of cost reduction, accompanied by attempts to maintain as much revenue inflow as possible.

The choice between early liquidation and harvesting can be a difficult one. If the business can be sold quickly, perhaps before others have appreciated its problems, then there is the prospect of a substantial and useful cash injection which is unlikely to be available from the sale of a business which has been fully harvested. On the other hand, if the firm has made an incorrect assessment of the status of the business, early liquidation may mean that it has sold and lost a cash cow and helped to establish or strengthen the competition. On the other hand, harvesting can be difficult to achieve effectively as customers and suppliers will have limited confidence in a business which has been singled out for milking and managers are hardly likely to feel highly motivated to work well in a situation where there is no long-term future.

Market development

The option indicated by the lower left hand cell in the Ansoff matrix involves maintaining the current product base, but developing a new mission, which implies the development of new markets for the existing products. This may be done either by extending the firm's segment scope, thereby serving hitherto unexploited groups of users in the home market, or by extending the firm's geographical scope, serving the same segment of users, but in a broader geographical area. Whichever route is adopted the firm needs to consider carefully the appropriateness of the new markets in the light of its generic strategy. A firm which is competing through cost leadership, for instance, would be ill-advised to attempt to develop geographically distant markets if serving those markets would involve a significant cost penalty in the form of transport costs or co-ordination across long distances.

Product development

The third basic option to consider lies in the top right hand cell of the Ansoff matrix, indicating the development of new products for sale in existing markets. Such an approach may be linked most directly to the generic strategies of differentiation or focus, but product development may also impact upon cost leadership as product design has 'makeability' as one of its major objectives (Davies (1989)).

The feasibility and desirability of new product development as a strategy depend upon both internal and external factors, which can be examined in the process of appraisal. To be successful by this route the firm needs to have strengths in research and development, and an organisational structure which is capable of effectively turning inventions into innovations (see Chapter 13 for details). It also needs to be operating in an environment where there are 'first-mover advantages' to be had by firms which introduce new products quickly, and to be serving a group of buyers who place value on having access to new products.

Diversification

The most radical strategic option identified by the Ansoff matrix involves both new products and a new mission, and is therefore concerned with **diversification**, the economic analysis of which is considered in more detail in Chapter 18.

Diversification can take three basic forms. The first involves increasing the degree of **vertical integration** in the firm by developing into activities concerning inputs (backward integration) or by moving further down the chain of production and distribution towards the final consumer (forward integration.)

The second form of diversification is known as **horizontal integration** where the firm maintains its current degree of vertical integration, but enters new products and markets which are closely complementary or competitive to its existing products and markets.

Both vertical and horizontal integration are forms of **related diversification** where the firm remains in the same industry, extending its scope within that industry, either vertically or horizontally. If the firm adopts these options it may be able to use its existing strengths and 'distinctive competences' as the basis from which to develop. The third form of diversification is very different in that it involves **unrelated diversification** or the development of a **conglomerate** enterprise where the firm moves into businesses which have no vertical or horizontal connection with the firm's previous experience.

The feasibility and attractiveness of diversification as a strategic option depends upon which mode of diversification is being considered and a complex balance of costs and benefits. In the case of vertical integration a number of major benefits may be identified.

The first possible benefit concerns **cost reductions through integration**. Vertical integration involves replacing market transactions with in-house transactions and thereby **avoiding the costs of using the market** – identifying buyers and sellers, negotiating contracts, monitoring and enforcing contracts. Cost reductions may also arise through **the sharing of facilities** and the **joint use of information**, through **improved control and co-ordination** and through the use of **more specialised facilities** made possible by the long-term **stable relationship** between the vertically related units. Clearly, if such cost reductions are available, vertical integration may assist in the development of cost leadership.

The second advantage of vertical integration is that it may provide **enhanced ability to differentiate** or focus. As a larger proportion of the total value added in the product is placed under the control of internal management it may be easier to gear all of the activities in the firm's more extensive value chain to the specific requirements of differentiation or focus, instead of relying upon suppliers or distribution channels to provide the required attributes demanded by users.

The third advantage of vertical integration is that it may alter the structure of competition, giving the firm **enhanced market power**. In terms of the five forces analysis vertical integration will reduce the power of suppliers or buyers. If the advantages of vertical integration are real then the threat of entry from unintegrated firms will be less important, and the increased capital cost of establishing an integrated operation will raise the barriers to entry into the industry.

If the benefits arising from vertical integration were absolute then it would be expected that all firms would be completely vertically integrated from raw materials production to retailing. Clearly that is not the case and the potential benefits of vertical integration have to be set against the costs, a number of which may be identified.

In the first place, a higher degree of vertical integration may **reduce the firm's flexibility**. If the firm sources its inputs from another part of the company it may be difficult to switch suppliers if the in-house source ceases to be the most cost-effective. Furthermore, the existence of an apparently captive market for part of the firm's output may **reduce incentives** to keep costs down and allow inefficient cross-subsidisation of one part of the firm by another. A higher degree of vertical integration will also **increase the capital costs** associated with the firm's operations and **increase the degree of operating leverage**, by increasing the level of fixed costs associated with the same level of sales. Vertical integration also raises the question of the **balance** between the level of output produced by each stage of the production process. If the level of output produced by one part of the firm is not equal to the level of output required by another there will be either excess supply, which will have to be sold in the open market, or excess demand, in which case the firm will have to continue to source some of its inputs from independent firms. In either case there may be difficulties and the advantages of vertical integration nullified.

This analysis makes it clear that the net advantage of vertical integration is by no means always positive and that firms need to give very careful consideration to the balance of benefit and cost before embarking on this strategic option.

Similar considerations apply to the option of increased horizontal integration which involves a movement into new but horizontally related activities. Porter (1985) goes so far as to state that the development of a **horizontal strategy** should lie at the heart of any overall corporate strategy. The existence of interrelationships between different business units may provide a means of developing competitive advantage and a rationale for horizontal integration. Such interrelationships may be of two types, **tangible relationships** and **intangible relationships**.

Under the heading of tangible relationships, there are five areas which warrant investigation. First, there are **market interrelationships** where different business units may serve similar buyers or use similar distribution channels. If this is the case then there may be gains to be had by co-ordinating activities and sharing resources. Second, there are **production interrelationships**, where fabrication, assembly and in-bound logistics can be shared. Then there are **procurement interrelationships**, involving joint procurement of commonly used inputs, **technology interrelationships** where technology development can jointly serve more than one business unit and **infrastructure interrelationships** where it may be possible to share activities like human resource management and government relations.

In addition to these tangible relationships, which are fundamentally based upon sharing activities, horizontal integration may also provide the opportunity to develop more intangible links between business units such as the **transfer of general know-how and skills** with respect to the implementation of a particular type of generic strategy, the handling of particular types of customers or the development of individual value-creating activities.

A firm which is considering horizontal integration as a strategic option therefore has to first consider whether the industry in which it is considering development is structurally attractive. If not, there is little point in proceeding. If the industry is attractive the firm then has to consider all of the possible interrelationships with its existing activities in order to see whether there are opportunities for sharing facilities or know-how in ways which will enhance its competitiveness. If such opportunities do exist then horizontal integration will be a viable strategic option to be exploited.

Just as in the case of vertical integration it is important to establish that the net advantages from exploiting interrelationships are real, rather than imagined, which requires careful appraisal. In the case of shared production facilities, for instance, two businesses may use the same type of machines but have very different requirements in terms of tolerances and scheduling, in which case the advantages of sharing may in reality be very limited. The construction of an effective horizontal strategy has to be based upon the identification of real opportunities for the enhancement of cost leadership or differentiation, not upon superficial overlaps between different business units.

The third type of diversification involves **unrelated or conglomerate diversification** into products and markets which have no relation to each other. Firms may consider such a move for a number of reasons. In the first place a firm may find itself in an industry or group of industries which is in long-term decline and continued survival and profitability may require a radical change of mission and product range. In the second place, firms may seek to reduce the level of risk associated with the corporation as a whole by diversifying into businesses whose fluctuations are negatively correlated with those of the existing business, so that a difficult period for one part of the business is counter-balanced by a good period for another part. Thirdly, they may seek uses for excessive amounts of cash which have been amassed, or fourthly they may seek to achieve a better corporate-wide financial balance by combining a firm with a high ratio of debt to equity with one which is much less highly geared.

The advantages and disadvantages of conglomerate development have been the subject of much debate. Supporters of the conglomerate point to the possibility of 'synergy', where the combined effect of two or more sets of activity produce superior results to those of the sum of the separate parts. Financial synergy, in the form of risk reduction or more appropriate gearing, is an example of such a benefit. However, it might be argued that risk reduction in particular is better achieved through the financial institutions' management of share portfolios than through the construction of a portfolio of businesses by a management team whose expertise and distinctive competences may not be able to cover the wide range of different activities involved. If there are none of the interrelationships identified by Porter amongst the business units then it is difficult to see how synergy can develop in practice. For this reason conglomerate diversification is often seen as a potentially risky strategic option, and is sometimes identified as a strategy which is more likely to stem from managers' pursuit of their own desire for prestige and risk reduction than from pursuit of the shareholders' interests. Nevertheless, the evidence on the issue is mixed, with at least one major study of diversification in the British economy (Reed and Luffman (1984)) finding that conglomerate diversifiers provided their shareholders with the highest level of return at the lowest risk. As many of these conglomerates have been built by 'superstar' management teams, acquiring firms with quite uninspiring performance and then turning them round into profit and growth, it may have to be accepted that there is a particular distinctive competence in the management of conglomerate development, which can be used to overcome the apparent disadvantages of this particular strategic option.

The implementation of strategy

Once a firm has decided upon the strategic option which it wishes to pursue it then has to consider how the strategy is to be implemented. As questions of implementation are largely concerned with the establishment of appropriate management structures and control procedures, the management of change and the relationships of power within the corporation, they lie beyond the scope of this managerial economics text. However, there is at least one essentially economic issue concerned with implementation which merits analysis here. This concerns the three major routes through which a strategy may be implemented. These are:

- internal development
- acquisition
- joint ventures

Internal development

Internal development involves entering a new industry by establishing a completely new operation under the aegis of the existing company, as opposed to acquiring an existing business. As this form of strategic development involves new entry into an industry its success depends upon the extent to which entry barriers can be overcome, and the potential impact of retaliation from incumbents. It will tend to be a more effective strategy if links between the new business and the firm's existing activities can be used to lower entry costs, if retaliation is likely to be ineffective and if the competitive structure of the industry has not yet become stable and well-established, so that incumbents have not developed working relationships with each other which might be threatened by a new entrant. Internal development will be a particularly appropriate strategy if the firm's entry changes the structure of the industry in such a way that it is made more attractive for all the incumbents, by raising entry barriers, for instance.

Acquisition

Internal development requires the establishment of a new business entity, which may be time-consuming and expensive. The obvious alternative is to acquire an existing business in the industry where the firm wishes to develop a presence. As this does not involve new entry it reduces the problems which may arise from a disturbance to the industry's competitive structure, and it may also give the firm immediate access to the expertise of the acquired firm's management, allowing a very rapid movement along the 'experience curve'. The most difficult questions concerning acquisitions, which are explored in more depth in Chapter 18, are the price which should be paid for the business being acquired, and the integration of that business with the other parts of the firm. If stock markets work efficiently, the value of a firm's shares will reflect its expected future profits. If an acquiring firm is to be certain of success it may need to offer a price which is higher than the current market price, in order to persuade sufficient shareholders to part with their holdings. In that case, there is a danger that the cost of the acquisition will exceed its value. This will not be so if the incumbent management of the firm being acquired is failing to make the maximum profit, because in that case the share price will reflect that poor performance, and the assets will be under-valued. However, if the firm is not performing well there is the danger that this will continue after acquisition. The simple economics of share pricing suggests that acquisition will only yield substantial profits if the performance of the acquired firm can be improved after acquisition. This could be achieved either by generally improving its management or by exploiting links between the activities of the existing businesses and the new acquisition, which provide 'synergy' and make the acquired business more valuable to the acquirer than to the market in general.

Joint ventures

A third means of strategic development is the joint venture, where a group of firms establish a new jointly owned business. In some instances, particularly in developing countries, this form of venture is forced upon companies by government insistence upon local participation in ownership. However, firms may also choose the joint venture as a means of spreading the risk of very large projects or pooling different areas of expertise when a new venture requires a combination of skills not available to any single firm. The establishment of joint ventures may also assist in securing 'orderly' competition between the partners in other arenas as they build relationships with each other and become reciprocally vulnerable to opportunistic behaviour on each other's part.

Illustration

The use of portfolio planning

Haspeslagh (1982) provides a useful overview of the introduction and uses of portfolio planning in large US corporations, having carried out a survey of its adoption amongst the 'Fortune "1000" '.

According to the survey returns, by 1979 45 per cent of the 'Fortune "500" ' companies in the US had adopted portfolio planning to some extent, as had 36 per cent of the 'Fortune "1000" '. However, the extent of adoption varied widely. Haspeslagh draws a distinction between 'analytic portfolio planning' and 'process portfolio planning'. In the former, the use of the technique is confined to the corporate level, with no intention of using it to negotiate explicit strategic missions with managers. In 'process portfolio planning', the technique becomes a central part of the management process, which includes the use of the technique to negotiate strategic missions with the managers of strategic business units (SBUs). The survey data suggested that only 14 per cent of the 'Fortune "1000" ' had gone so far as to introduce 'process portfolio planning'. Some of the others were still in the process of carrying out the grid analysis, others had completed that analysis but had not yet decided on strategic missions and another group had decided on those missions at corporate level but had not yet negotiated those missions with unit managers.

Survey data on the characteristics of the respondents suggested that the adoption of portfolio planning was most common amongst diversified industrial companies and least often adopted in conglomerates. The evidence also provided information on the process by which firms introduced portfolio methods. According to the theory of portfolio planning the first step is for the company to define the strategic business units (SBUs) to which the analysis is to be applied. The evidence showed that in fact 70 per cent of companies did begin with a comprehensive re-examination of their definition of the businesses in which they were engaged. Furthermore, in 75 per cent of those cases, the re-evaluation led to the classification of SBUs which differed from the existing operating units. However, that did not amount to an administrative revolution because the redefined SBUs usually consisted of aggregations of existing operational units. On average, companies using portfolio techniques identified just 30 SBUs and in only 7 per cent of cases did these clearly cut across existing organisational lines.

As many of the companies surveyed were very large, each of these 30 SBUs represented substantial businesses in themselves and it was common practice to treat portfolio analysis as a multi-level exercise. At corporate level companies looked at large SBUs which were existing organisational units, while within those SBUs a more disaggregated view was taken of strategic segments.

Although portfolio planning did not in general lead firms to change their administrative systems or organisational structure, some managers did informally adapt systems to fit the different needs of different businesses, and such informal differentiation seemed to characterise the difference between those companies where portfolio planning was treated as an isolated exercise and those where it became an integral part of the management process.

Managers' responses to the introduction of portfolio planning seem to have been almost entirely positive. Respondents felt that portfolio planning had a positive impact on management and only one out of 176 respondents felt that it would have less importance in the years ahead. The perceived gains were in the following three areas.

In the first place, 33 per cent of managers felt that the most important benefit lay in the improved generation and communication of strategies by promoting improved analysis, more substantive discussion across the levels in a company and the capitalisation of benefits arising from diversity. Secondly, 32 per cent felt that the most important benefit lay in more selective resource allocation. Trade-offs between SBUs are made possible by providing a focus for the issues and a vehicle for negotiation. Thirdly, 20 per cent of managers felt that the most important benefit lay in 'following through'. In Haspeslagh's own view the most significant gain which is possible from portfolio planning is in the quality of the management process. If the recognition of diversity leads to the development of a management process which is differentiated in ways which correspond to the nature of the business, then portfolio analysis has made its most useful contribution.

References and further reading

H.I. Ansoff, *Corporate Strategy*, (Harmondsworth, Penguin 1965)

D. Asch and C. Bowman, *Strategic Management*, (London, Macmillan, 1987)

H. Davies, 'The Designers' Perspective: Managing Design in the UK', *Journal of General Management* Summer 1989

J.K. Galbraith, *The New Industrial State*, (London, Hamish Hamilton, 1967)

P. Haspeslagh, 'Portfolio Planning: Uses and Limits', *Harvard Business Review*, January–February 1982

C.W. Hofer, *Conceptual Constructs for Formulating Corporate and Business Strategies*, (Boston, Intercollegiate Case Clearing House, 1977)

C.W. Hofer and D. Schendel, *Strategy Formulation: Analytical Concepts*, (St Paul, West, 1978)

M. Porter, *Competitive Strategy*, (New York, Free Press, 1980)

M. Porter, *Competitive Advantage*, (New York, Free Press, 1985)

R. Reed and G. Luffman, *The Strategy and Performance of British Industry, 1970–1980*, (London, Macmillan, 1984)

H.H. Stevenson, 'Defining Corporate Strengths and Weaknesses', *Sloan Management Review* Spring 1982

Self-test questions

1 Which of the following are concerned with the appraisal of a firm's current position?

(a) SWOT analysis
(b) the Boston Box
(c) Ansoff's matrix
(d) the value chain

2 In the Boston Box which of the following variables is used as a proxy measure of industry attractiveness?

(a) market share
(b) market growth
(c) industry size
(d) number of firms

3 List the activities which make up the value chain, distinguishing between primary activities and support activities.

4 Identify the dimensions of scope.

5 List the strategic options identified by the Ansoff matrix.

Exercise

Compare two techniques for the analysis of a firm's portfolio of businesses, identifying the strengths and weaknesses of each approach.

Answers on page 416.

12 Pricing decisions

This chapter examines various aspects of the pricing decision, including the prescriptions derived from the simple economic model of the firm, the links between pricing and market structure and the problem of pricing to deter entry. Attention is also paid to the practice of price discrimination and the relationship between pricing and the concept of the product life cycle.

Price in the simple economic model of the firm

The basic rules for optimal pricing

The simple model of the profit-maximising firm, developed in Chapter 3 and extended in Chapter 9, is one in which price and quantity are the only decision variables. The nature of the product is given, there is assumed to be no spending on promotion or advertising, and no attention is given to the question of distribution channels. In terms of the 'marketing mix', popularised by McCarthy (1960) as the '4 Ps – Product, Price, Place and Promotion', only one of the Ps is taken into account.

In this model of the firm, the rule for profit maximisation is simple. The firm should produce the level of output such that marginal costs = marginal revenue (the first-order condition) and the slope of the marginal cost curve is greater than the slope of the marginal revenue curve (the second-order condition). The price which should be charged is then derived from the profit-maximising quantity, being the price at which that quantity can be sold.

Price can be made to feature more explicitly in the model by re-writing the first-order condition (MC = MR), to give:

$$\frac{P - MC}{P} = \frac{1}{E_d}$$

where:
P = price
MC = marginal cost
E_d = elasticity of demand

As this condition makes clear, the margin between price and marginal cost is essentially a function of **elasticity of demand**. If demand is infinitely elastic, being equal to infinity, the profit-maximising price will be equal to marginal cost. As demand is less and less elastic, so the margin between price and marginal cost will be larger.

While the equation given shows the links between price, cost and elasticity, it only provides a simple prescription for setting price if both marginal cost and elasticity are constant over a wide range of output. In that case, their values may be simply inserted into the equation to give the profit-maximising price. If they are not, which the analysis of preceding chapters has suggested is almost certainly the case, the equation can only be applied by identifying the profit-maximising level of output first, then identifying marginal cost and elasticity at that level of output, and then solving for price. A number of commentators, including Gabor (1977), have suggested that this renders the model useless for any practical purposes.

Another specification of the basic model which can be used to shed light on the profit-maximising price involves restating the cost conditions in terms of an average cost function, giving:

Total cost = AC(q).q   where:
AC = average cost
q   = output

In this case, the basic profit-maximising equation is as follows:

Profit = Total revenue − Total cost

$$= P(q).q - AC(q).q$$

The first-order condition for profit-maximisation can then be written:

$$Price = AC + q\frac{dAC}{dq} - \frac{dP}{dq}$$

This approach has the apparent advantage of expressing the optimal price in terms of average cost plus a margin, which corresponds with much of the evidence on business practice (see below). On the other hand, if it is viewed as a decision-rule for managers, or as a prescription, it suffers from the same disadvantages as the previous formulation. It cannot be applied until the profit-maximising level of output is known, along with the values of dAC/dq and dp/dq at that level of output.

It should be clear, then, that the basic model of the firm does not produce a set of simple formulae which allow a manager to set a profit-maximising price. Dorward (1987) quotes the comments of Nagle (1984), to the effect that: '[marketers] are soon disillusioned if they turn to economics for practical solutions to pricing problems . . . the role of economics is not to price products, but to explain the economic principles to which successful pricing strategies will conform.' Before turning to examine some of the more complex issues raised by the problem of pricing, it is useful to consider the links between the determination of price and the type of market structure in which firms find themselves. As these market structures have been considered in some detail in Chapter 9, the coverage in this chapter is brief, being focused entirely on pricing.

Pricing and market structures

Pricing under perfect competition

In a perfectly competitive industry, as outlined in Chapter 9, the firm does not have to take a pricing decision. Price is set by the forces of supply and demand, the individual firm is too small to have any impact on that price, and firms are known as **'price-takers'**. Each firm simply accepts the price which is set by the market and takes a decision on the level of output which maximises profit, given the market price. As each individual firm faces a demand curve which is infinitely elastic, profit-maximising behaviour on the part of each firm requires that price (which equals marginal revenue in this case) will be equal to marginal cost, at the profit-maximising level of output. If firms are able to make supernormal profits at the prevailing price then in the long-run entry will take place and the price will be forced down by market pressures until the supernormal profits are eliminated.

Pricing under monopoly

A monopolist is not a 'price-taker', but a 'price-maker', in the sense that the price which it sets is not pre-determined by external market forces. That is not to say that a monopolist has complete freedom with respect to price. In order to achieve maximum profit the optimal combination of price and quantity has to be chosen by selecting the level of output at which marginal cost equals marginal revenue and then adopting the market-clearing price for that level of output. This is illustrated in Fig. 12.1, which is simply a reproduction of Fig. 9.6.

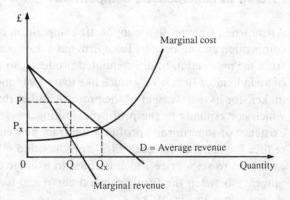

Fig. 12.1 A profit-maximising monopolist

As the figure shows, the profit-maximising level of output is Q and the profit-maximising price is P. A limit is set to the level of price by the buyers' ability to go without the industry's product, which in turn decides the elasticity of demand and the optimal price.

The textbook model of monopoly focuses attention on the short term, and by assumption the firm faces no threat of entry in the long term. As a result there are no long-term forces tending to eliminate any supernormal profits by forcing the price downwards. The only difference between the short run and the long run is that in the long run the firm can consider whether it has the most profitable set of plant and equipment, given the available technology and the demand curve facing it. If it does, then in the long run it will simply keep on replacing that set of plant and equipment. Cost and demand conditions will remain as shown in Fig. 12.1, as will the profit-maximising price and output. On the other hand, if there is an alternative set of plant and equipment which would allow greater profits to be made, that set will be built in the long run and there will be a new profit-maximising level of output and price corresponding to the cost conditions associated with the new plant.

As the textbook model of monopoly involves a firm which is protected from entry by assumption there is no possibility that the threat of entry may be affected by the price set and the profits made. In that case simple profit-maximisation will take place and, no matter how large the resulting profits, new firms cannot establish a foothold in the industry. Such a situation may arise if entry to the industry is absolutely blockaded by legal restrictions or some other absolute barrier. However, in many other situations the barriers to entry are not absolute and a monopoly firm may have to pay attention to the impact of its price and profits upon the behaviour of potential entrants. Earning maximum profit in the short run might encourage entry to take place in the long run and thereby erode the firm's monopoly position. The relationship between pricing and entry is considered further in the section on pricing and rivalry in oligopoly below.

Pricing in monopolistic competition

As shown in Chapter 9, monopolistic competition contains elements of both perfect competition and monopoly. Each firm has a downward sloping demand curve, arising from the production of differentiated products, so that in the short run the position of an individual firm is very much like that of a monopolist. Each business is a 'price-maker' for its own variant of the product, rather than a 'price-taker', setting a price which corresponds to the profit-maximising level of output. In the long run, the existence of supernormal profits will attract new entry into the industry, which will reduce the demand for each firm's product and eliminate super profits by forcing each firm to set a price which is equal to average cost of production at a point of tangency between the firm's demand curve and its long-run average cost curve (as shown above in Fig. 9.7).

Pricing and rivalry in oligopoly

The most complex form of market structure considered in Chapter 9 was oligopoly, a generic term used for many different types of industrial structure having the common feature of consisting of just a few firms, each of which is interdependent upon the others.

The analysis presented in Chapter 9 suggested a number of possible outcomes of the oligopoly situation, each of which has implications for pricing. A simple integrated treatment for some of these can be provided, following Dorward (1987), by using a straightforward mathematical framework. The starting point is with the case where all firms produce identical products. In this case, the demand curve can be written:

$p = p(Q)$ where:

p = price

Q = total output of all firms

$= q_i$

q_i = output of the i'th firm

The profit function for an individual firm is then given by:

$\$_i = p(Q)q_i - C_i(q_i)$ where:

$C_i(q_i)$ = total cost of q_i

and the condition for profit-maximisation is:

$$\frac{d\$_i}{dq_i} = p + q_i \frac{dp}{dQ} \cdot \frac{dQ}{dq_i} - \frac{dC_i}{dq_i} = 0$$

The most important term in this last equation is dQ/dqi which illustrates the importance of the links between changes in the i'th firm's output and changes in the outputs of the other firms and the industry as a whole. If the i'th firm increases its output by one unit, and the other firms do not respond to that change, then clearly:

$$\frac{dQ}{dq_i} = 1$$

On the other hand, if the other firms respond to the unit increase in output by raising their own outputs by a units, then:

$$\frac{dQ}{dq_i} = 1 + a$$

The term a is a measure of rivals' reactions. As the individual firm can only conjecture about the reactions of its rivals a may also be described as a measure of **conjectural variation,** as perceived by that firm.

Just as the simple profit-maximising condition (MC = MR) can be rewritten to give:

$$\frac{P - MC}{P} = \frac{1}{E_d}$$

The more complex oligopoly version can be re-written to give:

$$\frac{P - MC_i}{P} = (-) \frac{s_i(1 + a)}{E_d}$$

where:

s_i = market share, firm i
a = conjectural variation
E_d = market elasticity

Examination of this model shows that it encompasses both perfect competition (s_i and a both equal to zero) and monopoly (s_i equal to 1 and a equal to zero) as special cases.

In the oligopoly case, where a is non-zero, the firm's pricing behaviour depends upon the sign and size of the conjectural variation. If a is positive and large, indicating that other firms increase their output substantially when the firm under examination attempts to increase its own output (which implies lowering its price), then clearly demand for the individual firm's product will be very inelastic and the corresponding margin between marginal cost and the optimal price will be large. In the opposite case, if rival firms were to respond to an increase in output by reducing their own output, demand for the firm in question would be highly elastic (a reduction in price would lead to a large increase in demand as other firms reduce their output) and the optimal price/marginal cost margin would be lower.

The model set out above illustrates the importance of rivals' reactions for the optimal price in conditions of oligopoly. It can also be linked back to the more qualitative discussion of oligopoly in Chapter 9. In the case of collusion, for instance, if each firm conjectures that its partners in the joint monopoly will act in such a way as to maintain stable market shares then:

$$a = \frac{1 - s_i}{s_i}$$

This reduces the equation given above to:

$$\frac{P - MC_i}{P} = (-) \frac{1}{E_d}$$

which is exactly the same as in monopoly.

In the case of the kinky demand curve model, a takes different values for price rises (output reductions) and price falls (output increases.) If the individual firm attempts to increase its output by lowering the price, the assumption is that its rivals will also lower price and increase output so that a is positive. If the firm raises its price, thereby lowering its output, the assumption is that rivals leave their price at the initial level and increase their output, so that a is negative. As a takes multiple values around the existing price level, this makes the solution indeterminate, which brings the analysis back to the basic objection to the kinky demand curve theory, which is that it does not provide a prediction for the price level, but rather suggests that in oligopoly prices will tend to be stable.

Further extensions of this basic approach lie beyond the scope of this text but it may be extended in a number of directions to cover the case of differentiated products (Cubbin (1983)) and price leadership (Waterson (1984)).

Entry conditions and pricing

The analysis set out above has been placed in a short-run framework where firms pay no attention to the impact of their price setting upon the entry of other firms into the industry or market segment in which they are operating. Nevertheless, the models of perfect competition and monopolistic competition make it clear that the threat of entry is a major determinant of price in the longer run and some attention needs to be given to the links between barriers to entry and pricing.

The condition of entry

Entry barriers may be defined as advantages held by incumbent firms in an industry over potential entrants. In some situations these barriers may be absolute, so that new firms cannot enter the industry, no matter how high a price is being charged by the incumbents. In that case, following the seminal work of Bain (1956) the condition of entry is said to be **blockaded**. This is the condition of entry which is assumed in the pure monopoly model.

In other situations the condition of entry may be defined as **easy** if new firms are able to enter profitably when prices are set only slightly above costs, **ineffectively impeded** when pricing low enough to prevent entry is less profitable than maximising profit and allowing entry, or **effectively impeded** when it is more profitable in the long run to price at a level where no entry will occur other than to maximise short-run profit and allow entry to take place.

If the basic links between barriers to entry and pricing are to be understood, three issues need to be addressed. The first concerns the sources of entry barriers, the second concerns the determination of the entry-deterring price and the third concerns the factors which determined whether profit-maximising firms will choose to charge such a price.

The sources of entry barriers

In addition to legal barriers to entry, which may be erected by governments Bain (1956) identifies three major sources of entry barriers, each of which has been referred to above in Porter's 'five forces' analysis of competition. These are:

- absolute cost advantages
- economies of scale
- product differentiation

Absolute cost advantages may arise if incumbent firms have exclusive or low-cost access to resources needed in the industry, a proprietary technology not available to entrants, a favourable location or access to learning effects as a result of their longer experience in the industry. If incumbent firms do have such advantages they will be able to make profits at prices which are lower than potential entrants' costs, in which case entry can be deterred by setting prices appropriately.

Economies of scale have been discussed in some detail in Chapter 8. They arise mainly from the existence of indivisibilities and the advantages of specialisation in both production and management. If there are substantial scale economies then potential entrants will face a difficult dilemma. In order to enter the industry they must either produce at a lower volume than the incumbent firms, in which case they will suffer an important cost penalty, or they must establish a plant having very large scale, in which case they will have to secure a very large market share very quickly in order to avoid heavy losses.

Product differentiation will provide a barrier to entry if buyers have well-established preferences for the products of the incumbent firms. However, it seems reasonable to assume that new entrants can overcome these preferences through their own promotional spending in which case it can be seen that entry barriers attributed to product differentiation will only arise if new entrants have to spend more on promotion and advertising for the same volume of sales than the incumbent firms. Given the inertia of buyers and the time lags involved in building an effective brand image this is probably a reasonable assumption to make, but it does suggest that entry barriers attributable to product differentiation are simply a special case of absolute cost advantages.

Identifying the limit price

The **'limit price'** or **'entry-deterring price'** may be defined as the highest price which can be charged by incumbent firms without inducing new entry into the industry.

As a potential entrant will choose to enter the industry if it is able to earn at least normal profits, then entry will take place in any situation where a potential entrant's demand curve lies above its cost curve, for some level of output. The determination of the limit price therefore depends heavily upon the location of the entrant's expected demand curve. This in turn depends upon the entrant's expectations about the response of the incumbent firms to its arrival in the industry. The usual assumption in this respect is known as the **Sylos postulate** after Sylos-Labini (1962). This assumes that potential entrants assume that existing firms will maintain their output constant when entry takes place, and the incumbent firms know this to be the case.

If the Sylos postulate holds true, a potential entrant to an industry producing an undifferentiated product will be faced with a demand curve which is the segment of the industry demand curve lying to the right of the post-entry level of output produced by the incumbent firms. This is shown in Fig. 12.2.

The curve D_{ind} shows the market demand curve for the product. If existing firms produce a pre-entry quantity Q_1 then at price P_1 they satisfy the entire market demand, so that the demand for the additional output supplied by an entrant is equal

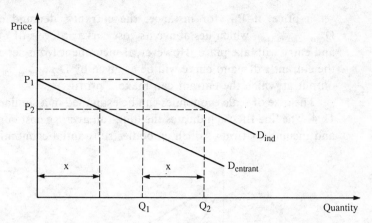

Fig. 12.2 Limit-pricing: the demand curve for an entrant's product

to zero at price P_1. If the entrant (and the incumbents) lowered the price to P_2 total demand would rise to Q_2. If the incumbent firms are expected to behave according to the Sylos postulate and maintain their output at Q_1 this would leave $(Q_2 - Q_1)$ units of output as the demand for the output of the new entrant, and the post-entry demand curve for the entrant is given by the line $D_{entrant}$. The position of the entrant's demand curve is determined by the pre-entry price and output of the incumbent firms.

This analysis allows the limit price to be determined for the two different types of entry barrier – absolute cost advantages and scale economies. Fig. 12.3 illustrates the position in the case of absolute cost advantages.

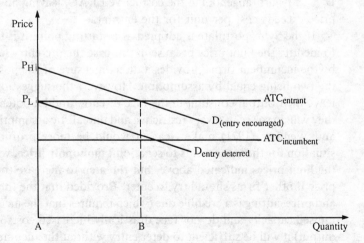

Fig. 12.3 Limit pricing: the case of absolute cost advantages

If incumbent firms have average cost curves given by the line $ATC_{incumbent}$ and the potential entrant has a cost curve given by $ATC_{entrant}$ then the entrant will expect to be able to make a profit if the incumbent firms set a price higher than P_L. If they set a price of P_H, for instance, the entrant's demand curve will be given by $D_{entry\ encouraged}$, which lies above its cost curve at levels of output between A and B and entry will take place. However, if incumbent firms set a price just equal to P_L, the entrant's demand curve will be as given by $D_{entry\ deterred}$ and there is no level of output at which the entrant can make a profit.

The case of scale economies can be examined in a similar fashion, shown in Fig. 12.4. The line LRAC indicates the long-run average cost curve facing both entrants and incumbent firms, which embodies substantial economies of scale.

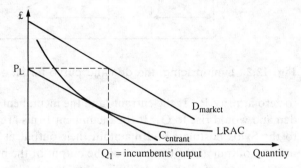

Fig. 12.4 Limit pricing: the case of scale economies

In this case, it is clear that the maximum price which can be charged without inducing entry is again indicated by P_L. At that price, the demand curve for the entrant, $D_{entrant}$, which is parallel to the demand curve for the market as a whole, D_{market}, is just tangential to the cost curve LRAC, leaving no level of output at which price exceeds cost per unit for the entrant.

If the Sylos postulate is adopted as a starting point it is therefore relatively easy to identify the limit price because in this case the pre-entry level of output produced by the incumbent firms provides a direct measure of the post-entry level of output, the two being equal by assumption. However, the suggestion that incumbent firms leave their output constant in the face of entry and let potential entrants know that they will do so seems a very restrictive and unrealistic assumption. As Pashigian (1968) and Wenders (1971) make clear, it would be more profitable in an oligopolistic situation for the incumbents to set a **joint monopoly price**, which will be higher than the limit prices indicated above, but threaten to increase their output and cut that price if other firms should try to enter. Provided that the threat of increased output and price cutting is a credible one (which requires that the incumbent firms have some unused capacity and do not face drastically increased costs in producing additional output) it will be sufficient to deter entry without the incumbent firms having to set a price at the entry-deterring level.

It would appear then that the Sylos assumption whereby incumbent firms will not increase their output in the face of entry, and entrants know that to be the case, is only tenable under oligopoly if the incumbent firms lack the capacity to increase output or if they face higher costs and the loss of their advantage if they attempt to increase output. The assumption will be more tenable in atomistic conditions of either perfect or monopolistic competition where there are too many firms for individual incumbents to react directly to entry.

The other major weakness of the Sylos postulate is the implicit presumption that entrants and incumbents produce identical products, so that buyers can have no preference for an entrant's product over an incumbent's. If this presumption is relaxed then an entrant who offers a product variant which is particularly attractive to buyers may be able to draw customers away from the incumbent firms, so that if they attempt to maintain their output at pre-entry levels they will simply be unable to sell all of that output, and the entrant may be able to make profits even if the incumbent firms charge very low prices. However, as soon as **product differentiation** is introduced into the model the whole analytical framework collapses as it is no longer possible to identify a market demand curve or the demand curve for an entrant, given the incumbent's output.

Limit pricing versus short-run profits

Even if the limit price can be identified, which is difficult unless products are identical and the Sylos postulate holds, there is no guarantee that firms will choose to set such a price. They may prefer to charge a higher profit-maximising price and make larger profits in the short run, accepting that this will induce entry and reduce profits in the longer run. Fig. 12.5 compares the time profile of profits for the two different strategies.

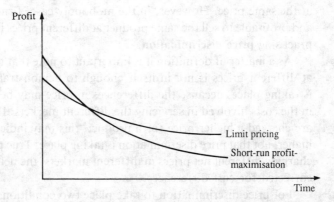

Fig. 12.5 The time-profile of profits for different strategies towards deterrence of entry

As the figure shows, short-run profit-maximisation leads to a higher level of profit in the short run, but this is eroded over time as entry takes place. Limit pricing leads to a lower level of profit in the short term, but profits are not eroded over time to such an extent. If firms are attempting to maximise the present value of future profits the choice between the two strategies will depend upon which yields the higher discounted cash flow, which in turn depends upon three factors. First there is the difference between the profits which can be made in the short run by not setting the limit price and the profits which would be earned at that price. Clearly, as this is larger, so is the incentive to opt for short-run profit-maximisation. The second factor is the speed with which entry can take place. If this is very rapid the extra profits made from short-run profit-maximisation will be short lived and limit pricing will be favoured. Finally, the decision will depend upon the discount rate applied. As this is larger, the more will firms value present as opposed to future profits, and the more likely they are to choose the option of short-run profit maximisation.

In practice, incumbent firms considering their strategy with respect to potential entrants do not have a simple choice between limit pricing and short-run profit-maximisation. They are also able to choose a range of intermediate prices, which may affect the rate at which entry and the erosion of profits takes place. Gaskins (1971), for instance, explores a model in which entry and the erosion of profit takes place more quickly if the incumbent firms choose a price which is substantially above the limit price and more slowly as it is closer to the limit price. Such complex dynamic models lie beyond the scope of this text but they do offer some explanatory value.

Price discrimination

Definition and necessary conditions

The analysis set out above has considered various characteristics of the price which will be set for a product, on the implicit assumption that every unit of output is sold at the same price. However, in the monopoly case, firms may find it both feasible and profitable to sell the same product at different prices in different markets, thereby practising **price discrimination**.

As a matter of definition it is important to note that the sale of the same product at different prices is not in itself enough to demonstrate that price discrimination is taking place, because the differences in price may be attributable to differences in the costs involved in servicing the different markets. If buyers in a distant market are charged a higher price for a product, this may indicate that transport costs are higher, not that price discrimination is taking place. True price discrimination involves charging different net prices in different markets, the net price being the actual price corrected for cost differences.

For price discrimination to take place two conditions have to be fulfilled. First, the total market for the product must be divisible into sub-markets which have different price elasticities of demand. Secondly, those sub-markets must be effectively separated, so that a purchaser in one market cannot resell to a buyer in another. If these conditions did not hold then price differences would either be unprofitable (if elasticities were the same in all markets) or impossible (if competitive arbitrage between one market and another meant that no buyer need pay the higher price because arbitrageurs buy in the low price market and then offer the product for resale in the high price market.)

Third degree price discrimination

Two basic forms of price discrimination are possible. The first is where the total market is divided up into a number of sub-markets, each containing a number of buyers, who will all be charged the same price set for that sub-market. This is known as **third degree price discrimination**.

Sub-markets may be separated in a number of ways. Most obviously, there may be different geographical markets in which separate prices can be charged. However, it may also be possible to segment the market by age, by social status or by a wide range of other variables. In the case of rail travel in Britain, for instance, several different types of market segmentation are employed. The use of Student Railcards and Old Persons Railcards allows segmentation by age. Family Railcards (giving discounts only when a party of travellers includes children) allow segmentation by social position (and also by the purpose of the journeys being made). The distinction between First and Second Class travel also allows segmentation by income (or by the purpose of the journey).

For goods which cannot be stored at reasonable cost, segmentation through timing may be possible. In the case of telephone calls or electricity or journeys for instance, it is not possible to purchase the good for one time period and then use it at another. As a result, suppliers will be able to charge different prices at different times without arbitrage taking place. If elasticities of demand differ at different times it will be profitable as well as feasible to introduce price discrimination in the form of peak and off-peak pricing.

Fig. 12.6 provides a formal graphical analysis of third degree discrimination for the case where the firm is selling in two sub-markets, within each of which a common price must be charged.

In Fig. 12.6(a) the demand curve D_1 indicates demand in the first sub-market and D_2 indicates demand in the second sub-market. Each has its own marginal revenue curve as indicated by MR_1 and MR_2. If the two markets are aggregated to give the firm's overall demand and marginal revenue curves the result is given by the lines $D = D_1 + D_2$ and $MR = MR_1 + MR_2$. In Fig. 12.6(b) the firm's marginal cost curve is added to the diagram, which shows that the profit-maximising level of total output is Q. The distribution of this total output across the two sub-markets can be seen by recognising that in each sub-market profit is maximised when marginal revenue in that market equals the marginal cost of supplying that market. As it is assumed in this simple case that the marginal cost of supplying the same unit to either market is the same, this implies that for profit-maximisation in each market:

$$MR_1 = MR_2 = MC$$

As marginal cost at the profit-maximising total output is equal to 25 it can readily be seen from the diagram that this equates to MR_1 at level of output 30 and MR_2 at level of output 50, which are the levels of output to be sold in each sub-market. The prices to be charged in each sub-market can then be read of from their respective demand curves, showing that a price of P_1 will be charged in the first market and P_2 in the second.

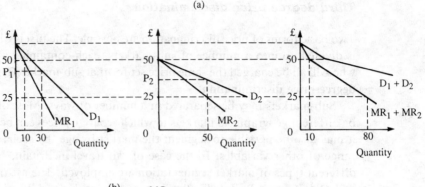

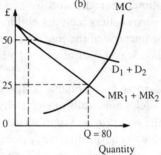

Fig. 12.6 Third degree price discrimination

First degree price discrimination

The second form of price discrimination is known as **first degree price discrimination** which is possible when every buyer of the firm's product can be charged a different price. In this case there is a separate market for each unit of output sold so that the supplier can extract the maximum amount which each buyer is willing to pay for each unit sold. This form of discrimination is feasible in situations where the product sold can only be used by the individual buyer, a situation which most obviously presents itself in the service industries. In the case of legal, medical, personal or financial services the product is 'customised' to the circumstances of the individual purchaser. It cannot be sold to another purchaser and first degree price discrimination is therefore possible. Fig. 12.7 provides a graphical analysis for the case of first degree discrimination, which is considerably simpler than that for third degree discrimination.

The curve MC indicates the firm's marginal cost curve. The curve DD shows the firm's demand curve. If first degree price discrimination is possible then the buyer of each unit will be forced to pay the maximum price he is willing to pay for that unit, so that the demand curve will also indicate the firm's marginal revenue. A profit-maximising firm will produce the level of output indicated by Q, and will charge a different price for each unit of output.

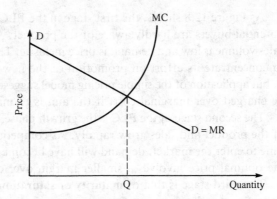

Fig. 12.7 First degree price discrimination

Pricing and the product life cycle

The product life cycle and elasticity of demand

The standard analysis of pricing embodies a static view of the demand for a product. The volume which can be sold is determined by the factors discussed in Chapter 5. Unless any of these factors change, demand is assumed to remain constant, so that time itself has no influence upon the level of demand for a product. However, marketing analysts frequently find it useful (Kotler (1984), Chapter 11) to introduce the concept of the **product life cycle** into the discussion of pricing and marketing strategies.

The product life cycle hypothesis consists essentially of the assertion that products have limited lives and that in the course of those lives they pass through a a series of distinct stages. Fig. 12.8 shows a typical product life cycle (PLC).

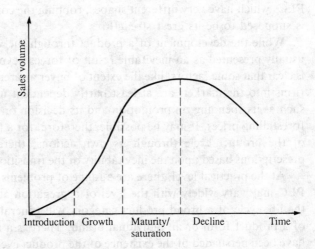

Fig. 12.8 The product life cycle

As Figure 12.8 shows, the first stage in the PLC is the **introductory period** when potential buyers are hardly aware of the product. At this stage in the product's life sales volume is low and demand is price inelastic. The marketing department is likely to concentrate its effort on promotion of the new product, rather than on pricing it, but application of the simple pricing model suggests that a substantial margin should be charged over marginal cost, if the aim is to make maximum profit.

The second stage of the PLC is the **growth phase**, when buyers become more aware of the product and sales grow rapidly. As competitors will also have had sufficient time to enter the market, demand will have become more price elastic, implying that the optimal price involves a smaller margin over costs.

The third stage is that of **maturity** or **saturation** when the growth of sales slows down, eventually to zero. Customers are well-informed about the product and experienced in its use and competitors are well-versed in the production of substitutes, leading to an increase in the elasticity of demand, and a further reduction in the optimal margin between price and marginal cost.

The fourth and final stage is that of **decline**, arising from changes in buyers' tastes or requirements, increasing competition, or technological progress. In this phase, sales volume declines, competition amongst incumbent firms is fierce and demand is highly price elastic, leading to very narrow margins between cost and price.

It is possible to identify a relatively simple relationship between the different stages of the PLC and the optimal level of price, the two being linked by the gradually increasing elasticity of demand over time. However, both the theoretical rationale and the practical usefulness of the product life cycle concept are the subject of much debate.

At the theoretical level it is possible to provide a justification of the S-shaped PLC as a logical consequence of the way in which innovations are diffused through a population of potential users (Rogers (1962)), and some empirical studies have found evidence to support the hypothesis for some product categories (Polli and Cook (1969)). On the other hand, other observers (Swan and Rink (1982)) have identified PLCs which have very different shapes, robbing the concept of the generality which is supposed to be its great strength.

While the development of a product through the various stages of the cycle is usually presented as an inevitable result of forces beyond the control of the firm it is clear that some factors, like the extent of buyer awareness or the entry of competing firms into the market, are at least partly dependent upon the firm's own actions, such as its spending on promotion and its decision on whether or not to set entry-forestalling prices. It may be possible, therefore, for a firm to alter the development of the product cycle through its own actions, thereby rendering valueless any prescriptions based upon the inevitability of the transition from one phase to another.

At the practical level, there are a range of problems. The form and timing of the PLC may vary widely with the level of aggregation at which it is applied, so that the life cycle of a broad product category will generally be much longer than that of a product form or an individual brand. There is a real danger that if managers have been persuaded of the existence of the product cycle they may act on that belief in ways which reduce the firm's profits and simultaneously confirm the managers' mistaken confidence in the usefulness of the PLC as a forecasting tool. For instance, if sales of a product have been growing for some time, believers in the PLC hypothesis will be expecting a slowdown in sales as maturity is reached, at which point they will reduce the level of promotion and advertising for the product, and probably reduce its price, on the grounds that these are the appropriate actions for a product which is in maturity and is about to decline. However, these actions in themselves may lead to the fulfilment of the prediction. Price cutting may stimulate retaliation from competitors and the reduction in promotion will erode buyer loyalty and alter buyers' perceptions of the product. As a result, a product which might have yielded healthy profits for a number of years goes into decline, not as a consequence of real changes in the environment but because the decision-makers had an inappropriate faith in the product life cycle hypothesis.

Pricing new products

Another issue in the analysis of price, which brings together aspects of the basic pricing model, the product life cycle and price discrimination, is the question of pricing new products. The best known contribution to this topic, frequently quoted in both the economic and marketing literature on pricing, is that of Dean (1950), who drew a distinction between two basic strategies for pricing new products.

The first approach is known as a **skimming strategy**. In this case the firm sets an initially high price for the product, deliberately selling it to a relatively select group of users who are prepared to pay a high price. As the product moves through its life cycle and imitation takes place, price can be gradually reduced as demand becomes more elastic until the margin between price and cost is much lower.

The alternative strategy is known as a **penetration strategy**. This involves setting a low price at the outset, in order to build a relatively large market quickly.

Various commentators, including Dean (1950) and Kotler (1984) have identified the conditions which determine the choice between the alternative strategies. Skimming is recommended when there are sufficient buyers prepared to pay a high price, when demand is price inelastic, when a high price will not attract rapid entry, and when the cost penalty for operating at relatively low volume is small. Penetration is recommended when demand is price elastic, when new firms can enter quickly if attracted by high price and when there are cost advantages to be had by operating at higher volumes of output.

It might be argued that this analysis of the choice between skimming and penetration pricing is nothing more than a naive restatement of the basic pricing model, which predicts a high price when demand is inelastic (skimming) and a low price when demand is elastic (penetration). On the other hand, the discussion of the choice between the two approaches does allow the introduction of more sophisticated considerations. In the case of skimming it is often argued that if there is great uncertainty about the level of demand and buyers are hostile to price increases then such a policy will have an additional advantage in that setting an initially high price is a safe way to test the market. If it should prove too high, the price can be lowered without incurring adverse reactions from buyers. To begin with a low price and attempt to raise it later would be more difficult.

It is also argued that when the market contains identifiable groups of buyers having different elasticities of demand a policy of skimming provides a means by which the firm can practice price discrimination over time (Phlips(1983)). If some groups of buyers are prepared to pay a higher price in order to acquire the product earlier then it will be possible to schedule prices over time so that the segments which are prepared to pay the highest prices are served first and prices are then lowered sequentially in order to bring groups of users with progressively higher elasticities into the market.

The theoretical analysis presented here appears to suggest that a policy of skimming prices has a great deal to recommend it, being consistent with the basic model of pricing, the progressive increase in the (absolute) value of elasticity of demand over the product life cycle, and the exploitation of profitable opportunities for price discrimination. Certainly there is evidence that firms in a number of industries, including pharmaceuticals (Reekie (1978)), adopt this approach. However, the conditions under which penetration pricing is to be preferred do prevail in some circumstances and the evidence does not provide universal support for the conventional view with respect to the profitability of high initial prices, followed by a programme of reductions. Dorward (1987) quotes Simon's (1979) finding for some consumer goods that price elasticities were high in the early stages of the PLC, falling in maturity and then rising again in the decline stage. Such a pattern would imply a policy of low initial prices, followed by a price rise, followed by a fall in the closing stages of the product's life. Jeuland and Dolan (1982) modelled a wide variety of different circumstances and found that optimal price paths could vary widely, from conventional skimming strategies to a policy of low initial prices followed by continuous price increases. Clearly, the choice of pricing strategy becomes a very complex matter when dynamic considerations are taken into account.

Illustration

Price elasticity and the life cycle of brands

Various authors have put forward hypotheses concerning the changes which take place in the price elasticity of demand for a product over its life cycle. This text has argued that elasticity simply rises through each of the stages. Mickwitz (1959) and Kotler (1971) suggest that elasticity increases over the first three stages (introduction, growth and maturity), but falls in the fourth (decline), while Parsons (1975) seems to argue somewhat inconsistently that elasticities decline over time, but are high in maturity.

Simon (1979) points out that throughout these analyses there is a degree of confusion on whether the life cycles in question refer to products, as implied by the term product-life cycle, or brands. In order to overcome this confusion, Simon provides an empirical analysis of the brand life cycle. The starting point lies in data for 43 brands, 28 of which were pharmaceuticals and 15 were detergents. A statistical model was then developed, having the general form:

$$q_{i,t} + A_{i,t} + B_{i,t} + C_{i,t} + U_{i,t} \qquad \text{where:}$$

$q_{i,t}$ = no. of units sold
$A_{i,t}$ = non-price effects
$B_{i,t}$ = the impact of own price on sales
$C_{i,t}$ = sales response to price differentials between brands
$U_{i,t}$ = error term

Various different equations were developed to represent each of the A, B and C effects, giving 20–25 different estimating equations. Each of these was fitted for each brand, giving a total of around 5,000 regressions to be computed. The equations which provided the best fits were then selected for interpretation. Examination of the best-fit equations revealed that the own-price term, $B_{i,t}$ was not significant for any products, but the $A_{i,t}$ terms, which represented the carryover and obsolescence effects, and the $C_{i,t}$ terms, representing competitive price effects, were well represented. Having estimated the regression equations, the actual values for prices and quantities were inserted, in order to calculate the value of elasticity and its growth rate, for each brand. This produced a number of findings.

With respect to the values of elasticity there were two major conclusions. First, as might be expected, the pharmaceutical brands exhibited much more inelastic demand than the detergents. Secondly, there was a clear pattern in the values of elasticity over the different stages of the life cycle, as shown in the diagram below.

As Fig. 12.9 shows, elasticity fell successively from introduction to growth and to maturity, but then rose again in decline.

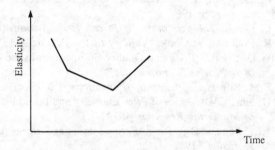

Fig. 12.9 Elasticity and the brand life cycle

The results with respect to the pattern of elasticity growth across the different life cycle stages was also highly uniform for all of the brands. During the growth stage of the life cycle elasticity decreased, while during the decline stage elasticity increased. For the maturity stage, the results were less clear, with elasticity for some brands rising and for others falling. However, although the sign of the elasticity growth rate varied from brand to brand in the maturity stage its size was uniformly smaller than in either growth or decline.

Simon's results clearly have implications for the optimal pricing strategy to be practised over the brand life cycle. If elasticity is relatively high during introduction and growth, then the optimal price mark-up in those stages is low, indicating a 'penetration' strategy for the pricing of new brands. As elasticity falls in maturity, so the mark-up should rise in that stage, falling again in decline, as elasticity rises again.

References and further reading

J.S. Bain, *Barriers to New Competition*, (Cambridge, Harvard UP, 1956)

J. Cubbin, 'Apparent Collusion and Conjectural Variations in Differentiated Oligopoly', *International Journal of Industrial Organisation*, 1983

J. Dean, 'Pricing Policies for New Products', *Harvard Business Review*, 1950

N. Dorward, *The Pricing Decision: Economic Theory and Business Practice*, (London, Harper and Row, 1987)

A. Gabor, *Pricing: Principles and Practices*, (London, Heinemann, 1977)

D.W. Gaskins, 'Dynamic Limit Pricing: Optimal Pricing Under the Threat of Entry', *Journal of Economic Theory*, 1971

A.P. Jeuland and R.J. Dolan, 'An Aspect of New Product Planning: Dynamic Pricing' in A. Zoltners (ed.) *Marketing Planning Models* (TIMS, 1982)

P. Kotler, 'Competitive Marketing Strategies for New Product Marketing over the Life Cycle', *Management Science*, **12**, December 1971

P. Kotler, *Marketing Management*, (Englewood Cliffs, Prentice-Hall, 1984)

E.J. McCarthy, *Basic Marketing: A Managerial Approach* (Homewood, Richard D. Irwin, 1960)

G. Mickwitz, *Marketing and Competition*, (Helsingfors, Centraltrykeriat, 1959)

T. Nagle, 'Economic Foundations for Pricing', *Journal of Business*, 1984

L.J. Parsons, 'The Product Life Cycle and Time-Varying Advertising Elasticities, *Journal of Marketing Research*, **12**, August 1975, pp.476–800

P. Pashigian, 'Limit Price and the Market Share of the Leading Firm', *Journal of Industrial Economics*, 1968

L. Phlips, *The Economics of Price Discrimination*, (Cambridge, Cambridge UP, 1983)

R. Polli and V. Cook, 'Validity of the Product Life Cycle', *Journal of Business*, 1969

W.D. Reekie, 'Price and Quality Competition in the United States Drug Industry', *Journal of Industrial Economics*, 1978

E.M. Rogers, *Diffusion of Innovations*, (New York, Free Press, 1962)

H. Simon, 'Dynamics of Price Elasticity and Brand Life Cycles: An Empirical Study', *Journal of Marketing Research*, 1979

J.E. Swan and D.R. Rink, 'Fitting Marketing Strategy to Varying Product Life Cycles', *Business Horizons* , 1982

P. Sylos-Labini, *Oligopoly and Technical Progress*, (Cambridge, Harvard UP, 1962)

M. Waterson, *Economic Theory of the Industry*, (Cambridge, Cambridge UP, 1984)

J.T. Wenders, 'Excess Capacity as a Barrier to Entry', *Journal of Industrial Economics*, 1971

Self-test questions

1 Which of the following are required if the simple model of the firm is to be used directly to set the price of a product?

(a) constant marginal costs
(b) constant average costs
(c) scale economies
(d) constant elasticity of demand
(e) inelastic demand

2 Set out the equation which links price to marginal

cost, market share and conjectural variation.

3 List the major sources of entry barriers and define the term 'limit-price.'

4 Set out the conditions required for price discrimination, and the difference between first and third degree discrimination.

5 List three factors which will make a 'skimming' approach to pricing the most appropriate strategy.

Exercise

Consider the issues raised when setting prices for the following products:

(a) a new, major dictionary
(b) telephone calls
(c) a garden spade

Answers on page 419.

13 Pricing practice, transfer pricing and pricing for public enterprise

This chapter builds on the theoretical analysis of earlier chapters to consider three further issues concerning the setting of prices. The first concerns the evidence on pricing in practice, the second concerns the establishment of prices for internal transfers and the third covers pricing in public, as opposed to private, enterprise.

Pricing in practice

Having outlined the major theoretical issues raised by the pricing of products for sale by the private sector, it is possible to consider the relationship between the theory of optimal pricing and the evidence on the ways in which firms take pricing decisions in practice. This is a potentially difficult area of analysis because it has already been pointed out in the section on basic rules for optimal pricing in Chapter 12 that economic analysis does not provide directly applicable practical solutions to pricing problems, but rather outlines the principles to which optimal solutions must adhere. It is not therefore to be expected that companies' pricing policies and methods correspond in any direct way to the prescriptions of the optimising models. The links between the theory and the practice have to be examined in a rather different way.

In order to examine pricing in practice this part of the chapter directs attention towards two major issues. The first can be described as **pricing objectives** and the second as **pricing methods**.

Pricing objectives

If the objective of the firm is to maximise profits then pricing may be regarded as one of the issues on which optimal decisions have to be taken in order to reach the objective set. In that case the objective of pricing is the maximisation of profit and there is little to be gained by considering the separate and independent objectives of the pricing process. Nevertheless, a number of important pieces of business research (Lanzillotti (1958), Weston (1972)) have addressed the specific question of pricing objectives and they merit brief consideration. Two questions in particular are worth exploring. The first concerns companies' perceived objectives for pricing and the second concerns the extent to which these perceived objectives are consistent with profit-maximisation as the fundamental objective.

The most common objective for pricing, referred to by approximately half of the American companies interviewed by Lanzillotti (1958) and two-thirds of British companies surveyed by Shipley (1981) was the achievement of a **target rate of return**. Clearly, if this target rate of return is equivalent to the maximum return achievable, then there is no conflict between the stated objective for pricing and the hypothesis of short-term profit-maximisation. Alternatively, if the target rate of return is less than the maximum achievable, but is set at a level designed to deter entry into the industry, then the establishment of the target return as a pricing objective could be seen as an aspect of long-term profit-maximisation, taking account of the threat of entry. It could be argued, then, that there is no conflict between the establishment of a target rate of return as an objective for pricing and the assumption that the firm's basic aim is to maximise profits. However, as is shown by Dorward (1987) and outlined below if a target return is used as the basis for a pricing method, rather than as a statement of the pricing objective, the results may be in conflict with profit-maximisation.

While target rates of return, or other profit related objectives, are commonly cited as the most important objectives for pricing, the research suggests three other aims towards which pricing policies are directed.

The first is the achievement of a **target market share**. Whether or not this is consistent with profit-maximisation clearly depends upon the particular target which is set. Firms may seek larger market shares than are consistent with maximum profits, for the 'managerial' reasons which have been outlined in Chapter 3, or they may set a market share target which is consistent with maximum profit, using it as a managerial tool to assist with the achievement of the more fundamental objective.

The second alternative pricing objective is the **stabilisation of output and price**. Some firms attempt to set price with the aim of maintaining full order books, in order to avoid expensive fluctuations in output and painful changes in the size of the work-force. For instance, Harrison and Wilkes (1973) found that maintenance of production was a major objective for Jaguar when pricing the XJ12. If fluctuations in output or price are expensive to manage or deter buyers then clearly their avoidance is compatible with long-run profit-maximisation. On the other hand there must be a suspicion that the fundamental reasons for desiring stability have their basis in managers' desire for a quiet life, rather than in serving the shareholders.

The third objective for pricing, which is often referred to in the textbooks, consists of **meeting** or **matching the competition**. Whether or not this can legitimately be described as an objective for pricing is open to question. It is perhaps better to see it as a description of a method of setting a price. However, if all firms in an industry set prices by matching the competition the logic of price setting is confusing and circular as each firm sets price with reference to that set by the others which in turn are set with reference to that set by others, and so on. Such a situation could only be resolved if either prices are set by market forces, as in perfect competition, or prices are set by a price leader, who is followed by the others.

Pricing methods I: the prevalence of cost-plus pricing

Having considered the question of pricing objectives, it is possible to examine the procedures which firms actually use to set prices and to consider the links between these methods and the economic models of optimal pricing.

By far the most common pricing method adopted in practice is to calculate the average direct cost of production for a product and then to add a margin for overheads and a further margin for profits, thereby arriving at a **full-cost-plus price**. This procedure was first brought to the attention of academic economists by a group of researchers at Oxford, reported by Hall and Hitch (1939) and that finding has since been confirmed by most other studies of pricing practice (Skinner (1970), Atkin and Skinner(1975), Govindarajan and Anthony (1983)).

Pricing on a cost-plus basis does not correspond directly to price setting as described in the standard profit-maximising model and some of the economists who first drew attention to the prevalence of cost-plus pricing, including Hall and Hitch (1939), Andrews (1949) and Barback (1964) fell into the trap of believing that because firms did not explicitly adopt marginal cost and marginal revenue methods the marginalist models had necessarily failed in their purpose. However, that conclusion was erroneous, for a number of reasons.

In the first place, it should be remembered that it is not the purpose of the economic model to provide either descriptions of real firms or simple prescriptions for setting prices. The model simply shows the conditions which must hold if firms have set profit-maximising prices. They are intended to predict those prices, not to show how they were arrived at. There is no reason to suppose, therefore, that a description of price setting procedures in firms will show price setters referring to marginal costs and marginal revenues. It is perfectly possible for firms to arrive at profit-maximising prices through procedures which they describe as cost-plus.

This point can be seen most clearly in a simple example which allows the reconciliation of the two different approaches. The profit maximising condition may be written in the following form:

$$\frac{P - MC}{P} = \frac{1}{E_d}$$

which is simply rewritten as:

$$P = MC \left(\frac{E_d}{E_d - 1} \right)$$

If average variable cost (AVC) is constant then it equals marginal cost (MC) and the equation can be rewritten:

$$P = AVC \left(\frac{E_d}{E_d - 1} \right)$$

As the value of elasticity of demand must exceed one, the expression in brackets also exceeds one, and may be interpreted as a mark-up. For instance, if elasticity has a value of three, the price (P) will equal 150 per cent of the AVC. Provided that elasticity of demand is constant, adding a mark-up of 50 per cent to average variable cost will give the profit-maximising price.

This example has restricted validity because it can only be applied in the very simple case when both AVC and E_d are constant. Nevertheless, it provides a formal demonstration that cost-plus procedures can in principle lead to profit-maximising prices. While the relationship between the two is rarely so simple, a closer examination of the details of cost-based pricing procedures shows quite clearly that many of the important influences identified in the theoretical model of pricing do in fact have an influence on the prices set by firms, even when the process is described as simple 'cost-plus'.

The method of cost-plus pricing involves two basic steps. The first is to identify the *unit cost* which is to form the basis of the pricing calculation and the second is to identify the *margin* which is to be added to that cost figure in order to determine the price.

At first sight both the cost and the margin appear to be objective factors, easily subject to mechanical calculation. However, closer examination makes it clear that this is not in fact the case. The estimation of cost per unit for an individual product depends very heavily on the accounting procedures which are used to allocate overhead costs across the different products produced. Cost per unit also depends upon the level of output being produced, which introduces a problem of **circularity**. If the level of cost is sensitive to the level of output then a firm needs to know the level of output it is likely to produce before it can calculate the cost per unit, on which to base the price. On the other hand, the level of output which it can sell depends upon the price. In this case the firm needs to know the price it intends to charge, in order to know the level of output it will produce, in order to calculate the cost, in order to set the price! Clearly, if the firm is to set price on the basis of cost per unit it will have to make its own series of assumptions about costs, which introduces a good deal of flexibility into the apparently objective measure of unit cost. In fact the evidence on cost-plus pricing suggests that firms allow the measure of cost which they use to be adjusted in the light of market forces, in ways which suggest that the resulting prices may be perfectly consistent with those predicted by the marginalist analysis. When defining cost for pricing purposes, firms usually rely upon the accounting concept of **standard costs**, which involves assuming some 'normal' level of output and then applying standard budgeted labour and materials costs per unit of output, augmented by an allocation of overheads to each product. This process involves a good deal of informal discussion within the firm, which provides plenty of opportunity for firms to take market conditions into account, as Edwards (1952) found. When Fog (1960) investigated pricing in Danish industry he found that firms nearly always described cost-based procedures, but that demand-side influences crept into the estimation of costs. In the case of one firm, for instance, cost per unit was calculated on the assumption that the firm would be operating at full capacity when no-one expected that to be the case, and actual costs were expected to be substantially higher. When questioned on why it adopted this apparently very odd procedure, the firm replied 'for competitive reasons.' In other words, it was recognised that the price which would be arrived at by using actual costs would be higher than the market would bear, so the firm adjusted its estimate of costs downwards in order to arrive at a price which was consistent with market conditions. One observer (Smyth (1967)) has suggested that instead of referring to 'cost-plus pricing' methods it would be more accurate to label them a 'price-minus theory of cost'.

Similar considerations apply to the size of the margin which is added to the unit cost figure in order to arrive at a price. The early studies which 'discovered' the phenomenon of full-cost pricing noted that firms made a '. . . conventional addition (frequently ten per cent) . . .' (Hall and Hitch, p.19) to the cost figure, in order to arrive at the final price. However, the evidence also shows that such a figure is by no means standard across industries, and that firms adjust the size of the margin in the light of the demand conditions and the competition facing them.

If firms simply calculated a figure for cost per unit, using some objective method of measurement, and then added a pre-determined margin, it could be said that prices are entirely cost-based and the marginalist model would only predict pricing behaviour with any accuracy when elasticity of demand and average cost are constant, and the margin is related to elasticity as shown in the example above. In other cases, such a procedure would lead to the setting of sub-optimal prices. There are undoubtedly cases where this occurs and firms lose profits as a result, as witness Jaguar's pricing policy in the 1970s (Harrison and Wilkes (1973)). However, such behaviour is inconsistent with the drive for profits and the balance of the evidence shows that most firms use a full-cost-plus figure as a benchmark in the pricing process but allow this figure to be adjusted in the light of market conditions, and the advice of the marketing department, in order to reach a final result which better serves to meet the firm's objectives. Much of the evidence also suggests that firms regard price as only one aspect of the marketing mix, whose determination cannot sensibly be separated from the determination of product quality, advertising, packaging, promotion, service and product development.

Pricing methods II: other approaches to pricing

In addition to the full-cost-plus approach to pricing, managerial economists have identified a number of other approaches which merit a brief outline.

The first of these is **target return pricing**, which can be linked to the pursuit of a target rate of return on capital as a pricing objective. In order to link the target rate of return and the price a firm first calculates the total profit required, which is given by the simple formula:

Required profit = aK   where:

a = target rate of return

K = capital employed

The margin to be charged over unit cost can then be arrived at by dividing the total profit required by the expected, or budgeted, level of output, to give:

$$m = \frac{aK}{Q^b}$$

where:

m = the margin

Q^b = budgeted level of output

Firms which use this approach are reported to do so because they wish to take a long-run view of pricing and because they wish to prevent short-term cyclical influences from leading to erratic price changes (Lanzillotti (1958)). As a result, it can be shown to be inconsistent with short-run profit-maximisation (Dorward (1987)). Nor is it necessarily of assistance in maximising long-run profits because the target rate of return which is aimed for and used in the pricing calculation is usually an accounting rate of return, not a true economic rate which would reflect the time-value of money.

Another approach to pricing, which has also been referred to briefly above in the section on pricing objectives, is **going rate** or **market-determined** or **competition-oriented** pricing. In its simplest form this is the type of pricing policy which is imposed by market forces on firms operating in a perfectly competitive industry. Each firm is obliged to charge the same price as the others, or lose all of its customers. In more complex situations a firm may not simply set exactly the same price as its competitors, but may use their prices as a 'benchmark' against which it adjusts its own price to take account of differences between them. For instance, a firm which is producing a high cost/high quality variant of the product will set its price above that of the competition, while a firm aiming for cost leadership may set it lower. A firm attempting to enter a new market may set its price lower than that of rivals in order to overcome existing brand loyalties and build a large enough volume of sales to allow economies of scale and capacity utilisation to be achieved.

In so far as competition oriented pricing takes proper account of rivals' prices and their impact on the demand conditions facing the individual firm then it potentially offers a means of securing maximum profit. Whether it actually does so or not depends upon the firm's ability to judge the appropriate differences between its own price and that of the competition. In the case of perfect competition this judgment is simple as the difference must equal zero. In other market conditions it may be more difficult, especially in oligopoly where a firm's rivals will react to its price setting. One situation where this problem may be resolved is that of price leadership, discussed in Chapter 9. If one firm in an oligopolistic industry acts as a price leader, followers may respond by setting the same price, or one which has been adjusted in a way which is mutually understood by all, so that the rivals know how each other will react, thereby creating an 'orderly' form of competition.

A final approach to pricing which merits attention is the process of **competitive tendering** or **sealed bid pricing**. In this situation, which is commonly associated with government purchases of large quantities of goods or services, or with major construction projects, the purchaser advertises the specification which it wishes to meet and invites potential suppliers to submit the prices at which they are prepared to supply to that specification. Bids are made in confidence (hence 'sealed bids') in order to avoid collusion and the firm which offers to meet the specification at the lowest price is awarded the contract, provided the purchaser is satisfied that the supplier will be able to deliver on time and to a satisfactory quality.

Firms attempting to set a price at which to bid for a competitive tender face a number of difficult problems. In the first place, if their own costs depend upon the **degree of capacity utilisation**, they will have to make some assumption about the level of orders they will be meeting at the time when they will be fulfilling the tender contract, in order to estimate the cost of fulfilling the contract. If they fear that they will have idle capacity they will be willing to tender at a relatively low price, because the marginal cost of meeting the order will be low and it would be profitable to accept business at a relatively low price. However, if this expectation turns out to be false, and the firm finds that it has no spare capacity with which to fulfil the order, meeting the contract may involve incurring higher costs than revenues. On the other hand, the firm could have the opposite problem. It could fear that meeting the order will be expensive, as it expects its capacity to be fully utilised, in which case it would offer to fulfil the contract at a relatively high price and then find that it fails to secure the order and has under-used capacity. Clearly this is only a problem if costs are sensitive to the degree of capacity utilisation, but that is almost always going to be the case. For very large and long-term orders the problem may be resolved by including the cost of the production capacity in the price which is bid, but that will not be possible for smaller contracts.

The other major problem concerns the behaviour of competing companies and the prices at which they are likely to bid. If rivals have very similar cost structures then each firm will be well-informed about the minimum price at which others will be prepared to bid, but does not know where the actual bid is likely to be placed. In order to secure a high probability of winning a contract firms may offer to meet the specification at a price which is very close to the incremental cost of production. As this incentive applies to them all, the prices which are offered and accepted will tend to be very low (which is, after all, the purchaser's objective). This effect may be tempered by the purchaser's fear that suppliers may go bankrupt if they offer prices which are too low, but there is clearly an incentive for suppliers in this situation to collude with each other in order to ensure that prices are fixed at higher levels than would otherwise be the case.

If collusion is ruled out, the major problem facing a firm which is bidding for a competitive tender lies in taking account of the likely behaviour of its competitors. If their identity is unknown, or there is little information about their bidding behaviour, there is very little that can be done. However, if there is an established record of competitors' bids for a large number of previous contracts it is possible to use this information to adopt a rational strategy towards bidding. The starting point is to assume that a competitor faces roughly the same costs in meeting a contract as the firm which is developing a strategy. In that case the competitor's previous bids can be expressed as a percentage of costs, and a frequency distribution can be set out, showing how the competitor has bid on those previous occasions. Fig. 13.1 gives an example.

Competitor's price as % of cost (C)	Relative frequency
.75C	.20
1.00C	.20
1.25C	.50
1.50C	.10

Fig. 13.1 Frequency distribution

The firm attempting to construct a bid can then identify a number of possible prices at which it may bid and construct a pay-off matrix showing the pay-offs for each bid, given the price at which its competitor has bid. Fig. 13.2 shows such a matrix for an example where the bidding firm considers five possible prices, ranging from 70 per cent of cost to 150 per cent of cost.

Firm's bid	Competitor's bid			
	.75C (Pr = .2)	1.00C (Pr = .2)	1.25C (Pr = .5)	1.50C (Pr = .1)
.70C	− .3C	− .3C	− .3C	− .3C
.90C	0	− .1C	− .1C	− .1C
1.10C	0	0	+ .1C	+ .1C
1.30C	0	0	0	+ .3C
1.50C	0	0	0	+ .5C

Fig. 13.2 Pay-off matrix
Source: J.H. Wilson and S.G. Darr *Managerial Economics*, (New York, Harper and Row, 1979) p.322.

As the figure shows, it is assumed that the firm which tenders the lowest bid will secure the contract. For each different price which might be bid an expected monetary value can be calculated, as explained in Chapter 4, and the bid price which yields the highest expected value can be chosen. In the example given, this yields a bid price equal to 110 per cent of cost, which leads to an expected profit of .06C.

This technique can be adjusted in a number of ways, to take account of additional information. For instance, if the competitor is known to be operating at full capacity then he is less likely to submit a low bid, and the probabilities can be adjusted accordingly. If the competitor is known to have a large amount of spare capacity the probabilities can be adjusted in the opposite direction as he is more likely to be prepared to submit a low bid.

The example given here is a very simple one, with a single competitor, who is not aware of the technique being used to construct a bid. If there are multiple competitors the situation becomes more difficult and it becomes even more complex if the competitor comes to realise that there is a pattern in the bids being made. In that case the competitor may use his knowledge of the bidding pattern to amend his own bids in which case the situation becomes a game between interdependent players which may be best modelled through the techniques of game theory.

Transfer pricing

The prices discussed thus far have been those which the firm sets for transactions between itself and its customers. However, in an era of large multi-divisional firms prices may also need to be set for transactions which take place between one part of the firm and another. These are known as **transfer prices**.

If a firm wishes each of its divisions to behave autonomously, choosing its own level of output and maximising its own profits, and yet still achieve maximum profits for the firm as a whole, the question of transfer prices becomes an important one. There are a number of different cases which need to be considered.

Transfer pricing in the absence of an external market

The first case which can be considered concerns the situation where a firm has two divisions, manufacturing and distribution. The manufacturing division produces an intermediate product which is sold to the distribution division, and for which there is no external market. In this case the amount which the manufacturing division chooses to produce and sell internally must equal the amount sold externally by the distribution division, and that amount must equal the profit-maximising level of output for the firm as a whole. The analysis can be seen graphically in Fig. 13.3.

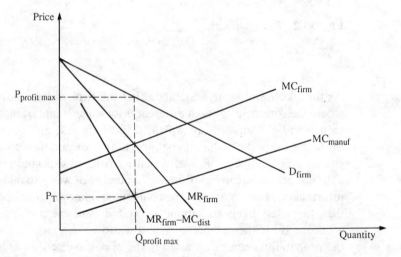

Fig. 13.3 Transfer pricing in the absence of an external market

In Fig. 13.3, the curves marked MC_{firm} and MR_{firm} show the marginal revenue and marginal cost for the firm as a whole. The profit-maximising level of output is given by $Q_{profit-max}$ and the price to be set for external sales is $P_{profit-max}$.

If the firm is composed of two different divisions, manufacturing and distribution, it is necessary to identify the cost and revenue conditions facing each of those divisions. For the distribution division, revenue conditions are given by the revenue conditions for the firm as a whole. Its costs are given by the costs of distribution plus the cost of purchasing the intermediate product from the manufacturing division. For the manufacturing division, costs are equal to the costs of manufacturing and revenues are given by the transfer price at which it sells to the distribution division, multiplied by the number of units which yield it maximum profit.

The appropriate transfer price can be found by first considering the net marginal revenue curve for the distribution division, shown on the diagram as $(MR_{firm} - MC_{dist})$. This is arrived at by taking the marginal revenue to the firm as a whole and subtracting the marginal cost of distribution. For each marginal unit this gives the net marginal contribution to the distribution division, before taking account of the cost of purchasing units from the manufacturing division.

The next step is to identify the marginal cost of manufacturing, which is equal to the difference between the marginal cost to the firm as a whole and the marginal cost of distribution, given in the diagram as MC_{manuf}. As the diagram shows, this must intersect the net marginal revenue for distribution curve at the profit-maximising level of output. This must be so because at that level of output:

$$MC_{firm} = MR_{firm}$$

and subtracting MC_{dist} from both sides gives:

$$MC_{firm} - MC_{dist} = MC_{manuf} = MR_{firm} - MC_{dist}$$

It can now be seen that if the manufacturing division is to choose to supply level of output $Q_{profit-max}$, the transfer price will have to be set at P_T. That price represents the marginal revenue for the manufacturing division, which will maximise its own profit by equating that to its own marginal cost, at level of output $Q_{profit-max}$.

In a similar way the distribution division will choose to purchase quantity $Q_{profit-max}$ from the manufacturing division because, in order to make maximum profit it will wish to distribute every unit of output for which the net marginal contribution, given by $(MR_{firm} - MC_{dist})$ exceeds the cost of purchasing the unit from manufacturing. In other words, the curve $(MR_{firm} - MC_{dist})$ is essentially the distribution division's demand curve.

To summarise the analysis in this case, if there is no external market for the intermediate product, the optimal transfer price is equal to the marginal cost of manufacturing the intermediate product, at the level of output which maximises the firm's overall profit. If central management sets the transfer price at this level it can then simply order each division to maximise its own profit and the result will be consistent with profit-maximisation for the firm as a whole. Alternatively, instead of actually setting that price, central management could provide the divisions with information about each other's situation which would lead to that price being arrived at without central intervention. If the distribution division is informed of the manufacturing division's marginal cost curve and told that this represents the supply function which determines the amount which manufacturing will supply to distribution at each price, distribution will choose to offer the transfer price P_T, which will induce manufacturing to produce just the correct amount. In a similar way, central management could provide the manufacturing division with information on the distribution division's net marginal contribution curve and order it to treat that as its own marginal revenue curve when deciding how much to supply.

Transfer pricing in the presence of a perfect market for the intermediate product

The second case to be covered in the analysis of transfer pricing is where the intermediate product may be bought or sold in a perfect market. In this case, examined by Hirschleifer (1956), the quantities supplied by the manufacturing division need not equal those required by the distribution division and the analysis can be explained with the help of Fig. 13.4.

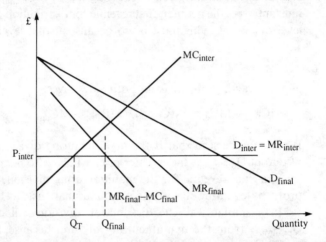

Fig. 13.4 Transfer pricing with a perfectly competitive external market for the intermediate

The starting point lies in the demand and marginal revenue curves for the final product, shown by the sloping curves marked D_{final} and MR_{final}, and the horizontal demand curve for the intermediate product, shown by D_{inter}, which also represents the marginal revenue for the intermediate, indicated by MR_{inter}. The analysis also requires information on the marginal cost of producing the intermediate product, labelled MC_{inter}, and the marginal contribution made by units of the final product, before making payment for the transferred intermediate product. This curve is labelled $MR_{final} - MC_{final}$.

For the department producing the intermediate product, profits will be maximised at level of output Q_T, where the marginal cost of producing the intermediate product is equal to its marginal revenue. However, for the department selling the final good profits are maximised at level of output Q_{final} where the marginal cost of purchasing the intermediate product is just equal to the marginal contribution earned by units of the final product.

As Fig. 13.4 shows, the division selling the final product requires more of the intermediate product than will be produced within the firm. However, that poses no difficulty as the difference can be made up by purchases on the open market. If the firm itself were to supply all of the intermediate product needed profits would fall as the cost of supplying the additional units of the intermediate product beyond Q_T is higher than the cost of purchasing them on the open market. Similar considerations apply if the division producing the intermediate product should wish to produce more than is required by the final product division. In that case the excess internal supply would simply be sold on the open market.

More complex issues in transfer pricing

The analyses set out above have considered two simple transfer pricing situations and identified two simple rules. If there is a perfect market for the intermediate product, the transfer price should equal the market price. If there is no such external market the transfer price should be equal to the marginal cost of producing the intermediate product, at the profit-maximising level of output.

Unfortunately these cases are much too simple to be of very general application, and a full treatment of the complex cases lies beyond the scope of this text. A number of complications are worth noting. First, there may be an external market for the intermediate, but it may be imperfect, a situation examined by Hirschleifer (1956). Secondly, there may be differences in the cost and the degree of risk associated with transactions carried out internally and those carried out between independent firms (Gould (1964)). Thirdly, there may be many different divisions competing for the use of the intermediate product and finally there may be interdependencies between the costs and the demand for the intermediate and the final product. If all of these complicating factors occur together it becomes extremely difficult even in theory to identify the appropriate transfer price. As firms rarely have the kind of cost and demand information which would be required to calculate optimal transfer prices in such situations it is hardly surprising that the evidence on transfer pricing in practice suggests that external market prices are used wherever possible (Emmanuel (1976), Vancil (1979)) and where there is no external market for an intermediate most firms use some form of simple cost-plus formula for the setting of such prices (Hague (1971)). This latter practice can lead to inefficiencies in the supplying division which is able to pass excessive costs on to 'downstream' users, unless some form of standard cost is used in the calculation, rather than costs actually incurred.

Pricing in public enterprises

The marginal cost pricing rule

The basic assumption which has been maintained throughout the analysis of this chapter is that the aim of price setting is to maximise profits. However, in the case of publicly owned firms this is not always appropriate as public enterprises often have a different set of objectives. In so far as these are frequently complex and sometimes confused (Rees (1976)), it can be difficult to analyse appropriate pricing policies for such firms. Nevertheless, it is possible to proceed with the economic analysis of public sector pricing by assuming that the basic objective of such organisations is to be **economically efficient** or to **maximise social welfare**.

It has been shown in Chapter 9, in the analysis of perfect competition, that a perfectly competitive industry will automatically be economically efficient because market forces ensure that price is equal to marginal cost, which is the basic requirement for welfare maximisation. This provides the starting point for the economic analysis of public sector pricing which simply states that price should be set equal to marginal cost (Webb (1976). That proposition in turn raises a number of other issues which merit brief consideration.

Pricing at short or long-run marginal cost?

One of the questions which is raised with respect to public sector pricing concerns the choice between short-run and long-run marginal cost as the basis for setting the optimal price. In fact, this problem disappears if the firm is utilising the correct set of plant and equipment for the level of output which it is producing, for in that case short-run and long-run marginal cost will be the same. This can be seen with reference to Fig. 13.5.

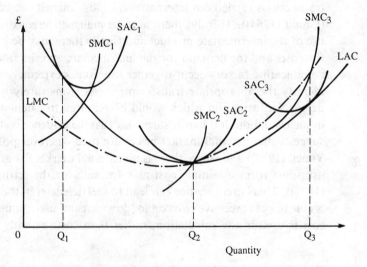

Fig. 13.5 Long- and short-run marginal costs

As Fig. 13.5 shows, for three different sets of capacity, at each level of output where the short-run average cost curve just touches the long-run cost curve (Q_1, Q_2, and Q_3) both short-run and long-run average costs and short-run and long-run marginal costs are equal to each other. It is easy to see that the average costs are equal but some brief mathematical analysis may be needed to understand why the marginals are also equal. Short-run marginal cost at output Q_1 is given by the equation:

$$SMD = \frac{dTC}{dQ} = \frac{d(SAC_1 . Q_1)}{dQ}$$

Long-run marginal cost is given by:

$$LMC = \frac{dTC}{dQ} = \frac{d(LAC . Q_1)}{dQ}$$

As SAC_1 is equal to LAC at output Q_1 and Q_1 is common to both equations, it follows that LMC = SMC at that level of output. To put it more crudely, at level of output Q_1, Q_2, or Q_3, total cost is the same in the short run and the long run, average costs are the same and the slope of the average cost curve is the same. As a result short- and long-run marginal costs must be equal. Provided the firm is utilising the lowest cost set of plant and equipment for the level of output there is no need to decide between short- and long-run marginal cost in order to set the price.

Marginal cost pricing and financial surpluses or deficits

It should be noted that the adoption of the marginal cost pricing rule has implications for the financial position of the enterprise. If average costs are falling, as at level of output Q_1 in Fig. 13.5, then marginal costs must be below average costs and setting marginal cost prices will necessarily involve incurring a financial deficit. On the other hand, if average costs are rising, as at Q_3, setting a price equal to marginal cost will imply making a surplus. Only if average cost is equal to marginal cost (at Q_2 where the average cost curve has a slope of zero) will the firm break-even exactly. In practice it is highly likely that public enterprises will have downward sloping long-run cost curves, if only because one of the most common reasons for locating firms in the public sector is the danger of monopoly power where there are substantial scale economies. As a result, it is to be expected that the adoption of the marginal cost pricing rule would lead to substantial financial deficits in many nationalised industries, (Webb (1976), Rees (1976)).

Various solutions may be offered to this problem. The classic theoretical prescription is for government to cover the deficit by imposing lump-sum taxes (Hotelling (1938)). As these do not affect the marginal conditions for consumers or firms they will leave economic behaviour unchanged and will therefore not introduce any distortions into the economy's price mechanism.

If lump-sum taxes (like a poll tax, for instance) are not feasible then some other solution to the deficit must be found. One of the most useful is the device of the **two-part tariff**. In this case the price which a buyer is charged is made up of two components. The first is a price which is set equal to marginal cost, so that consumers taking decisions at the margin are comparing the benefit they receive from an additional unit of the commodity with the additional cost of that unit. The second part of the tariff is a lump-sum per period, paid by all consumers of the good, which corresponds quite closely to the lump-sum tax.

Whichever method is adopted to cover public enterprise deficits attributable to marginal cost pricing there are associated difficulties, either with maintaining undistorted marginal conditions, or with non-economic considerations such as equity, or fairness. There is also the managerial difficulty that if a public enterprise is implicitly ordered to make losses it may do so not because of the marginal cost pricing but because of general X-inefficiency and the two different causes of the losses may be difficult to disentangle in practice.

Second-best considerations

A third, and potentially very complex, issue which is raised in respect of marginal cost pricing concerns the question of '**second-best**'. It has been shown above that economic efficiency requires that prices be set equal to marginal cost. An economy is said to be at a '**first-best**' optimum when all prices in all industries are equal to marginal cost. This would be the case if every industry were either perfectly competitive or a public enterprise following a policy of marginal cost pricing. However, it may be the case that in some industries there is a degree of monopoly power so that prices exceed marginal cost and it may be impossible to force them down to the marginal cost level. In this case, the 'first-best' will be unattainable and the important question becomes 'what is the second-best optimum?', i.e. the best position actually achievable. This is a question to which the theoretical answer is rather depressing, because it is simply not possible to identify the precise nature of the second-best solution. What is even more depressing is that theoretical analysis does show that if one of the conditions needed for the first best optimum is not achieved, then the others may no longer be desirable and might even be counter-productive. In other words, if marginal cost pricing cannot be achieved in every industry, there may be no benefit in achieving it in any!

This last point can be made more clear with an example. If every industry in the economy practised marginal cost pricing except the coal industry, which charged higher prices, the result would be an allocation of resources in which too little coal was produced, relative to the optimum. This would divert demand towards substitutes for coal, like gas, and as a result too much gas would be produced relative to the optimum. In this case the appropriate action could be for the gas industry to 'lean against the distortion' by also charging prices above marginal cost, thereby invalidating the rule that prices should equal marginal costs.

There are two potential solutions to the second-best problem. The first would be to build a complete and detailed general equilibrium model of the economy, which would identify all inter-connections between all activities in the economy, thereby allowing the model to be 'solved' in a way which would identify the necessary prices for everything. Clearly, that is quite impossible to achieve. The alternative is to adopt a piecemeal approach, applying the marginal cost pricing rule as a starting point and then making adjustments to compensate for the most obvious and significant distortions. This approach is at least operational, although serious doubts must remain concerning the soundness of its rationale. The final conclusion with respect to public sector pricing, then, has to be that there are no entirely satisfactory solutions. This difficulty provides one aspect of the rationale for the 'privatisation' of public utilities, examined in more detail in Chapter 17.

Illustration

Accountants misunderstand economists: interpreting evidence on the use of cost data in price decisions

Economists and management accountants both deal with the links between costs and price, but they approach the issue from different perspectives and often fail to adequately understand each other's position. A good example of this misunderstanding, accompanied by some very useful data on costs and prices is to be found in a paper by Govindajaran and Anthony (1983), referred to below as G−A.

G−A begin by declaring that economists and their courses disseminate two 'myths'. The first is that allocated costs are irrelevant to pricing decisions, and the second is that historical costs are irrelevant. According to G−A, economists advocate variable-cost-pricing, which ignores fixed costs, allocated costs and full-costs. In order to 'prove' that the economists are wrong, G−A carried out a survey of the 'Fortune ''1000'' ' companies, designed to identify whether these firms used variable cost pricing, as advocated by the economists, or full-cost pricing. Out of 505 respondents only 84 (17 per cent) used variable costs as the basis for pricing, while the other 83 per cent used some version of full-costs. G−A explain that managers use full-cost pricing because: 'the profit-maximising model cannot be applied in most real-world situations.' This, they claim, is because managers do not have perfect information, particularly with respect to the demand-curve. Price is but one element in the marketing mix, and in any event some decisions which would increase profit are considered unethical by managers who would not take unethical decisions(!). In order to further support their claim that economists adhere to a set of myths, G−A go on to examine the use of historical cost versus replacement cost, finding that the vast majority of managers use historical cost depreciation instead of the replacement cost recommended by economists.

Taking these two pieces of survey evidence together G−A suggest that their results 'will make many economists uncomfortable' and claim that at least one of their economist colleagues was 'somewhat shaken by the results of the survey.' They even go so far as to claim that: 'the results of our survey unequivocally destroy the two myths'.

Such a claim is entirely unfounded, revealing substantial ignorance of the nature and purpose of economic theory, and of the links between theory and evidence. Ever since the findings of the Oxford group in 1938, it has been well known amongst economists that managers do not set prices in the way which is described by the simple profit-maximising model. The G−A survey results are not in the least bit surprising to economists. Indeed, they simply (but usefully) replicate results which are well known. The fact that managers do not describe their price-setting behaviour in terms which directly mirror the profit-maximising model does not mean that the profit-maximising model is a 'bad model' or that the concepts associated with it have no value. The purpose of the model is not to describe how managers behave, but to identify the characteristics of the optimal price when profit is the objective, and to make predictions about the level of price and how it will respond to changes in the environment. For instance, the profit-maximising model, which G–A claim to have destroyed, predicts that when demand for a product rises, its price will rise. That prediction is constantly being validated by the behaviour of prices in practice, and yet it is absolutely inconsistent with G–A's finding that prices are set on a full-cost-plus basis. If the G–A survey really showed how prices are set in American industry it would imply that US companies completely ignore the market environment in which they operate, using costs as the sole basis for pricing. In fact we know from other evidence that firms are not usually so short-sighted as to set prices with sole reference to costs. Although they use a figure for full-cost or standard cost as a rough bench-mark, their calculation of that cost, and the margin which is added in order to arrive at a price, is sensitive to market conditions in a way which allows them to at least approximate the profit-maximising model. If competition is intense, and customers are thin on the ground, firms often reduce their prices. If the firm has a strong market position and customers who are able and willing to pay, prices will be higher, independent of cost. The economists' model is a much better 'real-world' predictor of prices and their changes than a naive accountants' model which imagines that prices are set through the use of mechanical cost-plus pricing rules which completely ignore the existence of both customers and competition! G–A need to think again about the real implications of their evidence.

References and further reading

P.W.S. Andrews, *Manufacturing Business*, (London, Macmillan, 1949)

B. Atkin and R. Skinner, *How British Industry Prices*, (London, Industrial Market Research Ltd., 1975)

R.H. Barback, *The Pricing of Manufactures*, (London, Macmillan, 1964)

N.M. Dorward, *The Pricing Decision: Economic Theory and Business Practice*, (London, Harper and Row, 1987)

R.S. Edwards, 'The Pricing of Manufactured Products', *Economica*, 1952

C.R. Emmanuel, *Transfer Pricing in the Corporate Environment*, PhD thesis, University of Lancaster, 1976

B. Fog, *Industrial Pricing Policies*, (Amsterdam, North-Holland, 1960)

J.R. Gould, 'Internal Pricing in Firms When There Are Costs of Using an Outside Market', *Journal of Business*, 1964

V. Govindarajan and R.N. Anthony, 'How Firms Use Cost Data in Price Decisions', *Management Accounting USA*, 1983

D.C. Hague, *Pricing in Business*, (London, George Allen and Unwin, 1971)

R.L. Hall and C.J. Hitch, 'Price Theory and Business Behaviour', *Oxford Economic Papers*, 1939

R. Harrison and F.M. Wilkes, 'A Note on Jaguar's Pricing Policy', *European Journal of Marketing*, 1973

J. Hirschleifer, 'On the Economics of Transfer Pricing', *Journal of Business*, 1956

H. Hotelling, 'The General Welfare in Relation to Problems of Taxation and of Railway and Utility Rates', *Econometrica*, 1938

R.F. Lanzillotti, 'Pricing Objectives in Large Companies', *American Economic Review*, 1958

R. Rees, *Public Enterprise Economics*, (London, Weidenfeld and Nicolson, 1976)

R.C. Skinner, 'The Determination of Selling Prices', *Journal of Industrial Economics*, 1970

R. Smyth, 'A Price-Minus Theory of Cost', *Scottish Journal of Political Economy*, 1967

R.F. Vancil, *Decentralisation: Ambiguity by Design*, (New York, Irwin, 1979)

M.G. Webb, *Pricing Policies for Public Enterprises*, (London, Macmillan, 1976)

J.F. Weston, 'Pricing Behaviour of Large Firms', *Western Economic Journal*, 1972

J.H. Wilson and S.G. Darr, *Managerial Economics*, (New York, Harper and Row, 1979)

Self-test questions

1 Which of the following statements is true and which is false in the light of the evidence on cost-plus pricing?

(a) prices are set with sole reference to costs
(b) the figure for cost is the actual cost incurred
(c) margins are calculated with reference to industry norms
(d) demand side factors influence the calculation of cost

2 Hall and Hitch argued that their evidence on pricing showed that the standard model of the firm was inappropriate. Was this because:

(a) firms made no reference to marginal cost and revenue
(b) firms did not see profit as their objective

(c) firms did not have perfect information as assumed in the standard model

3 Draw a diagram showing the optimal transfer price between a manufacturing division and a distribution division where there is no market for the intermediate product.

4 In which of the following situations will marginal cost pricing not lead to a financial deficit.

(a) economies of scale
(b) constant returns to scale
(c) diseconomies of scale

5 Write one sentence explaining why the theory of second-best is potentially so destructive of the case for marginal cost pricing?

Exercise

Explain why the evidence on cost-plus pricing was first felt to cast doubt on the value of the economic model of the firm and then to support it.

Answers on page 421.

14 Non-price competition and the marketing mix

This chapter is concerned with the analysis of non-price decisions. It begins by outlining the components of the 'marketing mix', and goes on to examine each in turn. Attention is paid to the level of advertising and promotional expenditures, to decisions concerning products, and to the choice of marketing channels. The chapter also considers the location of production and the role of research and development spending as aspects of a firm's competitive strategy.

The marketing mix

Economic analysis and the marketing mix

The 'marketing mix' has been defined by McCarthy (1960) as the 'four Ps'. These are;

- Price – including policy and practice with respect to discounts, allowances, payment periods and credit terms.
- Product – the attributes of the goods or services offered to buyers, including the range of products and their quality, brand names, packaging, service agreements and warranties.
- Promotion – advertising, publicity, sales promotion and personal selling.
- Place – the location in which the firm's products are offered to potential buyers and the marketing channels through which they reach that location.

The economic analysis of the firm pays some attention to each of these issues, though not at the level of detail which would be required to offer managerial prescriptions. As in the case of pricing decisions it has to be remembered that the central concern of economic model-building is to strip away the complications which bedevil the real world situation in order to identify the major factors which determine the optimal solutions to business problems. Detailed formulae for the day-to-day determination of operational decisions like branding or packaging are therefore not likely to be available.

The need to balance the four components of the marketing mix

Despite this reservation, even a simple approach to the economic modelling of the marketing mix illustrates the importance of achieving the correct balance between the different components of the mix.

If the firm is assumed to be a profit-maximiser, then:

Profit ($) = Total revenue (q) − Total cost (q)
or

$$\$ = TR(q) - TC(q)$$

In the simple model of the firm, both revenue and cost depend upon a single variable, which is the level of output produced and sold (q). As each component of the marketing mix affects both the demand for the firm's output and the cost of producing and selling it, the extension of the model to include these four factors gives the more complex version:

$$\$ = TR \text{ (price, product, promotion, place)} - TC \text{ (price, product, promotion, place)}$$

If each of the marketing mix variables could be measured quantitatively then this model could be solved for the profit-maximising level of every variable. In principle, this is simple enough, the first-order conditions for profit-maximisation being:

$$\frac{d\$}{(d)price} = \frac{d\$}{(d)product} = \frac{d\$}{(d)promotion} = \frac{d\$}{(d)place} = 0$$

In order for profits to be maximised, the marginal contribution of each element in the marketing mix should be equal to each other and equal to zero. If this were not the case then it would be possible to increase the level of contribution and profit by spending more on some marketing activities and by shifting the emphasis from one component of the mix to another.

While this simple exposition provides little assistance to a company attempting to establish the details of its own marketing mix, it does show very clearly that for maximum profit there has to be an appropriate balance between the four different components.

Advertising, promotion and selling

A formal model of advertising and promotion expenditures

Economic models of advertising and promotion are generally concerned with quantifying the optimal level of advertising and promotional budgets, rather than with the specific activities which should be carried out. Spending upon advertising and promotion affects the firm's demand curve and also increases costs, so that the model of the firm can be written as follows:

$$\$ = TR - TC - A \qquad \text{where:}$$

TR = Total revenue = $P[Q(P,A)]$

TC = Total cost of production = $C[Q]$

A = Spending on advertising and promotion

P = Price

Q = Quantity produced and sold = $Q(P,A)$

So that:

$$\$ = P[Q(P,A)] - C[Q(P,A)] - A$$

The decision variables in this version of the model are price and advertising expenditure. If the firm maximises profit the first order conditions are:

$$\frac{d\$}{dA} = \frac{P.dQ}{dA} - \frac{dC}{dQ} . \frac{dQ}{dA} - 1 = 0$$

$$\frac{d\$}{dP} = \frac{P.dQ}{dP} + Q - \frac{dC}{dQ} . \frac{dQ}{dP} = 0$$

The first of these conditions can be simply re-arranged to give:

$$\frac{dQ}{dA}(P - MC) = 1$$

and multiplying both sides by $\dfrac{A}{PQ}$ gives:

$$\frac{dQ}{dA} . \frac{A}{Q} \frac{(P - MC)}{P} = \frac{A}{PQ}$$

Closer examination of this equation reveals that the term $\dfrac{dQ}{dA} . \dfrac{A}{Q}$ is simply **advertising elasticity of demand (E_a)**.

The second first-order condition can also be re-arranged, to give the familiar profit-maximising condition that:

$$\frac{P - MC}{P} = -\frac{1}{E_d}$$

Combining these last two equations gives a result which is often referred to as the **Dorfman-Steiner condition**, which states that:

$$\frac{A}{PQ} = \frac{E_a}{E_d}$$

This shows that, for profit-maximisation, the ratio of advertising expenditure to sales revenue should be equal to the ratio of advertising elasticity of demand to price elasticity of demand.

Instead of presenting the model in terms of the ratio of elasticities, it can also be re-worked in terms of the familiar marginal conditions. In this framework it can be seen that the firm should be willing to spend an extra £1 on advertising, provided that the extra revenue raised is sufficient to cover both that £1 spent on advertising and the extra production costs incurred in producing the extra output for sale. The maximising condition thus becomes:

$$\frac{dR}{dA} = \frac{dC}{dA} + 1$$

The determinants of advertising elasticity of demand

The Dorfman-Steiner model illustrates the importance of advertising elasticity as a determinant of the profit-maximising advertising budget. Such a result is intuitively plausible because E_a is essentially a measure of the effectiveness of advertising, and the model provides a formal demonstration of the proposition that if advertising is highly effective it will pay to do more of it, which is hardly surprising. Rasmussen (1952) suggests a list of factors which will determine the advertising elasticity of demand.

The first is **the absolute level of advertising expenditure**. The links between advertising effectiveness and the level of spending may take a number of forms, the most plausible of which is shown in Fig. 14.1.

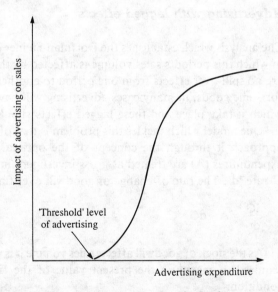

Fig. 14.1 The impact of advertising on the level of sales

As the figure shows, low levels of advertising expenditure have no effect upon the level of sales until a 'threshold' level is reached, at which point sales begin to be affected by the spending. As spending increases, effectiveness increases until eventually the point of saturation is reached and diminishing returns to advertising set in.

The second factor which determines the effectiveness of advertising is **the type of commodity involved**. Advertising elasticity will tend to be higher for new products than for old ones, and higher for luxuries than for necessities. There will also be differences between durable and non-durable goods, and those which are purchased frequently as opposed to those which are only bought occasionally. As theoretical analysis offers little guidance on the size of these effects rational decisions on the advertising budget will depend to a great extent upon the marketing department's skill in estimating them.

The third set of factors which will determine the advertising elasticity of demand concerns the **competitive structure and behaviour of the industry** and in particular the firm's market share and its rivals' reactions. The larger the firm's market share, the lower advertising elasticity of demand is likely to be. If rivals react to increases in the firm's advertising by increasing their own promotional spending, then these expenditures will tend to cancel each other out, reducing the advertising elasticity of demand.

Finally, the effectiveness of advertising will depend upon **the state of the economy in general**. If economic conditions are generally good and households have a high level of discretionary income they are more likely to respond to advertising than when incomes and expenditures are more tightly constrained.

Advertising with lagged effects

The analysis which establishes the Dorfman-Steiner condition is a single-period model in which this period's sales volume is affected by this period's advertising, but there are no spill-over effects from one period to another. While this may be appropriate for some goods, in many cases advertising will have an effect beyond the period in which it take place and these lagged effects should be taken into account.

One model which tackles this problem is that of Nerlove and Arrow (1962), who approach it through the concept of the optimal stock of goodwill. Advertising expenditures (A) are treated as gross investment in goodwill (G), which depreciates at rate 'd'. The rate of change of goodwill over time is then given by the equation:

$$\frac{dG}{dt} = A - dG$$

As the stock of goodwill affects sales volume it is possible to examine the conditions required to maximise the present value of the firm, which yields the following condition:

$$\frac{G}{R} = \frac{E_a}{E_d(r+d)} \qquad \text{where:}$$
$$r = \text{discount rate (see Chapter 15)}$$

As the equation shows, the result is essentially a multi-period version of the Dorfman-Steiner condition.

While the Nerlove-Arrow model embodies the important insight that advertising has lagged effects, it ignores the impact of past prices, and consumers' past purchases, both of which are also likely to affect the stock of goodwill. Schmalensee (1972) has therefore constructed an alternative variant which takes these into account and provides another long-run version of the Dorfman-Steiner condition. Such dynamic models can easily become too complex to be of any practical interest, although Dorward (1987) notes that if the lags which determine the impact of price and advertising on sales over time have the same structure, the optimal advertising to sales ratios will be the same in the short run as in the long run and the simple Dorfman-Steiner conditions holds for both. In that case, management can ignore the complexities introduced by the dynamic effects. In other cases, the results of the models are largely of academic interest, being too complex to have any practical value.

Advertising and market structure

The models described above have focused on the individual firm's advertising decision, without explicit reference to the market structure in which it operates. This is a shortcoming because market structure will affect the profitability of advertising, while advertising is itself a determinant of market structure (see Chapter 10, for example). Two issues in particular merit consideration. The first concerns the relationship between advertising and the level of concentration in the industry, and the second concerns the use of advertising as a means of raising entry barriers.

The link between advertising and concentration can be explored by considering the impact of concentration on the advertising to sales ratio indicated by the Dorfman-Steiner condition (see Waterson (1984) or Needham (1978) for a more extensive treatment). This can be written in expanded form as:

$$\frac{A}{R} = \frac{E_a}{E_d} = \frac{(E_A + E_{conj} \cdot E_{Ar})}{\dfrac{(E_m + E_s S_r)}{S_f}}$$

where:

E_A = the firm's advertising elasticity of demand, given that other firm's advertising remains constant

E_{conj} = responsiveness of rivals' advertising to changes in this firm's advertising

E_{Ar} = elasticity of this firm's demand with respect to rivals' advertising

E_m = market price elasticity of demand

E_s = elasticity of rivals' supply with respect to changes in the firm's price

S_r = rivals' market share

S_f = the firm's market share

As concentration increases, most of the terms in the equation will be affected so that the link between concentration and advertising is the result of complex interactions. Some observers have suggested that the most important effect derives from economies of scale in advertising (Kaldor 1950). If such economies are the dominant factor,

E_a will tend to increase with concentration and the advertising/concentration relationship will be positive. On the other hand, the evidence for such economies is less than convincing (Simon (1965)) and it might be argued that at very high levels of concentration, approaching monopoly, the returns to advertising are low because the firm has already attracted most of the buyers in the market. A number of authors (Cable (1972), Sutton (1974), Greer (1971)) have suggested that the most likely relationship between advertising and concentration is as shown in Fig. 14.2

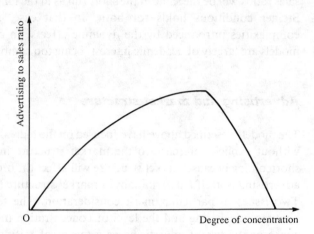

Fig. 14.2 Advertising intensity and concentration

At low levels of concentration (with perfect competition setting the limit) advertising intensity is low because price elasticity of demand is very high. As concentration increases and the industry becomes oligopolistic, A/R rises because price elasticity becomes smaller and rivals' reactions become more important. Once the highest levels of concentration are reached, A/R falls as the dominance of the leading firms reduces the returns to advertising.

The second aspect of market structure which is related to advertising concerns the condition of entry. If advertising creates entry barriers it will affect profitability in the long term by deterring entry into the industry where incumbents are earning high levels of profit, and allowing those supernormal profits to be maintained.

Advertising may contribute to entry barriers in three ways. First, it may give the incumbent firms an absolute cost advantage by creating buyer loyalty, which is expensive for new entrants to overcome. Secondly, if there are scale economies in advertising, newer and smaller firms will be placed at a disadvantage. Thirdly, the cost of advertising required to establish an initial market position will increase the initial capital requirement needed to enter the industry, and render the investment more risky, which may also act to deter entry.

The effectiveness of advertising as an entry barrier is a matter of debate. Some authors, notably Comanor and Wilson (1967), have argued that both theory and evidence support the view that advertising creates entry barriers and increases profits for firms in industries having high advertising intensities. Others are more sceptical

(Schmalensee (1974)), noting that advertising may be just as effective a competitive weapon for entrants as for incumbents. Most of the arguments suggesting that advertising creates entry barriers rely for their validity on a hidden assumption that there is some asymmetry between entrants and incumbents with respect to basic cost and demand conditions, which allows incumbents to secure a greater benefit from advertising than entrants. Whatever the general outcome of this unresolved debate, individual companies spending on advertising need to consider whether they are able to use that spending to deter other firms from entering their industry, perhaps by establishing 'first-mover advantages'.

Setting advertising budgets in practice

Just as many firms adopt cost-plus methods when setting prices, so the evidence suggests that firms adopt various **'rules-of-thumb'** when setting advertising budgets. Each of these may be considered in the light of the profit-maximising conditions identified in the Dorfman-Steiner model.

One of the most common approaches is the **percentage-of-sales** method. Many firms determine their advertising and promotion budgets as some pre-determined percentage of their current or expected sales revenue. This is seen by many as a 'safe' way to budget for advertising, as it restricts spending according to the amount of revenue available. It also provides for increasing advertising as sales grow, and the adoption of a common percentage by all firms in the industry could provide a means of securing competitive stability. However, there are serious disadvantages to the approach. In common with mechanical cost-plus pricing (see Chapter 13) it involves a problem of **'circularity'** in that the level of sales determines the amount spent on advertising, which in turn determines the level of sales.

While the percentage of sales method is consistent in form with the profit-maximising model, which specifies a ratio of advertising to sales revenues, it will only yield the profit-maximising solution if the percentage is calculated with reference to estimates of elasticity, or if the appropriate ratio is approximated in some other way. Furthermore, most of the evidence suggests that the percentage-of-sales which is spent on advertising is kept relatively constant, so that opportunities for a profitable increase in advertising spending, which will arise if general economic conditions improve or if competitors alter their behaviour, will be ignored. The percentage-of-sales approach also involves the danger that a temporary dip in sales may set up a self-reinforcing cycle whereby a reduction in sales leads to a reduction in the advertising budget, which leads to a further reduction in sales until a potentially profitable firm or product line is driven from the market altogether.

A second approach to the determination of advertising budgets is known as the **'all-you-can-afford'** approach. This involves the firm spending as much as it can without breaking the profit constraint. Clearly, there is no obvious mechanism through which this decision-process could lead to the profit-maximising result. It is perfectly feasible that where there are very high returns to advertising it would pay the firm to borrow in order to spend more on advertising than it can 'afford'. At the other extreme it would clearly be inconsistent with profit-maximisation to incur advertising expenditures up to a firm's profit constraint in a situation where the effectiveness of advertising is very limited. There is, however, one situation where the 'all-you can-afford' approach would lead the firm to achieve its maximising objective. That is where the firm's objective is sales-revenue maximisation, as in Baumol's model (see Chapter 3).

The third method which is commonly employed in determining advertising budgets is the **competitive parity** method, where firms set their budgets by matching the percentage of sales devoted to advertising by their rivals. If all firms had the same advertising and price elasticities and the percentage of sales set by all firms happened to coincide with the ratio of these elasticities at the optimal level of output, then the competitive parity approach would lead to profit-maximisation. However, as Kotler (1984) points out, companies within an industry often face such different opportunities that simply mimicking rivals' behaviour is unlikely to lead to the setting of optimal advertising budgets.

Each of the methods described above is concerned with setting a total advertising budget, after which individual activities can be planned within the total. The **objective-and-task** approach tackles the problem from the other direction. The starting point is to set a number of objectives which are to be met through advertising. For instance, the firm may wish to achieve a specified market share in a particular geographical area. Having set the objectives the firm then identifies the tasks which need to be carried out in order to meet those objectives. In the example given, it may be estimated that in order to meet the objective potential consumers need to be exposed to two television advertisements per day for two months. The costs of achieving the various objectives set are added together to determine the total advertising budget.

The objective-and-task approach to the advertising budget is not in itself likely to lead to profit-maximisation, because it does not directly take account of costs and revenues. However, if a firm identified a wide range of objectives and associated tasks and estimated the incremental revenues and incremental costs arising from meeting each objective that could provide the basis for reaching an optimal budget. If the firm simply agreed to meet every objective for which the incremental revenue exceeded the incremental cost then it would have a mechanism for at least approximating the profit-maximising advertising budget.

The promotional mix

It has been emphasised in the section on the marketing mix that the mix consists of a number of different components which have to be in balance if the firm is to meet its objective. Price, promotion, product and place all have to be considered together. Similarly, within advertising and promotion, there are various different activities across which the budget has to be spread. If the aim is to make maximum profit, then the general principle of marginal equivalency can be used to identify the optimal mix of activities.

For instance, if the total advertising budget has been set, providing the constraint within which the marketing department has to operate, and there are three different advertising media on which the budget might be spent (television, radio and newspapers) then as Reekie (1981) points out, the optimal allocation of the budget requires that the following condition be fulfilled.

$$\frac{MSR_{TV}}{P_{TV}} = \frac{MSR_{radio}}{P_{radio}} = \frac{MSR_{newspapers}}{P_{newspapers}}$$

where:

$MSR_{TV,radio,newspapers}$ = marginal sales response to a unit of advertising in each medium

$P_{TV,radio,newspapers}$ = the price of a unit of advertising in each medium

If the condition were not fulfilled then it would be possible to shift spending from one medium to another and increase sales volume with the same budget.

This analysis can also be presented graphically, which makes it clear that the problem being considered is fundamentally the same as that facing a consumer deciding which combination of goods to buy, given a limited income, or a firm involved in identifying the cost-minimising combination of capital and labour required to produce a given level of output. Fig. 14.3 sets out the position. The curves marked

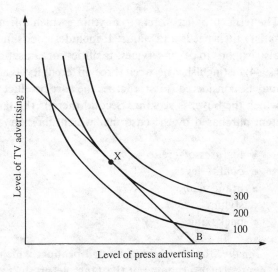

Fig. 14.3 Optimal media selection

100, 200 and 300 in the diagram, which closely resemble indifference curves or isoquants, are **iso-sales** lines, showing the different combinations of TV advertising and press advertisements which will lead to sales volumes of 100, 200 and 300 units of output. The line BB is the **budget line**, showing the different combinations of the two advertising media which can be purchased within the marketing department's budget. The optimal combination of TV and press advertising is given by the point of tangency, X.

This analysis illustrates the fundamental principles of promotional mix selection, but makes light of many of the practical problems. In order to apply the analysis, quantitative estimates are required of the responsiveness of sales to advertising through different media. These might be estimated through econometric techniques, but Chapter 7 has shown that such methods are not powerful enough to be relied upon with any confidence. A more practical approach would be to collect data on the number of potential buyers who are exposed to an advertisement, and to measure the extent of their awareness of the product as a result of that exposure. Media planning could then take place on the basis of maximising customer awareness, rather than maximising the sales response. If awareness is a good proxy for sales, this will be a perfectly adequate substitute and the method has the advantage of taking into account the 'creative' aspects of the advertising message. However, awareness and sales response are by no means the same thing and decision-making based entirely around buyer awareness could pose considerable risks.

Product policies

The scope of product policy

The term 'product' refers to anything which a firm may offer to buyers in order to satisfy their needs and wants. It includes goods in the sense of physical objects, but also extends to cover services, facilities, organisations, people and even ideas. Kotler (1984) distinguishes between three different levels at which the concept of the product may be considered. First, there is the **core product**, which is the fundamental benefit which the buyer is seeking. Second there is the **tangible product**. This is the actual item purchased by the customer which may vary in five major respects:

- features offered
- quality level
- brand name
- styling
- packaging.

Finally, there is the **augmented product** which includes additional services and benefits which accompany the tangible product. In the case of a motor car, for instance, the core product is mobility, the tangible product is the vehicle itself and the augmented product includes credit terms, delivery dates, guarantees and after-sales service.

Firms have two major types of product decision to take. The first are **product-mix** decisions, concerning the range of products which the firm should produce and the circumstances under which the product range should be expanded or reduced.

The second are **product attribute** decisions, concerning the characteristics of the individual products, including their branding, packaging and labelling and service components. Each of these may be considered in turn.

Product mix decisions

In simple models of the firm and the industry each firm produces only one product and the choice of product or industry is determined by the returns on capital which are available. Firms choose to produce the single product which they believe will bring the highest return on capital. In practice, most firms produce multiple products and it is necessary to consider the factors which will determine the range and variety of products which a firm will choose to produce.

A formal, and very limited, analysis of the product-mix decision can be carried out with the aid of a **production possibility frontier**. In Fig. 14.4 the line XY shows all the combinations of two different goods which a firm is capable of producing, given that there is a fixed level of resources available to it. The curve is concave, viewed from the origin, indicating that resources are not perfect substitutes for each other in the production of the two goods.

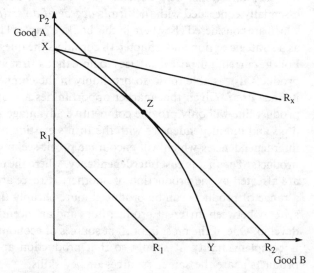

Fig. 14.4 The product mix

As the level of resources in use is fixed, total cost is constant for every combination of the two goods, and profits will be maximised when revenue is maximised. If it is assumed that there is a perfect market for both goods then any amount of either product can be sold for its market price. In that case, it is possible to draw **iso-revenue lines**, like R_1R_1 and R_2R_2 showing the different combinations of the two goods which yield the same level of revenue. These lines are straight as they represent a linear equation of the form:

$$TR = XP_X + YP_Y$$

where:

TR = a constant level of revenue
X, Y = amounts of product X and Y
P_X, P_Y = prices of X and Y

The optimal product-mix is that which allows the highest level of revenue to be earned, as indicated by point Z in the diagram. In that example, the firm chooses to produce both products. However, the combination chosen depends upon the shape of the production possibility frontier and the relative prices of the products. If the prices of the products should change so that iso-revenue curves have the slope given by the line XR_X then the firm would choose to operate at point X, producing a single product.

This analysis provides a formal statement of the rather obvious finding that the optimal product mix depends upon the prices which can be secured for different products (which determine the slope of the iso-revenue lines) and the opportunity costs of producing the two products (given by the shape of the production frontier). It also confirms that it will pay the firm to produce more of a product as its relative price is higher.

The question of product-mix may be approached less formally from a number of other directions. The decision to produce a number of different products is essentially concerned with the firm's *degree of diversification* and its *scope*, both of which are considered elsewhere in this book. Chapter 11 has considered diversification as a strategic option and Chapter 18 considers the question of 'scope' in more detail. For the current purpose it suffices to note that a firm will choose to produce multiple products if it is able to do so profitably in the competitive circumstances in which it finds itself. Given that market opportunities are open to all firms, an extended product line will only provide competitive advantage if it allows the exploitation of links and interdependencies with the firm's existing activities. There are three such interdependencies which will encourage profit-seeking firms to produce a range of products. The first is **cost interdependency**, where the costs of producing one product are affected by the production of another. If there are **economies of scope**, so that a range of products can be produced more cheaply than a single line, there will be synergy between different product lines and an incentive for multi-product firms to develop. One of the most important sources of economies of scope arises where there is **complementarity of supply** so that production and marketing of two or more products share the same resources or key skills.

In a similar way, there will be incentives to produce a full range of products if there are **demand interdependencies** so that the demand for one product is enhanced by the fact that the firm is producing other, related, items.

Thirdly there is the **reduction of risk**. If the returns associated with different products are negatively correlated with each other, so that poor performance in one product line is usually accompanied by good performance in another then the firm will be able to reduce the variability of its profits by producing and selling both lines.

The optimal product mix is therefore determined by a combination of cost drivers and demand conditions. As both sets of factors are subject to change over time a profit-seeking firm will keep its mix under continual review, pruning or expanding the product line when appropriate. Pruning the line will become necessary if a product ceases to make a contribution to profits, which will tend to happen as it reaches the later stage of its product life cycle and demand both falls and becomes more price elastic. Pruning will also be necessary if the firm has limited capacity and is unable to produce every product for which incremental revenues exceed incremental costs. In that case profit-maximisation requires that it concentrate its production and marketing effort on the most profitable lines. Conversely it will be appropriate to expand the product line if additional products will add more to revenues than they do to costs and the firm has the capacity to increase output.

The relationship between capacity utilisation and the optimal product mix implies that at times when demand is high, the number of products produced should be cut back in order to concentrate on the most profitable, while at times of low demand the firm should enhance its product range in order to produce all product variants which can make a contribution.

Product attributes

It has been noted in the section on the scope of product policy that the attributes of a product have at least five dimensions. These are:

- product features and performance characteristics
- the level of product quality
- styling and aesthetic considerations
- brand names
- packaging

Economic analysis tends to bundle these different dimensions together with advertising and promotion under the general heading of **product differentiation**. A profit-maximising firm will attempt to differentiate its product from that of its rivals in order to achieve two objectives. First, it seeks to raise the level of demand for its product, and secondly it seeks to reduce the price-elasticity of demand.

A firm may seek successful product differentiation in a number of ways. It may spend on advertising and promotion, rather than on the tangible attributes of its product. Alternatively it may attempt to configure the features and performance of the product and its packaging in such a way that it has enhanced appeal to buyers. In terms of Lancaster's 'characteristics' model of demand, outlined in Chapter 5, the firm may attempt to construct a product variant which has characteristics which consumers value highly in proportions which match their preferences. As part of the product differentiation process the firm may choose to opt for **branding** by attaching a **brand name** or a **brand mark** to its product, allowing for easier identification by consumers and creating an element of distinctiveness. While branding involves the firm in additional costs it offers a number of advantages over simply offering a **generic** product.

First, branding can provide legal protection for any special features of the product, preventing rivals from selling copies. Second, it allows the development of brand loyalty amongst consumers, reducing the price elasticity of demand and weakening the power of wholesalers and distributors. Third, branding can assist with market segmentation and price discrimination, by allowing different brands within the product line to be targeted on the needs of different groups of users. Finally, branding may be linked to the firm's overall **corporate identity**, reinforcing consumers' positive views of the firm and its products.

The appropriateness of product differentiation, and its form, can be linked back to the type of corporate strategy which the firm is attempting to pursue. If the strategy is one of **differentiation** then the firm needs to seek out those product attributes which buyers in general value highly, which the firm can provide cost-effectively, and which rivals are ill-equipped to provide. If the strategy is one of **focus** the product's attributes should reflect the needs of the target group of consumers. On the other hand if the strategy is one of **cost leadership** the major need will be to produce a product whose characteristics allow it to be produced at lower cost than that of rival firms, subject to its performance characteristics maintaining proximity to those of its rivals.

However the firm specifies the characteristics of its product and packaging, success will depend to a substantial extent upon whether or not the result can be considered '**good design**', for which there are three criteria (Davies (1989)). The first is **functionality** or **fitness for purpose** – the design should carry out the required functions effectively. The second is **makeability** – it should be possible to produce the design at an acceptable cost. Third, the design should have appropriate **stylistic and aesthetic qualities**. Successful achievement of all three objectives demands an effectively co-ordinated performance on the part of the marketing and production departments, in setting the design brief, and good creative skills on the part of the design team.

Marketing channels

'Place' as a component of the marketing mix

The fourth 'P' in the marketing mix is **place**, which refers to the locations in which the firm's product is offered to buyers and the distribution channels through which the product passes in order to reach those locations. In the textbook economic model of the firm no reference is made to these channels, the implicit assumption being that the product is sold directly to consumers. However, such **direct marketing** is comparatively rare and attention needs to be paid to the nature and function of other marketing channels or intermediaries.

The functions of marketing channels

Kotler (1984, p.541) defines the functions of marketing channels as follows:

- **Research** – gathering the information needed to make exchanges between buyers and suppliers.
- **Promotion** – disseminating persuasive communications about the product on offer
- **Contact** – finding and communicating with buyers

- **Matching** – adjusting the product to buyers' needs through activities such as grading, assembling and packaging
- **Negotiation** – setting final prices and other aspects of the offer so that transfer of ownership can be effected.
- **Physical distribution** – transport and storage.
- **Financing** – bearing the costs of channel work.
- **Risk taking** – bearing some of the risk associated with channel activities.

Each of these functions has to be undertaken by some organisation, but their allocation between the manufacturer of the product and other firms is variable, depending upon the relative efficiency of alternative channel configurations.

Alternative channel configurations

The marketing channel from manufacturer to consumer may have a number of levels. In the case of direct marketing, none of the channel activities are carried out by independent firms, and the configuration is known as a **zero-level channel**. At the other extreme, there may be a large number of intermediaries. In Japan, for instance, where the distribution system is notoriously complex and inefficient, it is estimated that the average consumer product passes through approximately a dozen different firms between the manufacturer and the consumer, in what marketing analysts would call a **twelve-level channel**. In Europe and the United States, channels more commonly have between one and three levels. A **one-level channel** consists of retailing organisations which either purchase from the manufacturer and sell to the consumer from a retail location or act as sales agents. A **two-level channel** includes wholesalers and a **three-level channel** also contains jobbers who purchase from wholesalers and then distribute to retailers.

Whatever the configuration of the marketing channel it co-ordinates the flow of goods and services (and the legal title to them), payments, information and promotional messages from the manufacturer to the final buyer.

Channel design and selection

In designing and selecting a marketing channel a firm has to take a number of major decisions. The first concerns the number of levels in the channel. The second is the number of intermediaries to be dealt with at each level, and the third concerns the selection of the individual organisations to be dealt with. It is also important to establish mechanisms for the monitoring, control and motivation of each component in the chain. This represents a complex set of decisions which lie beyond the scope of this text. Nevertheless, it is possible to briefly outline some of the factors which will influence the design of optimal channels.

Customer's characteristics will be a major influence. If buyers are very widely dispersed and buy small amounts very frequently, as in the case of convenience goods, then relatively long channels will be needed because the creation of direct links between the manufacturer and thousands of customers would be prohibitively expensive. On the other hand, if there are few buyers who purchase infrequently more direct marketing will be appropriate.

Product and company characteristics will be important. If the product is highly complex, customised to individual buyers' requirements, or has high unit value it will require close links between manufacturer and buyer which will be difficult to maintain down multi-level channels. Products which involve high transport costs will require a channel configuration which minimises those costs through bulk transport. Perishable products require speed and the minimisation of handling. All of these factors may be important in channel design. Similarly, the company's size, financial resources and the range of its product-mix will determine the balance between in-house channel activities and those which are handled by independent organisations.

Intermediary characteristics will also have an influence. A firm's own sales representatives will provide a substantial selling effort to each client contacted, as they are solely concerned with selling their own company's products. Sales agents, in contrast, will provide a less intensive sales effort as they will be selling the products of a number of companies. On the other hand, the sales agent will cost less per sales contact as his costs are spread across a number of clients. Individual intermediaries will each have strengths and weaknesses with respect to the effectiveness and cost with which they can carry out the various different channel functions which will affect optimal channel design. It should also be remembered that Chapter 10 has shown that 'buyer power' is an important determinant of the nature of competition in an industry, to be taken account of when considering how best to build competitive advantage.

This last point makes it clear that **competitive conditions and corporate strategy** will also be determinants of optimal channel selection. It has to be remembered that channel activities are an aspect of competition between firms, just like pricing and promotion. The extent of the firm's direct involvement in the marketing channel is an aspect of its scope, which determines the shape of the firm's value-chain and which has been shown to be one of the key features of corporate strategy. The form of the marketing channel will also be influenced by the firm's choice of **generic strategy**. If the business is aiming to compete through cost leadership a very different channel configuration will be required to that which will be suitable if the aim is to focus or differentiate.

Finally, it is clear that the **economic and legal environment** will affect channel choice. If economic conditions are generally depressed, there will be advantage in using 'stripped-down' marketing channels which deliver the product to the final buyer at least cost with the minimum of inessential services added. In more prosperous times and places, the buyer may seek additional services which can be used to add value to the product. The law, especially that on competition, (see Chapter 16) may place restrictions on channel designs which are seen to restrict competition or to create monopoly power.

To summarise, then, it can be seen that the design and implementation of appropriate marketing channels is an important and potentially complex component in the establishment of competitive advantage. As many of the determinants of the optimal configuration are subject to change, a successful firm needs to keep them under constant review and to modify the configuration with respect to levels, participants and management control whenever necessary.

The location decision

While place in the marketing mix is usually interpreted to mean the route by which the product reaches the final buyer, firms also have to consider the physical and geographical location of their production, distribution and administrative facilities. Selection of an optimal location is influenced by three major factors, namely:

- the impact of location on costs
- proximity to the market
- government policy.

The impact of location on costs

If the cost and quality of inputs, or their availability, varies from place to place this will give firms an incentive to locate in the lowest cost location, other things being equal. For some inputs, like capital, there is very little variation in cost from place to place, even at the global level, and they have little influence on firms' location decisions. For some other resources, like power, there are important differences from one country to another but relatively small differences within the same national economy, in which case only global location decisions will be affected. For most industries, the inputs whose costs may vary with location are **labour** and **raw materials**. As these are naturally less mobile from place to place (and almost completely immobile from one country to another), market forces do not completely eliminate locational differentials, providing incentives for firms to move towards lower cost sites.

Differences in relative labour cost are therefore one determinant of the location decision. As wages are considerably lower in mainland China than in Hong Kong, for instance, many Hong Kong companies have moved their labour intensive activities into China, in order to maintain cost leadership in a way that would be impossible if the activities were kept in Hong Kong. Computer companies, having produced the early versions of their machines in relatively high wage economies, have shifted the manufacture of mass-produced, technologically mature, machines to the Far East, where labour costs are low. At the global level, differences in labour cost remain a major determinant of the optimal location. Within an individual national economy differences in labour cost from region to region tend to be smaller, but they may still be sufficient to have an appreciable impact on costs.

The importance of raw materials as a factor determining location is more problematical. While there are a number of obvious examples where the availability of raw materials virtually dictates the location of an activity, like coal-mining or steel production, the improvement of transportation systems and the fact that in many industries raw materials account for smaller proportions of total cost, means that industrial activity has become less tied to the sources of such materials. As a result firms have become more free to choose locations on other criteria.

Another factor which may influence the cost of operating in different locations is the presence or absence of **agglomeration economies**, which are a form of **external economies of scale**. If a group of firms in the same industry, or involved in similar types of activity, are located in close proximity to each other, they may be able to secure cost savings which are available to them all, but could not be exploited by a single firm. Such savings could arise from a number of sources. Local educational institutions could specialise in the types of course needed by the industry. Local management consultants could develop specialist expertise. The transport infrastructure could be developed to suit the special needs of the industry, and the agglomeration of firms with similar requirements could produce a pool of workers and managers with the skills needed, thereby smoothing the workings of the local labour market. Such agglomeration economies are difficult to quantify, and have to be set against the costs of congestion which can arise if a large number of firms attempt to locate themselves close together. Nevertheless, it may be a significant phenomenon. In the famous case of 'Silicon Valley' in the United States, for instance, it has been shown that a large number of high technology firms chose to be located together in California, not only because the climate is very pleasant, but also because the area already had a high concentration of similar firms and related academic institutions which provided a source of the highly skilled manpower, and the new entrepreneurs, which the industry needed in order to develop.

While cost-minimisation may drive some activities to particular locations it is important to recall that managers may have their own preferences which will form an important input into the location decision. If a location is regarded as particularly desirable, like California in the United States, or the South East in the United Kingdom, that location may be chosen in preference to one involving lower costs.

The pull of the market

While the relative cost of resources is one factor determining location, another is proximity to the market. In part this is a question of the relative costs of transporting raw materials in comparison with the cost of transporting the final product. If the raw material can be transported more cheaply than the final product then profit-seeking behaviour will drive activities closer to the market and further away from the raw material. However, closeness to the market may also provide other advantages through better market intelligence, less extended marketing channels and closer liaison with buyers, allowing for a more rapid and flexible response to changing market needs. There may also be economies to be had through locating after-sales service and maintenance activities alongside production facilities.

Government policy

Government policy may affect the location of industry in two major ways. In the first place, at national level, governments may impose tariffs on imports or other restrictions on trade. In that case, a firm which seeks to exploit a particular market will be forced to locate production within it. Japanese motor companies, for instance, seeking to circumvent restrictions on their sales into the European market, have established production and assembly facilities in Europe in order to allow them to exploit the single European market of 320 million consumers, due to come into force at the end of 1992. When Britain first entered the European Economic Community there was an influx of American foreign direct investment, seeking to use a country with a common language as a base from which to develop the wider European market.

Within national economies governments may attempt to alter the location of industry in order to secure a more equitable distribution of income and employment, and in order to reduce the costs of congestion. This is attempted in a number of ways, examined in more detail in Chapter 17. Foremost amongst these is the provision of financial incentives which can reduce the costs of operating in some locations, thereby making them more attractive than they would be if market forces operated without any government intervention.

Technology development

Invention, innovation and science

In the elementary model of the firm, the starting point on the supply side is the existence of a production function, which represents a given state of technology which is exogenously determined. While this is useful for the analysis of the short-run problems facing the firm it abstracts away from the question of innovation and technological development which, some would argue, lie at the heart of the process of competition (see Chapter 16 for further discussion). It is important, therefore, to devote some attention to the process of technological change.

Schumpeter (1954) drew a useful distinction between **invention** and **innovation**. An invention is an idea, a sketch or a model for some new or improved device, product, process or system. Inventions do not necessarily, or usually, lead to an innovation, which is accomplished only when the first commercial transaction takes place involving the application of the invention. Innovation therefore involves making the connection between a new technical achievement and a potential market.

Innovations may be divided into **product innovations** which introduce new or improved products, or **process innovations** which change the way in which existing products are produced. Such new developments may arise from a number of sources. One of the earliest observers, Adam Smith (1776), identified three major sources of innovation:

- **Worker innovation** – where those intimately involved in the production process identify improvements which may be made.

- **The capital goods sector** – where product innovations in the sector become process innovations for other sectors.
- **Science** – where specialist workers trained in scientific principles identify the inventions on which innovations may be based.

Freeman (1974) has argued that 'science' has been increasingly important as the major source of invention and innovation in the twentieth century. The scientists who are responsible for innovations may be located in a number of different organisational situations. At one extreme there is the 'lone inventor', working on his own projects without direction from any firm or corporate body. At the other extreme there are workers in the Research, Development and Design departments of large corporations, working on projects with commercial objectives set by the company. In between these extremes there are research workers in educational institutions and specialised research establishments whose work may be placed anywhere on a very broad spectrum from the highly applied, for which there are known and immediate applications, to the most fundamental, for which there are no currently known commercial applications.

Innovation, firm size and competitive structure

One of the most important debates in the field of innovation concerns the extent to which technological progress has become the province of the largest firms and their Research and Development (R&D) departments. Some observers, following Schumpeter (1954), have suggested that the very largest firms, and those having substantial market power, tend to dominate the introduction of innovations. They have the financial resources needed to fund risky projects and their market share allows them to reap the returns on any new products or processes which they may introduce. However, the evidence on the issue is mixed. A number of studies have found that employment in R&D tends to increase with firm size but the relationship is weak and highly variable across industries and there is little evidence to suggest that **R&D intensity**, measured by the ratio of research workers to total employment, has a strong positive relationship with firm size. Similar findings have resulted from the examination of research outputs, in the form of patents, instead of research inputs.

If market power is measured by the level of concentration it might be expected, on the 'Schumpeterian hypothesis', that more concentrated industries would be more research intensive. Again, however, the evidence suggests that there is no such simple relationship. If the evidence does reveal any pattern it would appear that, for both firm size and the level of concentration, research intensity at first increases from small size and low levels of concentration but then peaks and goes on to decline as very high levels of firm size and of concentration are reached. The pattern varies very widely across industries which has led many observers to attribute the variation in technological effort to the intrinsic differences in the technological opportunities facing industries. In the 'science-based' industries like aerospace, electronics and chemicals there is a higher level of innovative activity, regardless of firm size and market structure, than in other sectors with more established technologies like textiles, clothing, furniture and food.

The sources of invention

Just as there has been debate over the impact of firm size and industry concentration on the rate of innovation, so there has been argument over the relative importance of the 'lone inventor' or the small entrepreneurial firm in comparison with the R&D departments of large corporations. While it is certainly true that a large proportion of the inputs to the innovation process are concentrated in large firms, and that the same applies to research outputs if measured by indicators like patents filed, that does not mean to say that the most important innovations have stemmed from inventions within large firms. A well-known study by Jewkes *et al.* (1969) found that a majority of major innovations in the first half of the twentieth century stemmed from inventions by outside inventors. Studies of the steel industry, petroleum refining and the chemical giant Du Pont all showed that important innovations tended to stem from developments outside the dominant firms in the industry. On the other hand, if the distinction between invention and innovation is remembered, it is equally clear that the vast bulk of the development work required to turn an invention into an innovation is carried out within large or medium-sized firms, and not by lone inventors or technology-based small firms. The overall judgment on the issue would seem to be that: 'corporate laboratories are responsible for a minority of major and a majority of minor or derivative inventions' (Devine, *et al.* (1979) p.221).

Given that the level of uncertainty is higher as the invention in question is more basic or fundamental it seems hardly surprising that profit-seeking firms concentrate their technological efforts on those parts of the process which are closest to the point of commercial application.

Technology development and corporate strategy

Porter (1985) defines technology strategy as:

'a firm's approach to the development and use of technology'.

Such a strategy has to address three major issues. The first concerns the nature of the technologies which should be developed, which in turn is related to the firm's overall corporate strategy. If the firm's generic strategy is one of cost-leadership then both product and process-related R&D should be directed towards building that type of competitive advantage. Product improvement can be geared towards cost reduction and process development can attempt to take maximum advantage of the various cost drivers in order to lower the cost at which buyers' needs can be met. The introduction of Flexible Manufacturing Systems (FMS), for instance, often reduces the minimum efficient scale of production, allowing the firm to produce smaller batches at low cost, and to compete on cost in much smaller market segments than was previously the case.

If the firm is attempting to compete through differentiation, its technological effort will be aimed at a different set of objectives. Both product and process development need to be geared towards enhancing the quality and features of the product, including the response time to orders and product 'deliverability'.

In a similar way a firm which is competing through a strategy of focus needs to direct its technological effort towards the specific requirements of the target sector it is aiming at, either by reducing costs for the targeted buyers or by differentiating in ways which are specific to that segment and less well met by more broadly targeted competitors.

Once a firm has established the objectives of its technology development programme it then has to consider whether it wishes to be a **technological leader**, being the first to introduce new technologies, or whether it would prefer to be a follower. The balance of advantage between the two approaches depends to a great extent upon the advantages and disadvantages associated with being **a first-mover**. If, for instance, there are pronounced learning effects in an industry, or if buyers can be 'locked-in' to the first supplier of a commodity through the effect of switching costs, or if the first-mover secures access to the most favourable market niches and distribution channels then it will pay to be a first-mover and technological leader. On the other hand, the first-mover often has to bear costs which can be avoided by followers, there is no certainty that its effort will be successful in either technological or commercial terms, and the lead gained may be very short-lived if the new technology can be cheaply and easily imitated by rivals. The choice between leadership and followership depends upon the competitive circumstances in which the firm finds itself, and the behaviour of its rivals.

If a firm decides to be a **technological follower**, then it has to consider how it will gain access to new technologies developed by leaders. In some cases, publicly available information concerning the new technology will be sufficient for the firm to develop its own variant of an innovation, while avoiding the full costs of reproducing the leader's own R&D effort. If this is not possible, followers may have to consider licensing-in new technologies from leaders. While this will be a viable route in some circumstances, it has to be remembered that licensed-in technology may still require development work and technological leaders will be anxious not to damage their own lead by licensing-out major components of their technological advantage. It may, therefore, only be possible to license-in relatively outdated technology, or technology owned by firms which have no major interest in the market in question.

Illustration

Marketing expenditures: an analysis of their determinants

One of the most important questions which marketing managers have to resolve concerns the amount they should spend on marketing and the distribution of that spending across different activities.

Buzzell and Farris (1976) attempt to provide insights into this issue, in the particular context of industrial marketing, by carrying out a statistical analysis of the relationship between measures of marketing spend and a range of other variables.

The objective of the study was 'to identify those factors which best explain variations in marketing cost among industrial manufacturing businesses.' The dependent variables which were chosen were as follows:

- total marketing expense as a percentage of sales
- advertising and sales promotion as a percentage of sales
- advertising as a percentage of sales
- sales force expenditure as a percentage of sales

For each of these variables a series of multiple regressions were carried out, using a set of independent variables which could be divided into five general categories. These were:

- product variables – purchase frequency, high amount of purchase, low importance of purchase to user, produced to order, importance of service to the product, R&D intensity.
- market factors – market growth, recent entry of competitors, decline stage of product life cycle
- customer factors – concentration of users, high number of users, low number of customers, percentage of individual users, percentage of institutional users
- strategy factors – percentage of sales through wholesalers, percentage of sales direct to end-users, common distribution channels, regional sales only
- cost structure and market share factors – trading margin, relative price, percentage of sales within the company, market share.

The regressions were run for three separate industrial groupings – capital goods, raw materials and components, and supply businesses – using data drawn from the PIMS (profit impact of marketing strategies) database.

The results showed that variations in the independent variables accounted for between 30 per cent and 45 per cent of the variation in the marketing effort variables, which is statistically significant though a weaker relationship than that found in consumer goods industries.

The detailed findings with respect to the signs and significance of the co-efficients on the individual independent variables are summarised in Table 14.1 below. Examination of the table suggests a number of features. In the first place, the signs show a remarkable consistency across the different dependent variables, suggesting that the different measures of marketing effort are related to the same independent variables in the same way. Scanning the results for common patterns suggests that marketing intensity for industrial products is positively related to:

- the importance of service
- R&D intensity
- high number of users
- percentage of sales through wholesalers
- trading margins

and negatively related to:

- high frequency of purchase
- high amount of purchase
- percentage direct to users
- market share

Table 14.1 Summary of regression results (signs and significance of co-efficients)

	Materials				Components				Supplies				Capital goods			
	(A+P)/S	A/S	SF/S	Mktg/S	(A+P)/S	A/S	SF/S	Mktg/S	(A+P)/S	A/S	SF/S	Mktg/S	(A+P)/S	A/S	SF/S	Mktg/S
Product variables																
High purchase frequency	n.s	*	***	***												
Low purchase frequency														*		
High amount of purchase	–*	–*	n.s	–***									**	n.s	–***	–***
Low importance to user									+**	+***	+**					
Produced to order	n.s	n.s	+***	+*									–***	–*		–**
Service importance	n.s	n.s	+***	+*									+***	+*	+*	+**
R&D intensity	+***	+**	+*	+***					n.s	+**	n.s	n.s	+***	n.s	+**	+***
Market factors																
Market growth	n.s	+**	n.s	+*												
Entry of competitors									+***	+*			+**	–**	–**	
Decline stage													–*	–*		
Customer factors																
User concentration	+**	+*	n.s	+*												
High number of users	+**	+**	+***	+***												
Low number of users	n.s	n.s	–***	–***												
% Individual users									+***	+***	–*	n.s				
% Institutional users									+***	n.s	n.s	n.s				
Strategy users																
% Through wholesale	+***	+***	n.s	+**									–***	–***	+*	n.s
% Direct to users													n.s	n.s	+***	–**
Common channels	n.s	+*	–**	–**									n.s	n.s	+**	n.s
Regional only									–**	n.s	+***	+**	n.s	n.s	+**	n.s
Shared programs	–*	n.s	n.s	n.s					n.s	n.s	n.s	n.s	–***	n.s	–*	–***
Cost structure/market share																
Trading margin	+***	+***	+***	+***					+**	n.s	+***	+***	+***	+**	+***	+***
Relative price									+*	+*	n.s	+*				
% Internal sales									n.s	–*	–*	n.s				
Market share	+**	n.s	–***	–***					n.s	n.s	–***	–***	n.s	n.s	–*	–*

Key:
n.s   not significant
*   significant at 10 per cent level
**   significant at 5 per cent level
***   significant at 1 per cent level
Blank cells indicate variables which were considered inappropriate for the industry in question

Adapted from: R.D. Buzzell and P.W. Farris, 'Industrial Marketing Costs: An Analysis of Variations in Manufacturers' Marketing Expenditures', *Marketing Science Institute Report No. 76–118*, (Cambridge, Mass., 1976)

The authors note that regressions never prove causality, merely association, so that the direction of causality could often be in either direction. However, they also note that many of the factors which are significantly related to the marketing effort lie outside the control of marketing managers, being inherent in the nature of the industry. The results suggest, then, that the degree of latitude which management has over its marketing costs may be more limited than is often supposed. They also suggest that the equations fitted might be used by the managers of new businesses to set the general level of their marketing budgets.

References and further reading

R.D. Buzzell and P.W. Farris, 'Industrial Marketing Costs: An Analysis of Variations in Manufacturers' Marketing Expenditures, *Marketing Science Institute Report* No. 76–118 (Cambridge, Mass., 1976)

J. Cable, 'Market Structure, Advertising Policy and Inter-Market Differences in Advertising Intensity', in K. Cowling (ed.) *Market Structure and Corporate Behaviour*, (London, Gray Mills, 1972)

W.S. Comanor and T.A. Wilson, 'Advertising, Market Structure and Performance', *Review of Economics and Statistics*, 1967

H. Davies, 'The Designers' Perspective: Managing Design in the UK', *Journal of General Management*, 1989

P.J. Devine, N. Lee, R.M. Jones and W.J. Tyson, *An Introduction to Industrial Economics*, (London, George Allen & Unwin, 1979)

N. Dorward, *The Pricing Decision*, (London, Harper & Row, 1987)

C. Freeman, *The Economics of Industrial Innovation*, (Harmondsworth, Penguin, 1974)

D.F. Greer, 'Advertising and Market Concentration', *Southern Economic Journal*, 1971

J. Jewkes, D. Sawers and R. Stillerman, *The Sources of Innovation*, (London, Macmillan, 1969)

P. Kotler, *Marketing Management*, (London, Prentice-Hall, 1984)

E.J. McCarthy, *Basic Marketing: A Managerial Approach*, (Homewood, Richard D. Irwin, 1960)

D. Needham, *The Economics of Industrial Structure, Conduct and Performance*, (London, Holt, Rinehart & Winston, 1978)

M. Nerlove and K.J. Arrow, 'Optimal Advertising Policy Under Dynamic Conditions', *Economica*, 1962

M. Porter, *Competitive Advantage*, (New York, Free Press, 1985)

A. Rasmussen, 'The Determination of Marketing Expenditure', *Journal of Marketing*, 1952

W.D. Reekie, *The Economics of Advertising*, (London, Macmillan, 1981)

R. Schmalensee, *The Economics of Advertising*, (Amsterdam, North Holland, 1972)

R. Schmalensee, 'Brand Loyalty and Barriers to Entry', *Southern Economic Journal*, 1974

J.A. Schumpeter, *Capitalism, Socialism and Democracy*, (London, Allen and Unwin, 1954)

J.L. Simon, 'Are There Economies of Scale in Advertising?', *Journal of Advertising Research*, 1965

C.J. Sutton, 'Advertising, Concentration and Competition', *Economic Journal*, 1974

A. Smith, *The Wealth of Nations*, 1776

M. Waterson, *Economic Theory of the Industry*, (Cambridge, Cambridge UP, 1984)

Self-test questions

1 List the four 'Ps' which make up the marketing mix and identify the components of each one.

2 Consider how price and advertising elasticities are likely to vary over the different stages of the product life cycle and consider the implications for the level of advertising in each stage.

3 How would you describe the following in the case of a micro-computer?

(a) the core product

(b) the tangible product

(c) the augmented product

4 List the advantages of branding.

5 How would you expect the marketing channels to vary between:

(a) machine tools

(b) breakfast cereals

Exercise

'The Modigliani–Miller proposition undermines the traditional view that there is an optimal degree of gearing, but is itself undermined by the recognition of the impact of bankruptcy costs and taxation.'

Explain this statement

Answers on page 423.

15 Investment decisions and the cost of capital

This chapter examines the major issues raised by long-term decisions concerning the firm's investment in capital goods and equipment. The first part examines the techniques which are available for the appraisal of investment projects and the second part addresses the problem of estimating the cost of capital for a firm taking such investment decisions.

Investment appraisal

The purposes and types of investment decision

The fundamental purpose of investment spending is to meet the firm's objectives, which were discussed in Chapter 3. As the central objective is taken to be profit, expressed in the long run as the maximisation of shareholders' wealth, then the usual starting point for any discussion of investment appraisal is the assumption that the ultimate objective of investment spending is to maximise the value of the firm.

Firms aiming for profit may invest in new capital goods and equipment for a number of reasons. First, they may invest in order to **replace existing equipment**, either because it is worn-out and cannot be used any longer, or because new equipment will allow cost savings to be secured. Secondly, investment may be needed **in support of expansion**, either of existing products and markets or into new products and markets. Thirdly, investment may be required **for reasons of compliance** with government regulations. Whatever the immediate objective of an investment project, its fundamental purpose is to enhance the value of the firm and the techniques used to appraise them are essentially the same.

Investment decisions may also be divided into three categories according to the nature of the conclusion which has to be reached. The first type of decision is simply to **accept or reject** an individual project. The second involves **ranking projects** and the third involves **choosing between mutually exclusive alternatives**. Each of these will be considered below.

Simple techniques for the appraisal of investments

The simplest criterion for the appraisal of investments is the **payback method**. This involves estimating the net profit generated by an investment project and calculating the number of years required to repay the initial investment. The results can be used in a number of ways. If the aim is simply to accept or reject projects then the firm's management may choose a cut-off period of (say) three or five years and accept any project which pays back its investment over that period. If the aim is to rank projects, those with the shortest payback period are ranked highest, while the choice between mutually exclusive projects is made by selecting that with the shortest payback period.

The payback method is widely used in practice because it is seen as a means of avoiding risk and ensuring that firms maintain adequate liquidity. However, it has a number of shortcomings. The first is that it ignores any returns which accrue after the payback period, which is itself chosen arbitrarily. For example, if two projects have identical payback periods of three years, but one of them yields very substantial profits in year four and the other yields nothing, the technique will not discriminate between them. The second shortcoming is that the pattern of returns within the payback period is ignored. Hence, a project which yields very rapid returns within the first two years of a five year payback period will be rated in exactly the same way as a project which pays back nothing until a full repayment in the fifth year. The third, and most fundamental, weakness of the payback method is that it ignores the time value of money. The returns to an investment are simply added together year on year until they equal the original outlay, at which point the payback period is established. As a result an amount of money which accrues in year one of a project carries exactly the same weight as the same amount of money accruing in year three, provided that the cut-off point for acceptance of a project is three years or more. However, this ignores the fact that money accruing in year one could be invested with interest for two years and be worth more than the original amount by year three.

The second simple technique for the appraisal of investment projects is the **accounting rate of return** method. This can take a number of different forms but consists essentially of estimating the net profits accruing to a project over its life, calculating an average profit per year, and then expressing that profit as a percentage of the initial outlay, to give an estimated rate of return. Projects are then accepted if the rate of return calculated exceeds the firm's minimum requirement and projects are ranked by their rate of return.

The accounting rate of return method suffers from the same fundamental flaw as the payback criterion in that it ignores the time value of money. If this is to be properly taken into account, more sophisticated methods have to be employed.

The principle of discounting

If the time value of money is to be taken into account, some method has to be found of assigning appropriate and comparable values to amounts of money accruing at different times. This is done through a method known as discounting, which is closely associated with the arithmetic of compound interest.

If £1,000 is invested at an interest rate of 'r' per year, payable in a single instalment at the end of each year, then the value of the sum invested at different times is as shown in Table 15.1 below, with a worked example for the case where 'r' is equal to 10 per cent.

Table 15.1 The value of £1,000, invested at interest rate 'r'.

Time	0	After 1 year	After 2 years	After n years
Value	1,000	$1,000(1+r)$	$1,000(1+r)^2$	$1,000(1+r)^n$

The value of £1,000, invested at interest rate 10%

Time	0	After 1 year	After 2 years	After n years
Value	1,000	1,100	1,210	$1,000(1.1)^n$

In a fundamental sense, each of the figures in the rows above are the equivalent of each other. At an interest rate of 10 per cent, £1,000 today is the equivalent of £1,100 in one year's time, or £1,210 in two years' time.

When calculating compound interest the value of a sum of money available today is being projected forwards in order to measure its value in future periods. However, exactly the same arithmetic may be used in reverse, in order to estimate the present value of a sum of money which does not accrue until some future period. If £1,210 is expected to accrue after two years, and the interest rate is 10 per cent, the present value of that £1,210 may be said to equal £1,000. The figure of £1,210 has been **discounted** by dividing it by 1.21, which is $(1+r)^2$, where $r = .1$.

In general, the present value of a sum of money 'X' which does not accrue until 'n' periods into the future is given by the formula:

$$\text{Present value} = \frac{X}{(1+r)^n}$$

The amount X is said to have been discounted 'n' times at interest rate 'r'.

Net present values

As the essence of investment appraisal lies in comparing the values of outlays and returns which accrue at different times, the principle of discounting provides a solution to the basic problem involved. The stream of returns accruing over the lifetime of a project may be reduced to a single figure, representing the present value of that stream of returns. This can be compared with the cost of the project, and the project can be accepted if the present value of the returns exceeds the present value of the costs. To put it more formally, an investment project should be accepted if it has a **net present value** (NPV) which is greater that zero, where NPV is given by the formula:

$$NPV = -K + \frac{NCF_1}{(1+r)} + \frac{NCF_2}{(1+r)^2} + \ldots + \frac{NCF_n}{(1+r)^n}$$

where:

K   = capital cost, accruing in full at the beginning of the project
$NCF_{1,2, \ldots n}$ = net cash flows arising from the project in years 1 to n
r   = the opportunity cost of capital

If the analysis is to be carried out correctly both the net cash flows and the opportunity cost of capital must be properly calculated. The figures for NCF in each year should include **all and only incremental cash flows after taxes**. Costs which the firm would incur even if it did not carry out the project should not be included, because they are not incremental and are therefore irrelevant. Depreciation should not be included directly as a cost because it is not an outflow of cash, although the impact of depreciation on the firm's tax position should be taken into account as that will affect outflows of cash arising from the project. If the equipment is to be sold for scrap at the end of the project's life, the revenue from that sale should be included in the NCF for the last period.

The calculation of an appropriate figure for the opportunity cost of capital is a complex issue which takes up the second part of this chapter. At this stage it suffices to note that when a firm puts resources into an investment project it is foregoing the opportunity to put those resources to an alternative use, and the figure for the cost of capital used in the NPV calculation should reflect the return which could be earned in that alternative use. This in turn depends upon rates of return in financial markets in general, and upon the riskiness of the projects involved.

Internal rate of return

A closely related technique for investment appraisal, which has its roots in the same discounting technique, involves calculating the **internal rate of return** (IRR) on a project. Instead of setting a value for 'r' in the NPV equation set out above, 'r' is treated as an unknown and NPV is set equal to zero. The IRR is then the value for 'r' which satisfies the equation. In other words, the IRR is the discount rate which renders the NPV of the project equal to zero. If this method is used to appraise investments, the criterion for acceptance is that the IRR on a project should exceed the opportunity cost of capital to the firm.

Precise direct calculation of the IRR may be mathematically difficult, as the NPV equation is a complex polynomial. However, the result may be arrived at through **linear interpolation**, which involves a series of steps. First, a guess is made with respect to the value of the IRR, and the NPV associated with that guess calculated. If the resulting NPV is positive, the guess is known to have been too low, and if the NPV is negative the guess is known to have been too high. A second guess is then made, with the intention of 'overshooting' the target. If the first guess yielded a positive NPV, the second guess should be higher by an amount which is expected to yield a negative NPV. The correct result is then known to lie between the two guesses and can be approximated by graphing the two results on NPV and IRR, connecting them with a straight line and reading off the rate of return at which NPV equals zero. Fig. 15.1 illustrates this procedure for a simple example.

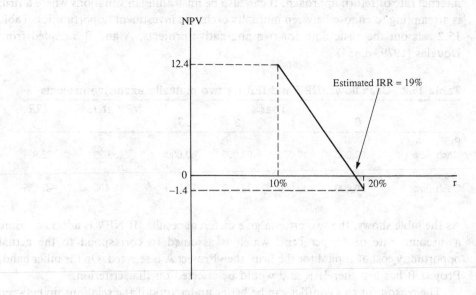

Fig. 15.1 Approximating the internal rate of return

In most situations the IRR method will yield the same results as the NPV method, as might be expected. However, there are a number of problems which can arise. The NPV formula is a polynomial and the mathematics of polynomials implies that there may be more than one value for the IRR which satisfies the equation. This will not happen in the most common type of investment project, where an outflow of cash at the beginning of the project is followed by inflows until the end of the project, because in that situation the sign of the cash flows changes only once, from negative to positive, which dictates that there can be only one positive value for 'r' (see Lorie and Savage (1955) and Pratt and Hammond (1979) for more detailed expositions). However, if the sign of the cash flows changes more than once in the life of the project, there may be multiple solutions to the equation and hence multiple IRRs, which lead to a number of difficulties. In the first place, having found one solution to the equation, the decision-maker may not be aware that others exist and may take a decision on the basis of incomplete information. Secondly, if there are multiple solutions, neither of them may be an appropriate figure for the appraisal of the investment project. Further exploration of these problems may be found in most financial management textbooks (van Horne (1980), Franks, Broyles and Carlton (1985), Copeland and Weston (1983)), which show that it is possible to adapt the IRR rule in order to cope with these difficulties. However, as Brealey and Myers (1984, p.75) note of such adaptations: 'Not only are they inadequate, they are unnecessary, for the simple solution is to use net present value'.

Choosing between mutually exclusive investment projects

The problem of multiple solutions is not the only difficulty which arises with the internal rate of return approach. It can also be misleading in situations where a firm is attempting to choose between mutually exclusive investment opportunities. Table 15.2 sets out the basic data for two alternative projects, A and B, adapted from Douglas (1979, p.454).

Table 15.2 Cash flows, NPV and IRR for two mutually exclusive projects

	Year				NPV at 15%	IRR
	0	1	2	3		
Project A Cash flow	−100,000	45,000	55,000	50,000	13,630	22.8%
Project B Cash flow	−60,000	30,000	37,000	28,000	12,496	27.2%

As the table shows, the two criteria give different results. If NPV is adopted, using a discount rate of 15 per cent, which is assumed to correspond to the actual opportunity cost of capital for the firm, then Project A is selected. On the other hand, Project B has a higher IRR and would be selected on that criterion.

The reason for this conflict can be better understood if the relationship between NPV and the discount rate is explored for each of the alternative projects. Fig. 15.2 shows the NPV of each project for every discount rate between zero and 30 per cent.

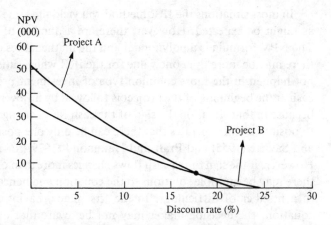

Fig. 15.2 Net present values and discount rate: projects A and B

As the cash flows associated with both projects are 'well-behaved', with no sign changes, the relationships between NPV and the discount rate are relatively simple. In both cases, the NPV declines as the discount rate rises, and in both cases there is only one IRR, where the discount rate equates the NPV to zero. However, the curves for the two projects have different slopes and intersect the axes at different points, while they intersect each other at a discount rate of approximately 18 per cent. For discount rates below 18 per cent, Project A has the higher NPV, while for discount rates above 18 per cent, the ranking is reversed and Project B has the higher value.

The conflict between the two different criteria can now be explained in a number of ways. The simplest is to note that when evaluating an investment the key issue is that the firm should take account of the opportunity cost of using its funds for the project. In the example used in Table 15.2 the opportunity cost of capital is 15 per cent, and that figure is of central importance. If the two projects are compared using present values at this discount rate, Project A is seen to be superior to Project B and that is the correct evaluation. The figures for IRR show the cost of capital where NPV would equal zero and would be useful if the cost of capital were actually at that level. However, as the cost of capital is actually 15 per cent and not 22.8 per cent or 27.2 per cent the IRR is essentially providing information with respect to a hypothetical situation in comparison with NPV, which is evaluating the actual situation.

Another way to explain essentially the same point is to note that the difference between the two criteria may be seen as involving two different assumptions with respect to the rate of return at which returns from the project may be reinvested. The NPV rule compares projects by using the actual opportunity cost of capital as the discount rate and is thereby implicitly assuming that shareholders can reinvest their money at that rate, which is correct. The IRR rule, in contrast, assumes that shareholders can reinvest at the IRR, which is in contradiction to the known fact that the opportunity cost of capital takes a different value.

The IRR method is inferior to NPV for a third reason: it is expressed in terms of a percentage rate of return, rather than in terms of a project's absolute effect on the wealth of shareholders. If a firm has a mutually exclusive choice between an investment costing £1, with an IRR of 100 per cent and an investment of £1,000,000, with an IRR of 15 per cent, the IRR criterion will dictate that the firm choose the investment of £1, whereas the investment of £1,000,000 will have a much more beneficial effect upon the wealth of the shareholders, which is the basic objective being pursued.

The conclusion with respect to the IRR rule, then, is that it has serious deficiencies in comparison with NPV and should only be used if careful thought is given to its shortcomings. Given that the IRR method is also more laborious than NPV it may be legitimate to wonder why financial management textbooks devote so much space to considering it. The usual argument put forward is that companies often use IRR, being intuitively more comfortable with the concept of a percentage rate of return, than with an absolute net present value, and that its disadvantages therefore need to be spelt out in detail.

Investment appraisal with capital rationing

If the aim of the firm is to maximise the wealth of its shareholders it should accept every investment project which has a positive net present value. However, there may be situations where this is not appropriate. If projects are mutually exclusive, the choice of one precludes investment in the others. A more general problem arises where a firm faces a number of projects which are not mutually exclusive but which cannot all be accepted because the amount of capital available is limited. Clearly, this situation could not arise in a world of absolutely perfect capital markets because it would be possible to borrow funds at the opportunity cost of capital to finance any project with a positive NPV at that cost of capital. Nevertheless, capital markets are not perfect and in practice firms may have to decide how to distribute the limited investment funds available amongst the opportunities which face them. They have to solve the problem of **capital rationing**.

Firms faced with this problem may a use variety of techniques in the attempt to find a solution. The simplest, which is referred to in most textbooks, involves the use of the **profitability index**, defined as:

$$PI = \frac{(NPV + I)}{I}$$

where:

PI = Profitability index
NPV = Net present value of the project
I = Initial investment outlay

The PI provides a measure of the present value per pound of initial investment outlay and may be used to rank projects by giving the highest priority to those having the highest PI. A solution to the capital rationing problem may then be found by sequentially accepting projects, beginning with those having the highest PI, until the capital constraint is reached. However, while this procedure 'can lead to a reasonable approximation for allocating funds that are limited in a single period' (Franks, Broyles and Carlton (1985) p.105) it is easily shown that the method may fail to identify the optimal grouping of projects, even in a relatively simple example. Table 15.3, for instance, shows an example adapted from Reekie and Crook (1982), showing five possible projects being considered by a firm facing an investment constraint of £4,000.

Table 15.3 Project selection under capital rationing

Project	Initial outlay	NPV	PI
A	2,000	1,000	1.5
B	1,000	400	1.4
C	2,000	700	1.35
D	1,000	250	1.25
E	1,000	200	1.2

If the PI criterion is applied as suggested, projects A and B will be selected first, yielding a present value of £1,400, and unused capital of £1,000. As that £1,000 is insufficient to fund project C, the firm then selects project D, using up all of the capital available and securing a total NPV of £1,650. However, simple inspection of the table shows that the firm could have secured an NPV of £1,700 by choosing projects A and C.

If the situation is more complex, with a large number of possible projects, capital spending constraints in every year, and the possibility of using cash flows generated from earlier projects to fund later ones, some more formal method of solving the problem is needed.

One possibility is to use **linear programming**. If we assume that each of the available projects is perfectly divisible, so that it is possible to carry out a proportion of each project, then the NPV for the total package of projects is given by the sum of the NPVs for the individual projects, each weighted by the proportion of the project which is undertaken. For the projects listed in Table 15.3 above, the total NPV for the package of projects, or part-projects, is given by the following equation:

$$NPV = 1000X_A + 400X_B + 700X_C + 250X_D + 200X_E$$

where: $X_{A,B,C,D,E}$ = proportion of each project undertaken

The problem is to maximise NPV, subject to the constraint that the total outlay in the first year does not exceed £4,000, and that the proportion of each project accepted must be between 0 and 1. If there are other constraints, perhaps on capital outflows in years other than the first, these can also be added in. The result is a linear programming problem which can be solved using standard techniques.

The obvious weakness of the linear programming approach to the capital rationing problem is that it assumes that every project is infinitely divisible. While this may be true in some cases and it may be possible to invest in 45 per cent of a project to install 1,000 square feet of floor space, for instance, most projects are either completely indivisible or only divisible into discrete 'chunks'. In this case, the solution to the linear programming problem may be impossible to implement and the technique has little value.

If fractions of projects are not feasible, decision-makers may have recourse to an alternative mathematical technique known as **integer programming**, in which the solutions are constrained to take the values of zero or one. This technique offers some assistance with the capital rationing problem, but a detailed examination of it lies outside the scope of this text. (See Franks, Broyles and Carleton (1985) pp.112–114 for a more extended treatment and further references on this issue.)

The cost of capital

The first part of this chapter has shown that the net present value (NPV) technique is the most appropriate way to evaluate investment projects and that use of the method requires the identification of a discount rate which is to be used in the calculations. However, little has been said about that discount rate, apart from noting that it should represent the opportunity cost of capital to the firm taking the investment decision.

The second part of this chapter considers how to measure the cost of capital, a topic which raises a number of fundamental issues and has led to a number of hotly contested academic debates.

The weighted average cost of capital

A firm may raise the funds for investment projects in a number of ways, including loans, debentures, retained earnings, and equity issues. Each of these may take a variety of forms in detail and each is subject to different accounting, legal and tax procedures, which render a detailed and comprehensive discussion impossibly complex. For simplicity, just two different types of capital will be considered. The first is **debt** and the second is **equity**.

The key characteristics of debt are that those who hold it have first call on any operating profits earned by the firm and they bear the risk of default. The key characteristics of equity are that its holders are the owners of the firm, they are the beneficiaries of any increase in the firm's value, they have the right to any profits made after interest payments have been made and they bear the equity risks associated with the variability of the firm's profits.

The cost of debt and the cost of equity need to be defined. The **cost of debt** consists of the interest rate which must be paid on new debt issues, adjusted for taxation. As the interest on debt is deductible for the purpose of corporate taxation, its cost to the firm is reduced so that the actual cost is given by the formula:

$$\text{After-tax cost of debt} = (\text{Interest rate}) \times (1 - \text{Tax rate})$$

The **cost of equity** may be defined as the rate of return that shareholders require on the ordinary shares of the firm in order to persuade them to continue holding those shares, or more formally: 'the minimum rate of return that the company must earn on the equity-financed portion of its investments in order to leave unchanged the market price of its stock'. (van Horne (1980) p.221.)

The calculation of this rate of return is a complex issue, which is examined in detail below. For the current purpose it is enough to note that it depends upon conditions in the capital market and the degree of risk attached to the operations of the individual firm.

If a firm is entirely financed through equity, it is clear that the cost of capital is the same as the cost of equity. At the other extreme, it is clear that for a firm which is financed entirely by debt, the cost of capital is the cost of debt. What is much more difficult, and contentious, is the calculation of the cost of capital for the vast majority of firms which are financed through a mixture of debt and equity, and the impact of **leverage** or the **gearing ratio** on that cost.

The traditional view of the weighted average cost of capital (WACC)

The starting point for the debate is to be found in the 'traditional' view of the issue which states that the cost of capital is given by a weighted average of the cost of equity and the cost of debt, as given by the formula for the weighted average cost of capital (WACC):

$$\text{WACC} = (\text{After-tax cost of debt} \times \text{Proportion of debt financing})$$
$$+ (\text{Cost of equity} \times \text{Proportion of equity financing})$$

Both the cost of debt and the cost of equity are held to vary with the gearing ratio, as shown in Fig. 15.3 below, which also shows the WACC.

As the figure shows, the cost of debt is held to be lower than the cost of equity, whatever the gearing ratio, because the holders of debt have the first call on the firm's profits. They are therefore exposed to less risk and will accept a lower level of return. As the gearing ratio increases, the cost of debt increases because the higher the level of debt, the higher the probability that the firm's profits are insufficient to service the debt and make repayments when due. At higher levels of gearing, the holders of debt are exposed to greater risk and therefore require a higher rate of return.

Similar considerations apply to the cost of equity. It begins at a higher level than the cost of debt because equity-holders bear a greater degree of risk, and it rises with the gearing ratio because a higher level of debt increases the risk to equity holders as well as to debt holders. The cost of debt and the cost of equity curves are therefore as shown in Fig. 15.3. The WACC which corresponds to these curves is U-shaped, as shown, because as the gearing ratio rises from a low level, the increasing proportion of cheaper debt lowers the average until it reaches the minimum point, after which the increasing risk attached to greater proportions of debt raise the WACC.

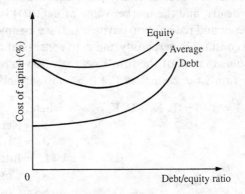

Fig. 15.3 The traditional view of gearing and the WACC

The Modigliani–Miller proposition

The traditional view of the relationship between the gearing ratio and the cost of capital has been challenged by Modigliani and Miller (M–M) in perhaps the most famous article ever written on the theory of finance (Modigliani and Miller (1958)). According to M–M, the cost of capital is not affected by the gearing ratio, as it is constant and equal to the cost of equity in a firm which has no debt. This result appears so unlikely at first sight that it requires closer attention.

The starting point for the M–M proposition lies in a very rigorous set of assumptions. These are:

- There are no taxes
- The capital market is efficient and competitive
- There are no transactions costs
- There are no costs associated with bankruptcy
- Shareholders can borrow on the same terms as corporations
- The cost of debt is constant, whatever the level of gearing.

If these assumptions hold, the total market value of two firms which are identical except for their levels of gearing must be the same, and their WACCs must be the same. If they were not, investors could improve their position by 'arbitrage', selling the shares of one and buying shares in the other, which would alter the relative prices of shares until the WACCs become equal. The level of gearing is therefore irrelevant to the WACC and the value of the firm.

This very striking proposition requires further explanation if it is to be fully understood. The total market value of a firm is given by the following equation:

$V = D + E$ where:

$\qquad$ V = Total market value
$\qquad$ E = Market value of equity
$\qquad$ D = Market value of debt

The market value of equity (E) is equal to the present value of the future stream of dividends, and the market value of debt (D) is equal to the present value of future interest and redemption payments. If we assume for simplicity that annual dividends are constant in perpetuity and debt consists of irredeemable debentures, and we also assume that all of the firm's net cash flow is paid out as interest or dividends, then the firm's net cash flow (Y) is a constant and is given by the equation:

$Y = d + I = [E . K_e + D . K_d]$ where:

$\qquad$ Y = Net cash flow
$\qquad$ d = Dividends paid
$\qquad$ I = Interest paid
$\qquad$ K_e = Cost of equity capital
$\qquad$ K_d = Cost of debt capital

The total value of the firm (V) is linked to the net cash flow (Y) and the WACC (K_o) in the following way:

$$V = \frac{Y}{K_o} \ or \ K_o = \frac{Y}{V}$$

If we now take two firms which have the same net cash flows and the same level of business risk, it is possible to show that they must have the same WACC and the same market value, even if they have different levels of gearing.

Consider an example of two firms, adapted from Lumby (1982). Firm A is financed entirely through equity in the form of 20,000 ordinary shares. Firm B is financed through £4,000 of debt at a cost of 4 per cent, plus equity in the form of 6,000 ordinary shares. Both firms have an annual net cash flow of £1,000, all of which is distributed in either dividends or interest payments. Table 15.4 shows how the WACC and share prices will be determined for firm A, which the stock market values at £10,000.

Table 15.4 WACC for firm A: an all equity firm

Annual net cash flow (Y)	1000
Market value of debt (D)	0
Cost of debt capital (K_d)	0
Annual interest flow ($D . K_d$)	0
Dividends paid ($d = Y - D . K_d$)	1000
Market value of equity (E)	10,000
Cost of equity ($K_e = d/E$)	.10
Total market value (V)	10,000
WACC ($K_o = Y/V$)	.10
Number of shares (N)	20,000
Price of shares (E/N)	.50

As the table shows, the WACC is equal to the cost of equity, at 10 per cent, the value of the firm is £10,000 and the share price is 50 pence.

A similar exercise can be carried out for firm B. This has the same risk attached as firm A and the same net cash flow, but is partly funded through debt. In contradiction to the M−M proposition, the stock market values the equity of firm B at £7,000, giving a total value for the firm of £11,000, compared with the £10,000 for firm A. The figures for B are shown in Table 15.5.

Table 15.5 WACC for firm B: partly debt funded

Annual net cash flow (Y)	1000
Market value of debt (D)	4000
Cost of debt capital (K_d)	0.04
Annual interest flow ($D . K_d$)	160
Dividends paid ($d = Y - D . K_d$)	840
Market value of equity (E)	7,000
Cost of equity ($K_e = d/E$)	.12
Total market value (V)	11,000
WACC ($K_o = Y/V$)	.091
Number of shares (N)	6,000
Price of shares (E/N)	116.66

Because the market values firm B more highly, the WACC differs between A and B and the M−M proposition does not hold. However, the central argument in the M-M debate is that if such differences do arise they represent a short-term disequilibrium in which firm B's shares are overvalued. Shareholders can improve their financial position by selling shares in B and buying shares in A. But if B's shares are being sold and A's shares being bought, the price of B's shares must fall while the price of A's rise. This process must continue until the value of both firms is the same, and their WACC is the same, despite the difference in their gearing.

Continuing with Lumby's example, the figures set out in Tables 15.4 and 15.5 above can be used to show how this process of arbitrage takes place. If we take an individual who owns 60 shares in company B, that investor's holding is worth £70 (60 × 116.66), it yields £8.40 per year, and it bears the level of financial risk associated with holding equity in a firm with a 4:7 gearing ratio. If the investor sells his holding for £70 and uses that money to buy shares in A, he can buy 140 shares yielding £7. However, he will also have altered the level of risk borne as his holdings are now in an ungeared firm. As the individual's original position involved the risk associated with a 4:7 gearing, and as we need to compare like with like, the investor can re-establish that level of gearing and risk by borrowing £40, at the cost of debt, and spending that £40 on a further purchase of shares in A. The individual investor then has a 'home-grown' gearing ratio of 4:7, a holding of £110 worth of shares in A, which yields £11, and a liability for interest payments of £1.60, giving a net return of £9.40, compared with only £8.40 on the original investment in B.

Clearly, there is an incentive to all investors in company B to sell their holdings and purchase shares in company A, which will tend to reduce the price of B's shares and raise the value of A's. These incentives will continue to be in place until the total values of the two firms, and their WACCs, are the same. In Lumby's example used above, this will produce an eventual share price of £1.05 for firm A and £1.08.33 for firm B, at which point the data for each firm is as given in Table 15.6 below.

Table 15.6 Post-arbitrage WACCs and values: ungeared firm A, geared firm B

	A	B
Net cash flows (Y)	1,000	1,000
Market value of debt (D)	0	4,000
Cost of debt (K_d)	0	.04
Annual interest flow (I)	0	160
Dividends paid (d)	1,000	840
Market value of equity (E)	10,500	6,500
Cost of equity (K_e)	.0952	.1292
Total market value (V)	10,500	10,500
WACC (K_o)	.0952	.0952
Number of shares	10,000	6,000
Share price	£1.05	£108.33

If the assumptions made by M–M are valid, the WACC is independent of the gearing ratio and is equal to the cost of equity in an ungeared firm. The relationship between the cost of debt, the cost of equity and the WACC is as given in Fig. 15.4. The WACC is constant, the cost of debt is constant and the cost of equity increases in a linear fashion with the gearing ratio (see Lumby, p.135 for further details).

While the M–M proposition provides a rigorous approach to the cost of capital, and illustrates the weaknesses of the traditional approach, its assumptions are extremely restrictive and the conclusions change if they are relaxed. The existence of transactions costs will affect the process of reaching equilibrium, although exactly how is not clear. If individuals and corporations cannot borrow at the same cost and risk, then 'home-made' gearing cannot provide a perfect substitute for corporate

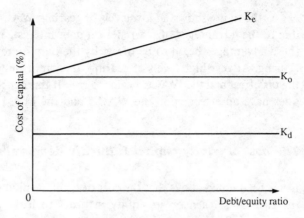

Fig. 15.4 The Modigliani–Miller view of gearing and the WACC

gearing, and the arbitrage process will be impeded. If there are costs associated with bankruptcy then the higher probability of bankruptcy which is associated with a higher gearing ratio will mean that investors require a higher rate of return from more highly geared firms.

Perhaps the most important issue of all in practice concerns the M–M assumption that there are no corporate taxes, which is clearly unrealistic. If the existence of taxation is recognised, and the interest on debt is tax deductible, then a higher level of gearing allows the firm to increase its net cash flows. The market value of the firm increases as gearing increases, and the WACC declines. As a result a firm seeking to maximise its total market value would have a capital structure consisting of 99.99 per cent debt and the minimum possible amount of equity. This is an uncomfortable result in many ways because while it is clearly more realistic to assume that taxes are present, the conclusion drawn as a result, is not one which matches firms' real-world behaviour where very high gearing ratios are rarely observed. As a result, the debate remains unresolved. Perhaps the most satisfactory, though tentative, conclusion (van Horne (1980) p.283, Lumby (1982) p.152) is that the combined effects of bankruptcy costs and taxation lead to a WACC curve as shown in Fig. 15.5.

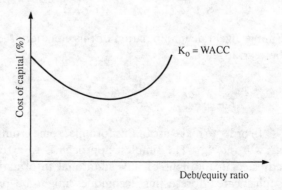

Fig. 15.5 WACC and gearing in the presence of bankruptcy costs and taxes

As the figure shows, at low levels of gearing, WACC declines with higher gearing, due to the advantages of tax relief on debt interest. However, beyond some point, these advantages begin to be offset by the bankruptcy costs associated with higher gearing. At very high levels of gearing, the bankruptcy effect is more powerful than the tax effect and the WACC begins to rise. If this conclusion is valid, capital structure does have an effect upon the WACC and the M–M proposition no longer holds.

The cost of equity capital I: the dividend valuation approach

It has been noted above that the cost of equity capital (K_e) is the rate of return which the firm must earn on its equity in order to leave the market price of its stock unchanged. The estimation of that rate may be approached in two different ways, based upon the **dividend valuation model** or the **capital asset pricing model**, each of which merit brief consideration.

The dividend valuation approach to the cost of equity capital is based upon the relationship between dividends, market price and the expected return on an investment. As the market price of a firm's equity (E) is equal to the present value of the dividends it earns (d), discounted by the required rate of return (K_e), the value of a firm which produces an annual flow of dividends which is constant (i.e. 'd' is the value of a perpetuity) is given by the equation:

$$E = \frac{d}{K_e} \text{ which rearranges to give } K_e = \frac{d}{E}$$

This is a very simple method to use for the estimation of the cost of equity and is restricted to the case where dividends are constant over time. A more sophisticated version may be developed for the case where **dividend growth** is constant over time, rather than the **dividend level**.

If 'd_1' is the dividend payable at the end of the first year, and 'g' is the growth rate of dividends, the market value of equity is given by the DCF calculation:

$$E = \frac{d_1}{(1 - K_e)} + \frac{d_1(1 + g)}{(1 + K_e)^2} + \frac{d_1(1 + g)^2}{(1 + K_e)^2} \cdots + \frac{d_1(1 + g)^{n-1}}{(1 + K_e)^n}$$

Simple algebraic manipulation of this equation (see Lumby (1982) p.78) allows it to be rearranged as:

$$E = \frac{d_1}{K_e - g} \text{ or } K_e = \frac{d_1}{E} + g$$

In order to make use of this formula, some estimate has to be made of the dividend growth rate 'g'. The simplest approach is to extrapolate the past rate of growth, adjusted in the light of any additional information which is available, or more sophisticated forecasting techniques might be preferred. Whichever method of estimation is chosen, the basic approach remains the same, using the present value of the expected future stream of dividends to establish the relationship between dividends, market price and the expected rate of return.

The cost of equity II: the capital asset pricing model

The dividend valuation approach makes no explicit reference to the degree of risk attached to the ownership of equity, being based entirely upon the future flow of benefits which it is expected to generate. An alternative approach, which places the valuation of risk at the heart of the analysis, is known as the **capital asset pricing model** (CAPM). This has its basis in a relatively complex body of financial analysis, known as portfolio theory, which lies outside the scope of this text. Nevertheless, it is possible to outline the basic principles involved, leaving a fuller treatment to the financial management textbooks.

The starting point for a brief overview of the CAPM is to note that the required return on a risky security may be divided into two components. The first is the return which could be earned on a riskless security and the second is a premium in compensation for the risk involved. (It is generally assumed that investors are risk-averse to some degree, and not risk-lovers.)

The risk-free return depends upon general conditions in financial markets and may be reasonably approximated by the return on Government bonds. The premium for risk which is to be applied for an individual firm is calculated by measuring the variability of the return on the firm's stock, and comparing it with the variability of the **'market portfolio'** of stocks, which reflects the variability of the stock market as a whole. This is encapsulated in a measure known as the **'beta co-efficient'** for the individual stock. If the shares of a firm have a 'beta' which is greater than one, investing in those shares is more risky than investing in the stock market as a whole. If the beta is less than one, the shares are less risky than the market as a whole, and if beta equals one investing in the share bears exactly the same risk as investing in the market as a whole. The expected return on a security is then given by the following equation:

$$K_e = R_F + b[K_M - R_F] \qquad \text{where:}$$

R_F = the return on a risk-free security
b = the 'beta' for the individual security
K_M = the return on the market portfolio of shares, representing the market as a whole

As the equation shows, if the security has a beta of one, the expected return will be the same as that for the market as a whole. If beta is larger than one, the return will be higher, if beta is less than one it will be lower, reflecting the lower level of risk associated with the individual security being assessed.

Clearly, the calculation of beta is of central importance to the application of the CAPM. It may be defined as the co-variance between the returns on a security and the returns to the market as a whole, divided by the variance of the returns to the market. Investment advisory services publish estimates of 'beta' for most stocks, which allow the CAPM to be used to calculate the cost of equity capital for the stock of most major companies.

Whether or not the CAPM is an entirely effective means of estimating the cost of equity capital remains a matter for debate and for empirical testing, which is extremely difficult. All of the returns referred to in the model are expected returns, which are not directly observable and may not be well approximated by historical returns. The market portfolio, whose returns and variability are central to the analysis, is very difficult to construct but should in principle contain every asset available to investors, including human capital, personal money and jewellery, and a whole range of assets which are non-marketable and whose returns cannot be directly observed. The empirical tests which have been carried out (see Copeland and Weston (1983) p.207) suggest that the CAPM has some predictive value, but have also tended to find that low beta stocks earn more than the CAPM would predict, while high beta stocks earn less. Factors other than beta, like price/earnings ratios and firm size also seem to have an influence on the rate of return, which reduces the usefulness of the CAPM equation which relies entirely upon beta as the determining variable.

Illustration

Investment appraisal: a worked example of NPV and IRR

The Wizzo Lollipop Company is considering the installation of a new production line, which will allow it to produce chocolate ice cream.

The initial investment required is estimated to be £1,000,000. The life of the new line is estimated to be five years and the marketing department estimates that initial sales revenue will be £1,000,000, rising at the rate of 10 per cent per year. The production department estimates that production of chocolate ice cream will incur fixed costs of £150,000 per year plus incremental variable costs of 50 pence for each £1 of sales revenue. Tax is chargeable at 40 per cent of profits, calculated as revenue minus costs, including depreciation. Wizzo uses the straight-line method to calculate depreciation over the five-year life of the equipment.

At the end of the project it is estimated that the equipment will be sold as scrap for £350,000. The cash flows from the project are shown in Table 15.7.

Table 15.7 Estimated cash flows

Revenue	1,000,000	1,100,000	1,210,000	1,331,000	1,464,100
Variable costs	500,000	550,000	605,000	665,500	735,050
Fixed costs	150,000	150,000	150,000	150,000	150,000
Depreciation	200,000	200,000	200,000	200,000	200,000
Profit before tax	150,000	200,000	255,000	315,500	382,050
Income tax	60,000	80,000	102,000	126,200	152,820
Profit after tax	90,000	120,000	153,000	189,300	229,230
Plus depreciation	200,000	200,000	200,000	200,000	200,000
Revenue from sale of scrap					350,000
Net cash inflow	290,000	320,000	353,000	389,300	779,230

As Table 15.7 shows, depreciation is first deducted, in order to arrive at profits before tax, and then added back in, in order to calculate net cash inflow. This is because depreciation is not in itself a cash flow, but it affects cash flows because of its impact on the tax deducted.

If the cost of capital to Wizzo is 12 per cent, the net present value (NPV) of the chocolate ice cream project is given by the equation:

$$NPV = \frac{290,000}{(1+0.12)^1} + \frac{320,000}{(1+0.12)^2} + \frac{353,000}{(1+0.12)^3} + \frac{389,300}{(1+0.12)^4} + \frac{779,230}{(1+0.12)^5}$$

$$- 1,000,000 = 466,193$$

At the given discount rate of 12 per cent, the project adds to the value of the firm, and should therefore be undertaken. If the discount rate had not been known, the firm may have preferred to use the internal rate of return (IRR) method, to evaluate the project. Most financial calculators allow this to be done directly, and there is a wide range of computer software which would carry out the task with ease. In the absence of such aids, or in order to have a better 'feel' for the project, the IRR could be estimated by making successive guesses and adjusting the estimate each time, in the light of the result.

Beginning with an estimate of 10 per cent, gives an NPV in excess of £500,000, indicating clearly that the IRR is higher than 10 per cent. Recalculation for 20 per cent still gives a positive figure, of approximately £170,000, showing that the IRR is above 20 per cent. At 28 per cent the NPV calculation yields a negative result and at 24 per cent positive one, indicating that this pair of estimates 'bracket' the true result. Confirmation with a calculator shows that the IRR is in fact 26.3 per cent.

In this example, calculation of the IRR raises no difficult mathematical problems because the sign of the cash flows changes only once and the solution is unique. When adopting the iterative approach to solving for IRR it should always be remembered that in complex cases there may be multiple solutions, which could be missed by this simple technique.

References and further reading

R. Brealey and S. Myers, *Principles of Corporate Finance*, (London, McGraw-Hill, 1984)

T.E. Copeland and J.F. Weston, *Financial Theory and Corporate Policy*, (Reading, Mass., Addison-Wesley, 1983)

E.J. Douglas, *Managerial Economics*, (Englewood Cliffs, Prentice-Hall, 1979)

J.R. Franks, J.E. Broyles and W.T. Carleton, *Corporate Finance: Concepts and Applications*, (Boston, Kent, 1985)

J.van Horne, *Financial Management and Policy*, (Englewood Cliffs, Prentice-Hall, 1980)

J.H. Lorie and L.J. Savage, 'Three Problems in Rationing Capital', *Journal of Business*, **28**, October 1955

S. Lumby, *Investment Appraisal and Related Decisions*, (Walton-on-Thames, Nelson, 1982)

F. Modigliani and M. Miller, 'The Cost of Capital, Corporation Finance and the Theory of Investment,' *American Economic Review*, **48**, 1958

J.W. Pratt and J.S. Hammond, 'Evaluating and Comparing Projects: Simple Detection of False Alarms', *Journal of Finance*, **34**, December 1979.

W.D. Reekie and J.N. Crook, *Managerial Economics*, (Oxford, Philip Allan, 1982)

Self-test questions

1 Which of the following statements is true?

(a) if there were no inflation it would not be necessary to discount the value of future cash flows in order to reach present values.
(b) discounting is necessary in order to recognise the time value of money.
(c) depreciation, using the straight-line method, should be included when calculating cash flows for NPV analysis.

2 Calculate the internal rate of return for the following stream of cash flows:

Year	0	1	2
Cash flow	− 100	+ 100	+ 20

3 List three reasons for preferring net present value to the internal rate of return as a criterion for evaluating investment projects.

4 Name the mathematical technique which may be used to solve the problem of capital rationing:

(a) when projects are perfectly divisible
(b) when projects cannot be sub-divided

5 Write down the equations which determine the cost of equity capital according to:

(a) the dividend valuation model
(b) the capital asset pricing model

Exercise

'The Modigliani–Miller proposition undermines the traditional view that there is an optimal degree of gearing, but is itself undermined by the recognition of the impact of bankruptcy costs and taxation.'

Explain this statement

Answers on page 425

16 Policy towards competition

This chapter examines the rationale for competition policy and outlines the major features of competition policies in the United Kingdom, the European Community and the United States. Alternative concepts of competition, including perfect competition, 'workable competition' and the 'Austrian view' are outlined and their implications for the social cost of monopoly power examined. The chapter then goes on to consider the legal control of 'dominant position', mergers and restrictive trade practices.

Alternative concepts of competition and monopoly power

Textbook approaches to competition and monopoly

In economics textbooks, and in large parts of the professional economics literature, the term 'competition' is synonymous with 'perfect competition' as described and analysed in Chapter 9. In this type of market structure an industry consists of a large number of small firms, producing identical products. New entry to the industry is completely free and this combination of circumstances guarantees that firms have absolutely no market power at all. The outcome of such a situation is that prices will be set equal to marginal cost, and it has been shown in Chapter 9 that the resulting allocation of resources is optimal, in the sense that social welfare is maximised, that being defined as the difference between benefits to consumers and costs to the economy.

In the same way, the textbook analysis of monopoly refers to the very restricted circumstance of 'pure' monopoly where there is only one firm in the industry and no possibility of entry. In this situation it can be shown that price will exceed marginal cost so that social welfare is not maximised, and firms will be able to exert considerable

---

* The first part of this chapter draws on the author's 'Economic Concepts of Competition', published as Chapter Two in J. Agnew, *Competition Law*, (London, Allen & Unwin, 1985). The author is grateful to the publisher for permission to draw on that material, and to John Agnew for providing advice on this chapter.

market power, allowing them to earn supernormal profits in the long run.

The case in favour of competition and against monopoly can be understood in terms of this analysis. Monopoly leads to a misallocation of resources because price is not set equal to marginal cost. Furthermore, the monopolist is under little pressure to keep its costs down and as a result will tend to be 'X-inefficient', incurring higher costs than are strictly necessary through organisational slack, laziness and general lack of tight control.

The limitations of the textbook models

The textbook analysis of competition and monopoly provides a basic rationale for anti-monopoly or anti-trust policy. However, this approach is subject to criticism on the grounds that the two cases examined are highly unrealistic and markets which conform to their very tight specifications are rare and perhaps even non-existent. It has been pointed out in Chapter 1 that for some of the purposes of economic analysis this lack of realism is not necessarily a weakness. If the models are to be used for purely positive and predictive purposes then unrealistic assumptions are quite acceptable, even necessary. On the other hand, if the analysis is to be used for 'normative' purposes, that is to make statements about how the economy should behave and what sort of policy should be introduced, the problems are real. If economic analysis is to be used to decide whether one real world situation is superior to another, and neither conforms closely to either 'pure' model then it is difficult to see how the models can be used convincingly.

It might be argued that most industries are a fair approximation to either perfect competition or monopoly and those which are roughly competitive could be left alone while those which are roughly monopolistic could be made subject to control. Unfortunately this argument is badly flawed. In the first place the dividing line between 'approximately competitive' and 'approximately monopolistic' is impossible to draw. In the second place, and more fundamentally, there is the **second-best problem**, touched on in Chapter 13. Although perfect competition in all industries can be shown to give a first-best optimal allocation of resources, it is not at all clear what is the second-best optimum if perfect competition is not achievable everywhere. It could well be the case that the lack of perfect competition in some industries means that the best available allocation of resources requires monopoly behaviour in some other industries. These difficulties have led economists to search for a variety of solutions to the problem.

The search for 'workable competition'

If the requirement that all industries be perfectly competitive is an unattainable counsel of perfection, then an obvious response is to try to identify 'workable competition', defined by Clarke (1940) as: 'the most desirable forms of competition, selected from those that are practically possible.'

The difficulty is that we have very little to guide us on the characteristics of such a market structure, and the theory of second-best makes it clear that simply approximating to perfect competition is not the answer. Clarke recognised this and his work on the issue provides an early intuitive statement of the second-best problem. Unfortunately, its implications have often not been taken up by other writers on the subject. Attempts to identify 'workable competition' have often consisted of long lists of structural and behavioural 'norms' to which an industry has to conform before being deemed workably competitive. However, many of the norms consist of nothing more than approximations to perfect competition, for which there is no sound rationale. As a result one observer (Stigler (1956)) has suggested, rather cynically, that it is a simple matter to decide whether an industry is workably competitive or not. All that is required is to have a graduate student write a thesis on it. There is, however, a further condition, which is that no other student should ever be allowed to decide whether the industry is workably competitive or not, because he would be bound to reach the opposite conclusion!

The search for 'workable competition' has not, therefore, proved very fruitful although it is worth noting (and somewhat worrying) that the law on competition often seems to assume that some undefined version does exist and is understood. Indeed, if the law on competition outlaws certain market structures, or certain actions on the part of firms, that does imply that such structures and actions are known to be incompatible with workable competition, which in turn implies that the concept is understood by someone.

Structure–Conduct–Performance

In view of the failure to clearly identify the characteristics of workable competition an alternative approach is to turn away from theory and examine the facts about industries' activities, in order to identify those factors which lead firms to behave in unacceptable ways, and those which lead to satisfactory performance. This approach was suggested by Mason (1937) who noted that: 'It is not sufficient to conduct purely analytical . . . studies . . . A further study of different types of industrial markets and business practices . . . is the only way in which economics can contribute directly to the shaping of public policy.'

This call has been taken up by groups of economists using increasingly sophisticated statistical methods in the attempt to identify the empirical links between industries' performance, their structure and the conduct of the companies within them. Many different relationships have been examined but the most common hypothesis to be tested is that profitability in an industry may be positively linked to the level of concentration, to the height of entry barriers, the extent of product differentiation and the rate of growth of demand.

As with so many issues, opinions vary widely on the value of this approach, which is known as the structure–conduct–performance paradigm. Many of the studies (though by no means all) have confirmed the existence of a positive relationship between the level of concentration in an industry and its profitability. That in turn has confirmed the view of many writers that concentration confers monopoly power and that government regulation of highly concentrated industries is therefore justified. Unfortunately, there are a number of reasons why such a conclusion cannot be held to with great confidence.

The first problem concerns the difficulties associated with the statistical methods used to identify the links between the various different variables. Many of the central concepts, like concentration, entry barriers and product differentiation, are difficult to measure and researchers are forced to approximate them using 'proxy' variables. As a result the findings of the different studies tend to vary widely with the sources of data used and the samples chosen. Very similar studies have often produced radically different, even diametrically opposite, conclusions!

There are also difficulties with the mis-specification of the relationships between the variables. In most structure–conduct–performance investigations it is assumed that the direction of causation runs from industry structure to industry performance. However, even a simple model like that of perfect competition makes it clear that performance (in the shape of a high level of profits) can affect structure (by inducing entry). If the relationships between structure and performance run in both directions, then the results of simple statistical techiques using just one equation provide very little meaningful information about how industry works.

The second problem is more fundamental, because it concerns the interpretation of the results and the use to which they are put. If it is accepted, for the sake of argument, that the evidence does show a positive link between concentration and profitability, the most common interpretation of that finding is that concentration bestows monopoly power and that there are gains to be had from an active policy against concentration and mergers. However, as Demsetz (1973, 1974) and others have noted, the same factual relationship between concentration and profitability could arise from a wholly different mechanism. Higher profits could simply be the result of greater efficiency, and high levels of concentration could simply be the incidental result of market share becoming concentrated in the hands of firms which have 'got it right'. If the cost structure of an industry exhibits substantial scale economies, or if a few firms have strong management teams while others don't, then the industry will become concentrated in the hands of a few highly profitable firms for reasons which have little to do with the pure monopolist's raising of price through the restriction of output.

There are, therefore, two completely different interpretations of the concentration-profitability relationship. The 'market power' interpretation sees it as evidence of powerful firms' ability to acquire and use monopoly power, to the detriment of the public. The 'competitive' view argues that concentration may be the result of a desirable competitive process. It is unfortunate, then, that Mason's challenge to economists to improve their understanding of the issues by examining the evidence has not fulfilled the aspirations of those who hoped that an appeal to the facts, over the head of theory, would help in the construction of policy.

Competition as a process, rather than a state

The 'competitive' interpretation of the concentration-profitability relationship clearly implies a completely different conception of competition from that embodied in the model of perfect competition, or approximations to it. The perfectly competitive world is completely static and there is no reference to behaviour over time. The basic picture of the economy which it represents is one of a group of households who have fixed tastes for a set of known products, facing a group of firms having a fixed set of technologies available to them. Everybody is perfectly informed about everything and the abstract forces of supply and demand ensure that consumer satisfaction is maximised. In that concept of competition there is no rivalry amongst firms, who simply face 'the market'. Emphasis is placed upon how an industry will behave in equilibrium and profits are simply a temporary aberration, which are eliminated in the long run by entry. Such a model has no room for the entrepreneur, for unthought-of innovations, or for rivalry between individual firms.

A very different view of competition, which links back to much earlier conceptions, and is much closer to the layman's interpretation of the term, is that which is sometimes referred to as **the Austrian View** (Reekie (1979)). In this view competition is not a state, but a process taking place through time in a world which is never in equilibrium. All of the possibilities are not known to everyone, firms have differing abilities and the entrepreneur who exercises creativity and foresight is able to alter the world he inhabits in ways which allow him to create profit opportunities. In this situation a company may develop a monopoly position. However, unless the monopoly arises from some government-imposed restriction, or the sole ownership of a resource which has no substitute, it will tend to be a temporary one as other firms recognise the opportunities and enter the industry, or devise substitute products for the one which is earning high prices and profits. In the Austrian view (which seems highly consistent with much of the management literature on corporate strategy) entrepreneurs are constantly trying to become temporary monopolists by being the first to invent a new product, or identify a new market, while others are constantly trying to break down existing monopolies by entering markets which are seen to offer the prospect of profits.

From this perspective, profits may arise in three different ways. First, there are true monopoly profits, arising from the firm being protected from competition in some way. These are undesirable and policy should prevent firms from having such advantages. Second, there are 'windfall' profits which arise as a matter of chance because cost and demand conditions turn out to be more favourable than anyone expected. Thirdly, there will be an element of 'entrepreneurial' profit, arising because some firms have a greater ability to identify profit opportunities or to go further and create opportunities which did not exist before. This last form of profit owes nothing to monopoly power, because the new opportunities are open to all, and it should not be seen as an indicator of misallocated resources.

Clearly, this interpretation has radical implications for the interpretation of profits, and for policy towards competition. If the notion of competition as a process is superior to the static conception set out in the economics textbooks then the existence of profits is at least partly the result of socially beneficial creative behaviour. Profits do not signal the existence of damaging monopoly power and it would be a mistake to introduce policies designed to eliminate the situations which lead to those excess profits.

The difficulty with this approach is that once the benchmark of perfect competition is abandoned there are no clear guidelines for deciding what kind of situations should be made subject to control through monopoly policy. Littlechild (1981) suggests that case studies of individual firms might allow some separation of the different sources of profits ('good' entrepreneurial activity, random variations in the environment and 'bad' monopoly power). Demsetz (1969) has suggested a 'comparative institutions' approach, comparing the likely development of the market process under different types of policy regime. However, it is difficult to see how this could be achieved in practice. Perhaps the only clear prescription which emerges, in common with the more orthodox approach, is that the removal of entry barriers should be a major focus for competition policy.

'Contestable markets'

The importance of entry conditions is also a key feature of a new approach to the analysis of competition, known as the 'contestable markets' approach (Baumol, Panzar and Willig (1982)). In some respects this development has elements in common with the Austrian view in that its general conclusions are that an industry may perform in a socially acceptable way even if it contains a very small number of firms and does not correspond even remotely to the specification of perfect competition. However, the origins of the new approach lie much closer to the mainstream of industrial economic theory, and it has the advantage of resting upon more conventional analytical foundations than the Austrian view. A full exposition of 'contestable markets' lies beyond the scope of this text but it is possible to provide an outline.

The most important new concept is that of 'contestability'. A perfectly contestable market is one in which entry is free, exit is costless, existing firms and entrants compete on equal terms and potential entrants are not deterred from entering by the threat of retaliatory price-cutting by incumbents. In such a market it can be shown that the benefits associated with perfect competition will accrue, even if there are very few firms in the industry. As the contestability theorists themselves put it:

'Monopolists and oligopolists who populate such markets are sheep in wolves' clothing, for under this arrangement potential rivals can be as effective as actual competitors in forcing pro-social behaviour upon incumbents, whether or not such behaviour is attractive to them. As we have seen . . . this may be true where observed market phenomena are far from the competitive norm, and even where they superficially assume some pattern previously thought to be pernicious *per se*.' (Baumol *et al.* p.350)

Clearly, the concept of a contestable market is related to the idea of entry barriers and such a market might simply be thought of as one where entry barriers are limited.

However, the new theory also suggests that in many instances barriers to entry are less formidable than has previously been supposed. In particular, the analysis points to the importance of sunk costs as the major real deterrent to entry. (Sunk costs are those which cannot be eliminated, even by cessation of production.) If sunk costs are small, entrants will have little difficulty in competing with existing firms on equal terms and the threat of this competition will force incumbents to behave like perfect competitors. Baumol *et al*. (1982) provide a good example in a small airline market. If we consider the market for air travel between two towns where the number of people travelling is only enough to fill one aeroplane, we have an example of a '**natural monopoly**'. It will always be cheaper for the route to be served by a single airline than for two or more to fly in competition. As a result the market will be monopolised, in the sense that there is only one supplier. However, that supplier will not be able to operate like a textbook monopolist. If aircraft can be rented, or if there is an active market for second-hand planes, then sunk costs are very limited. All an entrant need do, if the incumbent airline is creating a profitable opportunity by charging high fares, is to fly his aircraft on to the tarmac, undercut the incumbent and make a profit. If the incumbent then cuts his price the entrant can literally fly away and either use the plane on another route or sell it (or cease renting it). The absence of sunk costs makes entry cheaply reversible and the threat or the reality of easy entry will discipline the incumbent 'monopolist'.

The contestable markets approach has a number of implications for competition policy. First, it shows that it is not appropriate to decide on whether to intervene in an industry by making reference to the degree of departure from the conditions of perfect competition. Second, it provides an alternative benchmark to the unattainable criterion of perfect competition, that of 'contestability'. When considering the structure and behaviour of an industry, the first step is to decide whether or not it constitutes a contestable market. If it does, government interference is not needed, even if the industry exhibits symptoms which have in the past been accepted as indicators of poor market performance, such as high concentration, price discrimination, mergers and vertical integration. On the other hand, if the industry is not contestable then intervention to make it so needs to be considered. First and foremost governments need to consider means by which entry to and exit from an industry can be made easier. In particular, policy needs to reduce the level of sunk costs, which form the major barrier to exit and the main impediment to contestability. Measures could include having sunk costs borne by government, which would then lease facilities to firms, or by mandating that sunk costs should be shared by a consortium. Alternatively, sunk costs might be reduced by tax advantages for rapid depreciation, for retooling, or for the reuse of old plant in new activities. Anything which improves the efficiency of the second-hand equipment markets would also be useful.

The rationale for competition law

Measuring the cost of monopoly

If an anti-monopoly policy is to be introduced it will use resources and impose costs on the economy. It is important, therefore, to consider whether the losses caused by monopoly are sufficiently large to justify the expenditure incurred in correcting it. This in turn requires some estimate of the **cost of monopoly power**. It is hardly surprising, in the light of the preceding discussion, to discover that estimates of the cost of monopoly power vary widely with the method of calculation used and with the analyst's interpretation of the nature of competition and the source of profits. The mechanics of the measurement process are too complex to detail here, beyond noting that they begin from the proposition that monopoly power will reduce consumer satisfaction and increase profits. Published figures for profits are then used as the basis for measuring the size of the loss involved. The earliest attempt to make an estimate in this way was carried out by Harberger (1954) who concluded that the loss was very slight, at approximately 0.1 per cent of national income (for the United States), a figure which has been refined but not radically altered by others using similar methods who also found the losses due to monopoly to be small.

If such estimates are correct, there are empirical grounds for questioning whether monopoly policy is justified at all. However, as might be expected, other commentators have criticised the basic method and produced much larger estimates. Some, for instance, have suggested that monopoly not only results in losses arising from sub-optimal prices and levels of output but that would-be monopolists use up scarce resources in the attempt to secure their monopoly positions, and the cost of those resources should be added in to the social losses caused. Posner (1975), for instance, argued that if acquiring a monopoly position is in itself a competitive activity then the cost of becoming a monopolist will just equal the monopoly profits to be made. In that case, the cost of monopoly is much higher than that estimated by Harberger and others using similar methods. Cowling and Mueller (1978) extend these arguments to calculate a number of different estimates of the cost of monopoly in the United States and the United Kingdom, using information on individual companies rather than whole industries. Their conclusion was that for the United States the losses attributable to General Motors alone amounted to $1.75 billion, which exceeded Harberger's estimate for the whole economy. For the 734 largest firms in the economy the loss attributable to monopoly power was equal to 13 per cent of the gross output of those firms. In the British case it was concluded that monopoly losses could be as high as seven per cent of output, with three firms alone (Shell, BP and BAT) accounting for losses of £186 million.

If these latter estimates are correct, the case for anti-monopoly policy is strengthened and the estimates of losses attributable to individual firms could provide the starting point for enforcement. However, that takes the debate back to the differences between the 'market power' and the 'competitive' approach to concentration and profits. Littlechild (1981) has argued that the whole conceptual framework used by Cowling and Mueller introduces an upward bias into the calculations, which therefore give highly exaggerated results. The basic problem is that all the attempts to measure the cost of monopoly power take place within a framework of long-run equilibrium. The investigators assume that the profits which they observe will be maintained in the long run and are entirely due to the monopoly position held by the firms. Under that assumption, all profits represent welfare losses. But that is a very strong assumption and if the industries were not in long-run equilibrium at the moment of observation then the profits and price/cost margins observed cannot be attributed to monopoly power. Even in a perfectly competitive industry, where there is no monopoly power at all, large profits can be made in the short run if demand increases. It has also been noted above that there are three components to supernormal profit – true monopoly profit, windfall gains and 'entrepreneurial' profit. Only the first arises from socially harmful behaviour and to assume that all profit is of this type seems certain to lead to over-estimates of the cost of monopoly.

Economics and competition law

As in so many other areas of economic analysis, there is no consensus on the importance of the need for competition law. Some economists argue that monopoly power is a major impediment to the efficient use of the economy's resources, imposing substantial costs on the economy. Others take the view that the dangers have been exaggerated and that the need for intervention is much less marked. As a result, economic analysis has not provided the law-maker with a clear set of guidelines concerning the types of industrial structure and market behaviour which lead to acceptable levels of performance. Although the rationale for competition law is fundamentally economic, the connections between the law on competition and the economic analysis of competition are much more limited than might be expected or hoped for. The best that can be said is that economic analysis illustrates that there are three dimensions to the concept of competition. The first concerns the **structure of an industry,** where the number of firms, their market shares and the condition of entry are of central importance. Second there is the dimension of **company behaviour,** encompassing firms' objectives and the methods they adopt in order to achieve those objectives. Third, there is the industry's **performance** with respect to prices, costs, profits, productivity, efficiency and equity. The law on competition is concerned with both structure and behaviour because of their perceived impact on performance, as is shown below.

Different approaches to monopoly policy and competition law

The debate on 'rules versus discretion'

There are two fundamentally different approaches to the law on competition. The first, which forms the basis for much of the American system of anti-trust legislation, is known as the 'rules' approach. In a system based upon rules certain types of market structure or behaviour are illegal '*per se*'. It is not necessary to show that the structure or the behaviour in question has been harmful because the illegality arises from the structure or the behaviour itself, not from any result which follows. The alternative approach is known as the '**discretionary**' approach around which the British system is largely based. In this type of system there is no automatic presumption that certain types of market structure or certain types of behaviour are necessarily harmful. Instead it is noted that some structures or behaviours may allow firms to damage the public interest, and it is that damage which the law aims to prevent. In other words, in the American system it is monopoly power which is illegal. In the British system it is the abuse of monopoly power which is illegal. The advantages and disadvantages of these alternative approaches to competition policy are themselves the subject of debate. The 'rules' approach has a number of advantages:

- firms have a clear understanding of what is permitted and what is not
- the criteria on which policy is based are objective
- the system is relatively inexpensive to administer
- the costs of legal procedures are lower than in a situation where the law has to be decided case by case (although the American example shows that the cost of lawyers does not become negligible!)
- firms have less encouragement to waste resources by lobbying those they believe will have influence in deciding their case, or potential cases.

The first major disadvantage of the 'rules' approach is that the system is potentially inflexible and unable to deal effectively with the special circumstances of individual cases. This could be overcome by having an increasingly complex set of rules, setting out how different circumstances are to be treated (Hay (1988), but as the rules become more complicated their application becomes more open to interpretation and the basic advantages of the 'rules' approach are lost. The second major problem, which follows from the discussion above, is that analysis has provided no clear indication of what exactly the rules should be. The 'rules' approach therefore involves the simple and efficient application of rules which may be incorrect.

The advantages and disadvantages of the 'discretion' approach are essentially the converse of the 'rules' approach. As there is no presumption that certain types of structure or behaviour are necessarily harmful each case has to be decided upon its individual merits. That allows a degree of flexibility which is not available under the rules approach. On the other hand, each case has to be investigated in depth, which is extremely expensive, and companies are uncertain with regard to the permissibility of some actions. As a result they may be deterred from carrying out legitimate activities for fear of government intervention, and there is the strong possibility that cases are decided on political, rather than economic grounds. Given the uncertain application of the law under this approach companies may also waste scarce resources in lobbying to attempt to influence the outcome of cases they are involved in, or to prevent their actions from being subject to legal proceedings at all.

Alternative institutional and legal frameworks

Apart from the differences between the 'rules' and 'discretion' approaches, competition policies may differ in the way in which they relate to the legal system, which may be through administrative controls, the criminal law or the civil law. In the American system, anti-trust policy is associated most closely with the criminal law, and it is a criminal offence to monopolise a market or to collude with others to restrict competition. Under European Community legislation, fines can be imposed upon offenders but civil sanctions involving injunctions and damages are also used to restrain anti-competitive activity. In the United Kingdom the system is based almost entirely around administrative controls and limited civil sanctions, with very little use being made of criminal sanctions.

Policy towards monopoly or 'dominant position'

The UK system

The British approach to monopoly or 'dominant position' can be traced back to the Monopolies and Restrictive Practices Act of 1948 and currently involves three main legal channels:

- a monopoly reference under the Fair Trading Act 1973
- a competition reference under the Competition Act 1980
- a prohibition of the abuse of a dominant position within the Common Market, under Article 86 of the Treaty of Rome.

Under the Fair Trading Act 1973 the Director General of Fair Trading has the power to refer a monopoly situation to the Monopolies and Mergers Commission (MMC). A monopoly situation is defined as one where at least 25 per cent of goods or services of a particular description are supplied in the UK by one firm, or two or more firms acting in such a way as to restrict competition between them. (Until the 1973 Act the proportion was 33 per cent.)

Clearly, the definition of the market to which the 25 per cent criterion applies is important, as any firm would be a monopolist if the definition were drawn narrowly enough. In principle the market which is defined should take into account a group of products or services which are very close substitutes for each other, having high cross-elasticities of demand, and the geographical area served by the firms under investigation. In practice it can be extremely difficult to decide on an appropriate definition of the market covered and companies coming under investigation could spend considerable time and effort attempting to redefine the boundaries of the market in such a way as to render them immune from investigation. In order to avoid this problem the Fair Trading Act 1973 simply states that in making the reference the Director General or Secretary of State should state the criteria on which goods and services are to be included. When a reference is made to the MMC, it has to consider a number of questions, namely:

- does a monopoly situation exist?
- in whose favour does it exist?
- are any steps being taken to exploit or maintain the monopoly position?
- are these steps contrary to the public interest and what are the adverse effects?

If the MMC should find against a firm, or group of firms, the Director of Fair Trading then usually seeks undertakings from them, designed to remedy the abuse which has been found. If such undertakings are not forthcoming, or not kept, the Minister responsible has quite wide powers to make an order prohibiting the anti-competitive behaviour, or even ordering disinvestment. Should such orders be breached, enforcement is by civil procedures.

A monopoly reference has a number of limitations, as it can only be used when there is a monopoly situation as defined. The whole of the market has to be investigated, which is expensive and time-consuming (some investigations take years to complete) and the sanctions are limited. As a result, the Competition Act 1980 gave powers to the Director to investigate the practices of a single firm if he believed it to be engaged in anti-competitive practices likely to restrict, distort or prevent competition in the UK. The Act makes no direct reference to monopoly or dominance in this respect, but it is unlikely that the terms could be applied to a firm which did not have substantial market power. The Director himself can make an investigation, rather than referring it to the MMC, and can try to obtain any undertakings deemed necessary from the firm in question. If these cannot be obtained satisfactorily then a 'competition reference' may be made to the MMC which must report back within six months.

Satisfactory evaluation of British policy on dominance or monopoly is difficult, given the failure of economic analysis to provide an adequate definition of workable competition, and given that the essence of a discretionary policy is to treat each case on its merits in the light of the public interest. It is certainly the case that 'contestability theory' casts very serious doubt on the market share criterion as a means of identifying situations in which market power is being abused (Hay (1988)). Various other commentators have suggested that the lack of clear rules has led to inconsistent judgments on the part of the MMC, which appears to have reached different conclusions in situations where the facts of the case appear to be substantially similar. At a more practical level it is also the case that practices like high prices, refusing to supply, or keeping other firms out of the market are not illegal under the British system unless there has been a monopoly report. As only a limited number of such reports can be produced, and as the process of investigation is often drawn out over a long period of time, the policy is unlikely to have a major effect on industrial structure, conduct or performance.

The impact of the European Community in respect of dominance

Since Britain joined the European Community, Community rules on competition form part of the law of the United Kingdom. These provide for a different approach to the control of economic power. Article 86 of the Treaty of Rome states that any abuse of a dominant position within the Common Market, or a substantial part of it, shall be prohibited in so far as it affects trade between member states. Dominant position is not defined, either in terms of market share or any other criterion, being left to judicial interpretation, which has defined it in one case (*Sirena v Eda* (1971)) as: 'the power to prevent effective competition in an important part of the market' and in another (*EC Commission v Continental Can* (1972)) as 'the power to behave independently without having to take into account competitors, purchasers or suppliers'. Under the European Community rules, evidence that a firm has a dominant position does not in itself lead to action being taken against the firm. The principle adhered to, as in Britain, is that it is abuse of a dominant position which is prohibited, not the position itself. Various such abuses have been condemned by the European Commission and the European Court of Justice, including unfair prices, discriminatory pricing, predatory pricing designed to drive rivals from the market, refusal to supply and unfair trading practices.

Under the Treaty of Rome such practices are not subject to Article 86 unless they affect trade between member states and in early judgments this was often taken to imply that imports and exports between member states had to be directly involved before the abuse of a dominant position could come within the remit of the Community's rules. However, as Agnew (1985) points out, more recent judgments have broadened this interpretation considerably, to the point where abuse of a dominant position affecting competition anywhere within the Community is interpreted as potentially having effects upon intra-Community trade. As a result, Community law on competition has begun to enter into areas previously reserved for national legislation.

Enforcement of Article 86 can take place in three different ways. The first is where the European Commission itself makes an order to end an infringement or imposes fines. The second is where national authorities themselves enforce the Article, although they can only do so if the Commission has not commenced proceedings, and the Office of Fair Trading has never taken such a step. Thirdly, an individual or company who has suffered harm as a result of an infringement of the Article could themselves bring an action for damages.

Evaluation of the impact of the European Community's rules on dominance has been very limited. In so far as they embody similar principles to those underlying the British approach, they are probably subject to the same shortcomings. Korah (1975) has suggested that Article 86 is being used to protect small and medium-sized firms from competition from larger rivals, which may be counter-productive if those rivals are more efficient. Agnew (1985) suggests that in at least one case a firm's attempt to rationalise its distribution system was put at risk because a former distributor who was excluded from the new, supposedly more efficient, system brought in an action for damages on the grounds of refusal to supply.

The American approach to dominance

American policy on anti-trust pre-dates British and European policy by a considerable margin, being traceable back to the Sherman Act of 1890. It also rests upon different principles, being much closer to the 'rules' approach where certain aspects of market structure are made illegal *per se*, as opposed to the discretionary approach where each case is considered on its merits. As Section 2 of the Sherman Act put it: 'Every person who shall monopolise, or attempt to monopolise . . . any part of the trade or commerce . . . shall be deemed guilty of a felony.'

In its original formulation emphasis was placed upon the word 'monopolise', in order to mean an active process of securing monopoly power, rather than simply possessing it, perhaps as a result of superior efficiency. As a result, the possession of large market shares was not itself seen as illegal, most notably in the early case of US Steel, which had a 65 per cent share of total output in 1901. In that case it was argued that a dominant position was only illegal if the firm actively attempted to use it or maintain it. However, this view was developed in the Alcoa case of 1954 in such a way as to effectively overturn earlier judgments. In the Alcoa case it was found that illegal monopolisation could be inferred without any evidence of unreasonable practices on the part of the firm in question. It therefore came very close to outlawing monopoly position *per se*, a position which was reinforced by other judgments. Some of the world's best-known firms, including Eastman Kodak, General Motors, and Xerox have been effectively forced, often through out-of-court agreements, to facilitate new entry by other firms into their industry, following the attentions of the Department of Justice.

The perceived balance between the costs and the benefits arising from these actions depends upon the concept of competition which is adopted. If firms have acquired a monopoly position through superior performance, to force them to assist less efficient firms to enter, and to allow those less efficient firms to survive is unlikely to be in the public interest. On the other hand, if dominant position secures monopoly power and misallocates resources such policies can be justified.

Policy towards mergers

Mergers may be of three main types. The first is the **horizontal merger**, where two or more firms in the same industry, and at the same stage of the distribution process, join together. The second is the **vertical merger**, where a firm becomes more vertically integrated by linking with another which is either closer to the final buyer ('forward' integration), or closer to sources of supply ('backward' integration). The third is the **conglomerate**, or **diversified merger**, where firms carrying on business in unrelated sectors come together. All three types of merger may have implications for competition but as both vertical integration and diversification are considered in more detail in Chapter 18, this chapter restricts attention to horizontal mergers.

Cost/benefit analysis of horizontal mergers

If a government has a policy towards dominant position and monopoly, it must also have a policy towards horizontal mergers, as they are one of the most common mechanisms through which a dominant position can be established. As in the case of monopoly, there are two basic approaches which policy can take. The first is to have rules, which would prevent firms from growing beyond a certain size, or having more than a certain specified market share. The alternative is to treat each case on its individual merits, measuring the costs and benefits which arise in each case and ruling accordingly.

Williamson (1968) puts forward a simple analysis which might be used to measure the costs and benefits associated with an individual merger, as shown in Fig. 16.1.

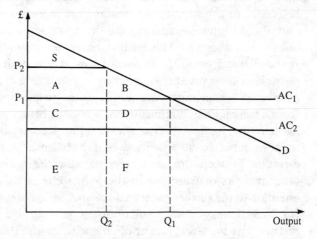

Fig. 16.1   Cost/benefit analysis of mergers

The starting point for the analysis is the assumption that if the merger takes place costs of production will fall, as a result of scale economies or synergy, but price will rise as a result of the monopoly power secured. In the simplest case it is assumed that before the merger takes place price is set at a level which equals average cost. In Fig. 16.1 the pre-merger position is given by the cost curve AC_1 and the price P_1. If social welfare is defined as in Chapter 9 (the difference between the benefit to consumers and the cost to the economy) it can be seen that the gross benefit to consumers is found by adding together the areas marked S, A, B, C, D, E and F. The cost to the economy is given by adding together the areas C, D, E, F. As net benefit is given by the difference between the two, it is equal to the areas S, A and B. If the merger leads cost to fall to AC_2 and price to rise to P_2 it can be seen that after the merger gross benefit to consumers is equal to the sum of areas S, A, C and E, while cost to the economy is equal to area E, giving a net benefit which is equal to areas S, A and C. Comparing the pre-merger and post-merger position it can be seen that on balance the merger leads to a gain given by area C and a loss equal to area B. The relative size of these effects determines the balance of advantage.

Clearly, the net advantage of a merger depends upon the particular circumstances, which are determined by the extent of the price rises, the size of the cost savings and the slope of the demand curve. Williamson sets out a table showing the relative size of cost and benefit for a range of different values for these variables, an exercise which suggests that a relatively small reduction in cost will compensate for quite a large increase in price. For instance, the table shows that if elasticity of demand is equal to $-.5$, and the merger leads to a price increase of 20 per cent, a unit cost reduction of only 1 per cent would be sufficient for the benefits to outweigh the costs.

This simple analysis suggests that in general mergers may be justified on cost/benefit grounds. However, as always, there are further complications which need to be taken into account. The model set out in Fig. 16.1 assumed that firms possessed no market power before the merger took place. If there was pre-existing market power, the analysis needs amendment in ways which suggest that larger cost reductions may be needed to compensate for similar price increases. The analysis is restricted to a partial equilibrium, examining the firms in question without any reference to their links to other sectors. This leads back to the second-best problem discussed above. If the characteristics of the overall second-best optimum are not known, it is not possible to know whether an apparent improvement in one part of the economy really involves an overall improvement. There are also questions of timing. If the costs arising from a merger are felt immediately, while the benefits do not accrue until some time in the future, a calculation which takes into account the value of time may show that the costs outweigh the benefits, even if the balance for a single period is in the opposite direction. Furthermore, the merger may slow the rate of technical progress, or trigger other mergers that are not in the public interest. Crew and Rowley (1970) draw attention to the further point that the analysis ignores the implications of the merger for X-inefficiency. If one result of the merger is to give the firm greater market power, this may give managers greater discretion to indulge themselves in organisational slack so that the potential cost savings are not actually achieved. In that case, the balance of the argument clearly shifts away from a general presumption that mergers will be in the public interest.

British policy towards horizontal mergers

In the British system, merger control is effected through the Fair Trading Act of 1973, which defines a merger to have taken place when two or more enterprises have ceased to be distinct from one another. This may happen either because they have been brought under common control or because one has ceased to carry on activities as a means of preventing competition with the others.

For a merger to be referred to the MMC, either the value of the assets taken over must exceed £15 million, or a monopoly position must be created or intensified. The criterion on which the latter is judged is the same as for a monopoly reference, namely that 25 per cent or more of the market referred to has come into the hands of a single enterprise or group of enterprises acting together. If either of the criteria are fulfilled, the Secretary of State may decide to refer the merger to the MMC, a decision which is taken in the light of advice from the Mergers Panel, chaired by the Director General of Fair Trading. If such a reference is made, the MMC is required to investigate first whether a merger situation which qualifies for reference has been created, and second whether that situation is expected to operate against the public interest. The term 'public interest' is not defined and it is the MMC's responsibility to identify the balance between costs and benefits for the individual case in hand.

In practice, policy appears to embody the view that mergers are, by and large, expected to be in the public interest. In the period 1977 to 1981 the Office of Fair Trading reviewed slightly more than 1,000 mergers, about 80 per cent of which were horizontal in form, and chose to refer only 27 in total. Of those, nine were set aside as the firms decided not to proceed, in ten cases the MMC reported in favour of the merger, and in the eight cases which received an adverse report three were eventually allowed to proceed. Only five mergers out of more than 1,000 were prevented. Whether this is appropriate or not clearly depends upon the view taken of competition. In the 'competitive' view of the economy, mergers are part of the process whereby more efficient firms take over the less well-run, leading to an improvement in the allocation of resources. Scale economies, 'synergy' and improved management are likely to be the result. In that case a lenient view of mergers is appropriate. In the 'market power' view of competition, horizontal mergers will lead to monopoly power, raised prices and X-inefficiency in which case British policy towards mergers offers considerable scope for more rigorous enforcement.

In June 1986 the British Government launched a review of competition law, including merger policy, which led to a Department of Trade and Industry Paper in 1988 (DTI (1988)). This examined various concerns expressed about existing policy but concluded that the broad thrust of current policy should remain unchanged. Nevertheless, it proposed two major legislative changes. The first suggests introducing a formal but voluntary merger pre-notification procedure, and the second provides for firms to give statutory undertakings without a reference to the MMC. In both cases the aim is to make policy more flexible, less time-consuming and to reduce the level of uncertainty for firms considering mergers. Firms choosing to give pre-notification of a merger will complete a standard questionnaire and will be entitled to automatic clearance of their proposal if they hear nothing from the OFT within four weeks. In cases where mergers pose a threat to competition which could be removed by some modification (including perhaps divestment of some activities, post-merger) the firm will be able to give undertakings to make those modifications which have statutory force without the cumbersome procedures of a reference being brought into play.

European Community policy on mergers

The Treaty of Rome provides no direct mechanisms for the control of mergers. Nevertheless, it can have an influence on them, through the Commission's interpretation of Article 86. In the case of *Continental Can*, for instance, the European Court of Justice found that:

'Article 86 is . . . aimed at . . . an effective competition structure . . . Abuse may therefore occur if an undertaking in a dominant position strengthens such a position in such a way that the degree of dominance reached substantially fetters competition.'

While this confirms the applicability of Article 86 to mergers it provides a very limited instrument of control. Action is only possible if a dominant position already exists, so that a merger involving the creation of a dominant position by two firms, neither of whom previously has a dominant position, could only be tackled after it had taken place. There have been proposals to strengthen European anti-trust law in this respect but they remain the object of controversy.

United States policy on mergers

While British policy towards mergers embodies a presumption that in general they are 'a good thing', American policy is based upon a much more hostile view. Under the Sherman Act any merger is forbidden if its effect would be to eliminate competition. In contrast to the discretionary cost/benefit approach adopted in the UK there are no exemptions to this prohibition and it cannot be argued that a merger be allowed because there are offsetting advantages in the form of scale economies, lower prices, improved management or the avoidance of unemployment. A horizontal merger is presumed to be illegal if it leads the merged firm to have a substantial market share or results in a significant increase in concentration.

While the Sherman Act adopts a comparatively tough stance towards mergers it only has effect if the merging firms are about to attain substantial monopoly power, which may mean that it can only be applied too late to save competitive market structures. For that reason the American Congress passed the Clayton Act in 1914 whose purpose was to: 'arrest the creation of . . . monopolies in their incipiency and before consummation.' Under this Act no firm engaged in commerce shall acquire any of the stock of any other firm if the effect will be substantially to reduce competition or to create a monopoly. The wording of this Act proved to have a loop-hole in that firms could merge through asset acquisition rather than stock acquisition until the loop-hole was plugged by the Celler-Kefauver Act of 1950, which also reinforced the determination of Congress to pursue a vigorous anti-merger programme.

Clearly, American policy towards mergers is much more active than its British counterpart. Nevertheless, the presumption against mergers is sufficiently strong in the United States for there to be continuing pressure to strengthen anti-merger controls, perhaps to the point where the onus is placed upon firms wishing to merge to demonstrate that there are positive benefits to be had from the merger, rather than the weaker requirement to show that competition is not weakened.

Policy towards restrictive practices

British policy on restrictive trades practices

While British policy towards monopoly and mergers is relatively permissive, the approach towards restrictive trades practices has been rather more firm. Controls first came into effect with the Monopoly and Restrictive Practices Act 1948 which has been followed by a substantial amount of legislation. The Restrictive Trade Practices Act 1956 established a Restrictive Practices Court, the Resale Prices Acts 1964 and 1976, abolished resale price maintenance, the Restrictive Trades Practices Act 1968 extended the scope of the legislation which was then drawn together with that concerning monopoly and mergers under the Fair Trading Act 1973 which established the Office and Director General of Fair Trading. Finally there has been a degree of consolidation through the Restrictive Practices Act 1976 and the Competition Act 1980.

The starting point for the policy has been the presumption that restrictive agreements between firms are against the public interest unless they can be proved otherwise, and that agreements should be registered with the Office of Fair Trading (OFT). Under the Restrictive Trades Practices Act 1956 only restrictive agreements concerning goods were to be registered. However, the scope of the legislation has been gradually expanded. It was realised that by exchanging information about prices firms could achieve much the same result as if they had a price-fixing agreement, a loop-hole which was covered in the 1968 Act which required that information agreements concerning goods should also be registrable. The Fair Trading Act 1973 and the 1976 Act extended the requirement to register to the service sector, covering both restrictive and information agreements so that both types of agreements for both goods and services come within the remit of the legislation. The legislation covers both 'agreements' in the sense of formal undertakings between firms and 'arrangements' in the sense of informal understandings. The legislation is therefore not restricted to legally enforceable relationships between firms but extends to much looser arrangements, the limits being set by decisions of the court, rather than by definition.

All arrangements covered by the legislation must be registered with the Office of Fair Trading and it is then the duty of the Director General to refer each agreement to the Restrictive Practices Court. In practice the Director General attempts to persuade the parties involved to withdraw any restrictions, or end the agreement, in order to avoid the expense of involving the Court. When the legislation was first introduced, more than 2,000 agreements were registered in the first few years, covering almost every sector in the Standard Industrial Classification. However, the vast majority were voluntarily abandoned by firms. By 1972 the Court had heard 37 cases, finding against the firms in 26 of them, and more than 300 cases referred to it had been abandoned by firms, because their agreements were similar to others which had been disallowed.

If the parties to an agreement do not abandon it, and wish to defend it in the Court, they are obliged to show that the agreement is capable of passing through at least one of eight **'gateways'**. These are defined as follows:

- The restriction is necessary to protect the public from injury.
- The removal of the restriction would deny the public substantial benefits.
- The restriction is necessary to counteract measures taken by someone who is not a party to the agreement.
- The restriction is necessary to enable those who are party to it to negotiate fair terms for the supply of goods or services from a person who is in a dominant position.
- The removal of the restriction would have a serious effect on the level of unemployment.
- The removal of the restriction would cause a reduction in the level of exports.
- The restriction is necessary to support another restriction which is not against the public interest.
- The restriction does not directly or indirectly restrict competition to any material degree.

In addition to being eligible to pass through one of these 'gateways', the Court must be satisfied that the restriction is 'not unreasonable', having regard to the balance between the benefits of the agreement and any detriment which might be caused to others.

British policy towards restrictive practices is clearly much more vigorous than that towards dominance and mergers and a very substantial number of restrictive agreements have been eliminated by the legislation. However, there continue to be reservations on at least three counts. The first concerns the rationale for the 'gateways', where Stevens and Yamey (1965) have argued that the first gateway is redundant in the light of other legislation and others have suggested that a concern for unemployment and exports is inappropriate for legislation concerned primarily with competition. The second reservation concerns the validity and consistency of the Court's judgments. In the case of the *Black Bolt and Nut Association*, for instance, a price-fixing agreement was upheld on the grounds that if firms charged a common price, buyers were saved the effort of shopping around, which seems a little dubious and which was not accepted as a valid defence in other cases of price-fixing. (On the other hand, the *Black Bolt* case involved 44 firms producing over 3,000 standard items of very low unit value, and it could be argued in these circumstances that the transactions costs incurred by buyers attempting to identify the lowest prices would be very high in relation to the value of the product, and could be avoided by the price-fixing agreement.) The third reservation concerns the very limited range of resources and sanctions available in support of the legislation. The Office of Fair Trading is only able to mount a small number of investigations at any one time, and if anti-competitive practices are taking place there is no power to impose fines under the national legislation, unlike the EC rules or those of other countries, including Germany.

As part of its review of competition policy, begun in 1986, the British Government produced a Review of Restrictive Trade Practices Policy in 1988. This concluded that, while the law had been very effective in the 1950s and 1960s it is less well-suited to current conditions. In particular it was argued that the law did not deter the formation of damaging agreements, that it catches agreements which do not restrict competition, that agreements can be drafted in order to avoid the law, that major sectors are exempt, and that the application of the law is complex and costly. In order to meet these criticisms, major changes are proposed. In the first place, UK law is to be defined in terms of the effects of agreements, rather than in terms of their legal form. Agreements with anti-competitive effects will be prohibited instead of being required to register, and the registration system will be abolished. There will be facilities for the granting of exemptions, framed to match the practices of the European Community (see below) which will include block exemptions for certain types of agreement, like franchising, and the OFT will be given greater powers of enforcement. It is also intended that some sectors of the economy, like professional services, which are currently exempt from legislation should not continue to be exempt without challenge.

Restrictive practices in the European Community

The creation of a single European market would be of little significance if restrictive practices amongst firms prevented competition from taking place within that market. Article 85 of the Treaty of Rome therefore provides that all agreements and concerted practices between undertakings, which have as their object or effect the prevention, distortion or restriction of competition within the Common Market, and which affect trade between member states, shall be prohibited. The Article also provides an illustrative, but not exhaustive, list of the types of practice which are forbidden, which includes price fixing, limiting production, sharing markets, discriminating between different partners to transactions and attaching supplementary obligations to contracts which have no connection with the subject of those contracts.

If firms are found to have infringed Article 85 then the agreement concerned is void in law, and cannot be enforced by any party which seeks to do so, which is the only sanction contained in the Article itself. However, further regulations give the European Commission considerable powers to enforce the rules on competition, including the ability to order the termination of an agreement or practice and the ability to impose fines of up to one million ECU (European Currency Units) or ten per cent of a firm's turnover, whichever is the greater.

Not all restrictive agreements between firms which affect trade in the EC are subject to proscription under Article 85, which provides for the **exemption** of some agreements and **negative clearance** for others. If an agreement contributes to improving the production of distribution of goods or to promoting technical or economic progress, while allowing consumers a fair share of the resulting benefits and if the agreement doesn't contain unnecessary restrictions or eliminate competition then it may be declared exempt from the rules. In addition to exemption for individual agreements the rules also allow for the 'bloc' exemption of certain classes of agreement including exclusive distributorships, selective distribution of automobiles, patent licensing agreements and research and development agreements. Such exemptions are necessary in part because the European Commission has been concerned to foster collaboration between small and medium companies and offers financial incentives to firms to enter into arrangements which might otherwise fall foul of the Commission's own competition policy.

Negative clearance is essentially a weaker form of exemption. The Commission may declare its opinion that an agreement or a class of agreements does not come within the scope of the competition rules. Such a declaration is not binding on the Commission or on national courts, but it is unlikely that significant action would ever be taken against agreements which have been given negative clearance which include agreements of minor economic importance, certain exclusive agency contracts, co-operation agreements, sub-contracting and a number of clauses common to patent licensing agreements.

Unlike the British system for dealing with restrictive practices there is no duty to notify restrictive agreements to the European Commission. However, exemption and negative clearance can only be given to agreements which have been formally notified, which provides a powerful incentive to notify.

Restrictive practices in the United States

Like other aspects of anti-trust legislation American policy towards restrictive practices has its origins in the Sherman Act of 1890, Section 1 of which provides that: 'every contract, combination . . . or conspiracy in restraint of trade or commerce . . . is hereby declared to be illegal.' As the Act itself makes no attempt to define those types of restrictive agreements which are illegal, any arrangement, formal or informal, which can be construed to be in restraint of trade could be illegal in principle. However, this extreme position has been moderated through the application by the courts of what is known as 'the rule of reason' whereby contracts in restraint of trade were held to be illegal in some cases only if they were unreasonable. This has led to two different categories of violation. The first are those which are illegal *per se*, and the second is those which are only illegal if **unreasonable**. Any agreement whose main object is to restrict competition is illegal *per se* which has led to the automatic prohibition of price-fixing agreements, market sharing, collective boycotts and limitations on supply. Other agreements may be anti-competitive, but that may not be their main object, in which case they are not illegal *per se*, but only if they are found to be unreasonable.

Illustration

Different approaches to the cost of monopoly

Different approaches to the nature of competition and the cost of monopoly are well exemplified by the debate between Cowling and Mueller (1978) (henceforth C−M) and Littlechild (1981) over the empirical estimation of the costs of monopoly in the UK and US.

C–M's starting point is with Harberger's analysis of 1954, which can be explained using a simple diagram (*see* Fig. 16.2).

In Fig. 16.2, the price and output for a perfectly competitive industry are shown as P_1, Q_1. If the industry becomes monopolised, price rises and output falls to the new combination $P_2 Q_2$. The welfare loss is given by the shaded triangular area ABC. Harberger attempted to estimate the sizes of these triangles for US industry by deriving a relationship between the welfare loss and profits earned and then using the figures for profitability to give estimates of the welfare losses. This produced an estimate of the losses associated with monopoly power in the US which was around 0.1 per cent of GNP. Such a figure was regarded as very small, implying that there need be little concern over the costs of monopoly.

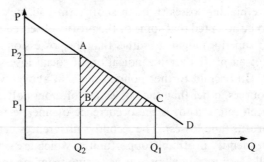

Fig. 16.2 Harberger's analysis

C–M took issue with the Harberger approach on a number of essentially technical points. First, they noted that Harberger assumed an elasticity of demand equal to -1 in every industry. When he then observed relatively small increases in price ($\triangle P$) due to monopoly this assumption about elasticity led to relatively small estimates of the change in quantity ($\triangle Q$) and to small estimates of welfare loss. Secondly, C–M noted that, when calculating monopoly profits, Harberger identified the competitive profit rate with the average rate, which could itself involve an element of monopoly profit. Monopoly profits were therefore under-estimated, again leading to small estimates of welfare loss. This problem was further compounded by the fact that industry profit rates were used, so that if some firms made losses these were subtracted from the profits of the monopolists, again under-estimating their importance. Thirdly, C–M argued that Harberger's estimates of the cost of monopoly were based solely upon the losses arising from the reduction in output and increase in price attendant upon monopoly behaviour, as shown in Fig. 16.2. However, if resources are also used up in the attempt to secure monopoly power, those resources represent an additional social cost which should be taken into account.

Having made these essentially technical criticisms of the Harberger approach, C–M produced a series of estimates of their own, based upon four alternative measures. Their conclusion was that in the US, the cost of monopoly could be as high as 13 per cent of the Gross Corporate Product of the major companies, while in the UK the figure could be as high as 7.2 per cent. Such estimates are very much larger than those found by Harberger and others, strengthening the justification for anti-monopoly policy.

The C–M estimates have been attacked by Littlechild (1981) in two different ways. First, he examined their calculations within the confines of their own model, making various technical comments which suggest that they have over-estimated the cost of monopoly, even if that framework is accepted. Secondly, and more importantly, he criticises the whole conceptual framework which C–M share with the Harberger study and others like it. The central assumption in all of these studies is that when firms are observed they are in long-run equilibrium. If that assumption is valid then the profits which are observed can be maintained in the long run and can be attributed to the abuse of monopoly power. However, the data used by C–M also includes examples of loss-making firms which cannot be in long-run equilibrium. If some firms are making losses through short-term bad luck or poor judgment then it also has to be accepted that some of the profits observed may be due to short-term good luck or superior judgment, rather than the possession of monopoly power. In other words, not all profits are an indication of social losses.

Littlechild further pointed out that above-average profits could arise from two sources, other than the possession of monopoly power. The first, which has already been referred to, is the occurrence of unexpected events, which lead to 'windfall' profits (and losses). The second is differences between firms in their ability to create or identify profitable opportunities which are open to everyone, but not noticed by all. To interpret all profits as arising from monopoly would be to ignore these other sources of profit.

Behind Littlechild's critique lies a conception of competition which is very different from that which underlies the textbook models. If competition is viewed as a process, rather than an equilibrium state, then it can be seen as a constant battle amongst firms to become temporary monopolists by being 'first in the field'. If a firm succeeds in spotting an opportunity which has gone unnoticed by its rivals, it will be able to make super-profits for a while, but they will soon be eroded as others imitate or improve on the original idea. In the meantime a truly entrepreneurial company will have spotted a new idea and will be making another round of super-profits from that new temporary monopoly. None of the profits which are observed can be interpreted as measures of social loss. Indeed, the diagram set out above can be reinterpreted in a completely different way. Instead of making a comparison between the situation under competition and that under monopoly, and suggesting that monopoly causes social loss, the diagram may be interpreted as showing the position adopted by an entrepreneur who has a monopoly because he is the only person to have spotted the opportunity. In that case, the appropriate comparison is not between the monopoly situation and that which would arise if everyone else had shared the monopolist's insight, because they did not. The appropriate comparison is between having the product as produced by the monopolist and not having the product at all. In that case the monopolist can be seen to have generated a social gain equal to his own entrepreneurial profit, plus the consumer surplus!

References and further reading

J.H. Agnew, *Competition Law*, (London, Allen & Unwin, 1985)

W. Baumol, J.C. Panzar and R.D. Willig, *Contestable Markets and the Theory of Industry Structure*, (New York, Harcourt Brace Jovanovich, 1982)

J.M. Clarke, 'Toward a Concept of Workable Competition', *American Economic Review*, 1940

K. Cowling and D.C. Mueller, 'The Social Costs of Monopoly Power', *Economic Journal*, 1978

M.A. Crew and C.K. Rowley, 'Anti-Trust Policy: Economics versus Management Science', *Moorgate and Wall Street*, 1970

H. Demsetz, 'Information and Efficiency: Another Viewpoint', *Journal of Law and Economics*, 1969

H. Demsetz, 'Industry Structure, Market Rivalry and Public Policy, *Journal of Law and Economics*, 1973

H. Demsetz, 'Two Systems of Belief About Monopoly', in H.J. Golschmid (ed.) *Industrial Concentration: The New Learning*, (Boston, Little Brown, 1974)

A.C. Harberger, 'Monopoly and Resource Allocation', *American Economic Review, Proceedings*, 1954

D.A. Hay, 'Competition and Industrial Policies', *Oxford Review of Economic Policy*, 1988

V. Korah, *An Introductory Guide to EEC Competition Law and Practice*, (Oxford, ESC, 1975)

S. Littlechild, 'Misleading Calculations of the Social Costs of Monopoly Power', *Economic Journal*, 1981

E.S. Mason, 'Monopoly in Law and Economics', *Yale Law Journal*, 1937

R.A. Posner, 'The Social Costs of Monopoly and Regulation', *Journal of Political Economy*, 1975

W.D. Reekie, *Industry, Prices and Markets*, (Oxford, Philip Allan, 1979)

R. Stevens and B. Yamey, *The Restrictive Practices Court*, (London, Weidenfeld and Nicolson, 1965)

G. Stigler, 'Report on Anti-Trust Policy Discussion', *American Economic Review*, 1956

O. Williamson, 'Economies as an Anti-Trust Defence: The Welfare Trade-Offs', *American Economic Review*, 1968

Self-test questions

1 Which of the following is an implication of the second-best problem?

(a) failure to achieve perfect competition in one industry means that it is not necessarily desirable in others.

(b) workable competition is not achievable by approximating perfect competition.

(c) monopoly power need not be controlled.

2 Which of the following variables represent market structure, which relate to conduct and which are indicators of performance?

concentration, growth of demand, advertising intensity, collusive agreements, productivity growth, entry barriers, profitability, degree of diversification, company objectives

3 List the three different sources from which profits may arise in the 'Austrian' view of competition.

4 Which of the following conclusions drawn from the orthodox analysis of the industry is rejected by contestability theorists?

(a) barriers to entry are important features of structure

(b) firms in an industry with a high level of

concentration will be able to exert significant market power

(c) monopolies charge prices which exceed average cost

5 **List the advantages and disadvantages of the 'rules' approach to competition policy.**

Exercise

Consider the view that policies designed to prevent the abuse of monopoly power are unnecessary and misguided.

Answers on page 428.

17 Industrial policy

This chapter examines various different forms of government intervention in industry, including regional policy, intervention in support of the small firm sector and privatisation.

The rationale for industrial policy

The scope of industrial policy

The term **'industrial policy'** is usually used loosely to cover a wide range of different areas of government intervention in the economy, including:

- competition policy
- regional policy
- support for the small firm sector
- privatisation versus public ownership
- support for innovation

The fundamental rationale for policy in most of these areas is the belief that market forces, based for the most part upon profit-maximising behaviour, cannot be relied upon to produce results which are satisfactory without some form of government intervention. The exception in some respects is privatisation, where the converse applies in that it is argued that public ownership is an inappropriate form of organisation for commercial activities and that closer involvement in the market would improve performance. However, even in that area of policy, faith in the results of uninhibited profit-maximising behaviour is not complete and privatisation often involves some form of government control or oversight of the enterprise after it has passed into private hands.

Alternative approaches to policy

Hay (1988) identifies three alternative approaches to industrial policy. The first, which includes the 'discretionary' approach to competition policy, is to analyse problems on a 'piecemeal' basis, examining each situation separately and weighing the costs and the benefits of intervention. In this approach there is no presumption either in favour of or against the free market solution, each case being examined on its merits.

The second approach may be labelled 'Austrian' after its best known proponent (Hayek (1960)). In this view, aspects of which have been explored in Chapter 16, the dynamic process of competition in a free market is seen as a good thing in itself and the only means by which the economy can be run satisfactorily. Provided that competition can be assured through the law, and those who are harmed by the actions of others can take action for damages against them, there is no need for further government intervention. In this view there is no valid justification for industrial policy, which should be replaced by the untrammelled operation of markets.

The diametrically opposite stance to that of the 'Austrians' is one which calls for an integrated industrial policy which develops an overall plan for the economy and then directs firms towards the fulfilment of that plan, taking them into public ownership if that is the most appropriate way to ensure conformance to the plan's requirements (Holland (1975)).

These three different approaches to policy can be located along a political spectrum running from left to right, which, as Hay (1988) points out, also relates to the relative importance given to markets, the balance between 'rules' and 'discretion', and the balance between competition policy and other aspects of industrial policy. At the extreme left of the spectrum, markets are seen as chaotic, inefficient and unfair. Competition policy is held to be relatively unimportant and discretionary intervention involving public ownership, central planning, protection and subsidies form the basis for policy. At the extreme right of the spectrum, markets are seen as the only possible way to secure efficiency and only a competition policy based on legal rules is of any value or consequence.

While governments of different political persuasion adopt different positions on this spectrum, neither extreme is seen as a realistic option in any major mixed economy, so that policy in practice tends to be located somewhere between the extremes.

Regional policy

The regional problem in the United Kingdom

The regional problem in the United Kingdom may be defined with respect to a number of different variables. The most obvious disparity between the different regions is to be found in the level of unemployment, as shown in Fig. 17.1. As the figure shows, the rate of unemployment in 1986 was more than twice as high in the worst hit region, Northern Ireland, as in the least affected South East. Levels of unemployment have been persistently and substantially higher than the national average in the North, Wales and the North West, Scotland, and Yorkshire and Humberside.

Similar regional disparities are revealed in the figures for incomes, which show that in 1984–5 average weekly income per person in the South East was £96.6, compared with only £59.9 in Northern Ireland and £65.5 in the North of England.

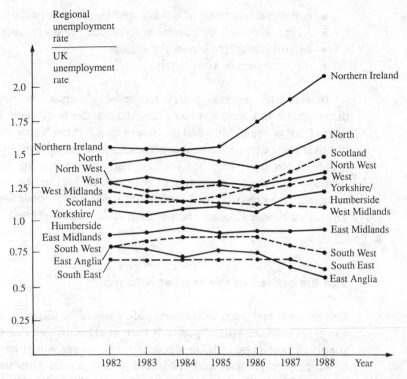

Fig. 17.1 Regional unemployment rates relative to the UK average

This pattern of regional differences is repeated in virtually every indicator of prosperity, whether it be house prices, the proportion of households owning cars, the rental of telephones or the taking of regular foreign holidays. However the picture is examined, the British economy exhibits very substantial regional differences in well-being, with the prosperous 'core' of London and the South East having very substantial advantages over the other parts of the country which form the 'periphery'.

These differences between the standard regions of the UK are by no means the complete picture. Within the prosperous South East there are pockets of poverty, most obviously within 'crisis locations' like the inner cities. Within the generally depressed regions there are pockets of prosperity which score at least as highly as the South East on a wide variety of indicators. Nevertheless, the general pattern is clear and the disparities are wide enough to warrant a consensus that the United Kingdom has a substantial regional problem which needs to be addressed.

The objectives of regional policy

Regional policy may have a variety of objectives, the most common of which are:

- acceptable levels of unemployment in the regions
- acceptable levels of income in the regions

- reduced divergences in income and employment across regions
- acceptable levels of migration from one region to another
- self-sustaining growth in the regions
- the reduction of congestion

In the UK, regional policy has most obviously been driven by the large discrepancies in unemployment rates and standards of living between the 'Greater South East' of the country and the outer regions of the North and West. Nevertheless, it should also be remembered that prosperity in the South East brings its own economic problems. In part these are the problems of congestion, high wages and skills shortages, but the concentration of economic activity in one part of the country also brings with it a need to provide additional expensive economic and social infrastructure while at the same time infrastructure remains under-utilised in other regions.

The limitations of the market solution

One possible approach to regional policy would be to leave the solution to market forces. If markets worked perfectly then in areas of high unemployment, where the supply of labour exceeds the demand for it, wages would be forced down relative to wages in other areas, and this would provide a number of incentives which would tend to alleviate the problem. Companies would find it attractive to relocate into areas of high unemployment, because of the savings in wage costs. House prices would be cheaper in these areas, making them still more attractive to companies and their executives. At the same time, higher wages in other areas would encourage workers to leave the depressed areas in search of work, thereby alleviating the unemployment problem still further. If labour and capital were perfectly mobile in this way, regional differences in factor rewards could not continue to exist and regional unemployment would disappear as markets equated the supply of and demand for labour in each region.

To a limited extent this model is borne out by the fact that there has been net migration from the relatively poor regions of the United Kingdom towards the Greater South East. However, the figures for net migration show the differences between inflows and outflows to a region, and disguise the fact that there have also been substantial outflows from the South East and inflows to the North and West. It is also clear that the flows of labour from one region to another have not been sufficient to either close the gap in incomes or to eliminate the problem of regional unemployment.

Closer examination of the problem suggests that markets are subject to a number of frictions which prevent them from providing a simple solution to regional difficulties. In the first place, differences in unemployment from region to region may not be fully reflected in regional wage differentials, partly because wages are 'sticky' downwards but also because in many firms and public sector organisations wages are negotiated on a national basis, leaving no mechanism through which regional labour market differences can have an effect. In that case labour markets will not clear, and there will be higher rates of unemployment in regions where the wage rate is above the equilibrium level. In such a situation regional differences in unemployment rates may provide some incentive for workers to move from one area to another but there are a number of reasons for supposing that this will not solve the regional problem. In the first place, if wages are sticky downwards so that the demand for labour is not equated to its supply there may be only limited job opportunities, even in the areas of relatively low unemployment. An excess supply of labour will be a national problem. As the evidence suggests that it is the 'pull' of job opportunities, rather than the 'push' of unemployment which encourages migration (Armstrong and Taylor (1985)) this will mean little movement from one location to another, and little benefit from that movement which does take place. Regional disparities in unemployment would be reduced by migration, but only by shifting the unemployed from one place to another.

In the second place, migration involves costs. Some of these are obvious and 'pecuniary', like the costs of moving house. Others are 'psychic', though just as real, like leaving familiar surroundings and friends and moving to an area with a different style of life and regional culture.

In the third place, the structure and performance of the housing market may erect additional barriers to mobility, especially in the British case. Tax incentives and the easy availability of credit for the purchase of property, coupled with the (possibly mistaken) belief that house prices provide a guaranteed capital appreciation has led Britain to become a nation of owner-occupiers. However, the difference in house prices between areas of high unemployment and areas of low unemployment has become so large in Britain that most owners of homes in the North and West could not afford to buy comparable accommodation, or anything at all, in the South East. Workers who occupy local authority housing have nothing to sell and will find it impossible to secure similar housing in areas where employment is available. Furthermore, the private rented housing market is so small in Britain that it offers no alternative to either owner-occupiers or local authority tenants who wish to migrate.

It seems clear, therefore, that regional problems are unlikely to be solved through labour migration. The other possibility suggested by the simple market model is that capital may migrate towards the less fortunate regions, attracted by lower wage rates. However, it has already been noted that imperfections in the labour market mean that wages will not necessarily be low enough to induce this movement. Movement from one location to another involves substantial costs, the evidence suggests that firms display 'satisficing' behaviour when seeking production sites (Townroe (1972)), and executives may exhibit strong preferences for locations with which they are familiar and where house prices have historically risen faster than the national average. As a result, capital may be at least as immobile as labour.

In summary, then, it would appear that frictions in the operation of markets prevent a simple market solution to the regional problem. If that is the case, government intervention will be justified, provided that the benefits accruing exceed the costs.

Types of policy for regional intervention

Armstrong and Taylor (1985) suggest that there are three major types of policy which may be brought to bear on the regional problem. The first, and most important in practice, are **micro-policy instruments**, designed to alter the location decisions of either a household's or firm's activities. The second are **macro-policy instruments** where macro-economic policies concerning fiscal, monetary or exchange-rate conditions are deliberately used in order to create regional effects (perhaps by having macro-policies which are regionally discriminatory in their application, like income taxes or interest rates which vary by region.) Thirdly, there are **co-ordination policies** which involve linking either different types of policy, like micro and macro policies, or the policies of different jurisdictions, like national government, local government and the European Community. As most regional policies are of the micro variety the discussion in this chapter is restricted to that aspect of policy.

Encouraging worker mobility

The market model has demonstrated that regional unemployment problems would disappear if wage signals directed workers towards appropriate areas and appropriate occupations and labour were sufficiently mobile to follow those signals. A first approach to regional policy, then, would be to ensure that appropriate wage signals do appear and to remove the barriers to mobility from area to area and occupation to occupation. This need not always involve a spatial re-allocation of labour because high levels of regional unemployment can be accompanied by vacancies and skills shortages, in which case providing the unemployed with skills which are in demand may reduce unemployment without the need for relocation.

In addition to the provision of retraining facilities an effective policy of moving the workers to the work has to fulfil three functions. First, regional differences in the labour market have to be reflected in wage signals. The most obvious means of bringing this about is to ensure that wages are set in response to local conditions of supply and demand, rather than at national level. Government has made a number of attempts to establish the principle of local and regional differentials, in the National Health Service for instance, and in education where a London Allowance is payable. A number of large private national firms, including banks and building societies, have also introduced additional payments for those working in the South East. However, much of the wage bargaining system is institutionalised at national level, trade unions fear an erosion of their influence if local pay bargaining is introduced and many workers feel that the principle of 'equal pay for equal work' is important for reasons of fairness. As a result regional and local differences in wages do not fully reflect differences in labour market conditions.

A second condition which is necessary if labour is to become more mobile is that workers are able to perceive the differences in labour market conditions from region to region. This requires that they are well-informed about pay and vacancies in other parts of the country, and are not simply provided with information concerning their local situation. The provision of nationwide labour market intelligence thus becomes an important function of government policy.

Even if differences in labour market conditions are reflected in wages, and workers are well-informed about those differences, labour mobility will not be substantially enhanced unless the costs of moving from one region to another can be reduced, and the rigidities in the housing market overcome. A third requirement for an effective policy, therefore, is that subsidies to cover both the pecuniary and the 'psychic' costs of moving are provided. There are schemes in Britain which provide some assistance towards the pecuniary costs of moving, but the 'psychic' costs are more difficult to deal with and developments in the housing market, where price differentials between North and South have increased in the late 1980s, have raised, rather than lowered the barriers to mobility. Government has been attempting to rejuvenate the private market for rented housing but the incentive to supply such housing, and the incentive to opt for renting rather than owner-occupation, remain weak.

On balance, then, it can be seen that a policy of encouraging workers to move to the work offers one means of overcoming the regional problem, but the institutionalised rigidities in labour markets and housing markets present very substantial obstacles to success. While many workers have found ways round such obstacles, and the phenomenon of the long-distance commuter has become increasingly common in managerial occupations, the injunction to 'get on yer bike' to find work continues to ring hollow for many, if not most, workers.

Direct control on the relocation of industry

If there are limits to a policy of having workers move to the work, an effective regional policy will have to take account of the alternative option of having the work move to where the unemployed workers are located. This can be carried out in a number of ways. One approach is to effectively force firms to choose locations which they would otherwise avoid by preventing industrial development in areas deemed not to be in need of additional employment. This could be achieved through national policy, as in the case of Industrial Development Certificates (IDCs), whereby until 1981 manufacturing firms in the UK required an IDC if they wished to establish new plant involving floor space above a set limit, or through a similar system of Office Development Permits for office space. As new development also requires planning permission from local authorities, restrictions placed by them on land available for industrial development could have a similar effect.

Such direct controls have a number of advantages. Most obviously, they are inexpensive, as they involve no financial assistance to firms. They can be used flexibly, allowing government to take account of the circumstances of individual firms, and they force firms to hold discussions with government officials who can then ensure that they are fully informed about the advantages of alternative locations, including any financial assistance which may be available. If firms do exhibit 'satisficing' behaviour with respect to location this process may force them to consider a wider range of options than they would otherwise do, which may demonstrate that alternative locations actually have real commercial advantages. Evaluation of such direct controls (Twomey and Taylor (1986)) suggests that they are extremely effective in achieving their objective.

The disadvantages of direct controls are obvious in that they force firms to select locations which they would not otherwise choose, which may have a harmful impact upon their efficiency. A firm which is not allowed to expand in its preferred location may opt to simply abandon an investment project, it may decide to invest abroad instead, or it may attempt to inefficiently 'shoe-horn' its expansion plans into the space for which it currently has permission. In any of these cases the impact of regional policy may be to reduce the international competitiveness of the UK as a location for business, or to reduce the competitiveness of UK firms, neither of which is desirable in an increasingly competitive global economy. More generally, of course, direct controls on location run counter to the philosophy of 'let the market decide', being placed towards the left of the policy spectrum described above. A government which is committed to the use of the market mechanism as the major means of stimulating economic development is bound to be uncomfortable with such a directly intervention-ist approach.

The provision of financial incentives

An alternative to the 'stick' of direct controls is the 'carrot' of financial incentives. Government may induce firms to transfer employment into depressed areas by offering financial inducements in the form of subsidies. Such subsidies could either be directed towards reducing the cost of labour in the regions, or towards reducing the cost of capital equipment and premises.

Labour subsidies are an intuitively attractive form of regional policy because they reduce the cost to firms of providing jobs in the regions, and the reduction of unemployment tends to be seen as the main indicator of success. If labour cost per unit is reduced, firms will be induced to select a more labour-intensive method of production and will increase their demand for labour. However, the actual impact of such subsidies on employment will also depend upon a number of other factors. Most obviously, it depends upon the technical possibilities for the substitution of labour for other factors. If these possibilities are limited by the nature of the available technology, the impact of subsidies may be limited. It may also be the case that despite unemployment the supply of the types of labour needed is limited, so that increased demand for labour from firms simply raises the price of that labour, weakening the effect. It is by no means certain (O'Donnell and Swales (1977)) that such subsidies do create a substantial number of additional jobs. In the British case, labour subsidies were an important feature of policy during the period 1967–76, in the form of a Regional Employment Premium. However, they were expensive and also fell foul of Britain's obligations to its European partners whose objections were partly responsible for their eventual abandonment.

The most popular form of subsidy to industry in the regions is financial assistance towards the provision of equipment and premises. In so far as these create an incentive to adopt more capital-intensive technologies they might appear to be at odds with the objective of increasing employment. However, like labour subsidies, they also reduce the cost of production for firms, which may allow price reductions for firms producing in the regions, which could stimulate demand and hence enhance both regional ouput and employment. Whether or not this actually happens depends upon the proportion of final product value which is added by the firm in receipt of the subsidy. If this is small, the impact on cost and price will be small. It will also depend upon the structure of the industry in question. If it is an oligopoly, firms may be reluctant to reduce their prices, for reasons which have been outlined in Chapter 9. On the other hand, if the prices of products produced in the regions does fall, demand for them is likely to be very highly elastic if there is a high degree of inter-regional and international competition.

The most that can be said on balance is that there is no clear '*a priori*' case for assuming that subsidising inputs for firms operating in the regions will have a very substantial effect.

UK regional policy in practice

British regional policy has evolved through a number of distinct periods since the Second World War. From 1945 to 1949 IDC controls were applied rigorously, accompanied by programmes of factory building and financial incentives, in a package of measures which appeared to be successful in that approximately half of all new industrial investment took place in assisted areas.

From 1949 to 1960 there was a period of 'policy-off', partly forced by the need to reduce public spending, and partly as a result of the lower priority given to regional policy by the Conservative government elected in 1951. In any event, this was a period of relative prosperity and the need for policy seemed much less urgent.

In the period 1960 to 1976 the regional problem emerged again as a number of industries located in the regions went into decline, and the issue returned to the political agenda. Concern began to mount over the UK's generally poor economic performance and regional policy was seen as an important component of an overall strategy for industrial development and growth. The Labour Government of 1964–70 extended the areas which were entitled to assistance and in 1967 introduced the concept of Special Development Areas which were areas within the assisted areas which had special problems meriting additional assistance. The Regional Employment Premium was also introduced and spending on regional assistance increased twelve-fold. Despite this spending, the Labour government lost the election of 1970 and it appeared that regional aid would again become a casualty, being inconsistent with the policy stance of the in-coming Conservative government. Nevertheless, the government made a 'U-turn' on policy and the 1972 Industry Act provided for financial assistance at three different levels – Special Development Areas, Development Areas and Intermediate Areas – each of which carried entitlement to a different range of benefits.

This regime remained in place until it came under heavy criticism in a White Paper in 1983, which led to the introduction of a new system in 1984, designed to provide more selective assistance and to reduce the very heavy drain on the public purse.

Evaluation of UK regional policy

It is notoriously difficult to measure the impact of regional policy because the question which has to be asked is 'counter-factual' – 'what would have happened if the regional policy had not been in place?' However, most studies (Moore and Rhodes (1976)) estimate that in the period of most active intervention approximately 325–375,000 jobs were directly created in the regions. If additional employment in 'dependent' activities is taken into account then the impact was probably as high as 500,000 jobs. However, this was at a cost of some £20 billion, 1960-84, and the 'cost-per-job' was estimated to be the enormous sum of £35,000. Furthermore, regional disparities had if anything become worse over the period. Dissatisfaction led to the reappraisal of regional policy, which had come in for criticism as early as 1973, when the House of Commons Expenditure Committee noted that: 'Regional policy has been empiricism run mad, a game of hit and miss, played with more enthusiasm than success.'

A number of more detailed criticisms were made. In the first place, the **capital** bias was attacked on the grounds that making capital cheaper was unlikely to create many jobs and much of the aid went in very large grants to plant-intensive industries like chemicals and metal manufacture, which use very little labour. Secondly, the **indiscriminate nature** of the aid was attacked as it seemed likely that much of the aid went to firms who would have located in the regions in any event. Thirdly, the **manufacturing bias** of the aid was seen to be inappropriate in a world where global and secular forces have been shifting employment away from manufacturing and into the service sector. Finally, it was argued that the aid regime led companies to locate branch factories in the regions, while maintaining higher level functions in the South East. This reduces the autonomy of regional economies and introduces a 'spatial division of labour' with low-skill, low-paid workers in the regions producing products at the later stages of the life cycle, while higher skill level activities remain in the more prosperous parts of the country. As branch plants are often only weakly integrated into the local economy, having limited linkages with local suppliers and customers, they offer limited prospects for self-sustaining growth.

These criticisms moved the Industry Secretary, Keith Joseph, to note in 1979 that despite the spending which had taken place the regions which required assistance in the 1970s were the same ones which had required assistance in the 1930s, reinforcing the Conservative government's general conviction that market forces are to be preferred to government intervention. As a result the map of the assisted areas was redrawn, a cost per job limit of £10,000 was set, the balance was shifted towards more selective assistance, IDC controls were withdrawn and the government signalled its intention to hold spending on regional policy down to a figure in the region of £250–300 million per year, at 1984 prices.

The current official view, then, is that direct financial intervention in favour of the regions is not likely to prove a very cost-effective means of solving regional problems. Such a view is clearly consistent with a general view of industrial policy which prefers to place emphasis on market forces. That is not to say that government currently has no policies which are of relevance to the regions. As the analysis above has shown, an alternative approach to the regional problem is to attempt to make markets work better by improving labour market intelligence, providing retraining facilities, introducing local wage-bargaining and revitalising the market for private rented housing. If the combination of these policies can make markets much more flexible then a market solution to the regional problem is much closer to becoming a real possibility. Needless to say, the government's critics believe that faith in market forces can be exaggerated and that substantial government intervention, perhaps through the reintroduction of direct controls, is the only way to solve the regional problem.

The small firm sector

The appeal of the small firm sector

Interest in the small firm sector grew substantially in Britain during the 1980s, as the result of a number of factors. In the first place there was a clear political and ideological commitment to self-help and individual initiative on the part of the Conservative government which first came into power in 1979. In the second place, as unemployment reached historically very high levels, the conviction was expressed that technological change meant that large firms were unlikely to ever rebuild their workforces to the levels which had been experienced before the shake-out in manufacturing, and that the small firm sector offered the only means of solving the unemployment problem. Thirdly, as has been noted above, traditional regional policy was seen as a failure and both national and local authorities turned their attention towards the small firm as a possible means of stimulating local economic development. Fourthly, as was noted in Chapter 14, there has been a technological dimension to the argument, in that small firms have been seen as an important source of inventions and innovations.

Taken together, these considerations suggest that policies geared towards support for small firms might assist in the simultaneous solution of the unemployment problem and the regional problem, while increasing the rate of technical change and developing the enterprise culture needed to secure more rapid industrial and commercial development.

The definition of a 'small firm'

While problems of definition may seem unimportant, the debate on policy concerning the small firm has often centred around statistical findings on their performance which depend heavily upon the definitions used. Fig. 17.2 shows some of the definitions which have been used.

Industry	Definition adopted by the Bolton Report (1971)
Manufacturing	200 employees or less
Retailing	turnover £50,000 or less
Wholesale trades	turnover £200,000 or less
Construction	25 employees or less
Mining/Quarrying	25 employees or less
Motor trades	turnover £100,000 or less
Miscellaneous services	turnover £50,000 or less
Road transport	5 vehicles or less
Catering	all excluding multiples and brewer-managed public house

Fig. 17.2 Definition of the small firm

Source: Bolton Report, p.3

Perhaps the most common definition used in manufacturing has been that adopted by the Bolton Report on Small Firms, which set an upper limit of 200 employees. However, as Fig. 17.2 shows, other definitions were deemed appropriate in other sectors. Furthermore, a definition which only sets an upper limit leaves a problem in respect of lower limits. If there is no lower limit then the definition includes the self-employed operating on their own account, which is a very difficult population to count accurately. Cross (1983) notes that Inland Revenue data suggests that there are 2.3 million such 'businesses' in the UK, while the figure drawn from VAT registrations is just 1.3 million. Problems also arise from the fact that a large enterprise may operate through a number of smaller, virtually autonomous units and the measurement of firm size may produce very different rankings depending upon whether the measure used is employees, output or turnover. An enormous automated factory may count as a small firm if it employs only a small number of workers, and a firm which expands its output and market share but reduces its labour force may find that its classification changes from being a large firm to being a small one! Any attempt to measure the size of the small business sector also has to confront the problems posed by the existence of the 'black economy', estimated in the UK to account for as much as 7–8 per cent of total output. (Dilnott and Morris (1981)).

The importance of the small firm sector

Given the complications outlined above, there is no single figure which can be drawn upon to illustrate the importance of small firms. Nevertheless, some broad indicators are useful, including:

- 2.3 million unquoted and unincorporated businesses in 1980
- 23 per cent of employees in manufacturing were in establishments having 20–200 employees in 1978
- 58 per cent of the working population were in small establishments in 1977
- the self-employed account for 10 per cent of the working population and 25 per cent of GNP

- approximately 8 million people work in the small business sector.

Changes in the small firm sector are even more difficult to monitor but the available evidence suggests that their numbers have been growing. There have been losses in agriculture and related industries but in some sectors like construction and furniture there have been large increases. The service sector has seen gradual increases, and in some parts of the country, notably the most prosperous parts in the South East and East Anglia the number of self-employed persons has increased substantially. Whatever the details, it is clear that the small firm sector is a very important part of the economy.

Small firms and employment growth

One of the key elements in the enthusiasm for small business stems from an American finding (Birch (1979)) that 66 per cent of net new jobs created in the US between 1969 and 1976 were in firms employing 20 people or less. Members of the British government were certainly influenced by that finding which led the Under Secretary of State for industry to declare that 'small businesses have a major part to play in providing the jobs for the future.' Unfortunately, much of the research done in the British context casts doubt on the validity of such sweeping statements. Studies on Clydeside (Firn and Swales (1978)), and in Manchester and Merseyside found low rates of job creation in small firms. While it could be argued that these studies concerned the least entrepreneurial parts of the country a further study of the South East (Mason and Lloyd (1983)) came to very similar conclusions. Storey (1981) identified one of the most important findings for policy towards small business, which is that small firms in the aggregate produce very modest growth in employment, and the growth which does take place is very heavily concentrated in a very small proportion of the total population.

The evidence suggests, for the British case, that small firms are not a major source of employment growth and that indiscriminate support for small business is unlikely to be cost-effective. However, a very small proportion of small firms do provide very rapid job growth and the most effective approach for policy may be to concentrate on identifying and assisting that very small proportion.

Small firms and innovation

Another claim made with respect to the small firm sector is that it plays an important role in the process of introducing innovations, and the Bolton Report devoted considerable attention to this issue. Certainly it can be shown that around 14 per cent of important innovations since 1945 have stemmed from firms having less than 200 employees. It has also been noted in Chapter 16 that small firms have often been the source of major inventions, as opposed to innovations. However, this is not the same thing at all as a claim that the small firm sector in general is more innovative than the larger firm sector, and much of the evidence suggests that the opposite is the case. Just as there are very small pockets of rapidly growing job producing firms in the small business sector, so there are even smaller pockets of highly innovative small firms. Nevertheless, their high performance should not be mistaken for high performance on the part of small businesses as a whole.

Constraints facing small firms

However ill-founded the mythology of the small firm, the sector is unquestionably important and governments will continue to be concerned to reduce the constraints facing the smaller business. There are a number of key areas where small firms in the UK face identifiable difficulties.

The first is in respect of **finance**. The inherent riskiness of new small firm activity makes it difficult and expensive for such firms to borrow and it is often claimed that the British financial system is insufficiently flexible and entrepreneurial, especially with respect to the provision of high risk venture capital. It was certainly the case for a large part of the post-war period in the UK that bank lending was restricted by controls which made it more profitable for the banks to concentrate their lending on a small number of safe borrowers than to risk lending to smaller companies. Since the early 1970s those controls have been abolished and greater competition has transformed the banks with respect to the effort they devote to securing new business. Nevertheless, it remains doubtful whether small firms can easily find access to the finance they need on terms which they can afford, unless their owners have very substantial personal assets with which to provide security.

A second constraint, though one which has been substantially eased in recent years, is the **availability of cheap premises** on flexible terms. Many small firms need very cheap, low-quality premises in their formative years, 'underneath the railway arches' being the classic cliche. In the 1960s in particular when local councils redeveloped many inner-city areas such locations were swept away in the name of progress and the clearance schemes unintentionally added to the problem of unemployment. Since the late 1970s this problem has been recognised and almost every British town and city has some form of 'incubator' premises for small firms, available at low rent on flexible terms, and often sharing some facilities with other firms in order to keep costs down.

A third constraint facing small firms is the difficulty of acquiring **trade credit** without an established credit history and the converse difficulty of ensuring that their own customers pay them without too much delay. One of the most common causes of business failure in small firms arises from cash flow problems stemming from their being squeezed between larger suppliers, who insist on rapid payment, and larger buyers, who keep them waiting for payment.

Perhaps the most important constraint of all on the development of most small firms is **limited marketing and managerial skills**. Small firms are often managed by the owner-manager whose core expertise lies in knowledge of the product and the production process but who has to function as a 'Jack-of-all trades', providing all of the major management functions. In this situation it is common for the firm to lack key business skills in finance or marketing and to become dangerously product-led without regard for the needs of the marketplace. It should be remembered that economies of scale are a very widespread phenomenon and that economies of specialisation are a major source of such economies. Unless the small firm can find ways to supplement its limited in-house expertise, it may find it difficult to survive.

UK policy towards small business

Both central and local government in the UK have established a wide variety of schemes to assist small firms, and the system of support has grown up in a rather 'higgledy-piggledy' manner. Unpublished work by the author and others showed that in 1984 there were no less than 170 different sources and schemes to which firms in the county of Humberside alone could turn to for assistance of one type of another. In principle at least, there are policies addressed to each of the major constraints which small firms face. Financial assistance is available from a variety of sources, as is support for training, support for innovation, and inexpensive premises. Perhaps most important in the light of the analysis above, substantial central government aid has been made available to subsidise the provision of consultancy in respect of marketing, business planning, design, production and quality assurance.

Perhaps the greatest dilemma facing policy-makers in this field concerns the degree of selectivity which should be applied in providing support, given that the amount of resources available is inevitably limited. One argument is that policy-makers should 'pick winners' in order to concentrate support on those firms which are most likely to succeed in the provision of additional jobs. On the other hand, it is argued that policy-makers are not noted for their ability to pick winners and such an attempt is doomed to failure. In that case, support should be made more generally available. Storey's finding, referred to above, is particularly relevant to this debate as it offers a means of resolving this dilemma. If the growth of employment is concentrated in the hands of a very small proportion of new firms, who then need assistance to sustain their rapid growth, it should be possible to identify such firms simply by observing their growth in the first few years of existence. Such winners would effectively pick themselves through their own performance and aid could then be effectively targeted on to them, without any of the problems associated with officials attempting to pick winners. While such an approach would seem to offer a rational way forward it is not difficult to see that it could face substantial political obstacles. A smaller number of firms would receive assistance, and those chosen would be the companies which had been most successful without aid. To focus aid on them would be to raise opposition from the rest of the small business sector, especially those less successful firms who might claim that they should have a higher priority for aid, on the grounds of equity.

However policy develops, the extent to which the small firm sector will live up to some of the claims being made for it is unclear. The only point which is absolutely certain is that a great deal of money, ingenuity and enterprise has been expended on devising new means of support and assistance. It is also clear that the small firm sector has produced a veritable bonanza for academics researching the issue, government officials devising new schemes and management consultants delivering reports to small firms paid for in part by the taxpayer. It is to be hoped for the sake of the taxpayer that future evaluation shows the effort to have been more effective than conventional regional policy.

Extending the scope of the market: privatisation and deregulation

The basic rationale for extending the scope of the market

It has been noted at the beginning of this chapter that there is a broad spectrum of different approaches to industrial policy. At the 'right-hand' end of that spectrum is the view that only market forces, in a competitive environment secured by the rule of law, can be relied upon to secure a dynamic and efficient economy. The arguments in favour of such a view may be put forward in a number of different ways. One approach is heavily ideological in that it sees the untrammelled operation of the market as a good thing in itself. Competition and market forces are identified with 'freedom', government intervention is seen as the thin end of a wedge which may lead to totalitarianism and 'rolling back the state' is seen as a major end in itself. Another approach is to concentrate on the improvements in economic and industrial performance which are held to flow from opening up a wider range of activities to competition and private sector management practices.

In Britain, the rationale for 'privatisation' has drawn upon both of these arguments. In the economic sphere at least, the writings of pro-market visionaries like Hayek (1948, 1978) have undoubtedly influenced the thinking of senior figures in the Conservative government to the point where a general ethos of 'public sector bad, private sector good' has permeated the national environment to an extent which would have been unthinkable in the 1960s and 1970s. At the same time, the more detailed arguments around particular aspects of the privatisation programme have tended not to rely on such a general justification but to point to improvements in efficiency, reductions in cost and the improvements in competitiveness and the quality of service which are deemed to flow from exposing public sector activity to the pressures and disciplines of the market place.

The diverse components of the privatisation programme

Heald (1984) identifies four major components of the privatisation programme. These are:

- Privatising the financing of a service which continues to be provided by the public sector − particularly the introduction of charges for services previously provided without charge.

- Privatisation of the production of services which continue to be financed by the public sector — tendering for refuse collection by private firms, school cleaning and similar services within the Health Service.
- De-nationalisation and load-shedding — selling off public enterprises and transferring state functions to the private sector.
- Liberalisation and de-regulation — the relaxation of statutory monopolies or other arrangements which prevent private sector firms from entering markets previously reserved for the public sector.

This is a very wide-ranging programme, testifying to Mrs Thatcher's (Prime Minister 1979–1990) declaration that 'nothing is sacred' and a detailed analysis of each component in the programme lies beyond the scope of this text. Nevertheless, each aspect of the programme merits at least brief discussion of the major economic issues raised.

The introduction of charges

The argument in favour of charges has two elements. The first lies in the need to finance the provision of services, and the effects of alternative financing methods on the public purse and the level of taxation. If services are to be provided free of charge this imposes a burden on the Exchequer which may be met either by running a larger public sector deficit or by having a level of taxation which is higher than it would otherwise be. If public sector deficits are abhorred because of the extent to which they create problems of monetary control, and higher levels of taxation are seen as inhibiting incentives then the introduction of charges can be supported on the grounds of financial prudence and the enhancement of the dynamic efficiency of the economy.

In economic analysis, however, prices are seen not simply as means of raising finance but as the central factor determining the efficiency of the allocation of resources. As has been seen in earlier chapters, static efficiency in the allocation of resources requires that all prices be set equal to marginal costs, so that each good is produced and purchased up to the point where the cost of producing a further unit is just equal to the value placed upon it by a purchaser. If charges have not been made then it can be argued that this will have distorted the allocation of resources in that rational utility-maximising households will consume goods which are provided free up to the point where the value they place on the final unit is zero. Resources will have been 'wasted' in the production of units of output whose additional cost exceeds the additional benefit created for consumers.

This argument provides a basic rationale for charges, but requires qualification in a number of respects. In the first place, the relevant marginal cost is **marginal social cost,** which may not be well-represented by the accounting costs which are usually the only cost information available. Second, there are **system effects** which need to be taken into account when setting charges for some goods and services in situations where others are not charged for. In the case of the National Health Service, for example, charging for prescriptions may lead to a reduction in the demand for medication, but a shift in demand towards other, uncharged for services such as acute hospital provision. In the case of charges for eye tests, for instance, it has been argued that such tests provide an early aid to the diagnosis of much more serious conditions than defective sight and that to deter some users from having eye tests could lead to the worsening of undetected illness to the point where much greater and more expensive demands are made upon the hospital services. Clearly, the 'piecemeal' application of accounting-cost-based charges offers little guarantee of an improved allocation of resources.

The other issue which is raised in respect of charging for services is that charges have distributional implications, which raise questions of equity or fairness. These arguments can be raised in both directions, especially as the concept of equity has no clear definition. In favour of charges it might be argued that it is 'unfair' in a situation of scarce resources to provide free services to the well-off. On the other hand, it could also be argued that to impose charges to be paid by the poor may effectively exclude them from the benefits of some services. Such arguments have featured substantially in the arguments over charges in the National Health Service and the growing debate on charging students for courses in higher education.

Contracting out

Services which continue to be financed by the public sector need not be supplied by public sector organisations. Refuse collection, for instance, has been 'contracted-out' to private sector contractors instead of being provided by local authorities' own direct labour. Private contractors have provided school and hospital cleaning services. Such arrangements allow for a degree of competition in that contracts for the provision of services may be awarded on the basis of competitive tendering, which exposes the provision of the activity to the pressure and discipline of the market.

While this exposure to competition may improve efficiency and lead to savings through the introduction of better working practices and greater incentives its opponents point out that the information required to measure the cost differences between direct production and contracting-out are bedevilled by the limitations of public sector cost accounting practices, so that real comparisons are difficult to make and might show direct production to be more efficient than had been believed. They also argue that private sector contractors may provide services for lower costs by providing inferior service or by adopting exploitative labour practices not open to public sector employers who are obliged to honour good practice in respect of employee protection, health and safety, and collective bargaining. The position of the trade unions is an important aspect of this debate in that the employees of private contractors tend to have much less bargaining power than public sector employees. This reduces the cost of private sector provision in a way which is applauded by some supporters of privatisation, but seen by its opponents as 'unfair competition.' The balance of the argument clearly depends upon the view which is taken of the trade unions and of collective bargaining. If trade unions are seen as impediments to the effective operation of markets, which should be allowed to drive down wages and conditions to an equilibrium level, privatisation is to be supported on these grounds. On the other hand, if trade unions are seen as necessary defenders of the interests of employees, privatisation is simply another means of weakening their influence.

These arguments are well-exemplified by the debate over the advantages and disadvantages of contracting-out refuse collection. A study by Domberger *et al.* (1988) found that where this service had been tendered out by local authorities, cost-savings in the order of 20 per cent had been achieved, both when outside contractors and in-house local authority organisations carried out the work. This appeared not to have reduced the quality of service offered to households, or to have been attributable to tendering companies offering 'loss-leaders' to establish their position in the market. On the other hand, a rejoinder to that study (Ganley and Grahl (1988)) argued that these results were heavily dependent on savings achieved by a small number of 'superstar' performers, all of whom were operating in the rather special conditions of rural areas, that working conditions for employees had deteriorated substantially, and that private contractors were found to be operating very high proportions of unroadworthy vehicles and to receive a high level of complaints from users.

De-nationalisation

Perhaps the most visible and spectacular aspect of the privatisation programme has been the de-nationalisation of such major enterprises as British Gas, British Aerospace, British Telecom and BP, with further plans for other major public concerns continually being put forward. Indeed, Beesley and Littlechild (1983) suggest that the term 'privatisation' is generally used to mean the transfer of nationalised activity to a Companies Act company and the sale of at least 50 per cent of the shares to private shareholders.

The issues raised by this aspect of privatisation can be approached in the first instance through the economic analysis of previous chapters. If a public enterprise is re-established as a private enterprise with ownership passing to the shareholders there will be a number of important changes. In the first place, the discussion in Chapter 3 of business objectives becomes relevant. Instead of having objectives set (or perhaps not set clearly) by nationalisation statutes, White Papers and direct government intervention the objectives will be those of a private company. The central objective will be profit, amended by the managers' own objectives to an extent determined by the degree of discretion which those managers are able to exert. This clarification of objectives is often seen as a major advantage of privatisation in itself, as clear objectives allow for more effective monitoring of managerial performance and give managers a much better directed set of tasks to perform. As Chapter 3 demonstrated, if a firm is under pressure to maximise profits it is also under pressure to eliminate 'X-inefficiency' and to keep costs down. This will only be the case if the pressure to maximise profit is powerful, exerted through shareholder pressure, the threat of take-over and the market for corporate control. The presumption made by the supporters of privatising public enterprises is that such pressure is powerful, so that the managers of the newly-privatised firms are not simply able to use the firm's resources to indulge themselves in 'organisational slack', perquisites and unnecessary costs.

The first major argument in favour of privatisation, then, is that pressure to concentrate upon the profit objective eliminates the X-inefficiency which is said to be inherent in the public enterprise. There are examples of firms in public ownership which have achieved quite remarkable improvements in performance while still in the public sector, British Steel being the most spectacular example (Aylen (1988)), but this is not typical and could be partly attributable to the knowledge that privatisation would soon take place.

The second issue raised by privatisation concerns the structure of the market which exists after privatisation and the degree of competition which the privatised firm faces. Private ownership in itself provides a source of market discipline through the market for corporate control which may force firms to eliminate X-inefficiency. However, if the firm then becomes a private sector monopoly instead of a public sector monopoly this will lead to all the disadvantages of monopoly which have been discussed in Chapter 16. Although the firm may be X-efficient, keeping its costs in check, it may charge exploitative prices and misallocate resources, thereby being **economically inefficient**. It may also be the case that if the market for corporate control does not achieve its full potential for exerting discipline, competition in the product market may be needed to provide a further stimulus to efficiency even in the narrow sense of X-inefficiency.

The full benefits of privatisation therefore require that vigorous competition and rivalry is established in the markets which the privatised firms are entering. This could be achieved in a number of ways. Most obviously, any statutory monopoly rights enjoyed by the firm should be abolished. Entry to the industry should be eased as far as possible, perhaps even by transferring some of the assets of the existing company to new entrants. The company could be dismembered into a number of horizontally separate competing units, which could only be allowed to re-merge if they could demonstrate benefits sufficient to satisfy the competition legislation. If privatisation does not provide for the establishment of competition, it is subject to the valid criticism that little has happened apart from transforming a public monopoly into a private monopoly.

The problem of introducing competition for privatised firms varies in the level of difficulty from firm to firm. In some cases, enterprises came into public ownership for political or historical reasons which had little industrial logic and the sectors in which they operate are already relatively competitive (the National Freight Corporation is an example.) On the other hand, some industries, like telecommunications, gas and water supply, were held in public hands at least partly because they exhibit many of the characteristics of **'natural monopolies'**. Sunk costs are very high indeed, making entry and exit difficult and expensive, and scale economies are so substantial as to almost reserve the market for a single firm. In these circumstances it is difficult to see how effective competition could be established. In the case of British Telecom, for instance, the company is required to lease part of its network to its much smaller competitor, Mercury, which reduces the sunk costs for entrants, rendering the market closer perhaps to 'contestability' but that is not likely in the short or medium term to establish a high degree of rivalry. In the long term as technology changes and new customer needs emerge this picture could change. Cable television networks or cellular radio could perhaps provide competition in some segments of the market. As the future is unforeseeable, and if competition is seen as a 'discovery process' (von Hayek (1978)) it might be that entrepreneurial activity will lead to the breakdown of monopoly powers, provided that government ensures that obstacles to entry are not established. In the meantime some privatised firms will enjoy substantial monopoly power and methods need to be found to prevent the abuse of that power. Two basic options offer themselves. The first is to regulate the industry, perhaps by limiting the profits earned. However, as Sharpe (1984) notes, the American experience with the regulation of privately-owned utilities suggests that the regulating agencies are soon either 'captured' by the industries they are supposed to be controlling, becoming vehicles for the companies' self-interest, or turned into 'political footballs' at the whim of trade unions and local political interests.

Another approach would be to directly limit prices, as in the case of the RPI − X formula applied to British Telecom which states that prices should not rise by more than the increase in the Retail Price Index minus X percentage points, X being negotiated with Government. Such a constraint provides reassurance for customers that privatisation will not lead to a massive and exploitative increase in prices, but it does little more than that. If maintained in the long term it could remove any incentive to be efficient if the industry could persuade Government that X should be very small because its costs have been increasing.

The alternative approach, which is clearly consistent with the general outlook on industrial policy which has led to the privatisation programme, is to place greater reliance on competition law. If the law had as its main aim the prevention of predatory practices and the protection of actual and potential competitors, and if such competitors were able to sue for very substantial damages it might be possible to prevent the abuse of monopoly power without resort to regulation.

Deregulation and liberalisation

The fourth component of the privatisation programme is the repeal of restrictions on entry into certain markets. In part this has accompanied the process of de-nationalisation discussed above, but there have been other examples, most notably the deregulation of bus services, beginning with the express coaches sector which was deregulated in 1980, and where sufficient time has elapsed for some evaluation to have taken place (Jaffer and Thompson (1988)).

The basic rationale for deregulation consists of the familiar argument that additional competition will improve efficiency and the quality of service, forcing cost-savings in sectors which have hitherto been protected from competition by artificial barriers to entry constructed by government. In the case of express coaches, monopoly rights to many inter-city routes were held by National Express, part of the National Bus Company, until they were removed by the 1980 Transport Act. Deregulation was accompanied by significant entry to the industry, falling fares and the introduction of various innovations including on-board meals, videos and bus hostesses (!). Robbins and White (1986) showed that in some markets fares fell by half, at the same time as the new services were introduced, in a process which very closely reflects the typical claims made for deregulation and privatisation in general. As might be expected, this experience was greeted with enthusiasm by supporters of deregulation and used in support of the argument for the extension of the policy into other areas of bus transport.

However, many of the entrants to the industry did not remain for very long and fares began to rise again, while National Express maintained a very high market share. This development illustrates a major problem for the evaluation of deregulation in that the increasing fares and continued dominance of a single firm do not necessarily show that deregulation has failed to be effective. It could equally well be the case that the dominant firm is able to maintain that position because it is more efficient than others, so that deregulation does not lead to it being ousted from its market position but does prevent it from exerting substantial market power. If the cost structure of the industry is such that efficiency requires only a small number of firms operating inter-city routes, and if entry barriers are low, an incumbent firm will not be able to exploit passengers but concentration needs to be relatively high in the interests of efficiency. On the other hand, the same observed situation might be attributable to the existence of entry barriers, in which case the judgment on deregulation is that it removed one source of entry-barrier, imposed by government policy, but left others in place which effectively prevented any gains from deregulation.

Distinguishing between these two alternative hypotheses is difficult but Jaffer and Thompson (1988) concluded that in the case of inter-city bus travel the explanation lay not in the 'effective competition' explanation, but in the existence of entry barriers. While the initial enthusiastic judgment on deregulation need not be completely overturned, it needs to be reassessed in the light of the evidence that entry barriers protect incumbent firms and keep prices substantially higher than they would be in their absence.

Illustration

Does the privatisation of refuse collection lead to efficiency gains?

The debate on the privatisation of public services in Britain is well exemplified by a series of papers on refuse collection which appeared between 1986 and 1988.

In 1986, Domberger, Meadowcroft and Thompson (henceforth DMT) published a paper which estimated that competitive tendering by local authorities had reduced the cost of refuse collection by an average of 20 per cent. This result was arrived at by first using regression analysis to estimate costs as a function of volume and service characteristics and then using that estimated relationship to compare the costs of refuse collection for authorities which had put the service out to collection with those who had not.

DMT's methods and conclusions were criticised by Ganley and Grahl (GG) on a number of grounds. In the first place, they noted that within the group of 'privatising' local authorities there were a small number of 6 to 8 'superstars' whose costs were as much as 50 per cent less than expected. The overall results with respect to the magnitude of the savings to be had from privatisation were heavily dependent on this small number of atypical points. Further examination of the 'superstar' local authorities showed that all of them were in rural areas, where collection rounds may exhibit much wider qualitative differences than in urban areas. DMT's results might, therefore, reflect the geographical characteristics of the local authorities under scrutiny, rather than their adoption of privatisation policies.

While GG's first line of criticism disputed the magnitude of the cost savings found by DMT it did not dispute their sign, accepting that some cost savings are apparent from the data. Their second line of attack concerned DMT's contention that those savings arose from increased efficiency attributable to competition.

GG point to a number of ways in which cost-savings may have been achieved without improvements in efficiency. First, they may have arisen from 'loss-leader' tactics on the part of the bidders, a suggestion which is supported by the fact that a number of successful bidders later applied for upwards revaluation of their contracts, having secured their position as suppliers. Secondly, bidders may have been given access to the local authorities' refuse collection facilities and equipment at prices which did not reflect their full value. Thirdly, the cost savings may have arisen because the quality of service declined and working conditions for employees also declined. GG quote the case of the largest contract moved to the private sector, where 84 per cent of the company's vehicles were claimed to be unroadworthy and to other cases where employees lost access to toilets and canteens and found their working day extended by two hours. Complaints from both the public and employees have been extensive and at least one of the 'superstars' had returned refuse collection to the public sector.

These criticisms of the original DMT approach led to a follow-up study by Cubbin, Domberger and Meadowcroft (CDM), published in 1987, which attempted to identify the nature of the efficiency gains found in refuse collection. In particular, given GG's arguments, they focused on measured of 'technical efficiency', which indicated the amounts of manual manpower and the number of vehicles used to provide the refuse collection 'outputs'. On this basis, local authorities which had tendered and contracted out had secured efficiency gains of 17 per cent over those which had not tendered, while those which had tendered but retained the services in-house had secured efficiency gains of 7 per cent. These results suggested, in response to GG's arguments, that the cost reductions found in local authorities which had 'privatised' were attributable to improvements in the physical productiity of men and vehicles, and not to pecuniary gains arising from lower output and poorer conditions for employees.

As might be expected, GG were not convinced by the follow-up study. A second version of their paper noted that the distribution of efficiency ratings for local authorities produced by CDM was completely different to that produced by DMT, but very similar to those produced by the Audit Commission which had not found examples of low-cost service through privatisation. They also noted that DMT's procedures implicitly assumed that the propensity of a local authroity to privatise is independent of its costs. However, a time-series analysis of the local authorities' costs showed that those which privatised had lower than average costs already, which in turn suggests that the cost-savings attributed to privatisation could at least in part be due to lower-cost operations before privatisation.

As so often happens in the analysis of the controversial policy matters, it is not possible on the basis of the evidence offered to conclusively pin down the impact of privatisation on the efficiency of refuse collection. Both sides in the debate appear to agree that costs are lower in privatising authorities, but whether those lower costs are attributed to productivity gains, losses incurred by clients and employees, or past practices independent of privatisation remains unresolved. While the application of the policy may reduce job opportunities for refuse collection operatives, it continues to provide grist to the academic mill. As GG note in conclusions, the results to date must be regarded as provisional until there is much more experience of contracting-out. 'Further analysis will then be necessary.'

References and further reading

H. Armstrong and J. Taylor, *Regional Economics and Policy*, (Oxford, Philip Allan, 1985)

J. Aylen, 'Privatisation of the British Steel Corporation', *Fiscal Studies*, 1988

M. Beesley and S. Littlechild, 'Privatisation: Principles, Problems and Priorities', *Lloyd's Bank Review*, 1983

D.L. Birch, *The Job Generation Process*, (Cambridge, Mass., MIT, 1979)

M. Cross, 'The United Kingdom', in D. Storey (ed.) *The Small Firm: An International Survey*, 1983

J. Cubbin, S. Domberger and S. Meadowcroft, 'Competitive Tendering and Refuse Collection: Identifying the Sources of Efficiency Gains', *Fiscal Studies*, Vol. 8, No. 3, 1987 pp.49–58

A. Dilnott and C. Morris, 'What Do We Know About the Black Economy?', *Fiscal Studies*, 1981

S. Domberger, S. Meadowcroft and D. Thompson, 'Competitive Tendering and Efficiency: The Case of Refuse Collection', *Fiscal Studies*, 1988

J. Firn and J. Swales, 'The Formation of New Manufacturing Establishments in the Central Clydeside and West Midlands Conurbations', *Regional Studies*, 1978

J. Ganley and J. Grahl, 'Competition and Refuse Collection: A Critical Comment', *Fiscal Studies*, 1988

D. Hay, 'Competition and Industrial Policies', *Oxford Review of Economic Policy*, 1988

F. von Hayek, *The Constitution of Liberty*, (Chicago, Chicago UP, 1960)

F. von Hayek, *Individualism and Economic Order*, (Chicago, Chicago UP, 1948)

F. von Hayek, *New Studies in Philosophy, Ethics and Economics*, (London, Routledge and Kegan Paul, 1978)

D. Heald, 'Privatisation: Analysing its Appeal and Limitations', *Fiscal Studies*, 1984

S. Holland, *The Socialist Challenge*, (London, Quintet, 1975)

S. Jaffer and D. Thompson, 'Deregulating Express Coaches: A Reassessment', *Fiscal Studies*, 1988

C. Mason and P. Lloyd, 'New Firms in a 'Prosperous' UK Sub-Region', *National Conference on Small Business Policy and Research* , 1983

B. Moore and J. Rhodes, 'Evaluating the Effects of British Regional Economic Policy', *Economic Journal*, 1973

A.T. O'Donnell and J.K. Swales, 'Regional Elasticities of Substitution in the United Kingdom in 1968: A Comment', *Urban Studies*, 1977

D. Robbins and P. White, 'The Experience of Express Coaching Deregulation in Great Britain', *Transportation*, 1986

T. Sharpe, 'Privatisation, Regulation and Competition', *Fiscal Studies*, 1984

D.J. Storey, *Entrepreneurship and the New Firm*, (London, Croom Helm, 1982)

P.M. Townroe, 'Some Behavioural Considerations in the Industrial Location Decision', *Regional Studies*, 1972

J. Twomey and J. Taylor, 'Regional Policy and the Inter-regional Movement of Manufacturing Industry in Great Britain', *Scottish Journal of Political Economy*, 1986

Self-test questions

1 List three factors which prevent market forces from eliminating regional disparities.

2 Why is the finding that firms exhibit 'satisficing' behaviour important to the arguments in favour of direct controls on industrial development? Answer in not more than two short sentences.

3 Which of the following are criticisms which were raised of British regional policy.

(a) it did not increase employment in the regions
(b) it did not eliminate regional disparities
(c) it exhibited 'capital bias'.
(d) it favoured the service sector
(e) the cost per job was £10,000
(f) the cost per job was £35,000
(g) it was provided too selectively

4 Which of the following correspond to the findings of research on small firms?

(a) small firms are generally innovative
(b) a substantial proportion of new inventions emanates from small firms
(c) job creation in small firms is concentrated in a very small proportion of the population
(d) support for small firms is a highly centralised activity
(e) lack of suitable premises continues to be the major constraint on the growth of small firms.

5 List the four different components of the government's 'privatisation' programme.

Exercise

Discuss the view that the de-nationalisation of public enterprises amounts to transforming public monopolies into private monopolies with little gain to the consumer.

Answers on page 430.

18 The growth and scope of the firm

This chapter outlines a general framework within which to analyse the 'scope' of the firm. It then examines the degree of vertical integration and diversification and goes on to consider the issues raised by mergers and take-overs.

The scope of the firm

A general framework: the firm as supersession of the market

The 'scope' of the firm was defined in Chapter 11 as a major aspect of corporate strategy, and scope was said to have four dimensions, following Porter (1985). These dimensions are:

- **segment scope** – the horizontal range of products which the firm produces
- **industry scope** – the range of industries in which the firm operates
- **vertical scope** – the extent to which the firm is vertically integrated
- **geographical scope** – the range of regions or countries in which the firm intends to operate.

Some aspects of scope have been touched on in earlier chapters. The question of product mix and range, examined in Chapter 14, is an aspect of scope. Chapter 11 has paid some attention to the advantages and disadvantages of company growth through vertical integration and diversification and to internal development versus acquisition. However, this treatment has been very brief and piecemeal with no attempt being made to place the discussion in a more general framework of economic analysis. This chapter outlines such a framework, which offers considerable insight into the issues raised by firm scope.

The 'Coasian' analysis

The starting point for discussion can be found in the work of Coase (1937), who attempted to consider 'the nature of the firm' in order to arrive at a realistic and manageable definition which could be used to make predictions and offer explanations.

In the market economy most economic analysis is concerned with the fundamental question of how the allocation of resources is brought about by market forces. The analysis of supply and demand, for instance, is essentially about the way in which prices act as a co-ordinating mechanism, answering the basic economic questions of 'what should be produced and how much?', 'how should it be produced?' and 'who gets it?'. The answers to such questions are not answered by a central decision-maker, or by a single firm, but by the price mechanism, acting as a decentralised system of social organisation. However, not all resource allocation is carried out in this way, as when a foreman or a manager in a firm orders a subordinate to move from one task to another. Coase quotes Robertson (1923) to the effect that there are 'islands of conscious power in this ocean of unconscious co-operation'. Outside the firm it is the price mechanism which co-ordinates the use of resources. Inside the firm, market transactions are replaced by the directives of the management. The essence of the firm, then, is that it is the supersession of the market mechanism.

Having established this starting point it is then possible to consider why the market is so often superseded and the factors which determine this supersession, thereby determining the scope of the firm. A number of possibilities offer themselves. The first is that individuals might actually prefer to be directed by other people, rather than simply taking part in abstract market transactions. Coase dismissed that explanation, although organisational psychologists might disagree. The second possibility is that some individuals may desire to exercise power over others, and would therefore be willing to pay others more than they would receive in a straightforward market transactions. That, too, can be dismissed as unlikely as it implies that those who exercise authority in firms would have to pay for the privilege, rather than being paid more than those they direct.

If these reasons for overriding the market mechanism are rejected, then the most obvious alternative explanation is simply that using the market involves costs which might be avoided. These costs are of various types, including the costs of discovering prices and the cost of negotiating and concluding contracts which have to specify precisely the obligations of the buyer and seller. This latter point, on the costs and disadvantages of precise or incomplete contracts, is particularly important. If transaction costs are to be kept as low as possible, then it would be preferable to establish long-term contracts, rather than a series of short-term contracts. However, the longer the period of the contract, the more uncertain are the purchaser's precise requirements. As a result, it will be desirable to establish a form of contract where the supplier is under an obligation to provide goods or services *within certain limits*, with the details left until a later date, to be decided by the buyer as and when his requirements become more clearly defined. Once such incomplete contracts are established, resources are directed by the authority exerted by the buyer *and a firm has come into existence*. Another general reason for preferring internalised transactions to external ones is that internal transactions are less accessible to governments and other regulatory bodies, so that it may be profitable in some situations to internalise transactions in order to avoid taxes or controls on output.

To sum up, the notion of the firm as supersession of the market mechanism leads naturally on to the existence of **transactions costs** as the major reason for the existence of the firm. Having established that proposition it is possible to go on to consider the factors which determine the optimal scope of the firm.

If there were no disadvantages to market transactions there would be no firms and all transactions would take place between individuals through markets. At the other extreme, if internalised transactions were always superior to market transactions the economy would consist of a single firm, in effect becoming centrally planned. As the reality lies in between these two extremes the question which remains is 'what factors determine the optimal balance between the two different types of transaction, and hence the scope of firms?'. Coase's analysis suggests that at small firm sizes internal transactions are generally superior. However, as size or scope increases so does the cost of organising the extra transactions until it becomes cheaper to organise the marginal transaction through the market or through the establishment of another firm. In this way the analysis of firm size and scope becomes amenable to the economist's standard marginalist tool kit.

A second factor which will set a limit to firm size will be 'managerial diseconomies of scale', whereby management makes less and less efffective use of resources as the number of transactions to be handled increases.

Finally, a limit might be set on firm size if larger firms have to pay more for resources than smaller firms. (It has been noted, for instance, in Chapter 3 that the salaries of executives have been found to be directly correlated with firm size, larger firms offering larger salaries. It is difficult to argue wholly convincingly that the executives of larger firms are necessarily superior to those in small or medium-sized companies.)

As a further step in the analysis, Coase considers three factors which could cause the cost of organising additional transactions to arise. The first is an increase in the physical or geographical space over which transactions are organised. If this is the case then any technological development which reduces the cost of organising across distance will tend to increase the size of the firm. The second factor identified by Coase is the dissimilarity of the transactions involved, an issue which is relevant to the development of the conglomerate, highly diversified, firm. The third factor put forward is the probability of changes in the environment and in prices. If prices change rapidly then the cost of organising a transaction within the firm may rise more rapidly than the costs of organising through markets.

The Coase analysis is pitched at a very general analytical level, rather than concerning itself directly with business decisions. Nevertheless, it is easy to see that it may be applicable in more detail to a number of different choices facing the firm, particularly with respect to the level of vertical integration, the degree of diversification and the choice of overseas operation. Vertical integration and diversification are considered below, and 'multinationalisation' is considered in Chapter 19.

Williamson's analysis

The most powerful extension and development of the Coase analysis has been that of Williamson (1975, 1986), which sets out a general framework within which to analyse the different institutional forms within which different types of transaction take place (see McGuinness (1987) for a more extensive summary). In the vocabulary of the Williamson analysis there is a distinction to be drawn between **markets and hierarchies** as the alternative modes for transactions.

In order to analyse the choice between markets and hierarchies Williamson draws upon two important concepts. The first is **'bounded rationality'** which has been introduced in earlier chapters. Perfect information is not available at zero cost so that individuals have limited information available to them and ᴊo not consider every possible option open to them. They are 'intendedly rational, but only limitedly so'. This implies that it is simply impossible to write complete contracts for the co-ordination of transactions between individuals. The second concept, which has not been introduced elsewhere, is that of **opportunism**. This is essentially guileful strategic ('sneaky') behaviour on the part of individuals of firms designed to give them an advantage in situations where they have information not available to the other party to a transaction.

The combination of bounded rationality and opportunistic behaviour raises serious problems for the organisation of transactions between individuals and through markets. If the parties to a transaction could be guaranteed not to behave opportunistically then uncertainty need not pose a problem. The parties to the transaction could simply agree to treat each other fairly and the contract between them could take the form of a 'promise', rather than a 'plan' with no fear of cheating on either side. In the same way, opportunism would not pose a problem if there were no uncertainty as contracts could be written to cover the perfectly anticipated eventualities. Only the combination of bounded rationality and opportunism leads to the problems outlined. In this situation the major question which has to be addressed is 'what factors decide the form which a transaction should take – market or hierarchy?' As in the Coase analysis it is clear that there are disadvantages to market transactions, but those disadvantages cannot be so crippling that hierarchies are always used, as many transactions do take place through the market.

In the Williamson model the starting point for an answer to this question lies in the presumption that 'economising' will take place and that, at least in the long run, transactions will be carried out in the way which minimises cost. It is then suggested that there are three major factors which determine the most appropriate **'governance structure'** or mode of transaction. They are:

- **The degree of uncertainty.** The greater the degree of uncertainty, the more appropriate it will be to organise a transaction within the firm, in what Williamson (1986) refers to as **'unified governance'**.
- **The frequency with which transactions take place.** If transactions take place only occasionally they will not merit the establishment of a unified governance structure as the threat of opportunistic behaviour will also be only occasional. On the other hand, if transactions are frequent there will be much greater justification for placing those transactions within a firm rather than between firms.

- **The extent of idiosyncratic investment** involved in the transactions. Idiosyncratic investments are those which are specific to the transaction in question and which lose value if the transaction should fail to take place. Clearly, if the extent of such investment is substantial there is a major incentive to establish a unified governance structure.

Having identified these factors, Williamson outlines four different types of governance structure which could provide a framework for the regulation of transactions.

The first is **'classical contracting'**, which is where the identity of the parties to the transaction is irrelevant, all future contingencies are accounted for, and transactions are self-liquidating. This corresponds to the ideal market transaction in economic theory, and is the way in which many of our day-to-day transactions are carried out. If a customer buys a pound of sausages from a supermarket, that transaction takes the form of classical contracting. Neither party to the transaction is concerned with the identity of the other party, the law of contract takes account of future contingencies, and the transaction is completely finished when the purchase is made.

The second type of governance structure is **'neo-classical contracting'**. This arises where it is not possible to account for all possible future contingencies, so that the agreement between two parties is recognised to be incomplete and there is some form of arbitration which can allow the transaction to be completed even if there is disagreement. Contracts of employment are an example of this type of governance structure.

The third mode of transacting is **'relational contracting'**, which departs still further from the classical concept of the discrete one-off transaction in that it encompasses relationships between the parties of greater duration and complexity, where the original agreement between the parties may cease to become a point of reference, being displaced by the relationship itself, which may become: 'a mini-society with a vast array of norms beyond those centred on the exchange and its immediate processes'.

Within the general category of relational contracting there are two variants. The first is **'unified governance'**, where transactions are internalised. The second is **'obligational contracting'** where the transaction takes place between independent firms. Transactions which take this form can include licensing and franchising agreements, long-term distribution agreements and a wide variety of 'networking' arrangements.

Williamson's model thus provides a general framework for describing different modes through which transactions can take place, and for identifying the factors which will determine which mode will be most efficient. The relationship between the two is shown diagramatically in Fig. 18.1.

As the figure shows, transactions will take place within a firm, through unified governance, when the level of idiosyncratic investment is high and when transactions take place frequently. This analysis can be borne in mind when considering both the level of vertical integration and the extent of diversification.

Extent of idiosyncratic investment

Frequency	Low	Medium	High
Occasional	Classical contracting	Neo-classical contracting	Neo-classical contracting
Recurrent	Classical contracting	Obligational contracting	Unified governance

Fig. 18.1 **Frequency, idiosyncrasy and governance structures**
Source: Based on O. Williamson *Economic Organisation*, (Brighton, Wheatsheaf, 1986) p.117.

The extent of vertical integration

Some general considerations

An important aspect of business operations to which the Coase analysis and Williamson's development of it can be applied is the **level of vertical integration**, defined as the extent to which different stages of production take place within the same firm. In this case, the transactions which are internalised link the flow of output between different stages of production, from the extraction and processing of raw materials at one extreme to retail supply at the other. It is important to recognise that all firms are vertically integrated to some extent in that most stages of production can be sub-divided into increasingly smaller stages. A firm which was totally 'disintegrated' vertically would have to carry out a single indivisible operation. The crucial question, then, is not whether a firm will be vertically integrated or not, but rather what level of integration will be optimal, and what factors will encourage more or less integration to take place. There are two general types of factor which can be identified. The first are 'Coasian' in the sense that they concern the cost savings and improvements in efficiency which may arise through the use of internalised transactions. The second type of factor concerns the possible impact of vertical integration on the degree of market power held by the firm. Davies (1987) provides a more comprehensive review of the literature on these issues.

Internalising vertical transactions

Perhaps the most immediately obvious advantages of co-ordinating vertically through internal transactions relate to technical economies in production, where close co-ordination between different stages of production can reduce costs. Bain (1968) has gone so far as to argue that unless such technical relations are involved there are unlikely to be substantial cost savings. The most common example used here is vertical integration in the steel industry where the direct transfer of hot metal from blast furnace to rolling mill saves considerable quantities of energy. This is a useful example, as Williamson notes, because it also shows that the fundamental issue is not actually technological, but is rooted in the disadvantages of market transactions. In principle, it would be perfectly possible for one firm to specialise in the production of molten iron, and another in the use of hot steel as an input, and the two firms could locate themselves physically next door to each other. However, that would require the negotiation, drafting, monitoring and enforcement of a contract between two independent firms, which could effectively substitute for the internal organisation of the flows of hot metal from one stage of the process to another. The provision of such a contract would be so difficult, expensive and risky that internal organisation is the preferred mechanism. This arises for a number of different reasons, identified by Williamson.

The first is that some of the information required to carry out one stage of the process will also be relevant for the others. As information is expensive to produce and disseminate it will be cheaper to integrate the two stages into a single process, thereby saving the duplication of information costs. It is just conceivable that the information needed could be provided through markets by a third party, or by one firm selling to another but the purchaser of the information could not guarantee its truthfulness, and there could be incentives for the information-provider to behave opportunistically, distorting the information to its own advantage.

Secondly, the world is a very uncertain place and firms only exhibit 'bounded rationality'. They do not consider all possibilities in advance and draw up plans for the decisions to be taken in every possible contingency. Instead, their decision-making consists of adapting to changing circumstances as unanticipated events and unforeseen opportunities for improvement occur over time. As a result it is not possible to write complete long-term contracts covering all possibilities. Nor would a series of short-term contracts suffice because of the cost of frequent negotiation and re-negotiation. In the case of steel production, then, vertical integration will be the preferred solution. This conclusion can be referred back to the analysis underlying Fig. 18.1. In the case of steel production, the frequency of transactions is very high and the level of idiosyncratic investment is very high. As a result, unified governance is indicated as the 'economising' way to organise the transaction.

Other observers have drawn similar conclusions in other industries. Monteverde and Teece (1982), for instance, suggest that in the production of components for the motor industry the extent to which development and production is carried on in-house depends upon the level of investment involved and the threat of opportunistic recontracting. If a component is technologically complex and expensive to produce, requiring close links between manufacturer and supplier, there will be a risk that a supplier will behave opportunistically by demanding better terms at the last moment, knowing that the vehicle manufacturer cannot simply take his business elsewhere. In that situation (frequent transactions, high level of idiosyncratic investment) the economising model requires that the transactions be organised through unified governance.

In some industries, most obviously the service sector, the main asset of a firm consists of human capital in the form of the specialist expertise and experience embodied in talented individuals, rather than in immobile plant and equipment. In this case, Williamson considers a slightly different way in which internal transactions may be superior to external transactions, with particular respect to the capital market. In such cases, bankers may be reluctant to invest in firms where the main asset is so difficult for them to value with any certainty. However, firms which have dealt with the individuals in question, as suppliers or customers, will be in a better position to value their worth and as a result will be willing to provide capital for such ventures at lower cost, through an internal transaction leading to vertical integration forwards or backwards.

It is clear, then, that the failure of the market provides an explanation for the internalisation of many transactions, leading to vertical integration. However, as Coase noted, there must be limits to this market failure because otherwise all firms would be fully integrated from raw material extraction to sales to final consumers. Williamson also extends the Coase analysis in this respect, pointing to some of the limits to internal transactions in the context of vertical integration. The first of these is the tendency for the **existence of internal sources of supply to distort procurement decisions**. Once a supplying division has been set up within a firm, the interests of the sub-group of managers concerned with that operation may militate against the use of outside sources of supply, if it should become more efficient and cost-effective to use those sources. Even if managers have guaranteed employment there will often be loss of status attaching to association with a 'failed' operation, and they may resist. There may also be a more general **resistance to change stemming from the bureaucratic nature of many organisations**, and the horse-trading which takes place as managers form shifting alliances with each other in support of their own 'pet projects'. This weakness of internal organisation is closely related to the 'persistence' phenomenon, whereby existing activities in organisations tend to be continued even in preference to demonstrably superior new projects, simply because the sunk costs associated with existing projects tend to insulate them from proper comparison with the cost of new approaches.

A second weakness of internal organisation lies in the **distortion of communications between managers**, who may tend to tell their supervisors or subordinates what they hope to hear, rather than the truth. If information about the firm's operations were easily checked, this tendency could be curbed through internal audit procedures. However, in many cases information is 'impacted', meaning simply that it is too deeply embedded in the details of operations for supervisors to be able to check its truthfulness at reasonable cost.

Clearly there are limits to the advantages of internal organisation and these set restrictions on the optimal size of the firm. There are also advantages to market transactions which are not considered in a very formal approach to the problem of incomplete contracts. While the legal position on contractual agreements between firms may be that of '*caveat emptor*' (let the buyer beware) and business lawyers may be very concerned to consider the worst possible consequences of a contract they draft, this position is often substantially qualified by the level of 'give-and-take' which businessmen exercise in their dealings with each other. Business reputation is important to firms, as a reputation for fair dealing and reasonableness may help in acquiring custom. This tendency is often reinforced through informal and social connections between executives, and in some cases by formal systems of experience-ratings where firms pool their knowledge of dealings with suppliers and customers (Leff (1970)). Even when complete contracts cannot be written or enforced, market transactions may still be possible through 'relational contracting' and informal enforcement. In industries where this informal network is strong, vertical integration need not proceed as far as would otherwise be the case, because long-term relationships between firms substitute for common ownership.

Vertical integration and monopoly power

The second set of factors determining the level of vertical integration concerns the possibility of the firm extending its monopoly power through forward or backward integration. This could take place in a number of ways.

The first is through **the ability to enforce profitable price discrimination**. As noted in an earlier chapter, price discrimination requires that there be different elasticities of demand in different markets, and that re-selling between different markets with different prices can be prevented. Vertical integration may assist this process in a number of ways. Integration forwards, towards the final consumer, may help the firm identify different segments of the market, where elasticities differ. Even if elasticities are known with ease, there may be advantages to vertical integration if it is difficult (or illegal, see Agnew(1985)) to establish contracts which preclude re-sale. If there are two categories of buyer, one of which will be charged a high price and one a low price then it may pay to integrate into the low price market in order to prevent re-sale from that market into the other. (Obviously the process of integration would need to take in all buyers in the low price market in this case.)

Crandall (1968) provides an interesting example of the use of vertical integration in the market for repair parts in the American automobile industry. Ideally, firms seeking maximum profit would wish to discriminate perfectly amongst buyers, charging each the maximum amount they would be willing to pay. Unfortunately for the manufacturer, that is made impossible by the ease of arbitrage between different customers. However, if the intensity of demand is related to the intensity of use (a crucial assumption in Crandall's analysis) it might just be possible for motor companies to rent vehicles, rather than sell them, charging identical rates per mile, but taking larger payments from the higher mileage users. However, such an arrangement would involve huge capital costs and added vulnerability to anti-trust legislation. An alternative approach would be to find a complementary product whose use varies with the intensity of use. Such a complementary product is to be found in spare parts. If motor vehicle producers integrate backwards into the production of components for use in original equipment, they are also able to produce the same parts for the repair market. If they can establish market power in the sale of repair parts, and if the demand for cars is more elastic than the demand for parts, then it will pay the firm to lower the price of cars and raise the price of parts, thereby effectively charging the more intensive user of cars a higher price for the motoring he acquires!

It is clear that a condition for success in this example is that the vehicle producer is able to prevent motorists from purchasing parts from other suppliers. This can be achieved in a number of ways. One is the backwards integration itself. If there are scale economies in the production of parts, and independent parts producers are denied the original equipment market by backwards integration by vehicle assemblers, then it will be difficult for independent producers to compete effectively. If this market strength is reinforced through a system of franchised dealers, bound by contract to use 'genuine spare parts only', by the ownership of the special tooling required to make the spare parts, and by frequent variation of the components, the assembling companies may be able to put together an effective package of market control.

In the case of auto repair parts, backwards integration may make market entry more difficult. However, there is a more general point to be made concerning entry barriers. If a potential entrant is required to enter two stages of production simultaneously, the capital requirements will be larger, as will the requirements for knowledge and skill and entry will be made more expensive and difficult. It can be argued, of course (Bork (1954)) that if entry is profitable then an increase in the capital requirement should pose no particular problem for an entrant. However, providers of capital have imperfect information on which to base their decisions and may be suspicious of providing capital to firms which cannot demonstrate experience in both stages of production. As a result, the cost of capital may be higher for a firm considering entry into a vertically integrated market, and the heightening of entry barriers may be real. Such barriers are additional to those created by scale economies, as in the spare parts case.

The extent of diversification

The importance of diversification

In the elementary model of the firm, the business produces a single product. However, virtually all firms in all industries are multi-product and the question is not whether to be diversified or not, but what extent of diversification should be aimed for. Companies may be diversified along a very narrow spectrum of closely related activities, or they may be **'broad-spectrum diversified'** or **'conglomerate'**, encompassing a range of activities which bear little technological or marketing connection with each other. There are a number of factors which are important in determining the extent of diversification, each of which bears a relationship to the discussion above.

Economies of scope

Economies of scope have been referred to briefly in Chapter 8 as a 'cost driver'. The term is used to refer to a situation where it is cheaper to combine two or more product lines in one firm, rather than producing them separately. A detailed technical analysis of scope economies involves a level of difficulty which goes beyond this text, but it is possible to outline a number of major points.

The key feature of economies of scope is that they are linked to the existence of inputs which are 'sharable' in the sense that once purchased or hired for the production of one product they are also available at little or no additional cost for the production of others. Generators for electric power, and the cables and equipment needed to distribute the power are an example as they can be used for different products at different times. Other examples are factory buildings, human capital like managerial skill or inputs like sheep and cattle which produce joint outputs (mutton and wool, beef and hides). The range of such sharable inputs is quite broad, and could extend as far as the marketing skills which can be used for a variety of products, or to the ownership of distribution channels down which a variety of goods could be sent. If such sharable inputs exist there will be economies of scope. Wherever such economies exist it is to be expected that the multi-product firm will be the norm, because any firm which is not producing an appropriate range of products will be at a cost disadvantage relative to those who do.

The exploitation of specific assets

A second factor which may make diversification profitable is the possession and development of specific assets which may be exploitable in a number of different activities, thereby giving rise to further economies of scope, and further opportunities for diversification. Companies may have 'core' skills which provide the foundation for a move into a wider range of activities. Penrose (1959), for instance, noted that as firms grow some of their assets are constantly regenerated in changing forms, which allow them to carry out new activities. One particular example concerns research and development activity (R&D). If a firm carries out R&D then it may produce new discoveries in products or processes which can be exploited outside the firm's current range of activities. Some of the empirical evidence (Gort (1962)) shows a distinct relationship between the level of R&D in firms and industries and the extent of diversification. This again raises the issue of the choice between an internalised transaction and a market transaction. If market transactions in knowledge were superior to internalised transactions, firms producing innovations outside their current range of activities would not become more diversified. Instead of producing unfamiliar new products themselves they would sell or license their innovations to firms specialising in that type of product. If a new discovery is easily identified and protected, if it can be cheaply transferred to a licensee, and if competition pushes the license fee high enough then licensing will be preferred (Davies (1977)) and new inventions will not lead to greater diversification on the part of the innovating firm. On the other hand, if it is expensive to transfer the know-how from one firm to another, and if the technological advantage is difficult to protect, then it will be more profitable to produce the product in-house and diversification will take place. Other factors are relevant to this decision. If there are economies of scope between the new activity and the firm's existing portfolio, then in-house development will allow cost reductions in both the new activity and existing ones, spreading the overheads over a wider scope. On the other hand, if the new discovery relates to an activity which is peripheral to the firm's existing activities, in the sense that the firm does not have the appropriate range of plant and equipment, managerial skills or distribution networks needed to exploit it, then licensing may be preferable.

The reduction of risk and uncertainty

Each of the issues considered above relates to diversification into activities which have some connection with the firm's existing activities, either through the structure of costs, the firm's core skills, or its research and develpment activity. However, none of these factors is sufficient to explain the existence of the true **conglomerate** firm composed of a completely disparate set of activities. One possible explanation for the existence of such firms lies in the reduction of risk and uncertainty. If the firm is viewed as an investment prospect, then it is easily shown that the risk associated with it, measured by the variability of its profits, can be reduced by grouping together a number of different activities. This can happen in two ways. First, the average risk will be reduced as activities are 'pooled'. Secondly, risk can be reduced particularly effectively by combining activities whose returns are negatively correlated with each other. As a result, the diversified firm may be a more attractive prospect to suppliers of capital.

The problem with this argument is that an investor could achieve the same result, or better, by investing in a diversified portfolio of shares, or a unit trust, rather than in a diversified firm. In fact, if investors are rational and dislike risk they will already have done so. However, this argument only applies completely when capital markets are perfect, and investors well-informed. There may be two reasons why a diversified firm may be more attractive than investment in a portfolio of shares. The first is that investors may rate the diversification skills of managers with inside information more highly than their own, or those of investment managers. Williamson has argued that the top managements of M-form, multi-divisional conglomerates have access to better and more detailed information on investment opportunities within the firm than does the external capital market. In a similar vein, Lewellen (1971) has noted that diversification within a firm may provide cheaper access to debt finance. One of the greatest worries for the providers of loans is that the borrower may default. This is known as default risk, as opposed to equity risk which arises from the variability of profits. Within a diversified firm, if one division makes losses, these may be compensated for by profits in another (provided that the returns to the different divisions are not highly positively correlated). As a result, the providers of debt finance, as opposed to equity, will be willing to lend to a diversified firm at a lower rate of interest. This will allow the firm to be more highly geared (have a higher ratio of debt to equity finance) which in turn may carry tax advantages as interest on debt is tax deductible whereas returns on equity are not.

Managers' desire for security

The analysis above has assumed that the aim of the firm is to maximise returns to the shareholders. However, Chapter 3 has indicated that in some situations the objectives of the firm may be the objectives of the managers, rather than the shareholders. For manager-controlled firms, diversification may be attractive as a means of reducing the variation in returns, thereby ensuring a quiet life, even if shareholders' interests are not best served by that policy. The choice of diversification as a strategy may also be affected by the functional background of those holding power within the firm. Sutton (1973) has argued that some functional specialists notably in marketing and R&D will be more aware of the diversification prospects than others (production or personnel), so that the firms controlled by some types of specialist will be more inclined to diversify than others.

Diversification and product life cycles

A further issue worth considering in respect of diversification concerns the gradual worsening of the prospects for a firm's current range of products as they move through successive stages of their life cycle. If demand for a firm's product begins to fall one response would be for the firm to simply go out of business, with its resources being distributed to other uses by the market mechanism. However, instead of this market transaction reallocating the resources to other uses, this is another situation where an internalised transaction could be more efficient. If the firm has built up a management team with skills which are usable in other activities that team may actively seek opportunities for diversification as existing products reach the mature and declining stages of their life cycle.

Mergers and taker-overs

Firms may diversify or vertically integrate through two different routes, which have been discussed briefly in Chapter 11. The first is through **internal development** and the second is through **merger** or **acquisition**, which merits further discussion.

Alternative forms of merger

A merger may be defined as the process by which a firm acquires resources which are already organised by another firm. If this process is uncontested it is usually referred to as a merger. If the incumbent managers of the 'victim' contest the process then it is usually referred to as a 'take-over.' In practice the distinction between mergers and take-overs is often blurred. Three types of merger may be distinguished, following the analysis above. These are:

- **horizontal mergers**, between potential competitors
- **vertical mergers**, between firms at different stages of the production process
- **conglomerate mergers**, between firms in unrelated activities.

Mergers in a perfect world

The simplest way to begin is to consider the situation where managers are all efficient, where the market value of every firm is an accurate reflection of expected future earnings, where there is no uncertainty, where managers are constrained to act in the interests of shareholders and where every investor uses the same discount rate in the evaluation of future returns. In this situation, every investor will place the same value on every company and no one will be willing to pay more for a firm than anyone else. Mergers will then only take place if the merged firm has a higher value than the sum of its parts. This could arise for a number of reasons, most of which have been touched upon above. These may be considered in turn.

Increased market power. A horizontal merger, or a vertical merger may give the combined firm more market power, allowing an element of monopoly profit to be made and enhancing the value of the merged firm above that of its pre-merger components. If restrictive collusive agreements between firms are outlawed, for instance, as under the UK restrictive practices legislation, mergers may take place in order to allow the same collusive arrangement to continue within a single firm. Needless to say, such mergers may also fall foul of the competition legislation.

'Synergy'. Synergy is a blanket term covering the general idea that 'two plus two may be greater than four'. In times of merger booms there are often rather vague claims made for the existence of synergistic effects, which amount to wishful thinking or ex-post rationalisation. Nevertheless the effects could be real and could arise through a number of different mechanisms, most of which have emerged in the analysis outlined above.

One source of synergy could be unexploited **economies of scope** in production, marketing or distribution. Similarly, if there are unexploited **economies of scale** a merger may allow the combined firm to produce at lower unit cost. One of the most important sources of such scale economies are **indivisible resources**. If a firm has an indivisible and under-utilised management team, distribution network or set of plant and equipment it may be able to reduce costs by applying these resources to a larger set of merged activities. Synergy may also arise in the case of vertical mergers if **transactions costs are reduced** by replacing market transactions with internalised transactions, as outlined above, if there are **economies in raising finance** or if the merged firm has **enhanced debt capacity**.

If any of these factors are present, there will be real synergistic effects arising from merger and the value of the merged firm will exceed the value of its pre-merger components. In a perfect world described mergers would only take place if such effects really exist.

Mergers as the transfer of resources to more efficient managements

If share markets work efficiently the value of a firm's shares will reflect the future profits which the firm is expected to earn. If some managers are more efficient than others, companies run by them will have higher expected profits and higher valuations. Conversely, firms run by less competent or X-inefficient managers will have relatively low valuations and relatively low share prices, as the market will value the company on the basis of the expected future profits to be made, which depend upon the competence of the management.

In this situation a strong management team will place a higher value than the market on the assets of a firm being run by a weak management team, the presumption being that the stronger team would be able to use the same assets to make a higher level of profit. As a result, the market for corporate control will ensure that mergers are a means by which the economy's resources are concentrated in the hands of more efficient managers (Manne(1965)). More efficient managements scan the market for less efficiently run firms who may be taken over, to the benefit of the shareholders.

One of the major problems with this explanation for mergers lies in the empirical evidence, which provides only very limited support for the view that mergers transfer resources from the weak to the strong. A key study by Newbould (1970) showed that in many cases firms considering merger carried out little or no analysis of their 'victim' in the pre-merger stage, and only about half of the firms examined even attempted to secure synergistic gains post-merger. Furthermore, the evidence concerning the impact of mergers on profits is highly contradictory. If the explanation for mergers set out above provides the whole story we would expect to find that after mergers take place the profits or the value of the combined firm increase. However, much of the evidence suggests that is not the case. Singh (1971), for instance, found that at least half of the firms involved in a sample of mergers experienced decreases in profitability after the merger. On balance 'there is little evidence that mergers lead to substantial real or pecuniary advantages'.

While some mergers do correspond to the view that resources become concentrated in the hands of the stronger firms, it would clearly be naive to assume that this is always the case. Other explanations need to be found. Koutsoyannis (1982) puts forward two further possibilities, amongst others. The first is that mergers may take place as a result of the manipulation of the market by merger promoters. The second is that discrepancies in the valuation of firms may arise in a number of ways other than differences in management competence.

Mergers as a result of manipulation

In the absence of well-informed investors it is possible that mergers could take place as part of a ploy by merger promoters. In the early American merger booms, for instance, the practice of 'stock watering' was common. This consists simply of a merger promoter planting rumours that there would be substantial gains to be had from a merger, leading investors to place an unrealistically high price on the stock of a merged firm, at least until the market recognises the fallacy, by which time the merger promoter has realised a substantial profit and sold any holdings. Koutsoyannis (p.244) also outlines a more sophisticated version of this technique, known as 'bootstrapping'. If a firm has a high price/earnings (P/E) ratio and acquires a firm with a lower P/E ratio by swapping shares then if investors can be persuaded that the combined operation should be valued at the higher ratio, the share price of the combined firm will rise. It is likely, of course, that the acquired firm had a lower P/E ratio because it had more limited prospects and that eventually the higher P/E ratio will be seen by the market to have been unrealistic. However, in the short term, substantial speculative profits could be made.

Mergers as a result of valuation discrepancies

In the model presented in the section on mergers as the transfer of resources to more efficient managements discrepancies in valuation arise because managements have different levels of ability. However, differences in the valuation of the same firm by different investors could arise in other ways. In times of economic disturbance, for instance, with rapid technological progress, shifting demand patterns and fluctuating share prices, different groups of investors may easily develop different expectations about the value of a business, and Gort (1969) has suggested that this could account for the existence of merger 'booms'. In this case, mergers are essentially the outcome of unpredictable changes in market sentiment with little foundation in the objective realities of the firms' position.

Are mergers really for managers?

A final explanation for mergers, which is consistent with points made in earlier chapters, is that they may come about because growth by merger is attractive to a firm's managers, even if there are no real gains for the shareholders. It has been noted above that conglomerate merger may reduce the level of risk, but that it is a relatively inefficient way of doing so for an investor, who could simply buy a more highly diversified portfolio of shares. For the managers, however, who are restricted to working in one firm at a time, the risk attached to their employment arises from the riskiness attached to that single firm's activities. From their point of view risk reduction through in-house diversification may be very attractive, providing for a more quiet life. Similarly, mergers may take place because firm size, or growth, is an important element in the managers' objective function, giving them status and prestige. In these cases, it is the needs and interests of managers which determine merger activity, not those of the shareholders or the economy as a whole.

Illustration

Vertical integration and transactions costs in the motor industry

The production of automobiles is essentially an assembly process which involves bringing together thousands of different components from dozens of sources. Some of these components are purchased from independent suppliers, while others are sourced internally through backward integration on the part of the vehicle producer.

Monteverde and Teece (1982) attempt to explain why firms take parts production in-house, using the theory of transactions costs as a framework. Their basic hypothesis is that assemblers will choose in-house sources when the production of the parts in question generates specialised, non-patentable know-how which yields substantial quasi-rents. Such know-how is essentially a transaction-specific asset which would be lost if the supplier ceased to supply. Switching to an alternative supplier would be expensive and time-consuming so that the vehicle assembler is highly vulnerable to opportunistic recontracting on the part of the suppliers of such components. Taking component production in-house through backward integration removes that risk.

In order to test this hypothesis, Monteverde and Teece had to find a way to measure the amount of transaction-specific know-how associated with different components and the quasi-rents arising from that know-how. There is no direct way in which such amounts can be observed, but they suggest that there will be a positive relationship between the 'applications engineering effort' associated with the production of a component and the appropriable quasi-rents. In that case, it is to be expected that components requiring more substantial engineering effort will be sourced in-house.

Having found a means by which the hypothesis can be tested it is possible to carry out the empirical analysis. A list of 133 vehicle components was obtained from an assembler, and each was classified as either internally produced or externally sourced, by Ford and General Motors (GM), giving a dichotomous dependent variable. A design engineer then provided an 'engineering cost rating' for each of the components, which was cross-checked with another set of ratings provided independently by another design engineer. These ratings took the form of a 10-point scale on which the extent of engineering investment varied from 0, which corresponded to 'none' to 10, which corresponded to 'a lot'. In addition to that cost variable, the analysis included a number of other independent variables. The first distinguished between components which are 'generic' (i.e. not designed for any individual car-maker) and those which are customised. The second distinguished between the two assemblers, Ford and GM, while the third attempted to capture the place of the component in the vehicles wider sub-systems. This last variable allocated each component to one of 5 sub-systems – body, engine, chassis, electrical, ventilation – and assigned a dichotomous dummy variable to each sub-system, on the hypothesis that different sub-systems would display different degrees of vertical integration.

The statistical analysis then examined the relationship between the dependent variable, representing the decision between in-house production and outside purchase, and the set of independent variables. As none of the variables have a continuous form the most appropriate statistical technique was probit analysis, which can be thought of as analogous to multiple regression.

Examination of the results revealed a number of features. In the first place the variable for 'engineering effort' bore a positive relationship to the choice of in-house production, at the .001 level, as did the variable for customisation and the variable which distinguished between Ford and GM. The evidence suggests that vehicle producers do internalise the production of components which require a substantial engineering effort, they do internalise the sourcing of customised parts and GM is significantly more vertically integrated than Ford. On the other hand, the variables reflecting the systems effects were of limited significance. Only 'electrical' systems gave any significant results, and those were at the .05 level.

The conclusion, then, is that vehicle assemblers' decisions on backward integration into component production may be explained in terms of the transactional superiority of internal production in situations where a substantial investment in know-how is required.

References and further reading

J. Agnew, *Competition Law*, (London, George Allen and Unwin, 1985)

J.S. Bain, *Industrial Organisation*, (New York, Wiley, 1968)

R.H. Bork, 'Vertical Integration and the Sherman Act', *University of Chicago Law Review*, 1954

R.H. Coase, 'The Nature of the Firm', *Economica*, 1937

R. Crandall, 'Vertical Integration and the Market for Repair Parts in the US Automobile Industry', *Journal of Industrial Economics*, 1968

S. Davies, 'Vertical Integration', in R. Clarke and A. McGuiness (eds.), *The Economics of the Firm*, 1987

H. Davies, 'Technology Transfer Through Commercial Transactions', *Journal of Industrial Economics*, 1977

M. Gort, 'An Economic Disturbance Theory of Mergers', *Quarterly Journal of Economics*, 1969

A. Koutsoyannis, *Non-Price Decisions*, (London, Macmillan, 1982)

A. Leff, 'Contract as a Thing', *American University Law Review*, 1970

W. Lewellen, 'A Pure Financial Rationale for the Conglomerate Merger', *Journal of Finance*, 1971

H. Manne, 'Mergers and the Market for Corporate Control', *Journal of Political Economy*, 1965

A. McGuiness, 'Markets and Managerial Hierarchies', in R. Clarke and A. McGuiness, *The Economics of the Firm*, 1987

K. Monteverde and D. Teece, 'Supplier Switching Costs and Vertical Integration in the Automobile Industry', *Bell Journal of Economics*, 1982

G. Newbould, *Management and Merger Activity*, 1970

E. Penrose, *The Theory of the Growth of the Firm*, (Oxford, Blackwell, 1959)

M. Porter, *Competitive Advantage*, (New York, Free Press, 1985)

D.H. Robertson, *The Control of Industry*, (London, Nisbet, 1923)

A. Singh, *Takeovers*, (Cambridge, Cambridge UP, 1971)

C. Sutton, 'Management Behaviour and a Theory of Diversification', *Scottish Journal of Political Economy*, 1973

O. Williamson, *Markets and Hierarchies*, (New York, Free Press, 1975)

O. Williamson, *Economic Organisation*, (Brighton, Wheatsheaf, 1986)

Self-test questions

1 List the different dimensions of 'scope'.

2 Identify appropriate governance structures for the following types of transaction.

(a) an infrequent transaction, involving no idiosyncratic investment

(b) a frequent transaction, involving a high level of idiosyncratic investment

(c) an infrequent transaction, involving some idiosyncratic investment

3 List three disadvantages of having an internal source of supply for an intermediate product.

4 Explain in one sentence why it is unconvincing to suggest that shareholders will seek to invest in diversified firms in order to reduce risk.

5 List four possible sources of synergy.

Exercise

Outline the factors which will encourage a firm to become more vertically integrated, and consider the disadvantages which may arise from such a move.

Answers on page 432.

19 The multinational enterprise

This chapter is concerned with the multinational enterprise (MNE). A brief outline of the MNE's development is followed by an examination of the ways in which economic theory has attempted to explain the pattern of multinational activity. This is followed by a short analysis of the impact of the MNE on host and source countries, and the chapter concludes with an outline of the main dimensions of global corporate strategy.

The development of the multinational enterprise

A definition of the MNE

Hood and Young (1979) suggest that a multinational enterprise (MNE) may be defined as:

> a corporation which owns (in whole or in part), controls and manages income generating assets in more than one country.

It might be argued that the definition should be more restrictive, perhaps by including only firms above a certain size, or by excluding minority ownerships abroad or excluding firms having operations in only two countries. On the other hand, to do so would be arbitrary and might exclude important and interesting phenomena. For the purposes of this chapter the broad definition will be adopted.

The significance and pattern of multinational activity

Problems in collecting and collating statistics on a comparable basis across countries can make it difficult to secure wholly satisfactory quantitative data on the activities of MNEs. Nevertheless, the figures which are available confirm the sheer size of multinational activity. At the end of 1978, according to Dunning, the book value of foreign investments in the major trading nations of the world approached $400 billion dollars. According to the Commission of the European Communities, the 260

373

largest MNEs employed more than 25 million people in 1973. Figures for turnover show that the total volume of sales for the very largest corporations exceeds the GNP of some countries.

Two aspects of the pattern of multinational activity warrant attention. The first concerns the spatial distribution of activity, by host-country and by source nation. The second concerns the sectoral distribution of activity. These are shown in Tables 19.1 and 19.2.

Table 19.1 The geographical distribution of foreign direct capital stock (1982, $US billion)

Country or area	Outward investment	Inward investment
Unites States	221.8	124.7
United Kingdom	87.4	51.3
Japan	53.1	4.2
Switzerland	42.1	not available
W Germany	40.1	32.1
Netherlands	39.7	18.0
Canada	27.5	56.3
France	19.3	14.8
Italy	8.1	7.4
Developing countries	2.0	129.0

Source: J. Dunning and J. Cantwell, *IRM Directory of Statistics of International Investment and Production* (Basingstoke, Macmillan, 1987)

As Table 19.1 illustrates, the United States was the most important source of foreign investment in 1978, with Britain second, followed by Germany, Switzerland and Japan. That pattern was radically different from that for 1914 which showed an almost total predominance of British investment overseas, followed by the US, Germany, France and Italy. The home base of multinational activity changes substantially over time, with a radical increase in Japanese activity during the 1980s, and the gradual emergence of MNEs based in developing nations beginning to make their mark.

Table 19.1 also shows the location of foreign direct investment by host countries and areas. As the table illustrates, the pattern of activity by host nation is very similar to that by source, except that Canada acts as host for a very much larger proportion of activity than it acts as source.

Table 19.2 The sectoral distribution of foreign direct capital stock (inward investment, 1982, $US billion)

Country or area	Sector Primary	Manufacturing	Services
EEC	25.3	70.8	46.9
US	20.6	44.1	60.0
Rest of the developed world	24.3	49.5	34.2
Developing nations	26.7	63.9	27.5
Total	96.9	228.3	168.6

Source: J. Dunning and J. Cantwell, *IRM Directory of Statistics of International Investment and Production* (Basingstoke, Macmillan, 1987)

MNE activity takes place to a very great extent between developed market economies, which host three-quarters of the stock of direct investment, in comparison to just one-quarter which takes place in developing nations.

As Table 19.2 shows, MNE activity spreads across all three major sectors of economic activity – primary, manufacturing and services. The largest proportion is to be found in manufacturing, at around 45 per cent, with the extractive and service sectors accounting for about equal proportions of the remainder.

An outline history of the multinational

According to Ghertman and Allen (1984) the first multinational, dating from the beginning of the nineteenth century, was the S.A.Cockerill steelworks established in Prussia in 1815. As might be expected from the pattern of global economic development the first multinationals were almost all European-based and included a number of firms which continue to be household names including British American Tobacco, Lever Brothers, Michelin and Nestlé. The geographical scope of many of these firms reflected the distribution of colonial influence and a large proportion of them were involved in backwards integration into agriculture and minerals in the colonies. This provided a means of securing raw materials to be processed in the imperial homeland for sale at home or for export.

While there were a number of such multinationals before the Second World War, they were largely restricted to the kinds of activity described and could not be considered to have been a major feature of the world scene. As Casson (1987) notes, a much more common approach to global competition, especially in the 1920s and 1930s, was the establishment of international cartels in many of the industries which later came to be dominated by MNEs.

The major period of growth for the multinationals, especially in manufacturing, was the 1950s through to the early 1970s, after which their expansion began to level off. This wave of development was led by American firms moving into the European market where their presence became so marked that **The American Challenge** (Servan-Schreiber (1967)) was seen as a serious threat to Europe's ability to achieve self-sustaining growth. European economies were said to be in danger of becoming dependent upon American firms for their higher level business functions, including research and development and marketing, and the European consumer was held to be at the mercy of American tastes and the market power of US corporations.

The American multinationals in this period had a number of characteristics which, for a time, were seen as the defining features of the post-war MNE. In the first place, they were drawn to the other major developed countries, rather than former colonies or other developing nations. Their purpose was to serve large markets like the European Community from a local base and they were involved in the production of import-substitutes, rather than vertical integration backwards towards sources of raw materials.

Secondly, research on the American MNE showed that its development was strongly associated with highly concentrated and research-intensive industries which also exhibited high levels of advertising intensity and made use of large proportions of highly skilled workers. The theory of the multinational (see below) produced explanations for this pattern, and for a while at least multinational activity as a whole was seen as conforming to this stereotype.

Various new developments in the 1970s and 1980s showed that the MNE could take other forms. The emergence of the Japanese multinational, focused until recently on offshore, 'export platform' activities in the newly-industrialising countries, ran counter to the stereotype of the skilled-labour, R&D-intensive activity associated with the American NME. The 'American Challenge' was reversed as European firms entered the American market and European ownership of American firms became at least as marked as American ownership in Europe (to the chagrin of some American observers). The emergence of MNEs based in developing nations like India ran counter to the established pattern and the realisation that there are many quite small multinationals, and that the service sector has an important MNE component, have all contributed to a re-assessment of the nature of the multinational. It has come to be recognised that multinational activity encompasses a much wider range of activities than had hitherto been appreciated.

Economic theory and the multinational

The application of alternative perspectives

One of the most interesting features of the multinational is that it brings together a number of different, otherwise unrelated, areas of economic analysis. The theory of international trade is relevant, as MNEs trade across national boundaries and the location of different types of economic activity is an important aspect to understand. Theories of industrial structure and behaviour are important, as MNEs are engaged in strategic actions which may affect rivals. Finally, the MNE is involved in co-ordinating transactions across national boundaries which raises the issues of 'internalisation' or 'markets versus hierarchies' discussed in Chapter 18. As Casson (1987) notes, the application of general theory to the specific issues raised by the MNE gives a special 'twist' to the theory in the course of the application, which makes it a particularly interesting area to explore.

The Hymer-Kindleberger proposition

The starting-point for almost any exposition of the theory of the MNE is to be found in the work of Hymer and Kindleberger. Hymer's PhD dissertation of 1960 remained unpublished until 1976, but some of its central points, which drew heavily on Bain's (1956) analysis of entry barriers were taken up by Kindleberger (1969) to begin a theoretical debate which extended the issues far beyond Hymer's original insight.

Hymer's initial observation was that firms operating abroad must face some disadvantages relative to incumbents in those markets. For them to compete in such markets, then, they must possess some form of offsetting competitive advantage. The development of the MNE, then, might be attributed to the acquisition of quasi-monopolistic advantages by firms who then find that these advantages can be exploited for profit in overseas markets.

Such advantages could take a number of forms, and the literature on the MNE contains a good deal of debate on the issue. Caves (1971) pointed out that the advantage in question needs to be a public good within the firm, so that its use in one location does not deprive the firm of its use in another. As corporate knowledge and skills are the most obvious assets to have this characteristic they would appear to provide the foundation for the development of the MNE.

Following on from that insight, corporate knowledge and skills were often identified with, and proxied by, in-house research and development spending. Examination of the links between these variables and the extent of multinationality showed that they had explanatory power in the case of American multinationals, hence the association referred to above between the MNE and technological superiority.

The possession of some form of advantage may provide a necessary condition for going abroad and competing with indigenous firms, but it cannot be a sufficient condition as there is always the option of selling or licensing the advantage to a local firm. If those firms do have advantages of 'localness' that would suggest that they should be able to make more profit from the use of the advantage than the would-be MNE. If there were competition to buy the advantage, driving its price up until it was equal to the extra profits to be made, that would suggest that licensing would be more profitable than foreign direct investment. The theory of the multinational therefore also has to explain why firms should choose to use their advantages themselves, rather than trade them. Hymer's suggestion was that the market for such knowledge is imperfect, so that MNEs cannot secure all of the monopoly rents accruing to their advantages by selling them. In that case there is a clear incentive to keep the transfer of the advantage in-house, and the MNE is seen as a conduit for the transfer of knowledge from one location to another.

Casson (1987) notes that at this point in the analysis Hymer's theory failed to distinguish between two very different aspects of market imperfections in knowledge. The first, which Hymer concentrated on, arises from imperfections in market structure. If, for example, there is only one potential buyer for a monopolistic advantage, and only one seller, the situation becomes one of bilateral monopoly in which it may be very difficult for the seller to extract all of the monopoly rents available. Such imperfections could provide the rationale for the MNE. However, there is another, conceptually quite distinct, type of imperfection which links to the work of Coase and Williamson, described in Chapter 18. That is imperfections in markets arising as a result of transactions costs and the difficulties of organising transactions between independent organisations in conditions of uncertainty.

'Internalisation' and transactions cost theory

The suggestion that the MNE could be explained through a similar set of analytical tools to that applied to vertical integration or diversification formed the basis for theoretical advances from a number of writers, most notably McManus (1972), Buckley and Casson (1976), Rugman (1981) and Casson (1982). While many of the ideas have close links with those of Coase and Williamson they are often expressed in different ways.

Buckley and Casson's analysis, in particular, has become the foundation for further developments around the concept of 'internalisation'. In their 1976 formulation they identified five advantages which an internalised transaction can have over the market. These are:

- increased ability to control and plan
- the opportunity for discriminatory pricing
- avoidance of bilateral monopoly
- reduction of uncertainty
- avoidance of government intervention

There is also a range of other issues which are relevant to the choice between foreign direct investment and the sale of an advantage through licensing. The first concerns the nature of the advantage which is being transacted. In some cases, where this consists of a patented machine, or a 'secret ingredient', it may be easy to identify the advantage and transfer it to another firm. However, in many cases a firm may not know exactly what gives it a competitive edge and it will be impossible to sell such an imprecisely defined advantage. Similarly , it may be expensive to transfer an advantage outside the bounds of the originating firm, which would make it preferable to invest, or there may not be competent local entrepreneurs to bid for the advantage. Both Rugman (1981) and Porter (1985) stress the possible loss of control associated with selling a competitive advantage to an independent firm which might use it to become an effective competitor in future. In principle, this might be overcome through the drafting and enforcement of contracts, but that raises the major points stressed in the Williamson analysis, namely that a combination of uncertainty and opportunistic behaviour will render such modes of governance inefficient. In the multinational context transactions between independent firms will be made more difficult by distance, different legal regimes and by the lack of regular informal business contacts between the parties to the transaction, who may inhabit very different business cultures.

While internalisation has a number of advantages over markets, and foreign investment therefore tends to be favoured over licensing, it is as well to note that these advantages are not absolute. Licensing does take place on a substantial scale and in some industries (chemicals and pharmaceuticals) is a major form of activity. Buckley and Davies (1979), Telesio (1979) and Michalet and Delapierre (1976) have outlined situations where licensing will tend to be important.

Casson (1982) takes up the issue of transactions costs in a rather different way, which leads to a refinement of the internalisation theory, providing a more general explanation for foreign direct investment in industries where the existence of advantages based upon technology or product-differentiation is less important.

If a market transaction is to be made, there are a series of 'market-making' activities which have to be carried out, each of which involves costs. These steps, taken in sequence, are:

- contact-making
- specification and communication of details to each party
- negotiation
- monitoring, including the screening of quality
- transport of goods
- payment or avoidance of taxes
- enforcement

These market-making services are provided by offices, showrooms and shops which could in principle simply specialise in providing these services (as do travel agents or estate agents). However, in most cases market-making is linked to the sale of the commodity itself, in order to avoid purchasers having to make two separate transactions. Furthermore, if buyers place a high level of importance on the monitoring of quality control it may pay them to integrate backwards into the production of the commodity, instead of relying upon independent market-makers to carry out the monitoring.

While Casson's analysis can be seen as a very general extension of the Coasian analysis, it offers a particular insight into the development of the MNE. If buyers are internationally mobile they will prefer to buy from a single market-maker, rather than deal with a different one in each location. However, the credibility and business reputation of the market-maker will depend crucially upon his ability to meet the same quality standards in each location. The incentive to integrate backwards into production will therefore be particularly strong, and a multinational is the result. Similarly, buyers may wish to place orders in one location for supply in another, which requires close liaison between branch plants in different locations. Finally, Casson's analysis can be integrated back into the Hymer−Kindleberger framework by noting that some firms may develop a competitive advantage in market-making itself, which is internationally transferable. In this case, it is that particular advantage which provides the foundation for 'going abroad'.

In terms of predictions the model suggests that MNEs will tend to be most heavily represented in market segments where high quality is most important. Two examples, which illustrate the ability of the model to explain the MNEs existence in market segments where neither technology nor product differentiation is particularly important, are to be found in the international hotel industry and in the export of tropical fruit. The major hotel chains (Dunning and McQueen (1982)) do not appear to provide highly differentiated products. What they do offer are international reservation systems (a market-making activity) and systems of hotel management which maintain product quality while using unskilled labour. In the banana industry two distinct sub-sectors can be distinguished. An unintegrated, market-directed trade exists, selling unbranded bananas to small retailers, on a seasonal basis. At the same time, there are multinational producers operating at the quality end of the market, advertising branded fruit (a market-making activity) and offering year-round supplies of optimally ripened fruit, delivered to retail chains through a fleet of special ships and subject to a system of quality control which allows any defective batches to be identified and the faults in either the delivery system or the plantation to be rectified.

The 'eclectic' framework

The 'internalisation' analysis provides a general theory in explanation of the MNE. However, whether or not it is complete remains the subject of debate. A closely related but different approach is Dunning's 'eclectic' framework, first put forward in 1976. That theory states that the extent, form and pattern of multinational activity is determined by the existence of three sets of advantages. The first, which relates back to both the Hymer analysis and internalisation, consists of **ownership advantages**. These may arise either because MNEs have assets not owned by other firms, or because their managerial hierarchies reduce the transactions costs associated with co-ordinating activities located in different countries.

The second condition for international production is that it should be in the best interests of the firms having ownership advantages that they be transferred through managerial hierarchies, rather than through markets. 'Internalisation' theory thus forms one of the three central strands in the eclectic paradigm. Buckley and Casson (1985) have argued that this amounts to double-counting and that the failure of intermediate product markets is itself a necessary and sufficient condition for multinationalisation to take place. Dunning (1985), on the other hand, argues to the contrary, suggesting that a distinction should be made between a firm's ability to internalise and their reasons for doing so. Whatever the balance of the argument it is clear that there are close links between the eclectic paradigm and the internalisation model.

The third strand in the eclectic paradigm concerns the location of production. For multinationalisation to take place not only do firms have to have ownership advantages, whose transaction is most effectively internalised, but there also has to be advantage in combining transferable inputs originating in the **home country** (like management skills or technological advantages) with other inputs in the **host-country**. Otherwise the firm would simply operate in a single location. Such advantages could arise in a number of ways. Most obviously there will be differences in local cost and revenue conditions, arising from different levels of wages and other input prices, or barriers to trade and factor mobility. Hirsh (1976) examines this choice in terms of cost-minimisation, and suggests the following inequalities as a decision-rule on whether to produce at home or abroad:

Export to country B if:

$$P_a + M < P_b + C \qquad \text{where:}$$

$P_a\ P_b$ = production costs in country A, country B

M = additional costs of export marketing

$$C = \text{extra costs of controlling a foreign operation}$$

Produce in country B if:

$$P_b + C < P_a + M$$

Production costs, marketing costs and the costs of control will depend upon a wide variety of factors, including:

- tariffs and trade barriers
- economies of scale and scope in each market
- factor costs
- government controls
- transport costs

These incentives to shifting the location of production arise essentially from market imperfections, without which they would cease to exist. However, even in the absence of such imperfections MNE activity would still occur if there are transactional gains to be had from common ownership of activities in different locations. Such advantages could include spreading foreign exchange risk or political risk, protecting supplies by multiple sourcing and the opportunity to use transfer prices to redistribute gains between different tax regimes.

The current state of theory

It should be clear from the brief outline above that the eclectic paradigm and internalisation theory are very closely entangled bodies of analysis. Casson (1987) has suggested that in fact there are few substantial differences between them, apart from terminology, and that it is possible to translate one theory into another and then back again, with minor qualifications.

Whether or not this combined set of theories is general enough to provide a complete explanation for the activities of the MNE is the subject of some debate (Buckley (1985)). Nevertheless, it represented the dominant theoretical framework in the 1980s. There have been attempts to suggest that 'Japanese multinationals are different' and Kojima (1982) has developed a 'macro-economic approach' to the MNE, which at first sight appears quite different from conventional theory. In particular, the Japanese theorists have argued that Japanese firms going abroad do not demonstrate ownership of the kind of monopolistic advantage associated with other MNEs. However, Giddy and Young (1982) show convincingly that the Japanese case is just another example of non-traditional foreign direct investment, which can be understood perfectly well in the broad terms of the general internalisation model.

The impact of the multinational on host economies

The debate over the multinational

The impact of the multinational on the world economy is an issue which has been hotly debated in a discussion which has had very substantial political overtones. On the radical left, the multinational has been exemplified by the large, monopolistic American corporation, acting as a vehicle for the exploitation of workers and consumers and the subornment of independent governments. On the right and in the centre the multinational has been regarded with much less suspicion, being seen as a means by which the impact of market forces may be felt on a global scale, bringing enhanced efficiency and an improved global allocation of resources. Such broad generalisations are an inadequate description of such a complex and important phenomenon as the MNE, and a more detailed analysis is called for.

The impact of the MNE on host economies

Multinational activity can impact on its host environment in a number of different ways, each of which merits some consideration. Following Hood and Young (1979) it is possible to identify four different types of effect, namely:

- resource transfer and technology transfer effects
- trade and balance of payments effects
- effects on competitive structure and performance
- effects on sovereignty and local autonomy

The transfer of resources and technology

The MNE may involve an inflow of both capital and 'technology', broadly defined, whose impact on the host economy depends upon a number of factors. In the case of capital, an inflow adds to the resources available for host-country production and the presence of MNEs which have identified profitable opportunities may help to mobilise domestic savings. In developing nations, which have tended to be the focus for much of the concern over the impact of the MNE, the presence of multinationals may also stimulate the provision of aid from the MNEs' home country, in support of their trading activities.

On the other hand, MNEs may not increase the amount of capital available, raising finance locally or re-investing profits made by local subsidiaries. In this case their impact depends upon the efficiency with which the capital is used. If MNEs put the capital to better use than local firms, making use of technological or other advantages, there may still be an improvement through the improved productivity of the limited capital available. Nevertheless this may still make it more difficult for local firms to raise capital for their own activities, which will be a disadvantage if local control of economic activity is seen as desirable for its own sake. There are also clear disadvantages if MNEs made less productive use of scarce capital than local firms.

In fact, capital flows are not seen as a major aspect of the the multinationals' activity. A much more important set of issues concerns the transfer of technology, broadly defined to encompass all kinds of ownership advantage including managerial skills as well as narrowly technological assets like patents and product designs. Technology transfer raises a number of questions (see Davies (1979) for a review.)

The first issue, particularly in the context of developing nations which have received a disproportionate amount of attention in comparison with the developed nations where most MNE activity takes place, concerns the **appropriateness** of the technologies transferred. In low-wage economies economic theory suggests that relatively labour-intensive techniques of production will be appropriate, both in terms of cost-minimisation and employment effects. However, much of the evidence suggests that MNEs often make only limited adjustment to the techniques of production they transfer (Davies (1977)), which could imply allocative inefficiency. On the other hand, there are reasons for supporting the transfer of more advanced techniques. In the first place, labour-intensive techniques for the production of many commodities may not be available. Standard economic theory, outlined in Chapter 8, assumes that the production function provides for an infinite range of production techniques, which is often unrealistic. Even if more labour-intensive techniques are available they will usually be older technologies, obsolete in the context of major industrial nations and these may have an adverse impact on the quality of the product produced, which may render it unsaleable in world markets. It may also be the case that more advanced technologies are absolutely efficient, using both less labour and less capital per unit of output than older methods.

The second issue concerns the transfer of managerial skills which accompany inward foreign direct investment. An inflow of entrepreneurial talent and better-trained managers may lead to improvements in efficiency in both the static sense of reducing costs and improving marketing activity and the dynamic sense of adjusting more quickly to changes in the environment and spotting opportunities for innovation. Dunning (1985), for instance, found that MNEs in the United Kingdom assisted in the restructuring of the economy more effectively than uninational indigenous firms and also responded more quickly to changes in Britain's locational advantages in respect of resource endowments, thereby improving the competitiveness of the economy. The mere fact that managers in a multinational are able to take a global perspective through internalised flows of knowledge about the global changes in their own industry may have advantages for the economies in which they are operating.

On the negative side of the balance sheet with respect to managerial skills there may be little diffusion of improved management practices throughout local industry if MNEs make substantial use of managers drawn from the home country, who either remain within the MNE or eventually return to work within the home country. On the other hand, if they bring with them improved working practices and management techniques, as is often claimed for Japanese MNEs entering the UK, these will involve workers, supervisors and indigenous junior managers in implementing the improved practices which may then diffuse through indigenous industry as these workers change jobs. Similarly, if local managements seek to emulate the practices of incoming MNEs in order to compete with them, new techniques may be effectively diffused. Certainly in the UK the number of seminars offered by management consultants on such Japanese-inspired practices as quality circles and 'Just-in-Time' methods of manufacturing suggests that this has been the case. It might be argued that this could be achieved without the Japanese firms actually moving to British locations, but the effect of demonstrating that Japanese practices are transferable into other locations provides a powerful stimulus to emulation.

Trade and balance of payments effects

An inflow of multinational enterprises may affect the balance of payments in a number of ways. If there is a capital inflow, this will improve the capital account, but this will be offset by any repatriation of profits and dividends to the source country. If the MNE is involved in producing for export, or producing import substitutes then the current account on the balance of payments will be improved. This depends to a great extent upon the extent to which value is added in the host-country, an issue which has been very sensitive in the case of Japanese investments into Europe. Some European policy-makers have been concerned that the local content of some Japanese firms' products produced in Europe is very low, with 'screwdriver plants' being established which import a large proportion of the total value of the final product in the form of components produced in the Far East. These are simply assembled and packaged within the European Community in order to evade controls on direct imports from Japan. Clearly such plants will do little to improve the balance of payments of host countries, but whether they should be outlawed on those grounds is a matter for debate. The fundamental question is whether the import controls are themselves inappropriate ways to improve the global allocation of resources.

Balance of payments issues also raise the sensitive question of **transfer pricing** within MNEs. One of the possible reasons for internalising multinational transactions is that it offers a means by which a firm may divert the profit from its activities from one location to another, by manipulating the internal prices which it charges for intermediate products. Such transfers may be worthwhile in the light of different tax regimes and fluctuating exchange rate. To take an extreme example, for instance, a firm which is making profits in the UK could transfer those profits to a tax haven by establishing a stationery supply office in the tax haven which supplies paper clips at very high prices to the UK subsidiary! Such practices would not only affect the balance of payments of the host country, but would also deprive local shareholders of their legitimate share in the profits and could reduce the earnings of local workers or increase prices to local consumers.

The degree of incentive to transfer price depends heavily on the differences in tax regimes from location to location, international taxation agreements and the volatility of exchange rates. In so far as governments attempt to collaborate on taxation, and exchange rates are either stable, or so unstable that it becomes impossible to make sensible predictions about their behaviour, the incentive will be reduced.

Nevertheless, transfer pricing raises some major questions about the global distribution of the benefits which flow from MNEs activity.

The competitive and structural impact of the MNE

While an influx of foreign direct investment may affect competition through its impact on the rate of technological change and the adoption of new management techniques, it may also affect the conduct and performance of industry in the host economy through its impact on industrial structure. In particular, if multinational transactions are internalised in order to ensure that the MNE receives the full value of the monopoly rents accruing to its knowledge-based assets the process of multinationalisation may in effect be a means of securing collusion by other means. As Casson (1987) puts it 'a firm that has developed a new technology can . . . only recover its costs through the exercise of monopoly power.' If MNEs are able to use their global interconnections to create additional entry barriers this may also give them additional market power which may be a cause for concern.

MNEs may also give cause for concern over their impact on industrial structure if the international division of labour which they find most profitable does not accord with that which governments consider to be in the host country's best interest. For instance, in the case of the alleged Japanese 'screwdriver' plants the parent firms find it most efficient to restrict the operations carried out in Europe to assembly and packaging, rather than the production of components. European governments found that unacceptable. In a similar way, MNEs frequently prefer to keep many of their higher level functions like research and development and headquarters activity in their home location, thereby limiting indigenous technological innovation in host nations.

Effects on sovereignty and local autonomy

This last point leads naturally into one of the most contentious areas of debate concerning the impact of the MNE on host countries. The very nature of the MNE implies that it is involved in co-ordinating activities on a global scale through internalised transactions which are effectively out of the reach of national governments. As a result, governments may lose a substantial degree of sovereignty. Monetary policies may be side-stepped through operations in global financial markets. Fiscal policies may be avoided through transfer pricing. National governments, and local authorities within them, may find themselves competing with each other to provide financial incentives to induce MNEs to locate within their jurisdictions to an extent which may ensure that it is the multinational which secures the gains to be had, rather than the local economies. It may also be the case that economic development in host countries is driven by decisions taken outside those countries, thereby reducing national governments' autonomy and their ability to determine the course of events within their own national boundaries. Such considerations open up very much broader aspects of the debate, including their implications for democracy and freedom. In a world made increasingly economically interdependent by the operations of the MNE the ability of any national government to pursue policies of its own choosing is heavily circumscribed.

The balance of judgment on the impact of the multinational depends heavily on the relative priorities given to their efficiency enhancing properties versus their impact on local autonomy. In the 1960s, when the multinational was best characterised as a powerful American corporation, and the global consensus (if there can be such a thing) was one of concern over their market power, there was much discussion of the ill-effects of the MNE, especially amongst the political left. In the 1980s, with the left wielding less influence, at least in Britain and the United States, with the development of a wider spectrum of multinationals based in many different countries, and with the loss of sovereignty arising from other developments, such as the European Community and relaxed exchange controls, the balance of judgment has shifted in favour of the multinational. Whether this will continue, or whether the pendulum of opinion will shift back towards hostility to the MNE remains to be seen.

The impact of the multinational on its home country

Converse problems: the MNE and source countries

Most of the discussion on the impact of the MNE has concerned its effects on host countries, especially developing nations. At the same time there has been some concern expressed, especially in the United States, over the impact of foreign direct investment on the source country from which the investment emanated. Much of this debate is a mirror-image of that concerning host-country impact, with doubts being expressed about the impact of such investment on the following areas:

- the balance of payments
- employment
- loss of technological advantage
- tax avoidance and loss of sovereignty

Each of these warrants a brief consideration.

Balance of payments effects

The impact of foreign direct investment on the balance of payments of the source-country is essentially the opposite of that on the host. An initial injection of capital will worsen the source country's capital account, but repatriated profits will improve the current account. Goods produced abroad may substitute for exports but expansion of the host-country economy may stimulate its demand for imports from the source. The overall balance is impossible to judge.

Employment effects

MNEs have sometimes been accused of 'exporting jobs' away from the source country and it is clear that direct job losses may arise if operations are transferred to an overseas location. On the other hand, the jobs created in foreign subsidiaries may be additional to those created at home and in activities which are not economic in the home location and could not alternatively be placed there. Outward investments may create additional demand for plant and equipment sourced from the home-country, and they may lead to the expansion of headquarters and other staff needed to administer an enlarged operation. There is clearly no fundamental reason to suppose that employment in the source-country will be lower than it would otherwise be as a result of outward investment, although the mix of employment may well be different as a result of the MNEs internalised international division of labour. From an analytical economic point of view it is also a mistake to see employment as being determined by the activities of individual firms, rather than by the structure and behaviour of labour markets.

Concern has also been expressed about the impact of outward investment on wage levels. If an MNE sees a locational advantage in transferring its labour-intensive activities to a low wage country this may reduce the source-country demand for the types of labour involved and lower wage levels in those occupations. In effect, source-country workers have to compete in a global labour market with workers earning very much lower levels of wages. On the other hand, as noted above, the demand for other types of labour is likely to increase and efficient labour markets would transfer workers from one occupation to another, leaving average wage levels higher than they would otherwise be. This point gets to the heart of much of the debate on the MNE. From one perspective the MNE is acting as a highly efficient global allocator of resources, placing each of its activities in locations where the opportunity cost is lowest. This will raise total global income allowing increased rewards for all, at least in principle. From another perspective this process involves adjustment costs which are likely to be borne by those workers who are forced to compete in global labour markets and who, as individuals, may not be able to simply move into new roles. A British or American production worker made redundant by the transfer of manufacturing to the Far East can hardly be expected to be impressed by the reassurance that his sacrifice has provided wages and employment in a poorer part of the world and more jobs for college boys at home.

The loss of technological lead

Just as a major advantage of foreign direct investment for a host country lies in the inflow of technological skills, so it has been argued, especially in the United States, that source countries are in danger of losing their technological advantages through transferring them to other countries. While this is primarily an economic argument, it also has a strategic military component in that there has been concern that foreign direct investment places strategically important technologies in the hands of foreign nationals who may in turn transfer them on to potentially hostile countries. Computer technology in particular has been placed in this category, as have sophisticated machine tool systems. While the military argument may be accepted, the economic argument is much less soundly based, for reasons which reflect many of the points already made above. In the short term, if a technological advantage is seen as a static 'one-off' asset, its use in a wider range of locations may reduce the returns to labour in its original location, and this may cause adjustment problems. However, technology is rarely static, and in many instances the technology which is transferred abroad is more mature, even obsolescent, in its home location where newer technologies have developed and the technological lead is maintained, to the advantage of those working with it. To attempt to restrict the use of technology to a particular geographical location would be to prevent the MNE from organising the most efficient global allocation of resources, thereby restricting the growth of world, as opposed to national, income. It should be remembered that the activities of the multinational do not represent a 'zero-sum game' where the benefits and costs to host countries are exactly cancelled out by costs and benefits to the source country. The overall sum is indubitably positive, although there are costs to some.

Tax avoidance and loss of sovereignty

The problems of tax avoidance and loss of sovereignty are essentially the same for source countries as they are for host countries. The multinational's ability to be everywhere and yet be effectively out of the reach of government is one of its most interesting characteristics. Those who approve of privately driven competitive activity see this as one of the multinationals' greatest achievements and one which need not be feared as competition ensures the achievement of global social goals. Others fear the power of the multinational and its lack of accountability to any power beyond that of its shareholders and managers.

Global competition and corporate strategy

The need for a framework for the analysis of global strategy

It is clear from the preceding pages that there has been very substantial attention paid to the development of theoretical analyses which are capable of explaining the existence and patterns of multinational activity. This analysis has been firmly within the basic traditions of economic analysis, being essentially 'positive' in nature, having the objective of producing testable hypotheses with respect to the patterns and effects of multinational activity. It has also concentrated on the explanation of multinationalisation '*per se*', rather than considering the full range of options open to firms in global markets, which may include serving world markets through trade, rather than through establishing production overseas.

One result of that emphasis has been that it provides little normative guidance to multinational firms with respect to the implications of '**globalisation**' for their development of business strategies, a criticism which has been made both by some of the leading economists involved (Buckley (1985)) and by Porter (1986) on behalf of business strategists. As the business strategy implications of the development of global industries have received only limited attention an extended treatment is not possible here. However, Porter (1986) has attempted to provide a conceptual framework which links back to some of the concepts outlined in Chapter 11. A brief outline of the framework is provided below.

Porter's conceptual framework

Porter defines an industry as **global** if there is competitive advantage to integrating activities on a world-wide basis. If the term 'activities' is taken to mean the primary and support activities which go to make up the 'value-chain', explained in Chapter 11, and it is recognised that international strategy is a matter of **geographic scope**, then those concepts can be used as a starting-point for considering global strategy.

A firm which intends to compete internationally has to decide how to spread its activities across the world. Some of the 'downstream' primary activities, like service, marketing and sales have to be located close to the buyer if they are to be effective. 'Upstream' primary activities and support activities are less dependent upon proximity to the buyer and competitive advantage in these activities may depend more on the firm's total global spread than on its position in individual countries. Porter puts forward two key dimensions of the way in which a firm may compete globally.

The first dimension is the **configuration** of the firm's activities, which refers to the locations in which activities are placed. The second is the extent of **co-ordination** between the different sites of activity. Each of these may vary widely. With respect to configuration, the options range from **concentrated**, where an activity, like technology development for instance, takes place in only one location, serving the whole global operation, to **dispersed**, where the activity is performed at every site or every country. If all activities are dispersed, every site has a complete value-chain of its own. With respect to **co-ordination** the options range from giving full autonomy to every plant to having very tight co-ordination with a common information system, common production technologies and common management practices.

A global firm's current strategy with respect to global competition may thus be characterised by its position with respect to these dimensions, and future strategies may be considered in these terms. For many Japanese car companies, for instance, their initial strategy has been tight geographical concentration within the home economy, keeping production and as many other activities as possible in that base, accompanied by a very high level of co-ordination of those activities which are carried out world-wide. Other firms, like General Motors, for instance have highly dispersed activities with low levels of co-ordination between them.

If a firm is to develop its global strategy it has to consider how different degrees of concentration or co-ordination can affect its ability to secure cost-leadership or differentiation. In the case of concentration the firm has to consider both **where** activities are to be located and in **how many** locations. For each activity in the value-chain the 'where' will depend upon factors like the comparative advantages of each location, determined by factors like labour cost, and the 'how many' will depend upon the significance of cost drivers like scale economies, economies of scope and learning effects. The optimal extent of co-ordination depends upon the advantages which may flow from a high level of co-ordination such as gathering information globally and identifying the implications of world trends for different locations set against the risk of control loss, the costs and the possible rigidities involved in co-ordinating across a wide geographical scope.

If the global options with respect to configuration and co-ordination are added to Porter's basic strategic 'tool kit' of 'generic strategies', 'the value chain' and 'scope' they offer a means by which firms may systematically consider how to build competitive advantage in global industries. The range of options taken in total is clearly enormous when it is considered that every activity in the value chain has to be considered in the light of the generic strategy, each aspect of scope and the two global dimensions. Whether firms will find such a complex conceptual framework too daunting remains to be seen. Nevertheless it does provide a means of considering and evaluating the global dimension of corporate strategy in a way which is integrated into the other parts of the Porter framework.

Illustration

Multinationals in the hotel industry

The term 'multinational enterprise' tends to conjure up a picture of a high technology company, usually American, engaged in some form of manufacturing activity. However, that is by no means the complete picture and Dunning and McQueen (1982) provide an interesting counter-example in their study of international hotels. They use the industry in order to test the applicability of the 'eclectic' theory of the multinational, in an unusual setting.

The first strand of the eclectic theory suggests that in order to operate abroad a firm must have 'ownership-specific advantages', that is some kind of competitive advantage over local firms. In the case of the international hotel chains, there are a number of such advantages which may be identified. Hotel services are essentially an 'experience good'. The consumer can only judge the quality of the commodity being offered by actually experiencing it. In that case international hotel chains can establish an ownership-specific advantage by providing and advertising similar standards of comfort and service world-wide. The business traveller and the one-time guest (who make up the market segment in which the international hotel chains are concentrated) can experience the good in one part of the world and be informed about its quality in others. The 'brand image' of the hotel thus becomes a major asset, which cannot be reproduced by the local competition.

A second type of ownership advantage held by international hotels lies in their experience of operating superior techniques of standardised production and control, often codified in detailed instruction manuals, and in supporting those systems through well-organised staff training. As these systems take a long time to be developed and are kept as secret as possible by their owners they constitute a type of proprietary 'know-how' or technology which is not available to the local competition.

In so far as the ownership advantages identified are all intimately connected with experience, the development of hotel chains based in different countries may depend upon the nature of the hotel industry in the home country. International hotel chains based in West Germany, for instance, own only two per cent of foreign-associated hotels, which is a substantial under-representation relative to West Germany's importance in international business travel. That phenomenon might be explained by the fact that the West German hotel industry is not characterised by chains of hotels, so that the experience required to run such chains overseas remained undeveloped.

If a company has ownership advantages which allow it to compete with indigenous competitors overseas it still has to decide between using these advantages in its home location (exporting the product) and transferring them overseas, combining the ownership advantage with locally available factors of production. In the case of the hotel industry, exporting is hardly an option so that servicing a market requires local 'production'. Nevertheless, hotel chains still have to decide which foreign markets to serve. As they are concentrated in the business travel market, and because they are themselves a form of multinational enterprise it is hardly surprising that the geographical pattern of hotel chain involvement closely mirrors the world-wide distribution of foreign direct investment.

After ownership advantages and location-specific advantages, the 'eclectic' theory of the MNE refers to the advantages of 'internalisation'. If a firm has an ownership advantage, and it is most profitable to transfer that advantage to a foreign location there remains the choice between transferring the advantage internally to another part of the company and selling it, or leasing it, to an independent company. International hotel chains are particularly interesting in this respect in that they exhibit quite complex combinations of internalised and external transactions. In some cases, MNEs in the hotel industry own their operations abroad. In others they operate leasing arrangements, in others they work through management contracts and in yet others they have franchise agreements. The pattern of involvement exhibits noticeable differences by area and by the origin of the hotel chain. In developed countries 48 per cent of hotel rooms are in hotels owned at least in part by MNEs, while the figure for developing countries, is only 18 per cent. American, French and Japaneses chains appear to favour non-equity participation, while UK-based chains prefer ownership.

In most industries, ownership and control are very closely associated. If an MNE wishes to have full control of its overseas activities, it needs to own a substantial proportion of the equity. However, in the hotel industry this relationship is much less marked. In some cases, as when Arab interests purchased hotels in London, the transaction was more akin to a portfolio investment in property than to a direct investment which would provide operational control. In other cases, MNEs in the hotel industry have almost total operational control with limited or no equity participation, through the vehicle of management contracts having 10 to 20 years duration. This phenomenon of low ownership/high control is a particularly interesting feature of the hotel industry, which may help to shed light on the whole issue of internalisation. The usual difficulties which arise from transferring ownership advantages to an independent company abroad are threefold. First, it may not be possible to transfer the ownership advantage across the boundaries between organisations. Secondly, there may be conflicts between the company's global interests and its local interests, which necessitate the integration of decision-making. Thirdly, it may be difficult to fully 'appropriate' the returns accruing to an ownership advantage which has been transferred to an independent organisation. On each of these counts, the hotel industry appears to have features which ameliorate the disadvantages of contract-based control. The ownership advantages which are being transferred consist essentially of human capital in the form of experience, which can be transferred through people, supported by manuals of operating and training procedures, both of which are easily transferred to independent companies. As each hotel provides services in one particular location, there cannot be any conflict with regard to which hotel serves which location, nor can there be conflicts over which hotel specilaises in which aspect of the production process. There is, therefore, little need to integrate decision-making across the chain. With respect to the appropriability problem, Dunning and McQueen argue that the economic rents arising from the ownership advantages possessed by hotel MNEs can be effectively protected by contract-based control. The use of the hotel chain's name is effectively protected, and the continuing success of the hotels depends upon its continuing involvement so that an independent firm could not simply purchase the 'know-how' and then renege on the contract.

All in all, then, the 'eclectic' theory of multinational production provides a useful framework within which to explain the pattern of MNE involvement in hotel chains.

References and further reading

J.S. Bain, *Barriers to New Competition*, (Cambridge, Mass, Harvard UP, 1956)

P.J. Buckley and M. Casson, *The Future of the Multinational Enterprise*, (London, Macmillan, 1976)

P.J. Buckley and M. Casson, *The Economic Theory of the Multinational Enterprise*, (London, Macmillan, 1985)

P.J. Buckley, 'A Critical View of Theories of the Multinational Enterprise' in P.J. Buckley and M. Casson, *The Economic Theory of the Multinational Enterprise*, (London, Macmillan, 1985)

P.J. Buckley and H. Davies, 'Foreign Licensing in Overseas Operations: Theory and Evidence from the UK', in R.G. Hawkins and A.J. Prasad (eds.) *Technology Transfer and Economic Development*, (Greenwich, JAI Press, 1979)

M. Casson, 'Transaction Costs and the Theory of the Multinational Enterprise', in A.M. Rugman (ed.) *New Theories of the Multinational Enterprise*, (Beckenham, Croom Helm, 1982)

M. Casson, 'Multinational Firms' in R. Clarke and T. McGuiness, *The Economics of the Firm*, (Oxford, Blackwell, 1987)

R.E. Caves, 'International Corporations: The Industrial Economics of Foreign Investment', *Economica*, 1971

H. Davies, 'Technology Transfer through Commercial Transactions', *Journal of Industrial Economics*, 1977

H. Davies, 'Technology Transfer through the MNE', *Management Bibliographies and Reviews*, 1979

J. Dunning, *Multinational Enterprises, Economic Structure and International Competitiveness*, (New York, Wiley, 1985)

J. Dunning and M. McQueen, 'The Eclectic Theory of the Multinational Enterprise and the International Hotel Industry', in A. Rugman (ed.) *New Theories of the Multinational Enterprise*, (Beckenham, Croom Helm, 1982)

M. Ghertman and M. Allen, *An Introduction to the Multinationals*, (London, Macmillan, 1984)

I.H. Giddy and S. Young, 'Conventional and Unconventional Multinationals: Do New Forms of Multinational Enterprise Require New Theories?' in A.M. Rugman (ed.), *New Theories of the Multinational Enterprise*, (Beckenham, Croom Helm, 1982)

S. Hirsh, 'An International Trade and Investment Theory of the Firm', *Oxford Economic Papers*, 1976

N. Hood and S. Young, *The Economics of Multinational Enterprise*, (London, Longman, 1979)

C.P. Kindleberger, *American Business Abroad*, (New Haven, Yale UP, 1969)

K. Kojima, 'Macroeconomic Versus International Business Approach to Direct Foreign Investment', *Hitotsubashi Journal of Economics*, 1982

J.C. McManus, 'The Theory of the International Firm' in G. Paquet (ed.), *The Multinational Firm and the Nation State*, (Toronto, Collier Macmillan, 1972)

C.A. Michalet and M. Delapierre, *The Multinationalisation of French Firms*, (Chicago, AIB, 1976)

M. Porter, *Competitive Advantage*, (New York, Free Press, 1985)

M. Porter, 'Competition in Global Industries: A Conceptual Framework', in M. Porter (ed.) *Competition in Global Industries*, (Boston, Harvard Business School Press, 1986)

A.M. Rugman, *Inside the Multinationals*, (London, Croom Helm, 1981)

J-J. Servan-Schreiber, *The American Challenge*, (New York, Athenaeum, 1967)

P. Telesio, *Technology, Licensing and Multinational Enterprises*, (New York, Praeger, 1979)

Self-test questions

1 Which countries were the most important sources and hosts of foreign direct investment in 1914 and 1975.

2 Which of the following words or phrases forms part of the stereotype of the MNE which emerged in the 1960s?

American, European, vertically integrated, labour-intensive, high wages paid, skill-intensive, technology-based, large size, undifferentiated products, raw material sourcing.

3 List three types of MNE whose development has led to the questioning of this stereotype.

4 List the three components of the 'eclectic' approach to the theory of the MNE.

5 Describe the following firms in terms of the extent of their global concentration and the extent of co-ordination.

(a) General Motors
(b) Toyota

Exercise

Explain the proposition that multinationals exist because of the difficulties of carrying out transactions through markets.

Answers on page 434.

Solutions to Questions

Solutions to Chapter 2 questions

Answers to self-test questions

1 (a)

2 (a), (b), (c), (d)

3 (a)

4 0.25, 0.75

5 (c)

Model answer to exercise

'De-industrialisation' is a term used to describe an aspect of structural economic change which has caused substantial concern in the United Kingdom. The simplest definition of 'de-industrialisation', put forward by Thirlwall, is 'a reduction in the absolute number of jobs in the manufacturing sector', although there are alternatives. One interpretation has been to identify the phenomenon with a falling proportion of total employment in manufacturing. On that definition, the United Kingdom has certainly experienced de-industrialisation but that experience has been shared by almost all other developed nations without raising undue concern. In many other countries, the decline in the proportion of the workforce employed in manufacturing has been accompanied by an increase in the absolute number of workers in that sector, so that there have been more jobs in manufacturing, not less. As these countries do not perceive the shifting proportions to be a problem it seems inappropriate to define de-industrialisation in this way.

A second alternative definition of de-industrialisation, attributable to Singh, is the failure of industry to sell enough exports to pay for the full employment level of imports at a socially acceptable exchange rate. If industry does fail in this way the imbalance will have to be put right, either by the exchange rate falling or by deflationary policies designed to reduce imports. In either case the adjustment will be painful and 'de-industrialisation' is clearly an economic problem. However, to define a phenomenon in terms of one particular explanation for it is not satisfactory. Similar criticisms hold for the 'Eltis and Bacon' interpretation of de-industrialisation which sees it as a process whereby growing employment in the public sector 'crowds out' private sector activity, including jobs in manufacturing.

Various explanations may be put forward for the decline in the number of manufacturing jobs in the 1970s and 1980s which may be summarised as:

- an inevitable process of economic development
- 'crowding-out' of private activity by the public sector
- poor competitiveness
- the impact of North Sea Oil.

The first approach to de-industrialisation is to see it as an inevitable part of the process of economic development whereby agriculture is first displaced by manufacturing, and manufacturing is then displaced by the service sector. In this view, increased productivity in manufacturing, coupled with relatively low growth in demand for manufactures, leads to de-industrialisation. While this analysis is convincing in the very long term, it doesn't provide an explanation for the very rapid loss of jobs in UK manufacturing in the 1980s. UK productivity growth at that time was very slow and countries which performed better in that respect experienced an increase in the number of jobs in manufacturing.

A second explanation for de-industrialisation might be found in Eltis and Bacon's thesis that the growth of the public sector 'crowded-out' resources from the private sector, including manufacturing. However, that hypothesis is not convincing in the case of labour, as the jobs which were created in the public sector were largely part-time jobs for women, while the manufacturing jobs which were lost were largely full-time jobs for men. There might be more of a case for arguing that 'crowding-out' has taken place with respect to finance, but various investigations, including the Wilson Committee, have found that shortage of finance has not put a constraint on investment.

A less sweeping explanation for de-industrialisation is that British industry has been uncompetitive, both in overseas markets and at home. In part this is a function of the exchange rate and labour costs, which have rendered UK products uncompetitive on price, but it extends further than that into non-price competitiveness, which takes into account factors like quality, technological level, delivery dates and after-sales service. There is some evidence to suggest that as the world becomes more wealthy, buyers place more emphasis upon non-price factors and that UK industry has taken insufficient account of that change.

Finally, it should be noted that the discovery and exploitation of North Sea Oil imposed a major structural shock on the British economy, by massively increasing the output of tradable goods, and reducing the UK's need to import oil from abroad. This boost to the balance of payments inevitably kept the pound higher than it would otherwise have been, making UK goods uncompetitive on price. A comparison of the trade performance of the oil versus the non-oil sectors shows very directly that the two have been closely and inversely related.

In summary, then, it does not appear convincing to explain the very rapid structural change which took place in the UK economy in the 1970s and 1980s in terms of long-term secular trends or crowding-out. It does seem more convincing to see it as a matter of poor competitiveness, caused partly by the advent of North Sea Oil and partly by poor general performance on the part of UK firms. Whether or not the process will go into reverse as North Sea Oil becomes less important remains to be seen.

Solutions to Chapter 3 questions

Answers to self-test questions

1 (b), (c)
2 More likely: (b), (c), (e)
   Less likely: (a), (d)
3 (b), (d), (e)

4 (a) – nothing (b) – output falls (c) output falls
5 (a)

Model answer to exercise

The neo-classical theory of the firm is based upon the assumption that the objective of the firm is to maximise profit, and that the firm is operating in a world of certainty. Revenue conditions are determined by consumer behaviour and by the structure of the industry. Cost conditions are determined by the form of the production function which represents the technology available. Neo-classical theory assumes that firms adopt the most efficient production technique available, and use up only the level of resources which is strictly necessary for the level of output being produced. In the language of model-building, the neo-classical model is an 'optimising' model, which assumes certainty, and which takes a 'holistic' view of the firm, treating it as an entity which can have objectives and take decisions. A graphical version of the resulting model is set out in Fig. Solutions 3.1, for the simple case of a firm in monopoly conditions. As the diagram shows, in

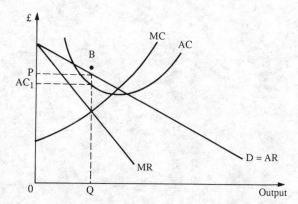

Fig. Solutions 3.1 The neo-classical model

the neo-classical model, the firm produces the level of output Q, at which marginal cost equals marginal revenue. Price is set at P, the level required to sell output Q, and cost per unit is AC_1 as shown by the average cost curve. The firm always operates on its cost curve, and never above it.

In the neo-classical model, the firm is always 'X-efficient' or 'operationally efficient', in the sense that it incurs no more costs than are strictly necessary for the production of the profit-maximising level of output. 'X-inefficiency' theory suggests that may not be the case. If the firm is not under powerful pressure from its shareholders, the market for corporate control, or competition, its managers may not be forced to maximise profits. In that case they will have a degree of freedom to indulge themselves in 'perks', and a 'quiet life', which will involve the firm in costs which are strictly unnecessary and which render the firm 'X-inefficient'. In terms of the diagram shown in Fig. Solutions 3.1, the firm will be above its cost curve, at a point like B.

The 'X-inefficiency' approach, therefore, does not assume that the firm is a profit-maximiser. Nor does it involve a completely holistic approach. Instead of treating the firm as a 'black box', X-inefficiency theory takes account of its internal workings by suggesting that workers and managers may have motivations other than profit. The extent to which a firm actually incurs unnecessary costs depends to a great extent upon the nature of those motivations, and the framework of relationships between managers, workers and shareholders. If shareholders exert powerful pressure on managers, forming an efficient 'principal/agent' contract, and if managers are effectively able to control workers, there will be no X-inefficiency. On the other hand, if neither of these links is strong, there will be room for 'organisational slack' and X-inefficiency.

This approach also identifies links between the opportunities for X-inefficient behaviour and the structure of the market in which the firm is operating. If the market is highly competitive, profit-maximising behaviour will be needed for survival, and the opportunities for incurring unnecessary costs will be limited. On the other hand, if competition is limited, firms will have the discretion to waste a proportion of the firm's resources in order to meet their own objectives. X-inefficiency theory therefore has an important application in the debate on competition policy. If a firm has monopoly power, not only will it tend to behave in ways which are economically inefficient, it will also tend to be X-inefficient, adding to the burden on the economy created by the monopoly power.

Solutions to Chapter 4 questions

Answers to self-test questions

1 (a), (b) **3** (b)

2 (c) **4** (b)

Model answer to exercise

The terms 'certainty', 'risk' and 'uncertainty' refer to differing 'states of information'. A situation of certainty exists when decision-makers are perfectly informed about the outcomes of actions they may take. 'Risk' is a situation where decision-makers are not perfectly informed about the outcomes of actions, but they are able to enumerate all the possible outcomes and to attach probabilities to each of those outcomes. 'Uncertainty' is a state of even more limited information, where a decision-maker does not know the possible outcomes of actions, or cannot attach probabilities to them.

In a situation of certainty, decision-makers can choose between alternative actions by comparing the known value of their outcomes. In the presence of risk, however, this cannot be done as each action has more than one outcome. If actions are to be compared some means has to be found of summarising the value of the various different outcomes, weighted in some appropriate way. The simplest way to carry this out would be to use **expected monetary values**, calculated according to the formula:

Expected monetary value $= \Sigma V_i P_i$ where:

$V_i =$ the value of the i'th outcome

$P_i =$ the probability of the i'th outcome

Expected monetary values involve weighting each outcome by its probability which seems intuitively plausible, at least at first sight. However, a simple example suffices to show the limitations of the EMV approach. If a fair coin is tossed for a bet of £1, the expected monetary value of taking part is equal to zero. If decisions are taken on the basis of expected values a rational decision-maker will be indifferent with respect to taking or refusing the bet, and a tiny inducement would be sufficient for him to accept the bet. A bribe of one penny would be enough to induce the decision-maker to take part. This analysis raises few problems if the size of the bet is small. Many people would be quite content to toss a coin for £1, £5 or perhaps £10. However, when the size of the bet becomes really substantial, the EMV approach begins to appear much less plausible. According to the arithmetic of EMVs, the expected value of tossing a fair coin for £1,000,000 is equal to zero, and a bribe of one penny would be enough to induce a rational decision-maker to take part. Intuition and casual observation suggest that this is clearly not a valid description of most people's behaviour. Few people would accept a fair 50/50 bet for £1,000,000 because the fear of losing is stronger than the prospect of gaining. In some sense, decision-makers 'care' more about losing £1,000,000 than they 'care' about winning £1,000,000.

Utility theory offers a framework within which to analyse this phenomenon. The example of the fair bet can be examined with the aid of Fig. Solutions 4.1.

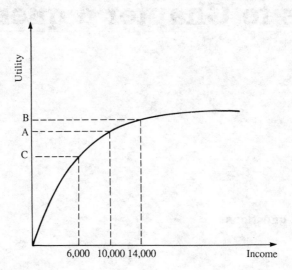

Fig. Solutions 4.1 Utility and income

The example shows a relationship between the level of utility accruing to a decision-maker and its level of income. The curve becomes flatter as it rises, illustrating **diminishing marginal utility of income**. If the link between utility and income is of this form, and decision-makers make their choices on the basis of expected utility instead of expected monetary values, the example can be explained.

Consider the case of a fair bet for £1,000 for a household whose current income is £10,000. If the household wins the bet, its income will rise to £11,000. If it loses the bet, its income will fall to £9,000. The increase in utility arising from a win is shown by the distance AB on the diagram and the loss of utility is shown by the distance CA. Clearly, the potential loss is greater than the potential gain. The expected utility of the bet is given by:

(.5 × distance AB) − (.5 × distance CA)

which is clearly negative.

If decision-makers behave in this way, they are said to be **risk averse** and the extent of their risk aversion will be reflected in the degree of curvature of their income/utility lines. If the line is almost straight, that implies a low degree of risk aversion. If the curve is highly curved, that implies a higher level of risk aversion.

Clearly, if the analysis is to be used to take decisions in practice, some method needs to be found to measure the extent of a particular decision-maker's aversion to risk. This can be a difficult task, but it could be tackled in principle by offering the decision-maker a series of hypothetical gambles and asking him which he would accept and which he would decline. Careful selection of the gambles offered would provide important information on the extent of risk aversion.

The usual assumption about decision-makers' attitude to risk is that they will be risk-averse. Nevertheless, it should be recognised that there are other possible attitudes. A decision-maker could be **risk-neutral**, having a linear income/utility line, in which case the expected monetary value criterion will be an acceptable way to evaluate decisions. Alternatively, a decision-maker could be a **risk-lover**. In this case, the income/utility line becomes steeper at high levels of income, indicating that such a decision-maker places a higher incremental utility on a gain than on a loss of equal value. Clearly, such a decision-maker will always accept fair bets and will be willing to pay to take part in them. In summary, then, utility theory provides a means by which different attitudes to risk can be modelled, allowing for a more sophisticated approach to decision-making than that embodied in the expected monetary values approach.

Solutions to Chapter 5 questions

Answers to self-test questions

1 (a), (d), (e)
2 See the diagram below
3 (Some approximation may be necessary) 35A
   and 33B gives 134 Juiciness and 169 Sweetness.

4 (b)
5 (a)

Model answer to exercise

Indifference analysis assumes that consumers are able to identify those combinations of goods which they prefer to other combinations and those combinations of goods between which they are indifferent. On the basis of this assumption, an indifference map can be drawn up which provides a graphical representation of a consumer's taste patterns. This map consists of a set of indifference curves, each of which shows combinations of the commodity amongst which the consumer is indifferent. Fig. Solutions 5.1 shows such an indifference map.

Indifference curves are shown as continuous lines, with increasing slope to the left and decreasing slopes to the right. (They are convex viewed from the origin.) This general shape reflects the further

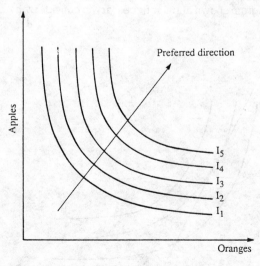

Fig. Solutions 5.1 An indifference map

assumption of a decreasing marginal rate of substitution, which implies that as a consumer has more of one commodity he is willing to exchange more of it for a given amount of the other commodity. Higher indifference curves represent higher levels of satisfaction and the aim of the consumer will be to reach the highest possible indifference curve. The indifference map can be used to identify the optimal basket of goods for a consumer. To find this, it is first necessary to consider the household's level of income, and the different combinations of goods it can therefore afford. This is shown using a budget line, as shown in Fig. Solutions 5.2.

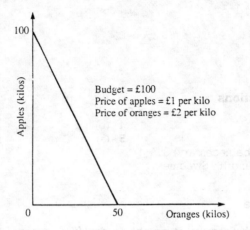

Budget = £100
Price of apples = £1 per kilo
Price of oranges = £2 per kilo

Fig. Solutions 5.2 The budget line

If the budget line is placed on the same diagram as the indifference map, it is then possible to identify the optimal combination of goods, shown at point X in Fig. Solutions 5.3.

It is now possible to examine the impact of a reduction in the price of one of the commodities. If the price of the commodity indicated by the horizontal axis falls, the budget line will shift, from its original position BB to the new position BB$_1$. This gives a new optimal combination of commodities at point Z. In the example shown, the consumer buys more of the good whose price has fallen. However, this could be a quirk of the particular diagram shown and it is necessary to consider whether this must be generally

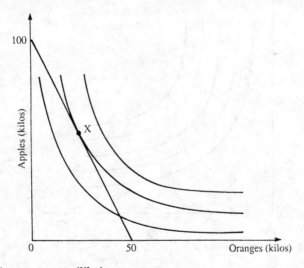

Fig. Solutions 5.3 Consumer equilibrium

true. This can be examined by recognising that the fall in price leads to two separate effects. The first, known as the substitution effect, arises because the relative prices of the two goods have changed. The second, known as the income effect, arises because a fall in price means that the consumer's real income has risen, a change which will also affect the consumer's purchases.

The substitution effect can be separated out by asking the question 'how would the basket of goods purchased change if relative prices changed, but the consumer maintained the same level of real income?' As 'real income' really means the level of satisfaction attained by the consumer this is equivalent to asking 'what would happen if the consumer stayed on the same indifference curve but relative prices changed?' This can be identified by changing the slope of the budget line so that it represents the relative prices of the goods, **after the price change**, but leaving the consumer on his original indifference curve. If the budget line is changed to B_2B_2 in Fig. Solutions 5.4 this shows that in those circumstances the consumer would purchase the basket of goods indicated by combination Y. This involves increasing purchases of the good whose price has fallen, and it is also clear that this must always be the case. If a good indicated on the horizontal axis becomes cheaper, the budget line becomes flatter and its point of tangency with the same indifference curve must move to the right. The substitution effect will always lead to increased purchases of the good whose price has fallen.

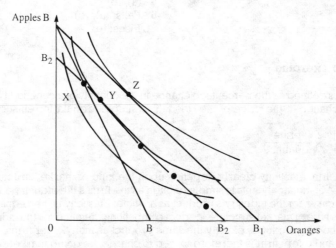

Fig. Solutions 5.4 Income and substitution effects

The income effect can now also be found. This is the change in the basket of goods which would be purchased if the consumer experienced the change in real income which follows from the reduction in price, but relative prices remained the same. That is indicated by the shift in the budget line from B_2B_2 to BB_1 and the shift in the basket of goods purchased from Y to Z. The income effect is less certain in its direction than the substitution effect. For 'normal' goods it will be in the same direction as the substitution effect, leading to more of the good whose price has fallen being bought. However, for 'inferior' goods, the effect will be perverse, leading to less being bought.

It can now be seen that the overall impact of a change in price (the 'price effect'), and the shape of the consumer's demand curve, depends upon the combination of the income effect and the substitution effect. It can also be seen that there are three possible cases. For 'normal' goods, lower prices must lead to more of a good being purchased and the demand curve must slope downwards. For 'inferior' goods, the two effects work in opposite directions and the outcome depends upon which is the most powerful. For most such goods, the substitution effect will outweigh the income effect, and the demand curve will slope downwards. For a very extreme class of inferior goods, known as 'Giffen goods', the perverse income effect will outweigh the substitution effect and the demand curve will slope upwards. For instance, if a consumer is very poor indeed and spending most of his income on a staple food, whose price then falls, the consumer may actually reduce his consumption of that staple food, replacing it with something else. However, this is a very extreme case and with that exception demand curves will slope downwards.

Solutions to Chapter 6 questions

Answers to self-test questions

1 (a), (d)
2 (a), (b)
3 (c), (d), (e)

4 (a), (e)
5 Falls: (a), (b)
   Rises: (c)

Model answer to exercise

Elasticity of demand is defined as the percentage change in the quantity of a commodity demanded, divided by the percentage change in the price of the good. The simple formula for elasticity is therefore:

$$\frac{\text{change in quantity}}{\text{change in price}} \times \frac{\text{price}}{\text{quantity}}$$

For an individual firm, elasticity clearly depends upon the kind of market structure in which the firm finds itself. In the case of monopoly, this is simple enough as the firm is the industry and the firm's demand curve is the demand curve for the industry's product as a whole. Elasticity is then equal to market elasticity. For the other extreme type of market structure, perfect competition, demand for the individual firm's product is infinitely elastic. The firm produces exactly the same product as many other firms, consumers are well-informed of that fact and every firm is therefore forced to charge the going market price. If a firm should charge a higher price it would lose all of its customers to the competition. In market structures other than perfect competition the position is rather more complex. In the 'kinky demand curve' model of oligopoly, demand is very elastic for price increases, because it is assumed that such increases will not be matched by a firm's rivals, but very inelastic for price reductions as it is assumed that rivals will match any price reduction. Another more general approach, which covers each of the above examples as special cases is to be found in the formula:

$$E_f = \frac{(E_m + E_s . S_r)}{S_f}$$

where:
E_f = elasticity of demand for the firm's product
E_m = market elasticity
E_s = elasticity of rivals' supply with respect to changes in the firm's price
S_f = the firm's market share
S_r = rivals' market share

In the perfectly competitive case, application of this formula yields a value of infinity as the firm's market share is very small. In the case of monopoly, elasticity is equal to market elasticity as there are no rivals to have market shares or responses to price changes. Intermediate cases depend upon relative market shares and rivals' responses. Looked at more descriptively, it can be said that elasticity of demand for an individual firm's product depends upon four main factors. The first is **market elasticity of demand**.

The second is the **extent of product differentiation** or brand loyalty, which determines how sensitive buyers are to differences in price between one firm and another. The third is **market shares**, and the last is **rivals' reactions**.

Solutions to Chapter 7 questions

Answers to self-test questions

1 (a)

2 (b), (c), (d)

3 (b)

4 1–D, 2–A, 3–C, 4–B

5 (c)

Model answer to exercise

'Estimation' involves attempting to quantify the causal links between one variable and another. In the case of the demand for a product this requires identifying the links between the quantity of the good demanded and such factors as its price, the level of advertising, consumers' income and the prices of substitute products. Estimation poses some very difficult and fundamental problems, which can only be partly resolved through sophisticated analytical methods. The most common method of estimating demand is through the application of econometric techniques to the available data on each of the variables. Estimation might also be carried out by attempting direct questioning of buyers on their response to changes in the values of the determining variables.

'Forecasting' involves attempting to quantify the future value of a variable without reference to its determinants. In a sense, forecasting involves an implicit assumption that time is the major determining variable. There are many different methods of forecasting, including:

- time-series analysis
- barometric forecasting
- surveys of buyers' intentions
- sales force opinion
- expert opinion
- market testing

Estimation through econometric forecasting usually involves the statistical technique of multiple regression, which fits an equation to the data, showing the 'best fit' which can be found for the data set. While this is a powerful technique it also carries with it a number of problems. In the first place, the 'best fit' may not be a very good fit, in which case the estimating equation only explains a small proportion of the variation in the level of demand. In the second place, the equation will provide individual co-efficients linking each of the determining variables to the variable which is being forecast. However, these will only be accurate estimates if a set of very restrictive assumptions is met.

Thirdly, econometric estimation has to deal with the 'identification problem'. If we focus on the link between price and demand, for instance, it is tempting to examine the set of observations on price and quantity, as shown by the set of crosses in Fig. Solutions 7.1 and conclude that a line drawn through them represents the demand curve. However, that set of points could have been generated by both the demand and supply curves shifting, as shown in the diagram. Sophisticated methods involving multiple equations can help to solve this problem but they have problems of their own which are difficult to resolve.

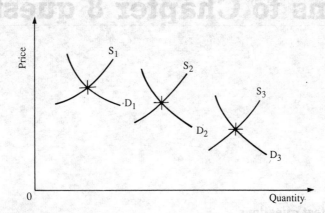

Fig. Solutions 7.1 The identification problem

As estimation is difficult and often unsatisfactory, companies often restrict themselves to forecasting. If they use barometric forecasting, the technique involves identifying some other variable whose value is known to foreshadow changes in the variable to be forecast. In attempting to forecast the number of children starting school, for instance, the figures for births five years ago will provide a very useful example of a 'leading indicator'. Companies may use more general 'leading indicators' of economic activity, like orders for machine tools, or even sunspot activity, which has been found in the past to have a close correlation with fluctuations in the economy.

The success of barometric forecasting depends upon finding a leading indicator which has a reliable and robust relationship with the variable to be forecast. If there is no obvious causal link between the two variables accurate forecasting will depend upon the continued existence of that past relationship. However, if there is a substantial change in any of the variables which determine the level of demand the link between the leading indicator and the variable to be forecast may break down. Other types of forecasting, such as sales force opinion, expert opinion or surveys of buyers' intentions may be more reliable because these provide a means by which expected changes in the environment may have appropriate influence upon the forecast.

Solutions to Chapter 8 questions

Answers to self-test questions

1 (b)
2 (a), (b), (c)
3 (b), (c)
4 The lowest possible cost per unit, given that the firm has selected the most appropriate set of plant and equipment for each level of output, selected from a given technology and with respect to a given set of factor prices.

5 (a) The contribution margin is £40 per delegate. Fixed costs are £500. Dividing the fixed costs by the contribution margin gives a break-even level of 13 delegates.
(b) Total contribution required is £1,000. Dividing that figure by the contribution margin gives 25 delegates.

Model answer to exercise

Break-even models have a number of characteristics, illustrated graphically in Fig. Solutions 8.1.

As the diagram shows, total cost is made up of two components. The first is fixed costs and the second is variable costs. The curve for total variable cost is drawn as a straight line, indicating that variable cost per unit is assumed to be constant. Similarly, the curve for total revenue is drawn as a straight line, indicating

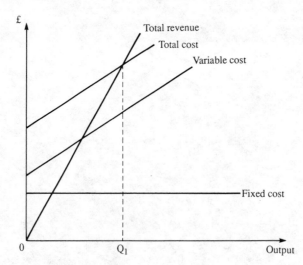

Fig. Solutions 8.1 The break-even model

that every level of output is sold at the same price. The level of output at which total revenue equals total cost, shown by Q_1, is known as the 'break-even' point.

If the cost component of the model is examined first, it is clear that the assumed structure of costs is very different from that which appears in the economic model of the firm. In the break-even model, whatever the level of output, and whatever the level of capacity utilisation, average variable cost remains the same. It is therefore assumed that the principle of diminishing returns, which leads to higher levels of variable cost per unit as more of the variable factors of production are combined with the fixed factors, does not hold. The break-even model appears to suggest that there is no limit to the output which the firm could produce, and no cost penalties for very high levels of capacity utilisation.

On the demand side, the linear form of the total revenue function reflects the assumption that every level of output can be sold at the price which is indicated. Different prices lead to different total revenue functions, with higher prices being reflected in steeper curves, and correspondingly lower break-even levels of output. The concept of elasticity of demand, and the possibility that different prices may lead to different levels of demand, has no place in the break-even model. If this model were used to answer the questions which are addressed by the economic model of the firm, it clearly produces nonsensical results. The profit-maximising level of output is infinity, as profits simply increase without limit as the level of output rises. Similarly, the profit-maximising level of price is infinitely high because the model contains no reference to the possibility that buyers may be deterred by higher prices.

If the break-even model were judged on the criteria applied to the economic model of the firm, which are that it should produce testable predictions with respect to output and price, then clearly it would be judged a failure. However, that would be to misunderstand the purposes of the model. The break-even model is not intended to predict or identify the profit-maximising level of output, or the profit-maximising price. Instead it is intended to examine cost and revenue relationships within a relatively narrow range of output, in order to assist in the planning and control of business activity. In particular, it is useful for short-term profit planning, and for considering the feasibility of particular business activities. Having calculated the break-even point for some activity, that result can then be the focus for further analysis. For instance, it can be used to consider whether or not the volume of sales required to break-even is felt to be feasible or not, at the price indicated. Different prices may be considered in order to examine their impact on the break-even level. If the firm has an estimate of the actual level of sales, this can be compared with the break-even level to consider the 'margin of safety' available, which provides a means of examining the firm's vulnerability to unexpected changes in the volume of activity.

In summary, then, break-even analysis is directed towards a set of questions which is different from those addressed by the economic model of the firm. The fact that it ignores the principle of diminishing returns and the concept of elasticity of demand does not imply that the model has no value.

Solutions to Chapter 9 questions

Answers to self-test questions

1 (a), (b), (d)
2 (a)
3 (a), (c), (d)

4 (a), (b), (d), (e)
5 zero in every case

Model answer to exercise

Perfect competition is a market structure in which the following conditions hold:

- firms aim to maximise profits
- a large number of small buyers and sellers
- firms produce identical products
- free entry to the industry
- perfect knowledge of market opportunities
- perfect mobility of factors of production.

In this situation, firms are 'price-takers', being forced to accept the price which is determined by the market forces of supply and demand. The situation for each firm, and for the industry as a whole, is shown in Fig. Solutions 9.1.

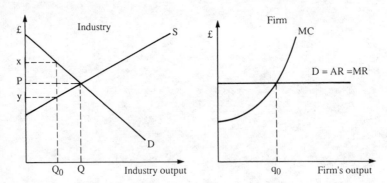

Fig. Solutions 9.1 The industry and the firm in perfect competition

The price, P, is set by the market. Each individual firm has a horizontal demand curve at the market price, indicating that it can sell as much as it chooses at that price, but nothing at higher prices. Because price is constant at different levels of output, marginal revenue and price are equal. Profit-maximising

412

firms will choose to produce level of output q_o, which gives an aggregate output for the industry of Q_o.

This result gives an optimal allocation of resources because it ensures that price is equal to the marginal cost of production. The individual firm, maximising its profit, chooses to supply the amount indicated by its marginal cost curve, which is also the firm's supply curve. The supply curve for the industry is simply the horizontal sum of the marginal cost curves for the individual firms, and may be thought of as the industry's marginal cost curve, as indicated on the diagram. As price is determined by the intersection of the demand curve and the supply/marginal cost curve, perfect competition guarantees that price equals marginal cost. The equality of price and marginal cost is the condition for an optimal allocation of resources because achievement of that condition implies that the economy has maximised the net benefit to consumers arising from production of the commodity in question. If the price of a good is recognised as a measure of consumers' 'willingness to pay' for it, and willingness to pay is seen as a measure of the value which the consumer places on a commodity, then maximising net benefit requires that output be set at the level where the price is equal to marginal cost.

This point can be seen more clearly with reference to the left-hand part of Fig. Solutions 9.1. If the industry were to produce level of output Q_o the allocation of resources would be sub-optimal as consumers would place a value of x on the production of an additional unit which would only cost y to produce. Net benefit to consumers would be foregone unless every unit for which the price exceeds marginal cost is produced. Only at Q, where price is equal to marginal cost, is this result achieved. Perfect competition therefore guarantees an optimal allocation of resources. However, a perfectly competitive market situation is only possible if there are no substantial economies of scale. This can be seen by examining the long-run equilibrium position for an individual firm in the industry, shown in Fig. Solutions 9.2.

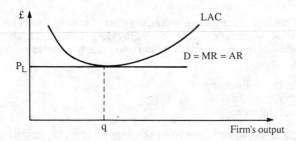

Fig. Solutions 9.2 Long-run equilibrium for a perfectly competitive firm

The curve LAC in the diagram indicates the long-run average cost curve for each firm in the industry. In the long run, price must settle at the level P_L because if it were any higher, new entry would take place forcing the price down, and if it were any lower firms would leave, pushing the price upwards. When the price reaches P_L, each firm has a horizontal demand and marginal revenue curve as shown, and chooses to produce level of output q where profit is maximised. This analysis makes it clear that the size of the firm is limited by the up-turn in the LAC curve. As there are a large number of firms in the industry, the level of output at which costs begin to rise must be a very small proportion of the total industry output. If there were any substantial scale economies, so that the LAC curve sloped downwards, rather than being U-shaped, there would be no long-run equilibrium. Larger firms would have lower costs than smaller ones and the industry would tend to become more concentrated, ceasing to be perfectly competitive. If scale economies exist, then, perfect competition will be impossible.

Solutions to Chapter 10 questions

Answers to self-test questions

1 (b)
2 (d)
3 (b), (d), (e)

4 (b)
5 (a), (b), (d)

Model answer to exercise

The economic models of perfect competition, monopoly and oligopoly are rigorously defined models of market structure, whose fundamental purpose is to provide a basis for making predictions about the behaviour and performance of firms. Each model is based upon a series of assumptions about market structure, which include:

- the number of firms in the industry
- the condition of entry
- the extent of product differentiation.

These formal models of competitive structure are not intended to be descriptively realistic or to provide decision-makers with a directly applicable tool for the analysis of individual industries. Their aim is to abstract away from the complexities of the real world in order to identify the major factors which determine the outcome of competitive situations. The method used is to set up tightly defined models for which equilibrium situations can be identified and then to examine the nature of those equilibria and the mechanisms through which they can be reached. The models show clearly how factors like the number of firms, entry barriers, economies of scale, rivals' reactions and product differentiation all affect the outcome of a competitive situation. Porter's 'five-forces' analysis, illustrated in the diagram opposite, differs from the economic approach in a number of ways.

In the first place, the objective of the analysis is quite different. Instead of aiming to make predictions on the basis of highly simplified 'ideal-types' of market structure, the five-forces analysis aims to provide managers with a means of systematically describing the nature of competition in the complex situations faced by real firms. This is achieved by examining a checklist of the factors which determine each of the five-forces, which are:

- the intensity of rivalry amongst incumbents
- the threat of entry
- the threat of substitution
- the power of buyers
- the power of suppliers

Having examined the factors determining the five forces they can each be summarised in a qualitative fashion in order to characterise the major features of competition in the industry in question. No attempt

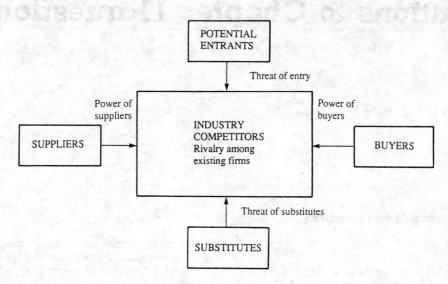

Fig. Solutions 10.1 The 'five forces' model
Source: M.E. Porter *Competitive Strategy*, (New York, Free Press, 1980) p.4.

is made to identify the equilibrium position towards which an industry will tend and the end result of the analysis is not a detailed description of its performance but a much more general categorisation of its structure as either 'attractive' or 'unattractive' to its incumbents.

Despite these major differences in their objectives and method, there are substantial overlaps between the two approaches to competitive structure. Each of the 'five-forces' identified in Porter's approach is a generalisation and extension of aspects of market structure which appear in the formal economic models. As a result, each of the formal models can be characterised in the Porter framework. Perfect competition, for instance, could be described in five-forces terms as an industry with a low level of rivalry, high threat of entry, limited buyer and supplier power, and a threat of substitution which varies from individual case to case. That suggests an industry which is likely to be relatively unattractive in five-forces terms, a conclusion which is reflected in the formal model by the fact that in the long run no supernormal profits can be earned. The five-forces model may therefore be seen as an attempt to develop the formal models in order to make them operational as a means of characterising the complex competitive structures which are to be found in real industries.

Solutions to Chapter 11 questions

Answers to self-test questions

1 (a), (b), (d)
2 (b)
3 Primary activities: inbound logistics, operations, outbound logistics, marketing and sales.
   Support activities: firm infrastructure, human resource management, technology development, procurement.

4 Segment, industry, vertical, geographic
5 Diversification, market development, product development, market penetration/consolidation/liquidation.

Model answer to exercise

The two best known techniques for the examination of a firm's portfolio of businesses are the **Boston Box** and the **General Electric Business Screen**. Each of these can be considered in turn. The Boston Box makes use of a simple matrix to categorise each business, as shown in the diagram opposite. On the horizontal axis, market share is measured, following the unusual convention of having larger shares to the left, smaller ones to the right. The vertical axis measures the growth rate of each business and the size of each business is shown by the diameter of the circle representing it. On each axis, a dividing line is set in order to distinguish between high and low growth and market share, and businesses in each of the four quadrants are characterised as either 'cash cows', 'stars', 'question marks' or 'dogs', as illustrated in the diagram. A general set of prescriptions is then set out which essentially consists of disinvesting in the 'dogs', which are seen as a drain on resources, and using the cash which is expected to flow from the 'cash cows' to develop the 'stars' and those 'question marks' which have the potential to become 'stars' or 'cash cows' in the future.

The key feature of the Boston Box, apart from its colourful terminology, is that it depends very heavily on just two variables. Market share is used as a measure of the firm's competitive position in an industry, and the growth rate of an industry is used as a proxy for its attractiveness. Hence it is argued that where a business has a high market share, but low growth (a cash cow), it will be producing profits for the business, while a dog, having low market share and low growth, is seen as putting a drain on resources.

This one-dimensional approach to competitive position and industry attractiveness is the major weakness of the Boston Box. Even the simplest economic analysis of market structure makes it clear that market share is not the same thing as competitive strength, and industry growth is not the same as industry attractiveness. Using single variables as proxies for such complex other variables may lead to dangerous misinterpretations of a firm's position. On the other hand, the strength of the technique lies in its simplicity and its very limited requirements for information, which can be met at relatively little expense. The General Electric Business Screen is a very similar technique to the Boston Box, with converse advantages and disadvantages. The GE matrix, shown in Fig. Solutions 11.2, has nine cells, in comparison with the four of the Boston Box. The horizontal axis of the GE matrix measures 'competitive position', and the vertical

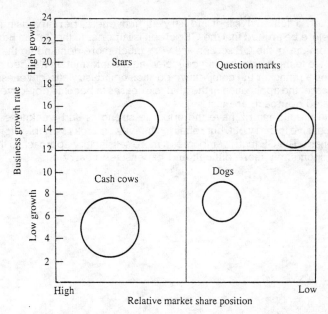

Fig. Solutions 11.1   The Boston Box Consulting Group growth/share matrix

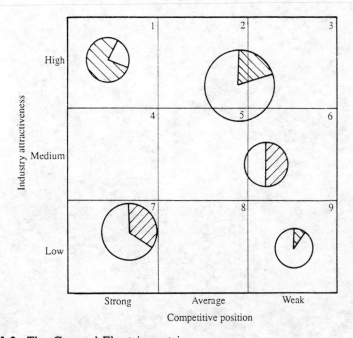

Fig. Solutions 11.2   The General Electric matrix

axis represents 'industry attractiveness'. Instead of a simple division into 'high' and 'low', an intermediate 'average' or 'medium' category is also included. The circles represent the size of each industry or segment, with the shaded areas showing the firm's market share in that segment. Because the axes represent multi-dimensional variables the GE screen is not subject to the criticism of over-simplicity which has been levelled at the Boston Box. A firm can take into account all of the variables which are relevant to its competitive position and can include a full analysis of industry attractiveness, perhaps using Porter's five-forces approach. It may therefore be argued that the GE screen is superior to the Boston Box. On the other hand, the information requirements of the GE screen are very much more demanding than for the Boston Box. They are very expensive to meet and, having collected all the information needed, executives may find it impossible to agree on a rating for the competitive position or industry attractiveness of some businesses and industries. In that case, the application of the analysis ceases to become objective, and the advantages of the more sophisticated approach are lost.

The Boston Box and the GE matrix have the opposite strengths and weaknesses. The Box is easily understood, and inexpensive to carry out, but relies too heavily on proxy variables for competitive position and industry attractiveness. The GE matrix embodies a more satisfactory approach to the complex variables involved, but is correspondingly more difficult and expensive to carry out.

Solutions to Chapter 12 questions

Answers to self-test questions

1 (a), (d)

2 $\dfrac{P - MC_i}{P} = \dfrac{s_i(1 + a)}{E_d}$

where:

s_i = market share, firm i

a = conjectural variation

3 Absolute cost advantages, economies of scale, product differentiation. 'Limit price' is the maximum price which can be set without inducing entry to the industry.

4 Markets must be separate, with no possibility of arbitrage between them, and elasticity of demand should be different in both markets. First degree price discrimination is where every buyer is charged the maximum amount they are willing to pay. Third degree price discrimination is where different prices are charged in different sub-markets, each containing a number of buyers.

5 Inelasticity of demand, a group of buyers who are willing to pay higher prices in order to secure the product before others, uncertainty about the level of demand.

Model answer to exercise

Joel Dean introduced the terminology of 'skimming' versus 'penetration' pricing to describe two different approaches to setting the price of a new product. A strategy of 'skimming' involves setting a high price, at least initially, and then reducing the price if necessary, in order to serve other, lower-price, market segments. A policy of penetration pricing involves setting a relatively low price from the outset, in order to rapidly penetrate the market. Elementary economic theory suggests that in order to maximise profits, a firm should set the price in such a way that the following equation holds true:

$$\frac{P - MC}{P} = (-)\frac{1}{E_d}$$ where: P = price

MC = marginal cost

E_d = elasticity of demand

This in turn suggests that a relatively high price should be set ('skim') when elasticity of demand is low, and a relatively low price should be set ('penetrate') when elasticity of demand is high. As the extent of elasticity is determined by the existence, price and performance of substitutes and by the proportion of buyers' total spending which is involved, these are the factors which determine the choice between the two different approaches to price. If the new product in question has no close substitutes and accounts for only a small proportion of buyers' total spending, its price should be set high, in order to skim. On the other hand, if there are close substitutes and buyers spend a large proportion of their income on the product in question, demand will be more highly elastic and a penetration price is indicated.

To this extent, the choice between the two different strategies may be seen as determined entirely by the extent of elasticity of demand. However, there are two other issues to be considered when choosing a pricing policy for new products. The first concerns the extent of uncertainty, and buyers' responses to changes in price. If the extent of the market is unknown, a firm may need to try both strategies, in order to find which is the most successful. In this case, if buyers respond in a hostile way to price increases, it may be appropriate to begin with a skimming price, reducing it later if necessary. The alternative of beginning with a low price, and then raising it, may be more difficult to implement.

The second consideration concerns the possibility of price discrimination through time. If the market for a product contains sub-markets in which buyers are prepared to pay more for a product in order to have it before others, it may be possible to maximise profits by first setting a skimming price, and selling at that price to the 'trendsetting' group of customers, and then gradually lowering the price over time to draw in other customers who are prepared to purchase the product at a lower price and are also prepared to wait for it. The market for books, for instance, would appear to conform to this pattern.

Solutions to Chapter 13 questions

Answers to self-test questions

1 False: (a), (b)
   True: (c), (d)
2 (a)
3 See Fig. 13.3
4 (b), (c)
5 While a first-best optimal allocation of resources requires that all prices should be equal to marginal cost, if some prices are not set at that level there is no reason to suppose that setting the others equal to marginal cost will lead to a second-best optimum.

Model answer to exercise

When a group of economists at Oxford first discovered, in the 1930s, that business pricing methods bore very little resemblance to the process described in the simple model of the firm, they were convinced that this showed the model to be inadequate. As businessmen showed no signs of even being aware of the vocabulary of marginal cost, marginal revenue and elasticity, preferring to describe their approach to pricing in terms of calculating the cost and then adding a margin, it was argued that the static, marginalist equilibrium model should be abandoned and replaced by some other form of model which bore a closer resemblance to reality as observed. However, 50 years later, the standard model remains at the centre of economic analysis and the consensus amongst mainstream economists is that the conclusions of the Oxford group were erroneous. This argument rests upon a number of foundations.

The first argument in favour of retaining the standard model is essentially methodological, or perhaps even philosophical. The question which has to be asked and answered is 'what is the purpose of a model, and what are the criteria for a good model?' The answer given is that the purpose of a model is to make predictions which are testable, and which are validated by the evidence. On those criteria, the descriptive realism or otherwise of a model is an entirely irrelevant issue. The standard model of the firm meets the criteria and is therefore perfectly acceptable. The Oxford economists made the mistake of assuming that the model was intended to be descriptive of firms' decision-making processes, rather than identifying the conditions which must hold if firms find some way of maximising profits.

The second foundation for the argument in favour of retaining the standard model of the firm lies in the evidence on the way in which firms go about the process of cost-plus pricing. At first sight, the procedure appears to be entirely mechanical, with a figure for cost per unit being calculated from cost accounting data, and a margin being added, in line with the custom within the industry. If that were actually the case it is clear that firms would be ignoring market conditions altogether. They would not be behaving like profit-maximisers, and the profit-maximising model would be unlikely to predict their behaviour with any accuracy. However, closer examination reveals that the calculation of both the cost per unit and the margin is a much less mechanical process than might have been thought and that both offer means by which market forces can influence the price eventually arrived at. In the case of calculating cost per unit, for instance, firms usually use some form of standard cost, which is set through a process of informal discussion during which market factors are taken into account. Firms often appear to have such factors in mind, as in the case of the firm which set prices on the basis of cost per unit at full capacity, even when it knew that it would not achieve full capacity. When asked why it used this apparently odd procedure, the firm explained that it did so for 'competitive reasons' – in other words it knew that if it calculated actual cost per unit and then added a conventional margin the resulting price would be higher than the one which was felt to yield maximum profit.

Just as the calculation of cost is actually very flexible, and is used as a vehicle for the introduction of market influences, so the addition of the margin provides an opportunity for firms to take account of buyers' response to different prices and competitors' pricing strategies. Firms are therefore able to make good, though rarely perfect, approximations to the profit-maximising price, through implicit adjustments rather than through explicit application of any economic model. The evidence on cost-plus pricing is therefore supportive of the standard model of pricing, rather than destructive of it.

Solutions to Chapter 14 questions

Answers to self-test questions

1 Product, place, price, promotion.
2 Price elasticity is likely to rise over the PLC. Advertising elasticity is likely to fall. Application of the Dorfman–Steiner model of the advertising to sales ratio suggests that the profit-maximising level of advertising intensity will decline over the PLC.
3 Core product – information processing.
   Tangible product – keyboard, screen, processor.
   Augmented product – hardware, software, peripherals.
4 Legal protection from copying, allows development of brand loyalty, assists segmentation and price discrimination, links and strengthens corporate identity.
5 (a) Machine tools are sold on a customised basis to a limited number of users, and there is value to be had from close links between the manufacturer and the buyer. The optimal marketing channel will therefore have a small number of levels and will often take the form of direct marketing.
   (b) Breakfast cereals are sold to a very widely dispersed group of buyers, which suggests a multi-level marketing channel. On the other hand, a small number of chain stores, who restock at very short intervals, are responsible for a large proportion of sales. There is likely to be at least two channel configurations. One will be relatively direct, serving the main chain stores, the other multi-level, serving smaller and more dispersed shops and stores.

Model answer to exercise

There are various different rules of thumb which companies may use in order to set their advertising and promotion budgets, the best known of which are:

- setting a percentage of sales
- spending all the firm can afford
- matching the competition
- setting objectives and tasks

If such rules are to be evaluated against the objective of profit-maximisation it is first necessary to consider what the profit-maximising model of the firm suggests with respect to the optimal level of advertising expenditure. This is to be found in the **Dorfman–Steiner condition**, which states that for profit-maximisation the ratio of advertising spending to sales revenue should be equal to the ratio of the advertising elasticity of demand to the price elasticity. Each of the rules of thumb can thus be evaluated against that condition.

Setting a promotional budget by allocating a percentage of sales is a common approach in many companies. It has the advantage of being relatively simple and its form corresponds to the form suggested by the Dorfman–Steiner condition. However, it will only correspond to profit-maximisation if the percentage chosen happens to coincide with the ratio of the advertising to the price elasticities. There is also a danger that if sales revenues fall for any reason, this leads to an automatic reduction in advertising, even if such a reduction is inappropriate.

One of the alternative approaches is known as the objective and task approach. A firm using this method establishes a number of objectives which advertising and promotion is intended to achieve, and then identifies the tasks which have to be carried out in order to meet those objectives. These tasks are then funded and the budget arrived at in that way. In itself, the objective and task approach is unlikely to achieve profit-maximisation. However, if each task were evaluated in terms of the additional revenues it would create and the additional costs it would incur, and all those tasks which add more to revenues than to costs were undertaken, that process would provide a mechanism whereby maximum profit might be approximated. When considering the establishment of budgets for advertising and promotion it is important to recall that this is only one element of the marketing mix. Effective profit performance requires an appropriate balancing of the mix, as well as careful evaluation of each component independently.

Solutions to Chapter 15 questions

Answers to self-test questions

1 (b)
2 19 per cent
3 IRR can give multiple answers, it involves an implicit assumption about the reinvestment rate which is inappropriate and it ignores the absolute size of projects.
4 (a) linear programming
  (b) integer programming

5 (a) If the stream of dividends is assumed to be a perpetuity, the cost of equity capital is given by:

$$K_e = \frac{d}{E}$$

(b) According to the Capital Asset Pricing Model

$$K_e = R_F + b[K_M - R_{F\pounds}]$$

where: R_F = the return on a risk-free security
b = beta
K_M = the return on the market portfolio

Model answer to exercise

The 'traditional' view of the cost of capital is shown in Fig. Solutions 15.1.

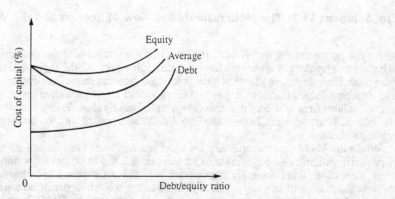

Fig. Solutions 15.1 The traditional view of gearing and the WACC

In the traditional view, the cost of debt is always lower than the cost of equity, as the holders of debt are exposed to less risk, having the first call on the firm's profits. As the gearing ratio increases both the cost of equity and the cost of debt increase because the holders of both type of capital face an increasing level of risk.

The weighted average cost of capital (WACC) which corresponds to these relationships has a U-shape. The WACC falls at first, as the higher proportion of lower-cost debt reduces the weighted average, and then rises as higher gearing ratios increase the risk held by holders of both debt and equity. As the curve has a U-shape there is an optimal capital structure where the cost of capital is minimised and the value of the firm maximised. This traditional view of the WACC has been challenged by Modigliani and Miller (M–M). They begin with the following set of assumptions:

- there are no taxes
- the capital market is efficient and competitive
- there are no transactions costs
- there are no costs associated with bankruptcy
- shareholders can borrow on the same terms as corporations
- the cost of debt is constant, whatever the level of gearing.

If these assumptions hold, M–M show that the cost of debt, the cost of equity and the WACC are as shown in Fig. Solutions 15.2.

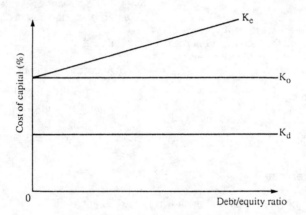

Fig. Solutions 15.2 The Modigliani–Miller view of gearing and the WACC

As the figure shows, the WACC remains constant, whatever the gearing ratio, and equal to the cost of equity in a firm which is entirely financed through equity. M–M argue that market forces must guarantee this result. If two firms are identical except for their gearing ratios they cannot have different costs of capital and different values because if they did there would be an incentive for shareholders to sell stock in the higher valued firm and buy it in the one with a lower value. This process of 'arbitrage' must even out the values of the two firms. In this case, the WACC is invariant with the gearing ratio and there is no optimal capital structure.

While the M–M conclusions may be valid under the assumptions they make, those assumptions are very restrictive and need to be relaxed if conclusions are to be drawn which are applicable to real-world firms. First of all, it is necessary to consider how the conclusions are altered if taxation is introduced. If there is taxation, and interest on debt is tax-deductible while dividends are not, a firm can improve its net cash flow by having a higher gearing ratio. In this case, the WACC simply falls as gearing increases and the value of a firm would be maximised by having almost 100 per cent debt finance. The optimal capital structure involves virtually no equity. On the other hand, if bankruptcy costs are introduced, the cost of capital will tend to be higher at higher gearing ratios, as the risk of default increases. If these two effects are both introduced together, the result is a relationship between the WACC and the gearing ratio as shown in Fig. Solutions 15.3.

At lower gearing ratios an increase in gearing leads to a lower WACC, because of the tax effect. However, as gearing increases, the risks and costs of bankruptcy begin to have an effect and eventually this is powerful enough to offset the tax effect. At higher gearing ratios the relationship between WACC

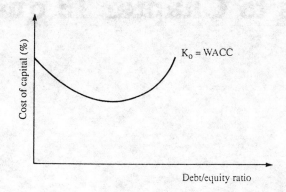

Fig. Solutions 15.3 WACC and gearing in the presence of bankruptcy costs and taxes

and gearing becomes positive. As a result, the curve linking the WACC and gearing is U-shaped, as in the traditional view, although for different reasons. There is an optimal capital structure and the level of gearing is not irrelevant.

Solutions to Chapter 16 questions

Answers to self-test questions

1 (a), (b)

2 concentration – structure, growth of demand – structure, advertising intensity – structure or performance, collusive agreements – conduct, productivity growth – performance, entry barriers – structure, profitability – performance, degree of diversification – structure, company objectives – conduct.

3 Monopoly power, chance, entrepreneurial activity.

4 (b), (c)

5 Advantages of the rules approach – easily understood, inexpensive to administer, less prone to political manipulation, firms waste less resources trying to influence decision-makers. Disadvantages – inflexible, difficult to accommodate the circumstances of individual cases, the rules established may have little real justification.

Model answer to exercise

In the conventional view, monopoly power is a common feature of industrial and commercial life, which reduces the efficiency of the resource allocation process in three different senses. First, it reduces static allocative efficiency, by leading to prices which are not equal to marginal cost. Secondly, it leads to X-inefficiency, as firms with monopoly power are not under pressure to keep their costs as low as possible. Thirdly, it leads to dynamic inefficiency as the rate of innovation is less than would prevail in more competitive circumstances.

The cost of these inefficiencies is difficult to measure, but various attempts have been made to provide estimates. In most cases, these are based around the idea that profits arise from monopoly power, and that profits can therefore be used as the basis for estimating the costs of monopoly power. It is also suggested that firms waste resources in the process of attempting to secure monopoly positions, so that at least some of firms spending on advertising and promotion should be included in the estimated costs of monopoly. The results of this process of measurement vary, as might be expected, but some suggest that the cost is very large indeed, so that considerable expense on anti-trust programmes would be worthwhile. This view can be attacked on a number of grounds, which centre around the view of competition which is adopted, and the source of profits. In particular, the 'Austrian' view of competition suggests that the dangers and costs of monopoly may have been over-estimated.

In the conventional view, on which the estimates for the cost of monopoly are based, profits can only arise, in the long run at least, from the ownership of monopoly power. In that case, profits are a direct reflection of monopoly power and can be the basis for such estimates. In the 'Austrian' view there are three possible sources of profit. The first is the ownership of monopoly power. The second is unexpected fluctuations in the environment, and the third is beneficial entrepreneurial activity. If a firm has a management team which 'clicks' better than others, or if it succeeds in finding a new market or creating a new product it will enjoy a high level of profits, at least for a while. These are not monopoly profits in any meaningful sense of the term because the opportunities from which the profits have been made were open to all.

In this view, competition is not a state, but a continuous process of attempting to gain monopoly power or attempting to break into the monopoly positions established by others. Most monopoly profits are not the result of exploitative behaviour but the relatively short-lived reward for firms which have been able to creatively develop new market opportunities. As a result, it is argued that estimates of the cost of monopoly power are greatly exaggerated and most monopoly legislation is a waste of resources. There is some real and costly monopoly power in the economy, arising from the existence of barriers to entry, some of which are government-induced, but its importance has been exaggerated and does not justify an expensive anti-trust effort.

It may also be argued that some anti-trust policy may be positively harmful. Anti-merger policy, for instance, is usually justified on the grounds that mergers may allow firms to establish dominant positions and use them to exploit consumers. However, if there is free entry to and exit from the industry, coupled with vigorous competition from firms attempting to break into the market, this power may be tightly constrained. The dominant firm will have little ability to exploit its position without attracting entry. There is therefore very little purpose served by having an anti-merger policy. Furthermore, a policy which prohibits mergers will insulate firms from an important aspect of competition, namely the threat of take-over and the market for corporate control. A firm whose managers know that they are safe from take-over because the monopoly legislation prevents it may indulge themselves in much more expensive X-inefficiencies. From this point of view, then, it may be argued that anti-monopoly policy is unnecessary and misguided.

Solutions to Chapter 17 questions

Answers to self-test questions

1 Sticky wages, costs of relocation, differences in house prices, lack of private rented accommodation.

2 Because it implies that they do not consider all the locational options available and may be locating themselves in congested areas as a result of this myopia, not because those locations are most efficient.

3 (b), (c), (f)

4 (b), (c)

5 introduction of charges, contracting-out, denationalisation, deregulation.

Model answer to exercise

The transfer of public enterprises into private ownership raises a number of issues which may be addressed through the application of economic analysis. In the first place, this form of 'privatisation' alters and clarifies the objectives of the enterprise in question. The objectives of public enterprises are rarely stated clearly, frequently involve multiple objectives which conflict with each other, and are subject to rapid change at the whim of politicians. Once transferred to the private sector, profit becomes the major objective, qualified to some extent by managers' ability to divert resources into their own 'perks' and the pursuit of a 'quiet life'. This clarification of objectives is in itself seen as a benefit from privatisation, as it provides managers with a clearer focus for their activities and avoids the constant shifting of objectives sometimes associated with the public sector.

The second change which results from privatisation is that the issue of shares brings the firm into the ambit of the market for corporate control. Once the shares are being traded the firm becomes subject to pressure from shareholders and vulnerable to take-over if its share price falls to a level at which the market sees its assets as being under-valued. As the share price depends fundamentally upon the level of profits which it is expected to achieve with its current management, this puts managers under considerable pressure to attempt to maximise profits and to be efficient. In particular, it forces managers to eliminate 'X-inefficiency' and operational inefficiencies which raise costs and reduce profits.

One major advantage claimed for privatisation, then, is that the profit objective becomes the major focus for managers and the market for corporate control puts them under pressure to keep costs down. Clearly, the effectiveness of this mechanism depends upon the efficiency of the market for corporate control and the extent to which the threat of take-over is real. If a privatised firm is subject to little pressure from shareholders and considers itself immune from take-over, perhaps because it is very large, or because anti-merger legislation prevents it from being acquired, managers will be under little pressure to keep costs down. In so far as take-over techniques have developed rapidly in the last decade, so that small firms quite often take over larger ones, the threat of take-over would seem to be very real. In an era when the Midland Bank almost came under the control of Saatchi & Saatchi, it seems clear that even the largest organisations cannot regard themselves as safe. On the other hand, anti-monopoly legislation may provide some managements with a degree of protection, and it is ironic that a policy intended to ensure competition may in fact have the opposite effect to that intended.

The other issue which is raised by de-nationalisation concerns the market structure of the industry in which the newly private firm is located. In some cases, the industry is relatively competitive and the de-nationalised firm has little monopoly power. On the other hand, many industries were originally nationalised because they were felt to be 'natural monopolies' in which scale economies and other entry barriers effectively prevented vigorous competition. In the case of such 'natural monopolies' privatisation may produce the hoped-for benefits of reduced X-inefficiency and lower costs, but this gain may be accompanied by a loss of allocative efficiency as the firm uses its market power to exploit customers by raising prices and lowering standards of quality. If this is to be avoided, there are two basic options. The first is to find ways in which competition can be stimulated, by ensuring first that there are no government-imposed barriers to entry into the industry, and then by attempting to reduce other entry barriers, particularly those arising from a high level of sunk costs. The other option is to regulate the industry by establishing some form of regulatory body. If at all possible, the first option is to be preferred as the American experience with regulation tends to suggest that the controlling bodies are soon 'captured' by the industries they are supposed to control.

To summarise the argument, then, de-nationalisation may involve replacing public monopolies with private monopolies unless steps are taken to ensure either competition or effective regulation. However, that is not the only change which takes place. A de-nationalised firm also becomes subject to shareholder pressure and the market for corporate control which, if effective, will yield benefits in terms of operating efficiency or X-efficiency. Naturally enough, the political opponents of privatisation tend to stress the dangers of monopoly power, while its supporters point to the benefits of having clear profit objectives imposed by an efficient stock market.

Solutions to Chapter 18 questions

Answers to self-test questions

1 industry, segment, vertical, geographical.
2 (a) classical contracting
  (b) unified governance
  (c) neo-classical contracting
3 Distortion of procurement decisions, resistance to change, distortion of internal communications

4 Because they could achieve a greater reduction in risk at lower cost by purchasing a portfolio of shares, or investing in a unit trust.
5 Economies of scope, economies of scale, reductions in risk, reductions in transactions costs.

Model answer to exercise

All firms are vertically integrated to some extent, as they carry out more than a single indivisible operation. The question they face is not whether 'to be vertically integrated or not?', but 'how vertically integrated should we be?'. The fundamental question is one concerning the firm's 'scope' - the range of activities in which it should become involved. The vertical integration of activities within a firm is essentially the organisation of transactions within the firm, instead of through the market place, and the advantages and disadvantages of additional vertical integration can be examined in that light.

The internal organisation of vertical transactions is rendered desirable by a number of factors. In the first place, there may be technological economies to be had by locating a number of activities in close proximity to each other – the most common example being the location of steel rolling mills next to blast furnaces in order to save on energy for heating the steel. In principle, the co-ordination of these transactions in hot steel could be carried out between independent firms through the marketplace, but that would be difficult and expensive to organise.

This last point raises a fundamental issue in respect of vertical integration, which is that such integration avoids using the market and therefore avoids the costs and risks of market transactions. These costs will be particularly high, according to Williamson, when there is a high level of uncertainty, when transactions occur very frequently, and when firms have incurred high levels of investment on assets which are specific to the transactions in question. In these circumstances, where uncertainty makes it impossible for complete contracts to be written, the dangers of 'opportunistic' behaviour are very high and firms will prefer to internalise the vertical transaction, as in the case of hot steel.

A third motive for vertical integration arises from the prospect of acquiring monopoly power through extension of the firm's scope. This has been the source of considerable debate as some analysts have argued that vertical extension cannot enhance existing monopoly power. However, it is clear that a higher level of vertical integration may raise entry barriers by increasing the capital requirements. It may also enhance market power by preventing downstream users substituting for the firm's intermediate products and by enhancing the prospects for price discrimination.

If the advantages of internalised transactions were absolute, they would always be preferred to market transactions and the economy would consist of a single firm. Clearly, this does not occur because there are also off-setting disadvantages to internalised transactions. The first disadvantage is that the existence of an in-house source of supply may distort procurement decisions. If the in-house source ceases to be the most cost-effective it may be difficult to switch to another because of the sunk costs involved and executives' commitment to an existing activity.

In a similar way, vertical integration may lead to a generalised resistance to change and the distortion of internal communications. If information is 'impacted', in the sense that important facts are well-hidden from view and very expensive to check, there may be incentives for workers and managers to report what they wish to report, rather than what they know to be true. This may make it extremely difficult to identify the real cost of procuring goods and services internally. Markets may provide much better information in the simple and unambiguous form of price signals.

To summarise, then, vertical integration may allow technological economies to be had, transactions costs to be avoided, and monopoly power to be enhanced. On the other hand, the internalisation of transactions may lead to inertia, a loss of flexibility and the distortion of information. For a firm considering an extension of its vertical scope each of these factors needs to be considered, and the balance of advantage struck.

Solutions to Chapter 19 questions

Answers to self-test questions

1 Sources: 1914, UK, US, France   1975: US, UK, Japan.
Hosts: 1914, developing countries 1970s: developed countries.

2 American, high wages paid, skill-intensive, technology-based, large size.

3 Japanese firms, firms based in developing nations, service-sector MNEs.

4 Ownership advantages, locational advantages, internalisation advantages.

5 (a) General Motors – dispersed, low level of co-ordination.
(b) Toyota – concentrated, high level of co-ordination.

Model answer to exercise

The establishment of a multinational enterprise (MNE) may be examined using Dunning's 'eclectic' framework for analysis, which draws together three themes in the attempt to explain the MNEs existence and the pattern of its activity.

The first element in the framework is the necessity for firms to have 'ownership advantages' which give them the ability to operate abroad in competition with indigenous firms. Such advantages may arise in a number of ways. Most obviously they may be technological, arising from carrying out R&D, or they may relate to the possession of well-known brand names or other forms of product-differentiation. Examination of the pattern of the MNE in the 1960s and early 1970s revealed that American MNEs were typically research, skill and advertising-intensive companies. For some time that pattern was felt to be typical until it was realised that Japanese MNEs, service sector MNEs and MNEs originating in developing nations had a very different profile. At that point in the debate, it was realised that 'ownership advantages' could take a wide variety of forms. Expertise and experience in general management, for instance, is often cited as the advantage upon which Japanese MNEs are based while service sector MNEs like international hotel chains rely upon their skills in managing labour and providing information systems.

While the possession of such advantages is a necessary condition for going abroad, it is not sufficient because the firm always has the alternative of selling or leasing its advantage to a local firm through a licensing agreement. Foreign direct investment will only take place, and a multinational be formed, if internalised transactions are preferable to market transactions. This basic insight forms the foundation for Buckley and Casson's 'internalisation' theory of the MNE.

According to the internalisation theory, the MNE only exists because of the imperfections and costs involved in making market transactions. The theory is therefore closely related to the writings of Coase on the scope of the firm and Williamson on markets versus hierarchies. If an internalised transaction allows closer control, perhaps through vertical integration, or the enhanced ability to discriminate on price, or the avoidance of uncertainty then it will be preferred to a market transaction. In Williamson's terminology, if there is a danger of opportunistic behaviour, transactions are carried out frequently, and there is a high level of 'idiosyncratic' investment in transaction-specific assets then the economising governance structure will be unified governance through the central authority of the firm.

'Internalisation' theory therefore makes it clear that the difficulties associated with market transactions lie at the heart of the MNEs existence. If there were no such difficulties, MNEs could not exist as transactions could all be carried out through markets. The 'eclectic' framework also draws attention to a third aspect of the MNEs activity which needs to be taken into account. This concerns the 'where' of multinational activity, which is determined by the relative advantages of different locations. Unless there are incentives to transfer activities to foreign locations, in order to secure lower costs or better market access, ownership advantages and internalisation will not be sufficient to lead to multinational activity.

It can be seen from this analysis that MNEs exist because there is an incentive to transfer ownership advantages and activities to different locations and to internalise the transactions within the managerial hierarchy of the firm. The difficulties of carrying out transactions through markets are therefore central to the existence of the MNE.

Glossary

Arc-elasticity of demand Elasticity of demand over a significant arc of the demand curve.

Back-forecasting Checking the validity of a forecasting method by using it to make a 'forecast' for a period for which the outcome is already known.

Barriers to entry Advantages which incumbent firms in an industry have over potential entrants.

Beta co-efficient A measure of the extent to which the returns on security vary with the returns to the market as a whole.

Bounded rationality A form of behaviour associated with uncertainty where individuals do not examine every possible option open to them, but simply consider a number of alternatives which happen to occur to them.

Branding Attaching a brand mark or brand name to a product in order to distinguish it from other product variants.

Capital asset pricing model A model which attempts to measure the return which investors will require from a security, as a function of its riskiness.

Cash cows Businesses which have large market shares but slow growth.

Cobb-Douglas production function A mathematical function showing a particular form of relationship between inputs and outputs.

Certainty-equivalent The risk-free return on capital which gives the same level of satisfaction as other combinations of risk and return.

Concentration The extent to which industrial activity is in the hands of a small number of firms.

Conjectural variation A measure of a firm's belief with respect to the response which its rivals will make to its own actions.

Contestable markets Markets in which entry and exit is costless.

Contribution margin The difference between revenue per unit and variable cost per unit, in the framework of break-even analysis.

Control loss Cost increases attributable to management's inability to monitor and control the performance of subordinates.

Cost leadership A 'generic' form of corporate strategy which involves producing at lower cost than the competition.

Delphi technique A forecasting technique whereby individual experts anonymously give an opinion, and their reasons for it, and the opinions are then circulated and amended until a consensus is reached.

Differentiation A form of corporate strategy which involves producing products which differ from the competition in ways which buyers value.

Diversification Carrying on business in a range of industries.

Dividend valuation model A model which attempts to estimate the cost of equity capital by examining the relationship between that cost, the flow of dividends and the market value of the firm.

Dogs Businesses which have low market share and low market growth.

Dominant position A market structure in which a single firm has a very large market share.

Dorfman–Steiner condition The condition that, for profit-maximisation, the advertising to sales ratio should equal the ratio of advertising elasticity to price elasticity.

Duopoly An industry containing only two firms.

Econometrics The application of statistical methods to the estimation of economic models.

Economies of scale Reductions in cost which arise from the utilisation of larger sets of plant and equipment

Economies of scope Reductions in cost which arise from producing a number of different goods together.

Engel curve A curve showing the relationship between a household's income and its consumption of a commodity.

Exit barriers Factors which make it expensive for a

firm to leave an industry.

First-best optimum The absolutely optimal allocation of resources, where all prices are set equal to marginal social cost.

Focus A corporate strategy which involves serving the special needs of a narrow group of buyers.

Game theory A technique for predicting the actions which interdependent rivals may take in their relations with each other.

Governance structure The framework which governs a transaction.

Group-think The process whereby the independent judgment of individuals is impaired by their desire to be seen as loyal and conforming members of the group.

Idiosyncratic investment Expenditure on assets which are specific to a particular transaction.

Income effect The change in a basket of goods selected by a consumer which takes place when the consumer's real income increases but relative prices remain the same.

Indifference analysis A method of modelling consumer behaviour.

Information agreements Agreements between firms to share information on issues like price, in order to establish a tacit form of collusion.

Institutional investors Financial companies who own shares in other companies.

Internal rate of return The discount rate which reduces the net present value (NPV) of an investment project to zero.

Iso-sales line A line showing all the different combinations of two promotional media which yield the same level of sales.

Isoquant A curve showing all the different quantities of capital and labour which may be used to produce a given level of output.

Leading indicators Indicators whose behaviour is believed to be closely correlated with the future behaviour of a variable which is being forecast.

Learning effects Reductions in cost which arise as a result of experience in carrying out some activity.

Loss-leaders Products sold at below cost with the aim of inducing buyers to purchase other products as well.

Managerial diseconomies of scale Increases in cost per unit at larger scales of output attributable to the loss of control associated with attempting to manage larger organisations.

Marginal product of labour The additional output arising from the use of an additional unit of labour.

Marginal rate of substitution The rate at which a consumer is willing to exchange one commodity for another, while achieving the same level of satisfaction.

Marginal sales response The change in the value or volume of sales arising from an additional unit of advertising or media exposure.

Minimum efficient scale (MES) The minimum scale of production at which all known scale economies have been achieved.

Net present value The discounted value of a stream of cash outflows and inflows associated with an investment project.

Normative theories Theories concerned with 'what ought to be', as opposed to 'what is'.

Opportunism Guileful behaviour designed to take account of asymmetries of information between parties to a transaction.

Organisational slack Unnecessarily high costs due to lack of tight control.

Own price elasticity of demand A measure of the responsiveness of the demand for a product to changes in its own price.

Penetration pricing An approach to pricing new products which involves setting an initially low price.

Perfect competition A market structure in which there are a large number of small firms producing identical products and where there is free entry to the industry.

Positive theories Theories concerned with 'what is', rather than 'what ought to be'.

Price effect The change in the basket of goods selected by a consumer which takes place when the price of one of the goods changes.

Principle of diminishing returns The generalisation that as more and more of a variable factor is added to a fixed factor, in order to produce more output, the additional output per unit of variable input must decline.

Proprietary technology Technological knowledge which can only be used with the permission of its owner.

Psychic costs of mobility The non-pecuniary costs of moving from place to place.

Pure monopoly A market structure in which there is only one firm and no possibility of entry.

Question marks Businesses which have low market shares but rapid market growth.

Restrictive agreements Agreements between firms which have the purpose of restricting competition.

Returns to scale The relationship between the unit cost of output and the scale at which the output is produced.

Revealed preference theory A theory of consumer behaviour.

'Satisficing' A form of behaviour where individuals seek to achieve a satisfactory target with respect to their goals, but do not seek more once that level has been achieved, at least in the short run.

Scope The range of activities, industries, markets and

countries in which the firm is involved.

Second-best optimum The best allocation of resources available, given that a first-best optimum is not possible.

Skimming pricing An approach to the pricing of new products which involves setting an initially high price.

Span of control The number of individuals under the direct control of another individual.

Stars Businesses which have both large market share and rapid market growth.

Stochastic economies of scale Economies of scale which arise as a result of the properties of random variations.

Strategic Business Unit (SBU) A sub-unit of a corporation which is large enough, or different enough, to have its own strategy.

Substitution effect The change in the basket of goods selected by a consumer which takes place when relative prices change but real income remains the same.

Time-series analysis A term applied to a number of different forecasting methods.

Value chain A concept used in the development of corporate strategy, whereby the firm's operations are divided into a series of activities.

Vertical integration The extent to which a firm carries out activities at different stages of the production process from raw materials to the final purchaser.

Weighted average cost of capital (WACC) The overall cost of capital to a firm, made up of a weighted average of the cost of debt and the cost of equity.

Workable competition The most desirable form of competition, selected from those which are actually possible.

X-inefficiency Where a firm incurs higher costs than are necessary, given the set of plant and equipment in use and its level of capacity utilisation.

Zero-sum game A game in which the gains to the winner are exactly equal to the losses to the loser.

Index